Nebraska Symposium on Motivation

Volume 64

Series editor

Debra A. Hope, Lincoln, NE, USA

More information about this series at http://www.springer.com/series/7596

Jeffrey R. Stevens
Editor

Impulsivity

How Time and Risk Influence Decision Making

Springer

Editor
Jeffrey R. Stevens
Department of Psychology and Center for
Brain, Biology & Behavior
University of Nebraska-Lincoln
Lincoln, NE
USA

ISSN 0146-7875
Nebraska Symposium on Motivation
ISBN 978-3-319-51720-9 ISBN 978-3-319-51721-6 (eBook)
DOI 10.1007/978-3-319-51721-6

Library of Congress Control Number: 2016962042

Printed on acid-free paper

This Springer imprint is published by Springer Nature
The registered company is Springer International Publishing AG
The registered company address is: Gewerbestrasse 11, 6330 Cham, Switzerland

Series Preface

We are pleased to offer this volume from the 64th Nebraska Symposium on Motivation.

This year the volume editor is Jeffrey Stevens. In addition to overseeing this book, the volume editor coordinated the 64th Symposium, including selecting and inviting the contributors. I would like to express my appreciation to Prof. Stevens and the contributors for a stimulating meeting and an excellent series of papers on impulsivity, an important factor in many behavioral problems.

This symposium series is supported by funds provided by the Chancellor of the University of Nebraska–Lincoln, Harvey Perlman, and by funds given in memory of Professor Harry K. Wolfe to the University of Nebraska Foundation by the late Professor Cora L. Friedline. Given Chancellor Perlman's retirement in 2016, we honored his long-standing generous support by naming the poster session and reception in his honor. We are also grateful for the University of Nebraska Foundation's support via the Friedline bequest. This symposium volume, like those in the recent past, is dedicated in memory of Professor Wolfe, who brought psychology to the University of Nebraska. After studying with Professor Wilhelm Wundt in Germany, Professor Wolfe returned to his native state, to establish the first undergraduate laboratory in psychology in the nation. As a student at Nebraska, Professor Friedline studied psychology under Professor Wolfe.

Lincoln, USA — Debra A. Hope

Contents

1 **The Many Faces of Impulsivity** 1
Jeffrey R. Stevens

2 **Delay of Gratification: Explorations of How and Why Children Wait and Its Linkages to Outcomes Over the Life Course** 7
Philip K. Peake

3 **From Risk and Time Preferences to Cultural Models of Causality: On the Challenges and Possibilities of Field Experiments, with Examples from Rural Southwestern Madagascar** 61
Bram Tucker

4 **A Fuzzy-Trace Theory of Risk and Time Preferences in Decision Making: Integrating Cognition and Motivation** 115
Shahin Rahimi-Golkhandan, David M.N. Garavito, Bertrand B. Reyna-Brainerd and Valerie F. Reyna

5 **Devaluation of Outcomes Due to Their Cost: Extending Discounting Models Beyond Delay** 145
Suzanne H. Mitchell

6 **Engaging and Exploring: Cortical Circuits for Adaptive Foraging Decisions** 163
David L. Barack and Michael L. Platt

7 **Dissecting Impulsivity: Brain Mechanisms and Neuropsychiatric Implications** 201
Trevor W. Robbins and Jeffrey W. Dalley

8 Toward Narrative Theory: Interventions for Reinforcer Pathology in Health Behavior 227
Warren K. Bickel, Jeffrey S. Stein, Lara N. Moody, Sarah E. Snider, Alexandra M. Mellis and Amanda J. Quisenberry

Index 269

Contributors

David L. Barack Department of Philosophy, Department of Neuroscience, Department of Economics, and Center for Science and Society, Columbia University, New York, NY, USA

Warren K. Bickel Virginia Tech Carilion Research Institute, Roanoke, VA, USA

Jeffrey W. Dalley Department of Psychology, University of Cambridge, Cambridge, UK

David M.N. Garavito Human Neuroscience Institute, Cornell University, Ithaca, NY, USA

Alexandra M. Mellis Virginia Tech Carilion Research Institute, Roanoke, VA, USA

Suzanne H. Mitchell Departments of Behavioral Neuroscience and Psychiatry, Oregon Health & Science University, Portland, OR, USA

Lara N. Moody Virginia Tech Carilion Research Institute, Roanoke, VA, USA

Philip K. Peake Department of Psychology, Smith College, Northampton, MA, USA

Michael L. Platt Department of Neuroscience, University of Pennsylvania, Philadelphia, PA, USA

Amanda J. Quisenberry Virginia Tech Carilion Research Institute, Roanoke, VA, USA

Shahin Rahimi-Golkhandan Human Neuroscience Institute, Cornell University, Ithaca, NY, USA

Bertrand B. Reyna-Brainerd Human Neuroscience Institute, Cornell University, Ithaca, NY, USA

Valerie F. Reyna Human Neuroscience Institute, Cornell University, Ithaca, NY, USA

Trevor W. Robbins Department of Psychology, University of Cambridge, Cambridge, UK

Sarah E. Snider Virginia Tech Carilion Research Institute, Roanoke, VA, USA

Jeffrey S. Stein Virginia Tech Carilion Research Institute, Roanoke, VA, USA

Jeffrey R. Stevens Department of Psychology and Center for Brain, Biology & Behavior, University of Nebraska-Lincoln, Lincoln, NE, USA

Bram Tucker Department of Anthropology, University of Georgia, Athens, GA, USA

Chapter 1
The Many Faces of Impulsivity

Jeffrey R. Stevens

Introduction

Can you resist the dessert tray when eating out at restaurants? Do you enjoy the thrill of pulling the arm on a slot machine in anticipation of the results? Do you succumb to purchasing candy or magazines in the checkout line of the grocery store? Have you ever bungee jumped or skydived? Have you ever blurted out something that you wish you would not have said? These questions all address *impulsivity*, a multifaceted concept that typically captures an inability to wait, a preference for risky outcomes, a tendency to act without forethought, an insensitivity to consequences, and/or an inability to inhibit inappropriate behaviors (Evenden 1999; Reynolds et al. 2006). Because it touches on so many different aspects of behavior, impulsivity connects to a number of other concepts including patience, self-control, delay of gratification, intertemporal choice, discounting, risky choice, risk taking, inhibitory control, and sensation seeking. So, when different researchers refer to impulsivity, do they mean the same thing? Is impulsivity a single construct across all of these usages?

A Taxonomy of Impulsivity

The shear breadth of behavioral phenomena labeled "impulsivity" already implies an answer to this question. It seems unlikely that impulsivity is a unitary construct that applies to such a diverse range of behaviors. In fact, researchers have created a

J.R. Stevens (✉)
Department of Psychology and Center for Brain, Biology & Behavior,
University of Nebraska-Lincoln, B83 East Stadium, Lincoln, NE 68588, USA
e-mail: jeffrey.r.stevens@gmail.com

J.R. Stevens (ed.), *Impulsivity*, Nebraska Symposium on Motivation 64,
DOI 10.1007/978-3-319-51721-6_1

taxonomy that carves up the concept into different types of impulsivity. A primary distinction divides impulsivity into impulsive choice (or decision making) and impulsive action (or disinhibition) based on both behavioral correlates across tasks and neural mechanisms (Evenden 1999; Reynolds et al. 2006; Dalley et al. 2011; Robbins and Dalley, this volume).

Impulsive Choice

Many cases of impulsivity involve making a choice: a choice between rewards with different costs. These costs can result from time delays to receiving the reward, probabilities of receiving the reward, or effort required to receive the reward. These choices typically involve a trade-off between a smaller reward with a smaller cost and a larger reward with a larger cost.

For *intertemporal choices*, the cost is a time delay to receiving a reward—individuals must choose between rewards that are available after different delays (Read 2004; Stevens 2010). Researchers often investigate explicit *delay choices* between a smaller, sooner option and a larger, later option (see Barack and Platt, Bickel et al., Mitchell, Rahimi-Golkhanden et al., Robbins and Dalley, Tucker, this volume). Choosing the smaller, sooner option is often labeled impulsive, whereas choosing the larger, later option signals self-control or patience. Psychologists and economists have proposed temporal (or delay) discounting as the mechanism generating delay choices—that is, they assume that decision makers subjectively devalue future rewards. Individuals who highly discount the future will show a strong preference for sooner rewards.

In addition to delay choice, other intertemporal choice paradigms explore *delay maintenance*, in which individuals must maintain a choice for a delayed reward in the face of alternatives (Mischel and Ebbesen 1970; Toner et al. 1977). Rather than making a single choice, delay maintenance requires making a constant stream of choices for the larger, later option. Walter Mischel's Marshmallow Test investigates the notion of delay of (or delayed) gratification by using delay maintenance tasks (see Peake, this volume). Though they are both measures of intertemporal choice, performance on delay choice and delay maintenance tasks are not strongly correlated (Toner et al. 1977), suggesting that even within intertemporal choices, levels of impulsivity are dissociated between making and sustaining choices.

For *risky choices*, the cost is the probability of receiving the reward, with the receipt of the small reward more certain than receipt of the larger reward. Impulsivity in this context refers to the willingness to take risks (Barack and Platt, Bickel et al., Rahimi-Golkhanden et al., Robbins and Dalley, Tucker, this volume). This ranges from gambling in games of chance to engaging in risky behaviors such as having unprotected sex. Conceptually, risky choices are analogous to intertemporal choices, and researchers refer to probability discounting as an analogous mechanism to temporal discounting.

Rewards can also be costly in terms of the effort need to obtain them. Increasing the effort or distance required to obtain a reward will reduce choices for that reward (Mitchell, this volume). So, like temporal and probability discounting, investigators can also measure effort and distance (or spatial) discounting, with impulsivity referring to choosing the option with the least effort/distance. Effort and distance preferences are not as well studied as time and risk preferences, but some evidence suggests that they are decoupled from time preferences (Mühlhoff et al. 2011; Mitchell, this volume), though they share some neural substrates (Mitchell, this volume).

Impulsive Action

Impulsive action refers to a failure of inhibition or the inability to withhold from making a response (Winstanley et al. 2006). This often involves acting without forethought, ignoring consequences of actions, and failing to inhibit inappropriate behaviors. Impulsive action can be divided into "waiting impulsivity" and "stopping impulsivity" (Dalley et al. 2011). Waiting impulsivity refers to situations in which individuals cannot wait and prematurely respond to a situation—for example, when drivers anticipate a traffic signal changing but accelerate before the signal actually changes. Stopping impulsivity refers to situations in which individuals fail to stop an action when required—for example, when a child is reaching to touch a forbidden object and fails to stop reaching when told not to touch the object. Robbins and Dalley (this volume) describe how different neural circuits underlie these two subcategories of impulsivity.

Scope of Impulsivity

Due to the many different varieties of impulsivity, this concept is wide in scope. It is of relevance to a large number of fields, including psychology, economics, biology, neuroscience, anthropology, nutrition, finance, and environmental sciences. Studying impulsivity requires investigation across a broad range of levels. Early work in this area began by focusing on the behavioral level of individuals. But impulsivity has important implications for society in terms of both differences across cultures (Tucker, this volume) and applications to critical societal problems such as physical health (Bickel et al., Mitchell, this volume), mental health (Barack and Platt, Bickel et al., Mitchell, Robbins and Dalley, this volume), financial well-being (Laibson et al. 1998), and environmental sustainability (Stern 2008). Given its potentially negative societal implications, interventions and nudges could be designed to reduce impulsivity. This raises interesting questions about whether impulsivity is a trait that people have or whether it is a response to the decision-making context (Peake, this volume). Therefore, investigating its cognitive mechanisms (Bickel et al., Mitchell, Peake, Rahimi-Golkhanded et al., this volume) could provide fruitful insights into impulsivity. Taking this a step further by exploring the biological mechanisms (e.g., neural circuits and neurotransmitters: Barack and Platt, Robbins and Dalley, this volume) can yield therapies to treat pathological impulsivity. Therefore, impulsivity connects numerous fields across many levels of analysis and has critical applications to human (and nonhuman) societies.

Due to this breadth, the current volume reflects the scope of impulsivity by including contributors from a wide range of fields who work at different levels of analysis. The volume begins with Philip Peake's review of the foundational work on the Marshmallow Test—a famous (and perhaps infamous) series of studies on delay of gratification in children (Chap. 2). This work has captured the public's interest in impulsivity by demonstrating important connections between the ability to wait for delayed rewards at a young age and life outcomes in adolescence and adulthood. It also highlights the underappreciated emphasis on how cognitive and contextual factors influence delay of gratification.

Bram Tucker then takes us on a bit of an adventure by describing the difficulties of and insights from studying questions of impulsivity in small-scale societies (Chap. 3). We learn that serious attention must be paid to cultural differences when translating the experimental paradigms used in Western populations to that of other cultures. These studies yield interesting insights into culturally specific contextual factors that shape understanding of risky outcomes.

Shahin Rahimi-Golkhandan, David Garavito, Bertrand Reyna-Brainerd, and Valerie Reyna provide an outside-of-the-box theory of memory, judgment, and decision making that challenges established models of risk and temporal preferences (Chap. 4). Fuzzy Trace Theory explores the social and cognitive mechanisms of these preferences by proposing that people use two different types of mental representations of the rewards, risky probabilities, and time delays inherent in these preferences: The gist representations give a "fuzzy," overall meaning of information (e.g., "now" vs. "later") in contrast to the precise verbatim representation (e.g., in 10 min vs. in 7 days). Incorporating this component of cognition captures many aspects of contextual effects on choice across the life span, with implications for the malleability of impulsivity and delay of gratification.

Suzanne Mitchell connects impulsivity in temporal discounting to psychopathology but also highlights an understudied form of discounting: effort discounting (Chap. 5). Though effort discounting shares some characteristics and neural circuitry with temporal discounting, it is distinct in many ways, as well. Given its potential effects on psychopathology such as depression and attention-deficit/hyperactivity disorder, effort discounting could provide a valuable tool to further understand impulsivity.

David Barack and Michael Platt provide a comprehensive review of the neural circuitry underlying time and risk preferences in foraging (Chap. 6). Foraging offers a decision domain critical to survival for all animals that combines both time and risk.

These authors describe a process model of foraging that incorporates both behavioral and neural data in humans and other species to implicate dysregulated neural circuitry for foraging as a key contributor to impulsive choice.

Trevor Robbins and Jeffrey Dalley synthesize behavioral and neural data in humans and other species to fractionate impulsivity into different subtypes (Chap. 7). Importantly, waiting impulsivity and stopping impulsivity show distinct neural circuits. Understanding the neural basis for the different types of impulsivity can translate into treatments for neuropsychiatric disorders such as substance abuse disorders, attention-deficit/hyperactivity disorder, Parkinson's disease, and other impulse control disorders.

Warren Bickel, Jeffrey Stein, Lara Moody, Sarah Snider, Alexandra Mellis, and Amanda Quisenberry introduce a novel approach to studying impulsivity with direct applications to physical and mental health (Chap. 8). Narrative theory is a framework that taps the power of storytelling to develop interventions for maladaptive health behavior, including addiction, overeating, and risky sexual behavior. Thus, narrative theory provides potential interventions for impulsivity in both temporal and risk preferences.

From neurons to societies, from mice to humans, from children to adults, these chapters cover a broad range of questions we can ask about impulsivity. Understanding the many faces of impulsivity requires continued integration across levels of analysis, species, and timescales. I am very grateful to the contributors to this volume for their participation in the Nebraska Symposium on Motivation and for their continued work to advance our understanding of impulsivity.

Acknowledgements Organizing the 64th annual Nebraska Symposium on Motivation was a joy and a privilege. But the success of the symposium relied on the goodwill and hard work of many people. I am grateful for the financial support from the University of Nebraska-Lincoln Chancellor Harvey Perlman and from the late Professor Cora L. Friedline's bequest to the University of Nebraska Foundation in memory of Professor Harry K. Wolfe. The symposium would not be possible without their generous gifts. I would also like to thank Professor Debra A. Hope, the symposium series editor, for shepherding me through the process of organizing the symposium—from advice on inviting speakers to help picking out the dessert tray. Finally, the symposium went off without a hitch, primarily due to the superb organization of Pam Waldvogel and the assistance of Emily Johnson and Juan Duque. Thank you for your time and hard work.

References

Dalley, J. W., Everitt, B. J., & Robbins, T. W. (2011). Impulsivity, compulsivity, and top-down cognitive control. *Neuron, 69*(4), 680–694.

Evenden, J. L. (1999). Varieties of impulsivity. *Psychopharmacology (Berl), 146*(4), 348–361.

Laibson, D. I., Repetto, A., & Tobacman, J. (1998). Self-control and saving for retirement. *Brookings Papers on Economic Activity, Brookings Papers on Economic Activity, 29*(1), 91–196.

Mischel, W., & Ebbesen, E. B. (1970). Attention in delay of gratification. *Journal of Personality and Social Psychology, 16*(2), 329–337.

Mühlhoff, N., Stevens, J. R., & Reader, S. M. (2011). Spatial discounting of food and social rewards in guppies (*Poecilia reticulata*). *Frontiers in Psychology, 2,* 68.

Read, D. (2004). Intertemporal choice. In D. Koehler & N. Harvey (Eds.), *Blackwell handbook of judgment and decision making* (pp. 424–443). Oxford, UK: Blackwell.

Reynolds, B., Ortengren, A., Richards, J. B., & de Wit, H. (2006). Dimensions of impulsive behavior: Personality and behavioral measures. *Personality and Individual Differences, 40*(2), 305–315.

Stern, N. (2008). The economics of climate change. *American Economic Review, 98*(2), 1–37.

Stevens, J. R. (2010). Intertemporal choice. In M. D. Breed & J. Moore (Eds.), *Encyclopedia of animal behavior* (Vol. 2, pp. 203–208). Oxford: Academic Press.

Toner, I. J., Holstein, R. B., & Hetherington, E. M. (1977). Reflection-impulsivity and self-control in preschool children. *Child Development, 48*(1), 239–245.

Winstanley, C. A., Eagle, D. M., & Robbins, T. W. (2006). Behavioral models of impulsivity in relation to ADHD: Translation between clinical and preclinical studies. *Clinical Psychology Review, 26*(4), 379–395.

Chapter 2
Delay of Gratification: Explorations of How and Why Children Wait and Its Linkages to Outcomes Over the Life Course

Philip K. Peake

Introduction

The ability to delay gratification, to forgo immediately available rewards in pursuit of more preferred but distal goals, is a hallmark of adaptive functioning across the life course. Delaying gratification is a behavioral manifestation of the larger umbrella construct of self-control (Moffitt et al. 2011) and is implicated in a wide range of self-regulatory regimens including maintaining a healthy diet (Herman and Polivy 2003), exercising effectively (Unkelbach et al. 2009), and doing well in school (Bembenutty and Karabenick 2013; Bindman et al. 2015) to name just a few. Inability to delay, on the other hand, has been linked to numerous maladaptive outcomes including obesity (Caleza et al. 2016), substance use (Abikoye and Adekoya 2010; Rossiter et al. 2012), relational difficulties (Ayduk et al. 2000), gambling (Callan et al. 2011), and clinical symptomatology (Ayduk et al. 2008; Campbell and von Stauffenberg 2009). Given the scope of life outcomes to which delay of gratification is linked, it is not surprising that the ability to wait for more desired outcomes is a vibrant field of inquiry within psychology (Tobin and Graziano 2010).

Although there a number of alternative operationalizations of delay of gratification, the paradigm developed by Walter Mischel and his students nearly 50 years ago has captivated both empirical and popular considerations of the topic. In the self-imposed delay of gratification paradigm, a 3–5-year-old child is brought to a "game room" by a familiar adult and asked to indicate a preference between, for instance, one small treat or two. Not surprisingly, children invariably opt for the larger of the two options. The preschooler is then told the adult needs to leave the room and that in order to get the preferred treats, the child will need to wait quietly for the adult to return. Should they decide they no longer want to wait, the child is

P.K. Peake (✉)
Department of Psychology, Smith College, Bass Hall, Northampton, MA 01063, USA
e-mail: ppeake@smith.edu

J.R. Stevens (ed.), *Impulsivity*, Nebraska Symposium on Motivation 64,
DOI 10.1007/978-3-319-51721-6_2

given the option to ring a small desk bell to signal the adult to return at any time. However, if the child terminates the wait, they only get the single treat. Although numerous types of treats (marshmallows, pretzels, M & Ms, mints, etc.) have been used in this research, the experimental paradigm has become popularly labeled simply as the "Marshmallow Test."

Originally designed during the late 1960s, the self-imposed delay of gratification paradigm became the methodological foundation for a decade-long experimental exploration of the cognitive and contextual factors that influence children's ability to wait (Mischel et al. 1989). The number of seconds children waited in those original experiments subsequently became the predictive base for a longitudinal research program that now spans four decades (Mischel et al. 2011). The research program that has evolved around the Marshmallow Test is widely recognized as contributing critical insights into the empirical understanding of childhood waiting and especially its connections to later life outcomes. Mischel et al. (1988) first reported that children who delayed gratification during preschool were perceived by their parents as adolescents who were more cognitively competent, socially competent, and able to cope with stress than their counterparts who did not wait. Subsequent research has extended these longitudinal findings to academic outcomes (Shoda et al. 1990), early adult interpersonal difficulties (aggression, peer rejection) and adaptive functioning (low self-worth, drug use) (Ayduk et al. 2000), borderline personality features (Ayduk et al. 2008), adult body mass (Schlam et al. 2013), and adult differences in neural functioning during impulse control tasks (Casey et al. 2011; Berman et al. 2013).

In popular culture, the Marshmallow Test has assumed a life of its own. The research was thrust into the public consciousness when Dan Goleman offered it as evidence for the importance of "impulse control" in his popular trade book on "emotional intelligence" (Goleman 1995). While there are serious empirical questions about whether delay of gratification is even a component of emotional intelligence (Mayer and Salovey 1997), Goleman captured widespread media and public attention by pitting the Marshmallow Test against traditional IQ tests as a predictor of "success" in later life. Although these claims have also been questioned (Amelang and Steinmayr 2006; Di Fabio and Palazzeschi 2009), they are rarely scrutinized in the popular portrayals of the research. Instead, the research findings are commonly reduced to the simple claim that terminating waiting in the Marshmallow Test portends all manner of later life challenges. These reductions are often buttressed by incredibly compelling, cute, and humorous depictions of children as they grapple with staged enactments of the Marshmallow Test. In outlets ranging from Sesame Street to Oprah, the virtues of impulse control are consistently extolled. The self-help industry has stepped in with numerous books cautioning parents about the fate foretold by early impulsivity. Through Internet blogs, TED Talks, and the like, the virtual life of the Marshmallow Test continues to grow largely unchecked. And like many things within this sphere, as hyperbole builds on hyperbole, complexity and nuance give way to simplistic reductions. Sadly, many academic and popular renditions of the lessons to be learned from this program of research run counter to the conceptual intent, empirical findings, and explicitly stated precautions of the published research.

What should we make of a child ringing a bell to summon the researcher to return during a Marshmallow Test? The direct answer to this question is that the child chose not to wait. In many scholarly and popular portrayals, however, terminating the wait is seen as an act of "impulsivity," the focal point of these conference proceedings. While the label impulsivity is descriptively convenient, it encourages inference about underlying process that may not be fully warranted. It implies more than that the child opted not to wait, and it suggests a reason for that choice. As an explanatory construct, impulsivity implies "acting on impulse" and is commonly defined as acting on emotion, without forethought or careful consideration of risks and consequences. For this reason, impulsive acts are often characterized as irrational, reflexive and stimulus bound. But is ringing a bell to summon an adult back to the room an act of impulsivity? Is the preschooler "acting on emotion, without forethought or careful consideration of risks and consequences"? Is terminating the delay and opting for the lesser reward an "irrational, reflexive, and stimulus bound response"? Labeling the termination of the wait as impulsivity both implicates an underlying process that may not be warranted, suggests that the root cause of stopping is dispositionally rooted in the child, and detracts from other prospective processes that might be implicated in the child's choice.

On the other side of this bipolarity, what should we make of the child who sticks it out, doesn't ring the bell, and waits in order to get the second treat? As noted above, effectively delaying gratification is commonly cast as an act of impulse control or "willpower" (Goleman 1995, pp. 80–82). Especially problematic in this labeling is the suggestion that differences in waiting time derive the individual's "self-control strength," an inferred limited resource subject to depletion under stress (Baumeister and Tierney 2011). Willpower also implies that the path to effective waiting involves "gritting it out" until one attains the desired outcome. Framed within this impulsivity/willpower dichotomy, individuals are viewed as navigating a continuing battle where the temptation to follow irrational impulses must be overcome by "willing" their way to more desired, reasoned choices. Rather than inferring that waiting is the product of willpower or impulse control and all that those terms imply, it is important to ask what children actually do to facilitate delay of gratification. It turns out that existing research provides rich and somewhat unexpected clues about these processes.

As the empirical span of this research program closes in on nearly half a decade, it seems timely to review the history of the Marshmallow Test from its early experimental roots through its various longitudinal forays. In the context of the current volume, any full consideration of impulsivity should rightfully include a review of this foundational research. The review offered here presents an historically annotated and purposely critical overview of what the original research program revealed about waiting, what the follow-up research has documented to date, and what those various explorations tell us about what might be guiding children's behavior as they navigate the challenge. The research reviewed will then be used to evaluate different factors that are commonly offered as explanations for why children wait and to explore academic and popular claims that are commonly attached to the Marshmallow Test.

Experimental Studies of Delay of Gratification (1967–1973)

Background and Setting

The series of experimental studies that constitute the empirical base of the Marshmallow Test evolved from the collective efforts of Mischel and a dedicated group of students during the latter part of the 1960s and continuing through the early 1970s. A number of theoretical and operational influences converged at that time that guided this program of research. Several of these are worth special consideration.

First, Mischel's interest in delay of gratification predated the Marshmallow Test by over a decade. Beginning with anthropological collaborations with his brother in Trinidad and Grenada that were initiated in 1955, Mischel conducted a series of investigations of preferences for delayed outcomes (Mischel 1958, 1961; Mischel and Gilligan 1964; Bandura and Mischel 1965; Mischel and Staub 1965; Mischel and Grusec 1967; Mischel et al. 1969). Throughout this line of research, the key dependent measure was the individual's choice between a small, but immediately available reward (one cent candy now) and a temporally delayed but larger reward (ten cent candy in one week). The expressed preferences were labeled as measures of "delay choice." The Marshmallow Test was designed with the recognition that expressed preferences for delayed outcomes are not always born out when people actually face the challenge of the wait itself. One only needs to think of the considerable challenges people confront holding to New Year's resolutions to understand this important distinction. People can express all manner of preferences for desirable distal outcomes only to see those preferences melt away when faced with the sacrifices and challenges of staying on a diet, maintaining an exercise regimen, or forgoing alcohol or cigarettes. Mischel and his students recognized the distinction between expressed preferences for delayed outcomes (delay choice) and the ability to actually maintain delay (delay maintenance) and focused the design of the Marshmallow Test directly on the latter.

The discrepancy that often exists between delay choices and delay maintenance was aligned with the then emerging literature on the differences that characterize people's attitudes and their actual behavior in other spheres (Fishbein and Ajzen 1972) and continues to be recognized as an important distinction in understanding self-control and impulsivity. Much of the current work on temporal discounting that is linked to the study of impulsivity, although impressively refined and operationalized over the early offerings of Mischel and others (Mahrer 1956), focuses almost exclusively on people's delay preferences despite reminders of the important distinction between those choices and delay behavior itself (Reynolds and

Schiffbauer 2005; Addessi et al. 2013). Although the term delay of gratification is often confusingly used to refer to either delay choices or delay maintenance, a key distinction between the two is that while self-reported preferences (and the discounting functions associated with them) yield static assessments of the person's desires, maintaining delay is a dynamic process that is defined by individual's option to defect from those choices as the waiting progresses (Young and McCoy 2015).

It is worth noting that children participating in the standard delay of gratification paradigm do state a preference between the two outcomes that are offered. Typically, this choice is between different quantities of the same treat (e.g., one marshmallow vs. two marshmallows) although it is not uncommon to use mixes (e.g., one pretzel vs. two marshmallows). When this preference is first expressed within the experimental paradigm, it is in the form of a straight choice (Mischel 1958) and is distinguished from a delay choice by the absence of a temporal element (e.g., one marshmallow now vs. two marshmallows in 15 min). Children are simply asked whether they would prefer one reward option or the other. The element of time is only introduced when it is later explained to the child that they must wait for the more preferred outcome, but even here the actual length of the wait is not specified. Indeed, one of the defining features of the Marshmallow Test is the child's uncertainty about how long they will need to wait. Preschoolers are only told that the experimenter needs to leave the room and that they must wait for the experimenter to return in order to receive the more preferred reward. Children might reasonably infer that the wait will be minutes versus hours or days, etc., but it is deliberately unclear whether the absence might be just a few seconds, a few minutes, or longer. One thing that is clear is that waiting alone to the required criterion time, which ranged from 10 to 30 min in the original experiments, is typically an unusual and challenging experience for preschoolers. Needless to say, subjective expectations about how long the wait might be are likely shifting as the experience unfolds (McGuire and Kable 2013). These shifting expectations contribute to the dynamic of most self-control situations where the individuals must continually re-evaluate whether the desired outcome is indeed worth enduring the wait and forgoing immediately available options. As in many real-life self-control scenarios, earnestly expressed preferences become subject to reappraisal and defection as the child sizes up the challenge, uncertainty, and experience of the task at hand.

A second major influence on the development and implementation of the experiments on children's waiting was undoubtedly the publication of *Personality and Assessment*, the classic critique of the field of personality theory and testing (Mischel 1969). In *Personality and Assessment*, Mischel provided a review of several lines of research that challenged key assumptions that had historically guided theory and research on the nature of personality. First, with the exception of some cognitive and intellectual measures, people show less consistency in their behavior across situations than was suggested by traditional dispositional approaches. Although people often demonstrate impressive stability in their behavior over time when observed in the same situation, observations taken across different contexts suggest that behavior is highly sensitive to contextual variation. Second, Mischel noted that efforts to predict how people behave in real-life situations based on static trait-based assessments of personality typically demonstrated modest efficacy. From these observations, Mischel questioned the utility of both conceptualizing and measuring personality using highly generalized dispositions such as impulsivity and willpower. Instead, Mischel challenged personality researchers to shift their focus to units of analysis that might more closely embody the observed contextual sensitivity of behavior. Rather than being driven by generalized dispositions, Mischel suggested that people's behavior is highly discriminative. People navigate the complexities of their social worlds actively processing situational cues that trigger sets of expectancies, goal systems, and competencies that guide their ongoing behavior.

The shift away from global, dispositional units to more contextualized, process-oriented constructs can even be seen in the very early work on delay choice. Rather than viewing these preferences as generalized traits, this research focused on identifying contextual and experiential factors that influence delay choices. In work based on Rotter's early social learning theory, Mahrer (1956) showed that children's experimentally manipulated expectancies that they will receive the preferred reward (e.g., their "trust" that the reward will in fact be delivered) powerfully impacts children's delay choices. Mischel (1958, 1961) similarly demonstrated that the trust-based expectancies that underlie delay choices can derive from children's cultural and familial history with agents who deliver rewards. Mischel and Metzner (1962) showed that delay choices varied in relation to age, intelligence, and the length of the wait. Also working within a social learning framework, Bandura and Mischel (1965) demonstrated that exposure to live and symbolic model's delay preferences produced sustainable shifts in children's delay choices. Mischel and Staub (1965) showed that when a work element was added to the requirements for attaining the desired outcome, delay choices were influenced by the child's expectancies of succeeding on the task. Additionally, Mischel and Grusec (1967) demonstrated that delay choices are related to beliefs about temporal delay and trust (probability of delivery) for both future rewards and punishments. This line of research illustrates the shift away from viewing delay choices as highly generalized dispositions to one where preferences are seen as the products of children sizing up the circumstances they face and using those contextual cues to guide their choices. From this perspective, delay preferences were not seen as fixed and enduring, but flexible and adaptive. Similarly, and importantly for the current review, children's delay choices were not seen as primarily reflecting of the child's impulsivity. The child expressing a preference for an immediate reward was not viewed as "acting on emotion, without forethought or careful consideration of risks and consequences." Instead, delay choices were seen as reflecting a reasoned evaluation of the current circumstances in light of child's beliefs, values, and expectancies regarding the proposed outcomes.

Similarly, as Mischel and his students shifted their focus of study from delay choice to delay maintenance, the child's ability to wait was not viewed as a fixed and enduring disposition, but as a competence that was likely influenced by an array of contextual and cognitive factors. The program of experiments that utilized the Marshmallow Test set out to identify and explore those factors. In the review that follows, the methods and key findings of each of the published experiments in that program are briefly described. Experiments are reviewed in the chronological order of their publication, which largely overlaps with the order in which they were conducted. It is important to note that the experiments employing the Marshmallow Test were but one part of a larger research program that explored different facets of children's self-control including children's generalized control beliefs (Mischel et al. 1974), coping plans (Mischel and Patterson 1976; Patterson and Mischel 1976), and knowledge of waiting strategies (Yates and Mischel 1979; Mischel and Mischel 1983). In addition, some experimental conditions that were part of the studies discussed here are not included in this review. Although all of this research informs our broader understanding children's self-control, these programmatic components do not employ an experimental variation of the Marshmallow Test or do so in examining something other than passive waiting (e.g., delay while working) and hence are not included in the longitudinal database to be discussed subsequently.

Reward Presence: Mischel and Ebbesen (1970)

The initial rendition of the Marshmallow Test was designed to address a straightforward but consequential question regarding the factors that might influence children's ability wait. It explored the impact of the physical presence of the rewards during the waiting period in research carried out by Ebbe Ebbesen at the Bing Nursery School during the summer of 1967. Mischel and Ebbesen introduced a new delay of gratification paradigm where preschoolers, typically 4–5 years of age, were asked to indicate a straight choice preference between either five 2-inch pretzels or two animal cookies (yes, the original "Marshmallow Test" did not include any marshmallows). After the child had indicated a preference, the experimenter explained they would need to leave the room and that the child would need to wait for the experimenter to return to receive the preferred reward. Unlike later versions of the paradigm, there was no bell in this first study. Instead, children were taught to consume a small ½-inch pretzel as a signal to the experimenter that they wanted to terminate the delay.

The key manipulation in this paradigm was which rewards were left in the room while the child attempted to wait. All combinations were included: both rewards, the delayed (preferred) reward, the immediate (less preferred) reward, or neither of the rewards. Mischel and Ebbesen reasoned that leaving different combinations of rewards in the room would allow children to focus attention on the rewards while they waited, and hence, this was offered as a manipulation of the child's attention to rewards. While it is clearly the case that children will pay more attention to rewards when they are physically present, it is not the child's attention per se that is being manipulated in this experiment but the physical presence or absence of the rewards.

Mischel and Ebbesen noted and subsequent research has since demonstrated that even with rewards physically available for attention, there are substantial differences in children's tendency to actually focus attention on the rewards (Peake et al. 2002).

The key finding of this research was that leaving the rewards physically present (and hence available for the child to attend to) was quite detrimental to waiting. Children facing both rewards during the delay period managed to wait on average just over 1 of the possible 15 min (Fig. 2.1). In contrast, when both rewards were removed, children waited on average over 11 min. If either one of the rewards (delayed or immediate) was left with the child, intermediate waits averaging around 5 min were observed. These findings demonstrate that having any reward present while waiting makes the delay more challenging, but having both rewards present makes waiting especially difficult. This indicates that the presence of both rewards encourages active comparison of the two outcomes that might encourage reappraisal and earlier defections from the desired path. It is one of the first empirical signs that children are actively processing and re-evaluating possible outcomes as the wait progresses.

In discussing the impact of reward presence, it is common to find the difference between the 1- and 11-min average waits highlighted (Mischel et al. 1989, 2011). However, Mischel and Ebbesen recognized that it was problematic in this paradigm for the "signal" to terminate delay (eating a small pretzel) to be so similar to one of the potential rewards. For this reason, in a section of the paper referred to as "follow-up data," they report a replication study where they introduced a small desk bell for children to use to signal the experimenter to return. This substitution eliminated the confounding of the signal to return with the desired outcome and became the standard procedure for all subsequent work in this paradigm. Interestingly, although average delay times remain significantly shorter when rewards are present than absent when using the bell as a signal (3 min vs. 9 min, see Fig. 2.1), they are no longer the extremely short times evidenced when pretzels

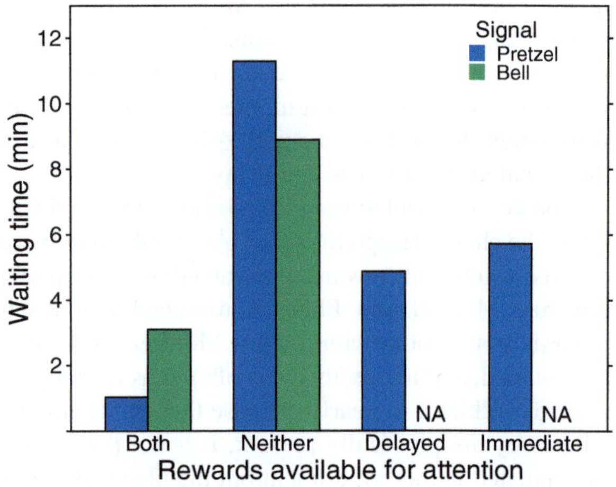

Fig. 2.1 Waiting time as a function of reward presence using either consuming pretzel or ringing bell as signal for experimenter to return. Adapted from Mischel and Ebbesen (1970)

were used as signals. This might again attest to the contextual sensitivity of delay behavior, but some caution is warranted here since sample sizes are quite small in most of these conditions (typically around $N = 10$ in any experimental condition), and hence, condition means can contain a substantial error component. It is worth noting that while reward presence almost always yields significantly shorter average wait times within a particular experiment, there is nonetheless sizable variation in the average wait time with rewards present across studies.

In retrospect, many suggest that it is obvious that leaving rewards present during the delay period should be detrimental to effective waiting. At the time, however, there were several compelling theoretical accounts that suggested just the opposite. Psychoanalysts, including Freud (1911), had suggested that the key to bridging time in pursuit of a blocked gratification involved constructing mental images of the desired but blocked object (see also Rappaport 1967). Working from a very different theoretical slant, social psychologists also weighed in on this issue suggesting that effective impulse control centered on self-instructional processes that increase the salience of delayed outcomes, thus facilitating "time-binding." From this perspective, any cognitive or contextual factors that increase the salience of the reward should make waiting easier (Jones and Gerard 1967). To this day, it is not uncommon to see self-help guides that steer individuals to repeatedly focus or remind themselves of desired outcomes. Within the empirical literature, there are still important questions regarding those circumstances where attention to rewards might facilitate performance (Peake et al. 2002). Whether obvious or not, the impact of reward presence remains one of the most robust and conceptually important findings in this program of research.

Distractions from Rewards: Mischel et al. (1972)

In discussing their findings, Mischel and Ebbesen commented on the activities of the children while they waited with the following:

> One of the most striking delay strategies used by some subjects was exceedingly simple and effective. These children seemed to facilitate their waiting by converting the aversive waiting situation into a more pleasant non-waiting one. They devised elaborate self-distraction techniques through which they spent their time psychologically doing something (almost anything) other than waiting. Instead of focusing prolonged attention on the objects for which they were waiting, they avoided looking at them. Some children covered their eyes with their hands, rested their heads on their arms, and found other similar techniques for averting their eyes from the reward objects. Many seemed to try to reduce the frustration of delay of reward by generating their own diversions: they talked to themselves, sang, invented games with their hands and feet, and even tried to fall asleep—as one child successfully did (1970, p. 335).

Mischel and Ebbesen saw these efforts as testimony to how frustrating waiting alone is for preschoolers. They noted that there were likely two components contributing to this frustration. First, merely waiting alone in a room with nothing to do is quite difficult and unusual for young children. The waiting task is boring, a quality shared with many self-control tasks. Children must invent ways to engage themselves during this monotonous period. Second, the presence of the rewards may increase the anticipation of the reward, adding to the frustration of the situation. The antics of the children as they attempt to wait, while often seemingly haphazard and quite amusing, were seen as strategic attempts to divert attention from these aversive components of the wait.

Working off this observation, Mischel and Ebbesen were joined in the spring of 1968 by Antonette Zeiss, then an undergraduate studying at Stanford, to explore the impact of providing children with different types of distraction during the delay period. In a series of three separate experiments, Mischel et al. (1972) explored the impact of both physical and cognitive distractions when rewards were either present (Experiments 1 and 2) or absent (Experiment 3) during the wait. In all three experiments, children indicated a preference for either one small marshmallow or one pretzel. Physical distraction was provided by allowing the child to play with a slinky toy. Cognitive distraction was provided by instructing the child to either think about fun things, about sad things, or about the rewards themselves during the wait depending on the experiment.

Mischel, Ebbesen, and Zeiss replicated the impact of reward presence in the absence of any distraction instructions with children showing very short delays when facing the both rewards (Fig. 2.2). Interestingly, when children had the opportunity to play with a slinky toy, a form of physical distraction, delay times were nearly 9 min despite the fact that the rewards remained available for attention. Thinking fun things, a form of cognitive distraction, was especially helpful, producing lengthy delays regardless of whether rewards were present or absent. In contrast, thinking sad thoughts, a cognitive distraction that children might be less likely to actually do or maintain, provided modest gains in waiting times.

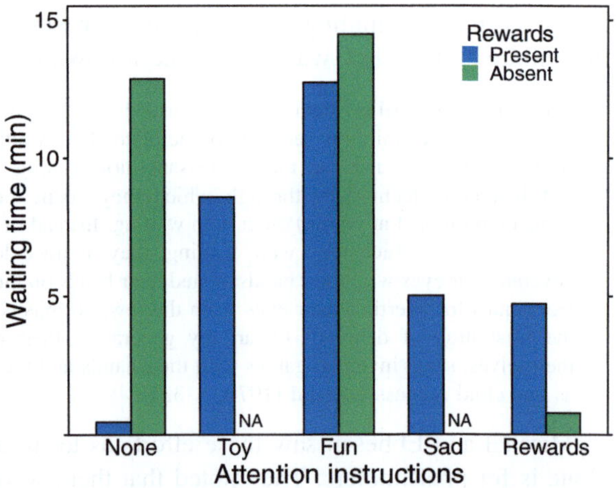

Fig. 2.2 Waiting time as a function of reward presence and type of attentional instruction provided. Results collapsed across three experiments. In replicated conditions, means across experiments are shown here. Adapted from Mischel et al. (1972)

In addition to demonstrating that physical and cognitive distractions during the wait period facilitate waiting, one of the more important findings in this work was seen when children are instructed to focus their attention on the rewards themselves. When the rewards are present, reward-directed attention yielded average delays somewhat but not significantly longer than when children were given no instructions, suggesting that in the absence of instructions to do something else, children were likely spontaneously engaging in reward-directed attention. Interestingly, when rewards were absent, asking children to think about the rewards had the same detrimental effect as placing the rewards directly in front of the child with no instructions. This finding suggested to the researchers that the cognitive representation of the rewards is as important as the physical stimulus itself. This is a theme that is born out throughout the remaining research program with the Marshmallow Test.

Symbolic Rewards: Mischel and Moore (1973)

Recognizing that distracting, irrelevant activities like playing with a slinky toy or thinking fun thoughts enabled waiting even in the presence of rewards, the research next focused more directly on reward representation during the delay period. During the time that he completed his graduate studies with Mischel, Burt Moore conducted a series of experiments examining the impact of symbolic versus real presentations of the rewards on waiting. The first of these experiments was initiated by Moore at the Bing School in the fall of 1970. Working off the prior finding that thinking about rewards in their absence was detrimental to waiting, Mischel and Moore sought to explore aspects of children's ideation about rewards while waiting. Even though the physical presence of rewards had been shown to debilitate rather than facilitate delay as previously theorized, Mischel and Moore noted that most theoretical accounts of delay of gratification made reference to people's thoughts and images while waiting, not their direct perceptions. Most waiting situations do not involve the actual physical presence of the rewards, so what mattered was how individuals thought or imagined the rewards in their absence during the waiting period.

Recognizing that children's cognitive activity was largely inaccessible during a waiting task, Mischel and Moore attempted to manipulate the child's cognitive representations by displaying symbolic presentations of the rewards while the child waited. This was accomplished by showing the child pictures of the rewards with a slide projector. In this first study, half of the children were asked to express a straight preference for either two marshmallows or one pretzel, while the other half selected between two pennies or a token. The reward pair for which the child expressed this preference was referred to as the "relevant rewards," while the other reward pair was referred to as the "irrelevant rewards." Using a crossover design, children observed slides of the relevant rewards, the irrelevant rewards, a blank slide, or no slide at all. For half of the children, the slide content was shown continuously, while for the rest the slide was shown "periodically" (5 s at 30-s intervals). This scheduling variation was intended to test the notion that periodic reminders of the goal might better serve the child than continuous exposure.

Contrary to the prior findings involving direct exposure to the rewards, Mischel and Moore found that exposure to symbolic representations of the reward did indeed facilitate waiting (Fig. 2.3). In both periodic and continuous presentation conditions, preschoolers exposed to symbolic representations of relevant rewards waited close to the maximum wait of 10 min utilized in this experiment. This is in stark contrast to both how children responded to irrelevant rewards in this study, and real and physically present rewards in prior experiments. There were only minor differences connected to whether the slides were continuously or periodically presented, and the research once again replicated the prior finding that when rewards were absent and children were given no instructions (no slide condition), children were able to demonstrate lengthy waiting capacity.

In interpreting the obtained pattern of findings, Mischel and Moore embraced Berlyne's (1960) distinction between two cueing functions that a reward might serve (see also Estes 1972). On the one hand, rewards can provide an arousal or motivational cue that stimulates the individual's desire for the outcomes. Second, rewards can provide an informational cue, reminding the child about properties of what they are striving to attain. Mischel and Moore speculated that the physical presence of the rewards likely served to cue arousal in the child, increasing the challenge of waiting. In contrast, symbolic representations of the rewards are less loaded with arousing physical cues and may serve mainly an informational function. This distinction about the different ways that children might cognitively process rewards lays the foundation for much of the theoretical formulations about delay that eventually evolved from this program of research (Metcalfe and Mischel 1999; Mischel et al. 2011).

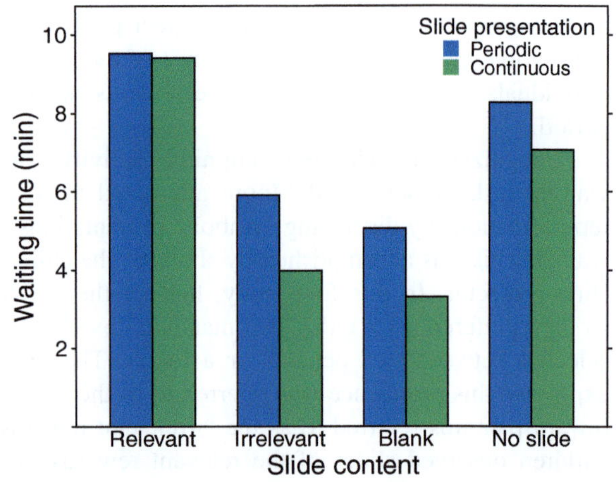

Fig. 2.3 Waiting time as a function of slide content for symbolically presented rewards. Rewards physically absent in all conditions. Adapted from Mischel and Moore (1973)

Beliefs About Instrumental Thinking: Mischel and Underwood (1974)

With the completion of Mischel and Moore's first exploration of symbolic presentation of rewards, Bill Underwood, another of Mischel's graduate students at Stanford, initiated a project in the spring of 1971 to examine instrumental ideation while children waited. Framed as a study to shift the research program from waiting to working situations, the "work" in Mischel and Underwood (1974) only involved children's beliefs about the instrumentality of what they are thinking as they wait. The research was an extended replication of the paradigm used by Mischel and Moore where preschoolers were exposed to either symbolic (slides) or real rewards that were either relevant or not. In this experiment, all rewards were presented continuously. To that core design, Mischel and Underwood added an instruction to make children believe that thinking about the rewards would make the experimenter return sooner. All children were told that they could think about the rewards while they waited if they wanted to, but those in the instrumental ideation condition were made to believe there was a contingency between this thinking and the return of the experimenter.

Mischel and Underwood found that making children believe there was an instrumental connection between thinking about the relevant rewards facilitated delay time regardless of whether the rewards were real or symbolic (Fig. 2.4). Similar but less lengthy delays were evidenced when children thought instrumentally about irrelevant rewards. Finally, delay times were modest across conditions without the aid of instrumental instruction. The most significant finding from this work is seen in the lengthy delays for children provided with instrumental instructions when rewards were real and relevant. This stands in stark contrast to all prior research conditions where rewards were present and children were not provided with instructions about how to think about them (including the "non-instrumental–relevant–real" condition of this experiment). Mischel and Underwood speculated that the instrumental instructions shift the child's reward focus to the informational properties of the reward and away from the arousing cues that they likely gravitate toward without instruction. In this way, the findings of Mischel and Underwood provide further indirect insight into what children might

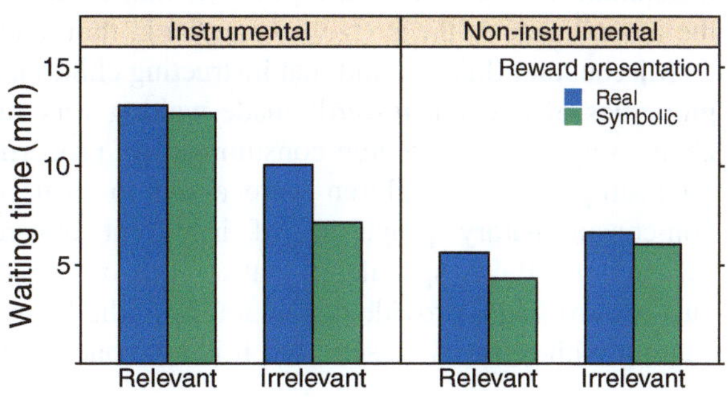

Fig. 2.4 Waiting time as a function of child's belief about instrumentality of thinking about real or symbolic rewards that are either relevant or irrelevant. Adapted from Mischel and Underwood (1974)

be doing spontaneously when trying to wait in the presence of the reward. It is noteworthy that delays are modest in all non-instrumental conditions.

Consummatory and Non-consummatory Ideation: Mischel and Baker (1975)

As the research program on delay of gratification progressed, a theoretical formulation was evolving. That formulation recognized first that the physical presence of the rewards made waiting difficult. However, the research also demonstrated that *how* children thought about the rewards could override the impact of their mere physical presence. The idea that rewards could function as either an arousing or an informational cue was evolving and supported, albeit indirectly, in the research. Mischel and Moore speculated that presenting rewards symbolically might be directing children's attention away for the salient motivational properties of real rewards. Similarly, Mischel and Underwood suggested that instructing children to think instrumentally about the rewards was also leading to an informational focus. These experiments demonstrated that shifting the form (mode of presentation) and function (instrumentality) of rewards altered their impact on children, but did not explore specifically how children cognitively represent rewards themselves while waiting. It was not until Nancy Baker, then an undergraduate at Stanford, tested children at the Bing School in the spring of 1971 that an experiment looked directly at the consequences of having children focus on the arousing properties of rewards while they waited.

Mischel and Baker (1975) employed a rewards physically present crossover design where children were exposed to and instructed to think about either relevant rewards or irrelevant rewards during the wait period that was lasted a maximum of 20 min. The rewards used were either 1 versus 2 marshmallows or 1 versus 2 pretzels. Children were told to focus on either consummatory (arousing) properties or non-consummatory (transformational) properties of the rewards. In the consummatory conditions, children were told to think about the how the marshmallows were "sweet and chewy and soft" or how the pretzels were "crunchy and salty." In the non-consummatory conditions, children were instructed to think about how marshmallows are "white and puffy … like clouds" and "round and white … like the moon" or how the pretzels were "long, thin, and brown … like logs."

Mischel and Baker found that instructing children to focus on the consummatory properties of relevant rewards made waiting very difficult for children (Fig. 2.5). Conversely, focus on non-consummatory properties leads to lengthy delays. Interestingly, when children were asked to focus on the consummatory versus non-consummatory properties of irrelevant reward, this effect was reversed. Mischel and Baker speculated that a focus on consummatory properties of irrelevant reward might provide distraction from the frustration typically associated with waiting with rewards present, but it is not conceptually obvious why transforming

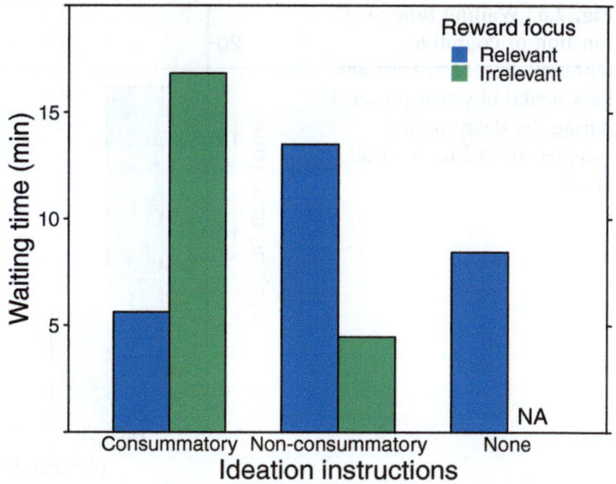

Fig. 2.5 Waiting time as a function of instructions to think about consummatory or non-consummatory properties of rewards. "None" represents a control condition where children are not provided with any instruction. Adapted from Mischel and Baker (1975)

an irrelevant reward would lead to shortened waiting times. Needless to say, these types of focus on irrelevant rewards, while experimentally convenient, do not have many real-life analogs. The key takeaway from this pivotal work is that the impact of physically present rewards can be either accentuated or attenuated by instructions that influence *how* children cognitively represent the rewards.

Transforming Real and Symbolic Rewards: Moore et al. (1976)

Mischel and Baker demonstrated that children could be instructed to cognitively transform rewards so as to focus on their less arousing properties. In work conducted in the summer of 1973, Moore et al. (1976) asked whether the prior findings obtained by Mischel and Moore (1973) concerning the impact of symbolically presented rewards using slide presentations would hold if children were asked to cognitively transform real rewards into symbolic ones, in this case pictures. During the 20-min delay period, children waited with either a picture of the rewards (two marshmallows vs. one pretzel), the real rewards, or no rewards physically present. Some children were instructed to look and think about the rewards that were in front of them (real or pictures). Other children were instructed to cognitively transform the rewards as they were presented. Hence, children who faced the real rewards were asked to imagine a color picture of the rewards in their head and then "put a frame around it." They were then asked to pretend that the picture was on a screen and that they could see it. Children who faced the picture of the rewards were asked to cognitively transform them to imagine that they were real and setting on the table in front of them.

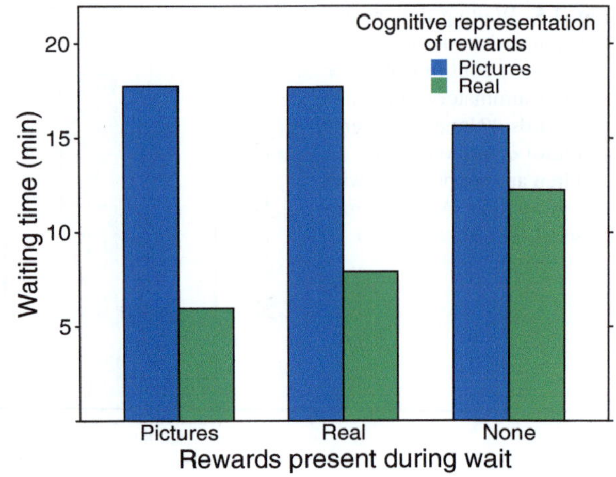

Fig. 2.6 Waiting time as a function of cognitive representation of reward and their actual physical presence during the delay period. Adapted from Moore et al. (1976)

Moore, Mischel, and Zeiss showed that having children imagine the rewards as pictures facilitated delay regardless of which rewards were physically present as the child waited (Fig. 2.6). In contrast, representing rewards as real yielded shorter delay times regardless of whether the child was facing real rewards or their symbolic representations. When rewards were not present in any form, children once again showed the ability to wait. The findings of Moore, Mischel, and Zeiss not only replicate Moore and Mischel's prior finding about how symbolic representations impact waiting, but more critically demonstrate that this impact can be obtained using just the child's imagination. Having a child "put a frame" around the real rewards transforms them in a manner that they have the same impact as actual pictures, bolstering the view that what really matters is the child's representation of the rewards.

Consummatory Focus on Symbolic Rewards: Mischel and Moore (1980)

In the final published experiment containing data that are included in the longitudinal follow-ups of the Marshmallow Test, Mischel and Moore (1980) once again examined the impact of symbolically presented rewards but now with a focus on how children were instructed to ideate about the slide content. Using a crossover design modeled after Mischel and Moore (1973), children waited while viewing continuously presented slides that pictured either relevant rewards, irrelevant rewards, or no rewards. Children were also instructed to think about the consummatory qualities of the relevant rewards, the irrelevant rewards, or neither. Children initially indicated their preference for either 2 marshmallows versus a pretzel or 2 candy mints versus a graham cracker. The reward pair employed in this choice was

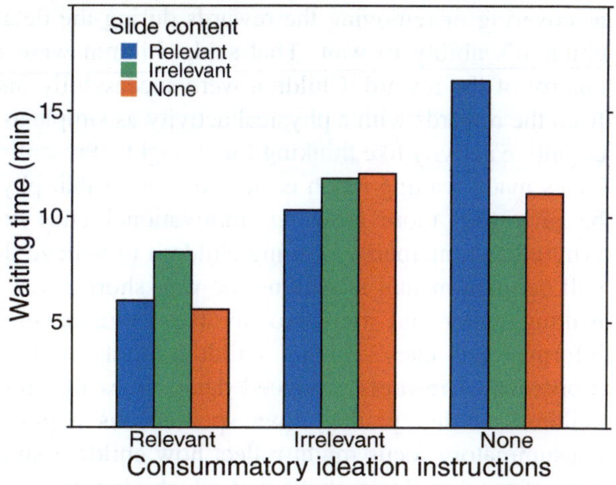

Fig. 2.7 Waiting time as a function of consummatory ideation instructions and type of slide content presented during the delay period. Adapted from Mischel and Moore (1980)

labeled the relevant rewards, and the other was referred to as the irrelevant rewards. If a child had chosen between the marshmallows and pretzels and was assigned to engage in the consummatory ideation for the relevant rewards, they were asked to think about how marshmallows are "sweet and chewy." If, on the other hand, they were assigned to the think about the irrelevant rewards while waiting, they would be asked to think about how mints are "sweet and melt in your mouth." As with Mischel and Moore (1973), real rewards were absent in all conditions of this experiment.

Mischel and Moore (1980) replicated Mischel and Moore's (1973) finding that symbolic presentations of rewards tend to facilitate delay as compared to exposure to real reward (Fig. 2.7). However, when children were asked to focus on the consummatory properties of the relevant reward, delay times resembled those obtained when the rewards were physically present and children had no instructions. Moreover, thinking about the consummatory properties of irrelevant rewards facilitated delay regardless of the slide content. These findings buttressed Mischel and Moore's prior claim that symbolic presentation of rewards (without instruction) leads children to focus away for the arousing properties of rewards and focus on their informational cues. Directing children's attention back to the arousing, consummatory cues debilitates their ability to wait.

Experimental Studies: Takeaways and Caveats

The experimental investigations utilizing the Marshmallow Test reviewed here paint a compelling picture of the capacities of preschoolers to wait for desired outcomes. The first general finding of this work is that a child's ability to delay gratification depends very much on the situation they face. A manipulation as subtle as covering or removing the rewards during the delay period powerfully impacted children's ability to wait. That said, children were not solely under the stimulus control of the reward. Children were successfully instructed to distract themselves from the rewards with a physical activity as simple as playing with a slinky toy or a cognitive activity like thinking fun thoughts. Presenting the rewards symbolically as slides made waiting much easier, indicating that physically present rewards might be providing more arousing, motivational cues compared to their informative symbolic counterparts. Leading children to believe that thinking about the rewards will be instrumental in making the wait shorter was also an effective way to make waiting easier and may also involve a similar shift in attentional focus toward informational cues. Having children think about the arousing, consummatory properties of rewards produced delay times that resemble those that occur when children are left to their own spontaneous coping strategies, suggesting that a consummatory focus might reflect how children spontaneously process physically present rewards. Instructions that ask children to transform the rewards by focusing on their non-consummatory properties, on the other hand, greatly facilitated waiting. Children proved to be remarkably adept at cognitively transforming rewards creating representations of real rewards as if they were pictures and pictures as if they were real rewards. In both cases, the impact of the rewards on waiting was driven by the cognitively transformed versions. Finally, even though symbolically presented rewards facilitated waiting, those gains quickly dissipated when children are asked to focus on the consummatory properties of the slide presentations.

The picture that emerges from this line of research is not one of children primarily driven by a general disposition like impulsivity or willpower. Rather, children are facile in their responsiveness to contextual cues and can readily adapt to instructional sets that assist (or debilitate) their coping efforts. Even those children who terminate the delay do not seem irrational, reflexive, and stimulus bound. Instead, they appear to be making reasoned choices that reflect both qualities of the challenge presented to them and how they come to represent that challenge cognitively.

All that said, it should be noted that the typical child left to wait in the presence of rewards found the task challenging. In many reports, the very short (less than one minute) delay times of some studies (Mischel and Ebbesen 1970; Mischel et al. 1972) are emphasized implying that virtually no child can cope long at this challenge. The research reviewed here suggests that these extremely short average wait times are not typical. Average wait time with rewards present varies from study to study, and it is difficult to make cross-study comparisons since the maximum delay time varies across studies and minor adjustments were made to the paradigm as the research progressed. Nonetheless, it can be said that wait times with rewards present typically averaged around 4–5 min and these delays were reliably significantly less than when children were waiting with the rewards removed or covered. Moreover, the average wait time of 4–5 min with rewards present is consistent with more recent research using the paradigm (Peake et al. 2002) with preschoolers including a large-scale testing of nearly a thousand children in the paradigm as part of the National Institute of Child Health and Development (NICHD) Study of Early Child

Care and Youth Development (SECCYD; https://secc.rti.org/) (for a descriptive summary, see Duckworth et al. 2013).

Recognizing that waiting with rewards present is generally challenging, there were nonetheless substantial individual differences in how long children actually waited in this experimental setting. Some children opted out and rang the bell within the first few minutes of the session, while others stuck out the wait and received the preferred rewards. The experiments reviewed here provide indirect insight into how children might typically process the experience and the types of strategies that might contribute to the observed individual differences. The consistent message across all the research reviewed here is that any experimental instructions that moved children's attentional focus away from the variously labeled arousing, consummatory, or motivational properties of rewards facilitated delay. In contrast, instructions that focused attention toward these properties increased the challenge of the wait. Collectively, the findings suggest that in the absence of experimental instructions on what to think or do while waiting, preschool children will tend to focus attention of the "hot" properties of rewards. Individual differences in waiting, then, are most likely connected to children differentially engaging in activities and cognitions that divert attentional focus away from the rewards (Metcalfe and Mischel 1999).

It is important to note, however, that the inferences offered here all derive from experiments focused on group differences. None of the original Marshmallow Test experiments examined individual differences in what children were doing while they waited. The strategies that the children might have been spontaneously deploying were neither directly observed nor measured. Informal direct observation of children in the delay situation raises important questions about whether the captivating behaviors they commonly display (singing, clapping, staring away), behaviors that seem to distract attention away from the rewards and task at hand, are actually deliberate and strategic attempts at coping or if children are merely emitting behaviors some of which happen to be helpful and others less so. If the former were the case, the resulting individual differences in waiting might be meaningful and connect with other aspects of the child's adaptive functioning. Alternatively, if children are just randomly stumbling across more or less effective strategies, the observed individual differences should not be especially meaningful or predictive. This key question is at the core of the Bing Longitudinal Study, a project that has now followed the lives of the participants in these experiments for over 35 years.

Longitudinal Explorations of Delay of Gratification (1981–2016)

Background

Data collection for the last of the experimental investigations reported above was completed in the summer of 1973. While completion of the published manuscripts for that work continued, Antonette Zeiss along with her husband Bob initiated a new project that they called the Bing Consistency Study. Recall that Mischel had previously raised important questions about the consistency of behavior, and Zeiss set out to explore the consistency of children's behavior on the Marshmallow Test. With the ambitious research program that was conducted at the Bing School from 1967 to 1973, many children found their way into the experimental game room on more than one occasion. In a typical scenario, a child might be tested in one experimental paradigm and then be brought back to participate in a pretest for subsequent research. This allowed the research team to explore modifications to the design and/or new manipulations without using previously untested children, a valuable commodity in such an active program. The purpose of the Bing Consistency Study was to organize all the data collected in connection with this research program in hopes of examining issues such as the stability and consistency of children's waiting in different experimental settings.

Mischel had conscientiously maintained the data sheets from the original experiments, and Zeiss initiated efforts to consolidate those data. It is important to recall that at the time of the original experiments, computers were only beginning to become utilized in academic settings, and they were large, expensive, and not easily accessible. Data from the experiments were all collected and recorded on large "green sheets," the paper-and-pencil forerunner of the modern spreadsheet. Interestingly, all data reduction and statistical calculation were also completed by hand, recorded on similar green sheets, and stored in crudely labeled file folders. To accommodate the sheer amount of data, Zeiss taped green sheets together to provide more columns and rows. Unfortunately, these early organizational efforts were not completed before Zeiss left for graduate school, and the resulting summary sheets were filed away with all the other data in Mischel's back office.

In 1978, I arrived at Stanford with no real interest in delay of gratification and fully intending to study the consistency of behavior. Powerfully influenced by reading *Personality and Assessment* as an undergraduate at Carleton College, I had initiated a major investigation into the consistency of student behavior along with my mentor Neil Lutsky and fellow student Linda Wray. Modeled after the seminal work of Bem and Allen (1974), the Carleton Consistency Study yielded boxes and boxes of data that I transported to Stanford hoping that it would form the basis of my dissertation work. The Carleton project was ambitious, and my early meetings with Mischel made clear that I needed to find a more manageable project that could be completed during my first year in Palo Alto to fulfill the entry requirements of the Ph.D. program.

After several false starts, we resolved on a delay of gratification project that examined Bem and Funder's (1978) template matching approach to understanding the personality of situations. Bem and Funder obtained parental ratings of children using Block's California Child Q-Set (Q-Set), an omnibus assessment that required sorting of 100 personality descriptions tailored toward the children's personalities and then correlated these ratings with children's behavior in two delay of gratification situations. One of these was a modification of the Marshmallow Test where the experimenter stayed in the room while the child waited. The second was a "gift delay" measure developed by Block (1977). In the gift delay, a child is told they can have a small colorfully decorated box after they complete a challenging puzzle. The child's behavior is recorded both during the process of completing the puzzle and upon its completion to see how long the child will wait to grab and open the gift. Although these are both putative measures of delay of gratification, they tap into conceptually distinct psychological processes, and this is what Bem and Funder's results seemed to show. A full discussion of the follow-up work on this project can be found in Mischel and Peake (1982).

While dutifully filing away copies of the data sheets from this work in Mischel's back office, a folder labeled simply "Bing Consistency Data" captured my attention. It contained Zeiss' prior efforts to organize the data from the experiments employing the Marshmallow Test for a consistency analysis. Calling this to his attention, Mischel agreed this might be a nice match for my interests, so I set about what would become a sizable effort to reorganize the original experimental data into a form that could be examined using the then rapidly improving computer systems at Stanford. Examination of these files led to the quick realization that many of the children who had participated in the delay experiments had familiar names. They were, indeed, the now teenage children of many Stanford professors. Aware of efforts to examine the longitudinal correlates of Block's operationalizations of delay of gratification including the gift delay (Funder et al. 1983), a similar longitudinal follow-up involving children in the Marshmallow Test seemed compelling. On proposing this idea to Mischel, the Bing Longitudinal Study was born. In the beginning, the research was viewed as relatively inexpensive and quick way to see whether connections might exist between preschool delay and adaptive functioning in adolescence. We had a hunch there might be linkages, but given the simplicity of the initial assessment and the complexities of developing lives, there was no strong conviction about what we might find. We certainly never anticipated that we were initiating what has now become a 35-year longitudinal exploration.

The pages that follow summarize all of the published results of the longitudinal explorations of the Marshmallow Test to date. Like the summary of the experimental studies, the review is organized around discussion of each publication that taps into the evolving Bing Longitudinal Study data set. The review focuses separately on those studies that explore direct correlations between early waiting and later functioning, those that explore delay as a moderator of relations to subsequent life outcomes, and those that incorporate preschool delay to examine the behavioral and neural correlates of different life course self-regulation trajectories.

Delay as a Direct Predictor

Relations to Adolescent Functioning: Mischel et al. (1988)

During the summer of 1981, phone books from around the San Francisco Bay Area were scrutinized in an attempt to locate the parents of children who had participated in the original delay experiments. Packets that included a California Child Q-Set and a brief competency questionnaire that was devised with the assistance of Antonette Zeiss were sent to those who were located. The Q-Set was included because it contains a comprehensive set of personality and behavior descriptors appropriate for young children and because this would allow comparisons with our own and prior research that had employed this assessment device. The competency questionnaire was an intentionally brief questionnaire that asked parents to rate their child's academic competence, social competence, frequency of problems, and ability to cope with problems, all included as general markers of self-regulation in adolescence. In the end, 95 parents responded to our request, and their Q-Set ratings and questionnaires became the first wave of data collected as part of the Bing Longitudinal Study.

One of the first analytic problems faced was to determine exactly what the predictor variable would be for these parental responses. Recall that the children were observed in numerous different experimental settings, many of which had powerful effects on the child's behavior. Because of this, the child's raw delay time was not a good candidate. By the time, the first wave of parental responses arrived at Stanford, so had a new graduate student, Yuichi Shoda. With Shoda's capable assistance, we classified different experimental conditions according to the type of objects available for attention (e.g., rewards, slides, and nothing) and the types of ideational instructions provided (e.g., think about the consummatory aspects of the rewards, think about the consummatory aspects of other objects not in the contingency, and think about fun events, no instructions). A delay deviation score was then calculated by computing the difference between a child's wait time and the average delay for all children who waited under similar circumstances. This delay deviation score is the standard index of the child's ability to wait that has been used consistently in all subsequent longitudinal explorations.

We first examined the correlations between preschool waiting and parental ratings of the adolescent's competencies (Table 2.1). Children who were able to wait as preschoolers were more likely to be seen by their parents as teenagers with more academic competence and more social competence. While they were not seen as experiencing problems in life more frequently, when they did experience

Table 2.1 Correlations between parental ratings of adolescent competencies and preschool self-imposed delay

Adolescent rating	*r*
Academic competence	0.24*
Social competence	0.35**
Frequency of problems	0.03
Coping competence	0.23*

Note Adapted from Mischel et al. (1988, p. 691). Copyright 1988 by the American Psychological Association
$N = 87$; all p-values are two-tailed
$^{*}p < 0.05$; $^{**}p < 0.01$

challenges, parent's reported that they coped with those challenges more effectively. This general pattern of surprising connections was consistent for both boys and girls. To obtain a broader picture of what these teenagers were like, we next explored the California Child Q-Set ratings that parents had provided (Table 2.2). Consistent with the competency profile, the positive correlates in the top portion of

Table 2.2 Correlations between parental California Child Q-Set ratings in adolescence and preschool self-imposed delay

Q-Set item	*r*
Positive correlates	
Is verbally fluent	0.47***
Is attentive and able to concentrate	0.44***
Uses and responds to reason	0.42***
Is competent and skillful	0.41***
Is planful and thinks ahead	0.40***
Becomes strongly involved in what he/she does	0.34**
Is self-reliant, confident, and trusts own judgment	0.33**
Is resourceful in initiating activities	0.32**
Is curious, exploring, and eager to learn	0.27*
Is self-assertive	0.26*
Is persistent in activities and does not give up	0.25*
Can be trusted and is dependable	0.23†
Is an interesting, arresting child	0.23†
Negative correlates	
Tends to go to pieces under stress	−0.43***
Is shy and reserved	−0.42***
Appears to feel unworthy and thinks of self as bad	−0.38**
Reverts to immature behavior under stress	−0.34**
Teases other children	−0.29*
Tends to be indecisive and vacillating	−0.29*
Is stubborn	−0.25*
Is inhibited and constricted	−0.24†
Tends to be sulky or whiny	−0.24†
Shows specific mannerisms or behavioral rituals	−0.23†
Is jealous and envious of others	−0.23†
Tends to become immobilized under stress	−0.23†
Tends to be suspicious of others	−0.22†
Has a readiness to feel guilty	−0.21†
Is unable to delay gratification	−0.20†

Note Adapted from Mischel et al. (1988, p. 692). Copyright 1988 by the American Psychological Association

$N = 67$; all p-values are two-tailed

†$p < 0.10$; *$p < 0.05$; **$p < 0.01$; ***$p < 0.001$

Table 2.2 suggest that children who waited longer on the delay task were seen as teenagers who were bright, adaptive, planful, etc. In contrast, the lower panel of Table 2.2 portrays children who terminated the delay as generally more challenged teens. Perhaps, most noteworthy in this profile is the array of items indicating that short delays in preschool signal adolescents who struggled significantly coping with stress.

The reporting format of these early reports was adopted to allow comparison with the work of other research examining delay of gratification (Funder et al. 1983). Consistent with much of Block's work using the Q-Set, lists of correlations are presented to allow one to surmise the general patterning and profiling of correlates, not to highlight the relation to any individual item. As an alternative to this atheoretical listing, Block and Block (1980) conceptualized delay of gratification as being fundamentally related to the underlying constructs of ego-control and ego-resiliency. Ego-control relates to the permeability of psychological subsystems and finds expression behaviorally in a spectrum of behavior that consists of impulsivity (undercontrol) at one extreme and excessive constraint and inhibition (overcontrol) at the other. According to the Block's conceptualization, the general tendency toward impulsivity represented by the construct of ego-control can be situationally modulated at times by one's ego-resilience, a reflection of elasticity of the psychological subsystems. Ego-resilience is seen as manifesting itself temporarily to increase ego-control in response to situational constraints and expresses itself as competence, intelligence, resourcefulness, and adaptability under stress. Funder et al. (1983) used Q-Set items to derive indices of ego-control and ego-resiliency and then showed that delay of gratification, measured in part by the Block gift delay task, was linked to ego-control for boys but ego-resiliency for girls.

Noting that we had found different patterns of relation of the Marshmallow Test to ego-control and ego-resiliency in prior work (Mischel and Peake 1982), we examined the relations of self-imposed preschool waiting to these Q-Set derived indices (Table 2.3) in the Bing Longitudinal Study sample. Interestingly, preschool waiting as measured by the Marshmallow Test was powerfully related to ego-resiliency and showed virtually no relation to ego-control. This was true for both boys and girls. This finding is provocative not only because of the strength of the longitudinal ties, but also because it sheds more light on what might be governing children's ability at the delay task. It suggests that the child's ability to be flexible and adaptive to the challenge is far more important than their dispositional impulsivity. This message is remarkably consistent with the message from the experimental research which showed that it is not so much the physical presence of

Table 2.3 Correlations between California Child Q-Set indices of ego-resiliency and ego-control and preschool delay

Sex	Ego-resiliency	Ego-control
Girls (n = 35)	0.56**	0.11
Boys (n = 32)	0.49**	−0.22
Combined (N = 67)	0.53***	−0.09

Note Adapted from Mischel et al. (1988)
$^{**}p < 0.01$; $^{***}p < 0.001$

the reward stimulus that regulates waiting. Rather, delay maintenance derives from how the child adapts to the situation through the strategies they use to distract their attention or transform the features of the task to make it less challenging.

Diagnostic Experimental Settings: Shoda et al. (1990)

The interesting linkages between preschool waiting and adolescent well-being captured our curiosity. First, it was impressive to see that a single assessment of the child's waiting at age 4 was correlated with psychological functioning over 10 years later. It is also curious because these correlations are calculated using a delay index that includes waiting in not just one but many different experimental conditions. The calculation of deviation scores within waiting situations was one tactic to eliminate the impact of experimental variations. But even with this centering around conditional means, the remaining variance in the scores should not have the same psychological meaning. First, individual differences in waiting should be meaningful, and hence "diagnostic," only in those situations that are psychologically challenging. In the case of the delay of gratification experiments, the differences in wait times should be most meaningful when the rewards were present. Second, in most of the experimental conditions, children were provided with instructions about how to cope with the situation at hand. They were told to play with toys, think happy thoughts, transform marshmallows into clouds, etc. Enduring individual differences should most likely be tapped in those situations where children are not provided with any instruction and hence are left to their own spontaneous coping strategies. Unfortunately, the sample size of the first outreach in the Bing Longitudinal Study was not sufficient to allow these comparisons.

During this period of the research, Mischel accepted a new position at Columbia University and Shoda opted to follow him there. Working with our conscientious assistant, Rhea Cabin, and the aid of the Stanford Alumnae Association, the search for more Bing children pressed on at Stanford. The second mailing to this expanded sample of parents included requests for information about the child's demographic, academic, and vocational history, an expanded survey of self-regulatory capacities referred to as the Adolescent Coping Questionnaire, and the California Child Q-Set, now presented simply as a questionnaire instead of the traditional sorting packet. Responding to complaints from parents about the sorting task, we were swayed by a personal communication from Lee J. Cronbach and the analysis of Green (1980), both of which asserted the functional equivalence of the complex sorting procedure and standard questionnaire methodology. The returns from this mailing were gathered at Stanford and shipped off to Columbia just as I left for a new appointment at Smith College.

Using data from this expanded sample, we first looked at the correlations between preschool delay and parent provided Q-Set ratings of the teenagers. In this analysis, we first divided participants into groups that represented the type of experimental setting to which they were exposed at preschoolers. Experimental settings were classified both according to whether rewards were present versus absent during the delay and according to whether children were provided with instructions about what to do or think about during the wait period or not. Our hypothesis was that meaningful individual differences should only be found in "diagnostic" conditions where children were exposed to the rewards (e.g., the task was challenging) and were not provided with instructions about what to do during the wait (e.g., were left to their own spontaneous coping strategies). The respective correlates for these four groups are presented in Table 2.4. Two main themes are clearly evident. First, most of the conceptually meaningful longitudinal correlates were found in the predicted diagnostic condition. When rewards were absent or children were provided with instructions about what to do, fewer correlates were detected and they made less conceptual sense. Second, the correlates found for children in the diagnostic condition were basically consistent with the portrait of delay that emerged in earlier studies with positive correlations indicating bright,

Table 2.4 Correlations between parental California Child Q-Set ratings in adolescence and preschool self-imposed delay in different diagnostic settings

Q-sort item	Spontaneous ideation		Suggested ideation	
	Rewards Present (n = 48)	Rewards Absent (n = 51)	Rewards Present (n = 32)	Rewards Absent (n = 35)
Positive correlates				
Has high standards of performance for self	0.44**			
Uses and responds to reason	0.43**			
Is attentive and able to concentrate	0.39**			
Is competent and skillful	0.37**			0.34*
Is planful and thinks ahead	0.36**			
Develops genuine and close relationships	0.36**	−0.36**		
Appears to have high intellectual capacity	0.34*			
Is verbally fluent	0.32*			
Tends to be proud of accomplishments	0.30*			
Is talkative	0.29*			
Is vital, energetic, and lively	0.28*			
Can be trusted and is dependable		0.26†		0.30†
Recognizes the feelings of others	0.25†			
Is suspicious and distrustful of others		0.32*		
Daydreams and tends to get lost in reverie		0.26†		
Becomes strongly involved in activities			0.42*	
Is persistent in activities			0.30†	
Is fearful and anxious				0.28†
Is aggressive (physically or verbally)				0.28†

(continued)

Table 2.4 (continued)

Q-sort item	Spontaneous ideation		Suggested ideation	
	Rewards Present (n = 48)	Rewards Absent (n = 51)	Rewards Present (n = 32)	Rewards Absent (n = 35)
Negative correlates				
Feels unworthy and thinks of self as "bad"	−0.39**			
Tends to imitate those he/she admires	−0.38**			
Tends to go to pieces under stress	−0.34**			
Is unable to delay gratification	−0.34*			
Tends to dramatize or exaggerate mishaps	−0.30*			
Is calm and relaxed and easygoing	−0.28†			
Has an active fantasy life	−0.27†	0.28†		
Prefers nonverbal communication	−0.25†			
Shows mannerisms or behavioral rituals	−0.25†			
Tends to arouse liking and acceptance in elders		−0.28*		
Is jealous and envious of others			−0.32†	−0.28†
Tends to brood, ruminate, and worry			−0.31†	0.32†
Reverts to immature behavior under stress				−0.51***
Is easily offended and sensitive to ridicule				−0.44**
Is afraid of being deprived				−0.38*
Overreacts to minor frustrations				−0.38*
Tends to be sulky or whiny				−0.35*
Looks to adults for help and direction				−0.34*
Tends to be judgmental of others				−0.30†

Note Adapted and expanded from Shoda et al. (1990)
†$p < 0.10$; *$p < 0.05$; **$p < 0.01$; ***$p < 0.001$

planful, and resourceful adolescents were linked to preschool waiting, whereas teens challenged in coping with stress had shorter delay times in preschool. This pattern was even more dramatic when focusing in directly at coping competencies that are implicated in self-regulation (Table 2.5). Here, virtually all statistically significant relations were found only when children were exposed to the rewards and left to their own coping strategies to work through the challenge. Finally, as part of this report, we examined the relation of preschool waiting to scores on the Scholastic Aptitude Test (SAT) (Table 2.6). Once again, predictive linkages were found to both verbal and quantitative components of the test but only for children who participated in the hypothesized diagnostic condition. These relations were especially powerful for females.

Table 2.5 Correlations between adolescence coping questionnaire and preschool self-imposed delay in different diagnostic settings

Coping questionnaire item	Spontaneous ideation		Spontaneous ideation	
	Rewards Present (*n* = 42)	Rewards Absent (*n* = 42)	Rewards Present (*n* = 21)	Rewards Absent (*n* = 28)
Gets sidetracked by minor setbacks	−0.30*			
Shows self-control when frustrated	0.58***			
Copes with important problems	0.31*			
Capable of doing well academically	0.37*			
Yields to temptation	−0.50***			
Settles for immediate gratifications	−0.32*			
Pursue goals when motivated	0.38*			
Is intelligent	0.42**			
Exhibits self-control when tempted	0.36*	−0.32*		0.39*
Skilled at maintaining friendships				
Is distractable when trying to concentrate	−0.41**			
Capable of self-control when frustrated	0.40**			0.38*
Effectively pursues goals				
Diverts attention from desired rewards	0.32*			

Note Adapted from Shoda et al. (1990)
$*p < 0.05$; $**p < 0.01$; $***p < 0.001$

Table 2.6 Correlations between SAT scores and preschool self-imposed delay in different diagnostic settings

Measure	Spontaneous ideation		Suggested ideation	
	Rewards Present (*n* = 35)	Rewards Absent (*n* = 33)	Rewards Present (*n* = 14)	Rewards Absent (*n* = 12)
SAT verbal	0.42*	−0.12	−0.40	−0.21
SAT quantitative	0.57***	−0.33	−0.26	−0.23

Note Adapted from Shoda et al. (1990)
$*p < 0.05$; $***p < 0.001$

Body Mass: Schlam et al. (2013)

The most recent research to look at a direct relation between preschool waiting and a later life outcome examined linkages to a self-reported body mass index (BMI) in adulthood. Schlam et al. (2013) tapped into data collected as part of the midlife follow-up of the Bing Longitudinal Study participants that was organized by Ozlem Ayduk at Columbia between 2002 and 2004. Respondents to this survey were 39 years of age on average. Since this follow-up consisted of two parts separated by about one year and each questionnaire asked for information about weight and height, BMI [weight in kg/(height in m)^2] was calculated separately for each assessment and then averaged. Because sex is known to correlate with BMI (women report lower BMI scores than men), Schlam et al. first entered sex into a hierarchical regression and found that this variable alone accounted for 13% of the variance in scores. Preschool delay was then shown to account for 4% of the variance over and above sex. Although the precise factors driving this relation are not clear, it is noteworthy that the number of seconds children waited for rewards at age 4 showed linkages to this general metric of physical well-being 35 years later. It is noteworthy that the relation between preschool delay of gratification on the Marshmallow Test and body mass have been replicated outside the Bing Longitudinal Study by examining BMI at age 11 for children who participated in the NICHD Study of Early Child Care and Youth Development (Seeyave et al. 2009).

Delay as a Direct Predictor: Takeaways and Caveats

The pattern of correlates between preschool delay and later life outcomes is both surprising and revealing. They are surprising in that a single assessment of a child in preschool at a task where the child's behavior is surely being impacted by numerous factors demonstrates useful predictive efficacy over the time frames examined. This suggests that the delay task is tapping into some fundamentally important psychological processes that have important lifelong consequences. Those processes appear to be connected to the ability to be flexible and adaptive in responding to contextual demands, to be cognitively competent in developing plans and strategies, and to be generally adept at coping with stress.

While much has been made of the longitudinal correlates of delay reported here, there are some necessary precautions that are often neglected in their popular portrayals. On the one hand, these are correlations and their causal implications should not be overstated. Far too frequently, popular presentations of the findings suggest that the Marshmallow Test foretells one's fate. "Failing" the test portends a life of struggle; "passing" the test foreshadows all kinds of good fortune. Despite the rather obvious fact that one cannot pass or fail the Marshmallow Test since it is not and never has been a "test," the number of seconds a child waits at the task in preschool is not determinative of anything later in life. It is safe to say that on most any follow-up measure, some children who did not wait will do quite well. On that same measure, some children who did wait will struggle. The correlations reported simply tell us that children who waited tend to also perform better on average in the longitudinal assessments. It is a basic but easily forgotten statistical truism.

Nonetheless, parents all around the world are subjecting their children to home versions of the Marshmallow Test and then fretting or celebrating their child's prospects. We strongly discourage this practice. First, be reminded again about the contextual sensitivity of the testing procedure itself. It is doubtful home versions of the Marshmallow Test could ever replicate the laboratory conditions structured into the original research. For example, it is not uncommon to hear of parents setting their child at the kitchen table and watching as they attempt to navigate the challenge. But, prior research in the laboratory has shown that merely leaving the experimenter in the room during the wait totally changes the dynamic of waiting situation and disrupts the diagnostic utility of the task (Mischel and Peake 1982). Staged demonstrations of the Marshmallow Test commonly found across the Internet are rarely faithful to the original procedures, and it is hard to imagine that a home test could do much better.

In reports that tout the predictive prowess of the Marshmallow Test, it is not uncommon to find specific correlates singled out and highlighted. For example, relations between preschool waiting and performance on the SAT have become a particular favorite in popular accounts (see, e.g., Goleman 1995). This is not advisable both due to the inherent unreliability of single assessments and due to the prospect of capitalizing on chance when calculating multiple individual correlations. There is much to be learned from the patterning of correlates documented to date, but it is not advisable to focus on or emphasize any single relationship. This is as true of SAT and BMI scores as it is for the ratings obtained using the Q-Set. And, as always, caution needs to be observed when making reference to correlates based on relatively small samples of individuals, an issue that is especially important in analyses where partitioning by diagnostic conditions constrains sample size. The findings from the Bing Longitudinal Study can only shed light on prospective relations that require replication and refinement before they are treated as fact.

Although the longitudinal correlates of preschool delay are commonly featured in presentations of this research, in terms of conceptual significance, the identification of diagnostic conditions by Shoda et al. (1990) may be one of the most important findings in the program. The fact that children's delay scores are only longitudinally predictive when they are tested in settings that are challenging and where they must use their own coping strategies speaks again to the contextual specificity of delay behavior. Subtle changes in the physical setting (e.g., removing the rewards) fundamentally shift the psychological dynamic of the experience. This is expressed not only in group differences as was documented in the experimental findings, but in the meaningfulness of the individual differences remaining once the group difference is removed. Second, the diagnostic value of reward presence tells us something more about the factors that are contributing to the longitudinal findings. Recall that one of the components of the waiting situations is the sheer boredom of the self-control task. This is a central aspect of many self-control situations and one aspect, independent of striving for desired rewards, that the child must cope with during delay. The diagnosticity findings demonstrate that coping with boredom does not account for the longitudinal linkages. Waiting without rewards present is also an extremely boring task, yet individual differences in waiting in these situations do not relate to adolescent outcomes, even when children are left to their own coping strategies. This suggests that the presence of the rewards is a defining feature of situations that tap into preschool competencies with longitudinal consequence.

Finally, the finding that conceptually meaningful longitudinal correlates are almost exclusively connected to situations where children are not provided coping instructions is critically important. This indicates that the behaviors that children spontaneously emit while waiting—playing with their hair, looking around the room, singing songs, etc.—are not simply random acts that happen to help the child endure the wait. These spontaneously generated activities reflect early differences in coping that may provide children with a head start toward later self-regulatory competence. Those behaviors that people find so cute and amusing when watching re-enactments of the Marshmallow Test are the child's self-generated strategies to temper and endure the challenge. It is noteworthy that the long-term individual differences are not found when the strategies employed result from experimental instructions that are not the child's own construction. This raises an extremely important question about what preschoolers actually do while they wait. What are the typical strategies that preschoolers spontaneously deploy in their efforts to delay gratification?

Delay as a Moderator

Rejection Sensitivity and Adolescent Life Outcomes: Ayduk et al. (2000)

The 1990s were a period of great transition for the Bing Longitudinal Study with its key partners now relocated to the East Coast. With the first round of publications on the longitudinal correlates of delay, Mischel and Shoda turned their attention back to issues of the consistency and stability of behavior. This effort was driven by Shoda's dissertation work on person-situation profiles that conceptualized personality as sets of conditionally sensitive "if-then" propositions (Shoda et al. 1993, 1994). This research laid the groundwork for the presentation of the cognitive affective processing system (CAPS), which was offered as an alternative to disposition-based approaches to personality (Mischel and Shoda 1995). Quite separately, work on the Bing Longitudinal Study continued at Smith College where a follow-up of a further expanded sample of now young adults was initiated in collaboration with Mark Lepper at Stanford.

During this period, Ozlem Ayduk, along with her partner Rudy Mendoza-Denton, was beginning their graduate training at Columbia, both working with Mischel. Ayduk also developed a working collaboration with Geraldine Downey, who had pioneered investigations into the construct of rejection sensitivity (Downey and Feldman 1996; Feldman and Downey 1994). Rejection sensitivity (RS) reflects an interpersonal vulnerability that leads individuals to anxiously expect rejection in relationships, to quickly see others' behavior as rejecting, and to overreact to those perceptions. Downey and her students and collaborators documented that persons high in RS were more likely to experience aggression, bullying, and violence in relationships, were more likely to experience loneliness, social anxiety, and depression, have a diminished sense of self-worth, and have an increased likelihood of substance abuse (see Pietrzak et al. 2005 for review). The Columbia University collaborators saw RS as a good example of the type of conceptual unit proposed in the CAPS framework where aspects of the interpersonal situation trigger a set of interconnected expectations, encodings, and emotions that lead to intense reactions. In this way, they conceptualized RS as a "cognitive affective mediator that links situational features to psychological processes operating in interpersonal relationships" (Ayduk et al. 2000, p. 777).

Ayduk tapped into the early adult data that had just been collected at Smith to explore whether self-regulatory capabilities might moderate the relation between RS and maladaptive outcomes. Specifically, she developed a proxy measure of RS using self-rated Q-Set responses from participants and then examined whether preschool waiting moderated the relationship between RS and a set of conceptually predicted life outcomes. These included measures of self (and parent)-rated positive functioning, as well as behavioral reports of educational attainments and substance (cocaine–crack) use. Positive functioning was indexed by compositing self-ratings of self-esteem, self-worth, and coping with stress into one measure so as to maximize reliability. Each of these component measures had been shown in prior work to be negatively correlated with RS. Ayduk et al. showed that preschool waiting moderated this relation such that the deleterious impact of increasing RS is only seen in those children who were not able to wait in preschool (Fig. 2.8a). From this vantage, the self-regulatory processes tapped by preschool waiting served to buffer the impact of RS. Ayduk et al. went on to show that this buffering effect applied additionally to educational attainments (Fig. 2.8b) and substance use (Fig. 2.8c). Related to the prior findings of Mischel et al. (1988) that preschool delay correlates strongly with the Block's construct of ego-resilience, Ayduk et al. also showed that the relationship between RS and ego-resilience in young adults is also moderated by preschool waiting. This result seems to follow since the ego-resilience measure derived from Q-Set ratings and the positive functioning rating derived from other personality scales are quite highly correlated.

After reporting these findings as they pertained to preschool delay and the Bing Longitudinal data, Ayduk et al. reported similar findings in a project that involved children from an inner-city school in the Bronx, New York. Assessments using the delay task were first performed when children averaged about 11 years of age. Follow-up assessments two years later showed once again that delay of gratification moderated the impact of RS for both self-worth and interpersonal functioning (peer acceptance and aggression [inversely scored]). These findings are noteworthy because they replicate the pattern of findings found with the Bing sample when working in a population that is both older (late elementary school) and far more economically challenged, partially allaying concerns about the generality of findings obtained at the Bing School to the privileged demographics of the original sample.

Rejection Sensitivity and Borderline Personality: Ayduk et al. (2008)

Following on the findings of Ayduk et al. (2000) that RS and preschool delay interacted in the prediction of metrics of early adult adaptive functioning, Ayduk et al. (2008) extended this analysis to explore behaviors in the clinical realm.

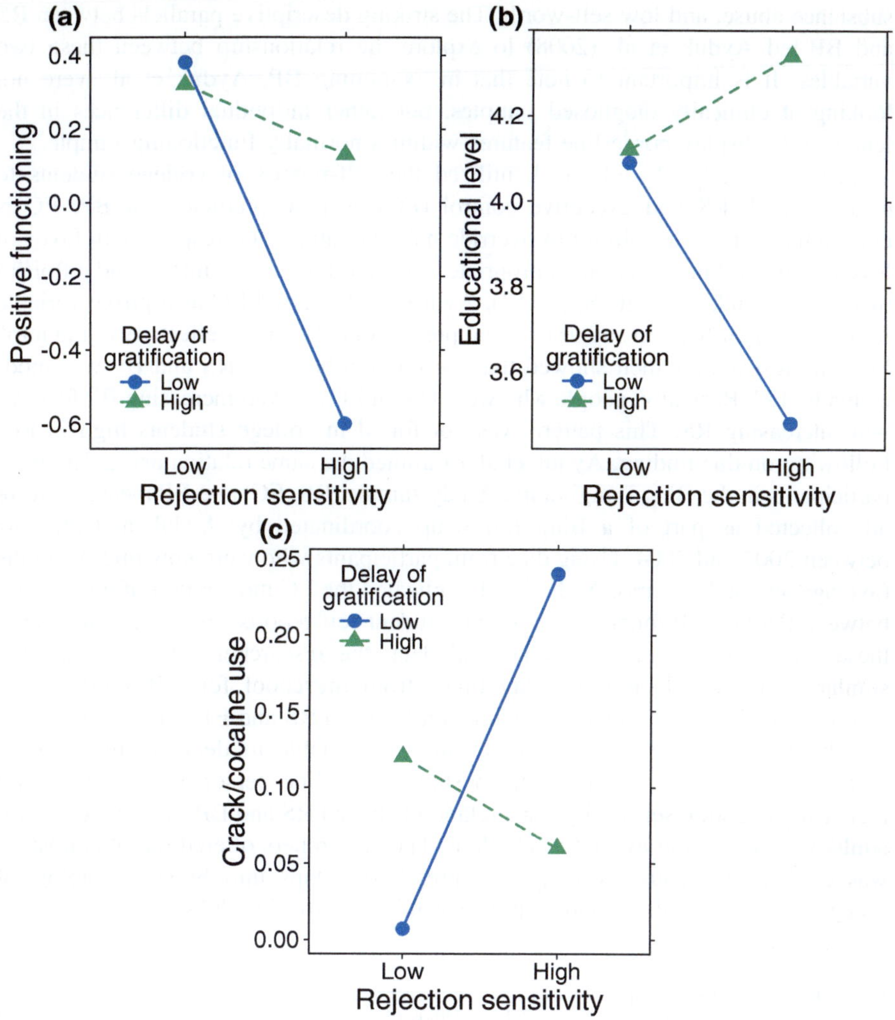

Fig. 2.8 Interaction of preschool delay of gratification and rejection sensitivity. **a** Impact of rejection sensitivity on early adult positive functioning is moderated by preschool delay of gratification. **b** Impact of rejection sensitivity on early adult educational attainment is moderated by preschool delay of gratification. **c** Impact of rejection sensitivity on early adult substance use is moderated by preschool delay of gratification. Adapted from Ayduk et al. (2000)

Specifically, they recognized the close parallels between some aspects of RS and the clinical features that define borderline personality disorder (BP). Specifically, RS and BP share common patterns of interpersonal interaction where individuals amplify and overpersonalize minor disagreements that can rapidly turn into personal attacks and outright aggression. The two syndromes also share common life outcomes including difficulty maintaining relationships and jobs, increased substance abuse, and low self-worth. The striking descriptive parallels between RS and BP led Ayduk et al. (2008) to explore the relationship between these two variables. It is important to note that in examining BP, Ayduk et al. were not looking at clinically diagnosed samples, but rather individual differences in the tendency to display borderline features within a normally functioning sample.

In a first study, Ayduk et al. utilized the self-reports of college students to examine both RS and executive control (EC) as joint predictors of BP. EC is conceptualized as the "ability to override habitual, automatic responses in favor of less dominant but situation appropriate responses in a voluntary and effortful manner" (Ayduk et al. 2008, p. 153). Ayduk et al. offered EC as a proxy variable for delay of gratification suggesting that preschool delay times effectively "tap into" EC. The researchers then showed that the relation between RS and BP was moderated by EC. Basically, people who were low in EC showed increasing BP features with increasing RS. This pattern was not found in college students high in EC. Following on this finding, Ayduk et al. examined the same relation using data from participants in the Bing Longitudinal Study sample. RS, EC, and BP measures were all collected as part of a Bing follow-up coordinated by Ayduk at Columbia between 2002 and 2004. Using data from participants who were now midlife adults (average age of 39 years), Ayduk et al. replicated the EC moderation of the relation between RS and BP found using college student self-reports. In an effort to extend these self-report findings to behavioral data, the researchers then conducted a similar analysis, substituting delay times from preschool for self-reported EC. Ayduk et al. found that, indeed, the relation between RS and BP was moderated by preschool waiting (Fig. 2.9). Adults who were unable to delay gratification as preschoolers were far more prone to show borderline personality features with increasing rejection sensitivity. This relation between RS and BP was attenuated for adults who were able to wait as children. The researchers offered that this relation was evidenced because waiting as a preschooler taps into basic psychological processes that form the foundation of executive control in adults.

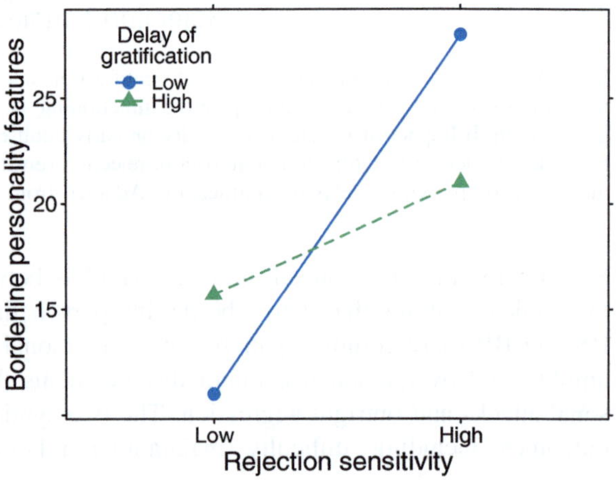

Fig. 2.9 Impact of rejection sensitivity on adult borderline personality features is moderated by preschool delay of gratification. Adapted from Ayduk et al. (2008)

Delay as a Moderator: Takeaways and Caveats

The repeated demonstration that delay ability during preschool buffers the impact of rejection sensitivity on a host of self-regulatory ratings and outcomes over the life course is provocative. Mischel (2014) has written that the finding that self-control as measured through the Marshmallow Test serves to protect individuals from the impact of other life-changing vulnerabilities is a far more important finding than the direct correlations that receive so much attention in the literature and in the popular press. The finding that the self-regulatory capacities that are reflected in waiting times on the Marshmallow Test buffer people from undesirable outcomes suggests a set of skills that might have more generality than is implied by direct correlates. To date, the work of Ayduk and colleagues elegantly demonstrates how this plays out in the realm of one interpersonal vulnerability: rejection sensitivity. One imagines that the interaction demonstrated here might accrue to many other variables impacted by RS. More importantly, the findings open up the prospect that self-regulatory capacities might similarly buffer people in other realms and with other vulnerabilities. The specification of those types of relations is one rich with conceptual and empirical possibilities for further investigation.

Self-control Trajectories and Neural Processes

Cognitive Control: Casey et al. (2011)

Behavior in the delay task appears to tap into a set of basic underlying skills, competencies, and/or processes that form the foundation for self-regulatory competence later in life. There are, of course, many possibilities, and it is likely that how preschool waiting links to later life outcomes is idiosyncratically organized. Nonetheless, the longitudinal findings indicate that some common processes are engaged. In the most recent phases of the Bing Longitudinal Study, teams of cognitive and neuroscientists have joined in the exploration searching for links between patterns of delay and basic cognitive and neural processes. Data collection for these efforts took place from 2008 through 2011 and consisted of two sets of activities. In one, laptop computers were sent to Bing participants and they were asked to complete a set of computer-driven cognitive assessments. In a second, a subset of the original Bing participants returned to Stanford where fMRI imaging was conducted as they completed different self-control-related tasks.

In the first of these studies, Casey et al. (2011) examined the relationship between life patterns of self-control and measures of cognitive control. Cognitive control (CC), a behavioral analog for the self-reported assessment of executive control previously used by Ayduk et al. (2008), refers to “the ability to suppress competing inappropriate thoughts and actions in favor of appropriate ones” (2011, p. 14999) and, as such, is a measure of one aspect of how individuals control attention. Since directing attention played such as pivotal role in the experimental studies with preschoolers, perhaps differences in CC in adulthood would relate to individual differences in the Marshmallow Test. Prior research with a different sample had demonstrated linkages between what preschoolers looked at while waiting (attentional focus), but not how long they waited, and CC during adolescence as assessed by performance on a go/no-go task (Eigsti et al. 2006). Casey et al. sought to examine whether differences in CC might be found in Bing Longitudinal Study participants nearly 40 years after the original experiments.

To examine this idea, Casey et al. first targeted subgroups of Bing participants who were classified as either high or low "delayers." Recall that over the course of the Bing Longitudinal Study assessments, participants were asked to repeatedly complete ratings of their personality using the California Q-Set. Using a subset of items from the Q-Set, Casey et al. created measures of the participants' self-reported self-control when they were in their 20 s and then again 10 years later. Participants who scored above the median in preschool waiting time and both of the subsequent self-control reports were labeled as "high delayers." Participants who scored consistently below the median on these three measures were labeled as "low delayers." In a first study, Casey et al. examined CC using two variations of a go/no-go task for 59 Bing Longitudinal Study participants. In one task, reaction time and accuracy were assessed as participants made "go" (press a button) or "no-go" (do not press button) judgments about emotionally neutral target images, the faces of males versus females. In a second variation of the task, participants made go/no-go button presses for more emotionally laden targets, faces that were either fearful (or not) or happy (or not). Casey et al. found no differences between low delayers and high delayers in reaction times or accuracy for go trials for either of the different target stimuli. Similarly, no differences were detected in the accuracy of no-go trials when the target stimuli were emotionally neutral. However, when the target stimuli were emotionally laden, low delayers showed far more false alarms, pressing the button to indicate the presence of a target when it was absent (Fig. 2.10). This decline in

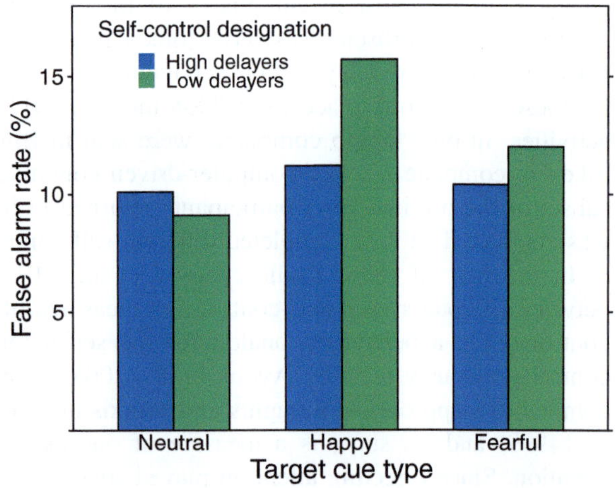

Fig. 2.10 No-go false alarms as a function of the emotional cue of target and lifelong self-control designation. Adapted from Casey et al. (2011)

accuracy of no-go target responding is a classic critical indicator of the inability to inhibit a prepotent response and hence a deficit in CC.

In a second study conducted nearly two years later, 26 of the participants from the prior study came to Stanford and were tested on a similar go/no-go task while having their brains scanned in an fMRI. In this follow-up, participants completed only the emotion-laden (happy and fearful faces) stimuli. The pattern of findings was similar to the first study with low delayers showing a trend toward increased false alarms in the no-go trials. Analysis of the fMRI scans revealed that accuracy at the task was supported by the ventral frontostriatal circuitry. Specifically, low delayers generally showed less polarization of the inferior frontal gyrus in response to no-go as compared to go trials, indicating less activity in this portion of the prefrontal cortex when trying to engage in CC. Additionally, low delayers showed greater activity in the ventral striatum when trying to suppress a no-go response, particularly when target stimulus was a positive cue (happy face). This indicates that this reward center within the limbic system may be activated by positive cues in a manner that interferes with the higher cognitive control systems ability to appropriately modulate reactions to emotionally laden stimuli.

In summary, Casey et al. identified behavioral differences in response to a go/no-go task administered in adulthood between groups of Bing participants who were selected because they showed patterns of self-control that were either stably high or low over the life course. False alarms to no-go tasks were not generalized over different types of stimuli, but were cue specific, only appearing when the cue was positively socially rewarding (happy faces). Follow-up brain scans of a subset of these participants on a similar task implicated two regions of the brain, both part of the frontostriatal circuitry, to account for the behavioral differences. High delayers showed more activation of the inferior frontal gyrus, an area commonly associated with CC, when required to make any no-go responses. Low delayers showed cue-specific activation for positive stimuli in the ventral striatum when required to suppress a no-go response. Together, the findings draw a picture of contextually specified, reward-oriented activation within the limbic system that is paired with attenuated prefrontal cognitive control as low delayers attempt to suppress a prepotent response.

Brain Network Dimensionality for Working Memory: Berman et al. (2013)

Berman et al. (2013) examined the hypothesis that controlling the contents of working memory is linked to lifelong patterns of self-control. Utilizing the same subgroup of high- and low-delaying Bing participants as Casey et al. (2011), Berman et al. conducted behavioral and imaging analysis while participants engaged in a different continuous performance task. In the directed forgetting task, participants were first asked to memorize a group of six words. Three words were presented with blue letters and the remaining three with teal letters. Participants were then presented with a cue instructing them to forget all of the words of one color. For example, they might be cued to forget all the blue words and hence remember the teal words. Over a series of trials, a single probe word was presented and participants pressed a "yes" key if the word was one of the words they were instructed to remember and "no" if it was not. Among the no trials were control words that were not part of the target array and that rarely occurred over trials and lure words that were drawn from the set of to-be-forgotten words on the current trial. Response time and accuracy were recorded on each trial, and the overall difference in these assessments between control and lure trials was used as an index of control over working memory.

Berman et al. found slower and less accurate performance on lure trials for both high- and low-delaying participants. Although the interaction between the two groups and trial type was not significant, a trend was observed where low delayers were less accurate and took longer to respond to lure trials. According to Berman et al. (2013, p. 3), "… these results hint at the possibility that low delay participants find it more difficult … to resolve interference between relevant and irrelevant material." Despite the behavioral performance similarities between the two groups, Berman et al. did document robust differences in the neural engagement. Low delayers recruited neural networks far less efficiently than high delayers. Using linear discriminant analysis to identify the optimal number of principal components required to achieve maximum classification between lure and control trials, Berman et al. document that high delayers recruited lower level neural networks (fewer principal components) and showed more homogeneity as a group in this recruitment (Fig. 2.11). Compared to low delayers, high delayers showed consistently more efficient recruitment of cortical networks in order to obtain similar outcomes on the working memory task. This led Berman et al. to conclude that neural dimensionality might serve as a key biologic marker of self-control ability.

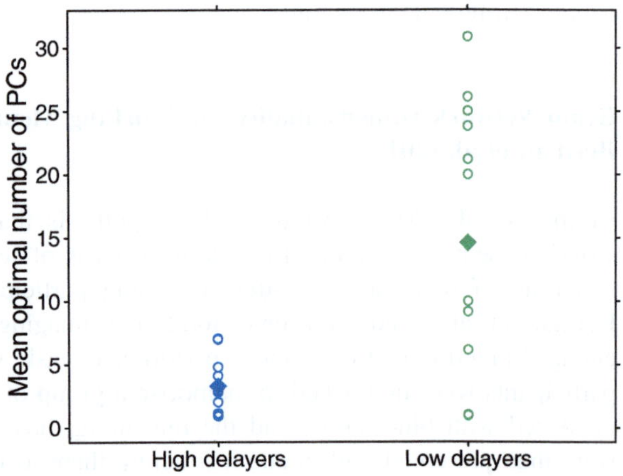

Fig. 2.11 Efficiency of working memory represented as mean number of linear discriminant principal component (PC) required to achieve maximum classification between lure and control trials for high- and low-delaying participants. Adapted from Berman et al. (2013)

Self-control Trajectories and Neural Processes: Takeaways and Caveats

The detection of differences in behavior and neural processing between groups labeled as low and high delayers provides a provocative glimpse of the cognitive and neural processes that might support individual differences in self-control. The work of Casey et al. (2011) and Berman et al. (2013) implicates two different neural systems. The involvement of the ventral frontostriatal circuitry by Casey et al. is consistent with other research examining performance on go/no-go tasks, suggesting that observed differences in self-control over the life course may derive from individual differences in cognitive control and the attentional processes required to suppress competing inappropriate responses in pursuit of a goal. These findings also map nicely onto Metcalfe and Mischel's (1999) hot/cool processing framework (and other dual-process models similar to it—see Rahimi-Golkhandan et al. and Bickel et al., this volume), which posits that effective self-control requires the suppression of hot, fast, limbic based response tendencies by cool, slow, prefrontal processes. In this case, the limbic processes are localized in the ventral striatum, whereas the competing "cooling" mechanism is localized in the inferior frontal gyrus. Casey et al. also suggest that the contextual specificity of the finding for emotion-laden stimuli illustrates how important it is that the stimuli in question be "hot" and hence provocative for the participant. Berman et al., in contrast, implicate a different system that is commonly associated with executive functions, namely working memory. Effective working memory is posited as essential for keeping long-term goals in mind during delay, and this research points to marked differences in the efficiency of this system between low and high delayers. Collectively, the two findings hint that individual differences in self-control can be mapped onto distinct neural processes that may maintain across the life course.

While the findings of these two studies are offered as evidence of the biologic underpinnings of self-control generally and the Marshmallow Test specifically, they might be more conservatively seen as preliminary explorations of the neural processes that support adaptive self-regulation. Interpretive caution is warranted on a number of fronts. The first of these traces to the classification of individuals in the research as either low or high delayers. While it is technically true that the groups compared differed in their tendency to wait as preschoolers, the additional selection criteria requiring participants to consistently report as being either high or low in self-control over the life course cloud the interpretation of this classification. So, for instance, there are many high delayer preschoolers who were not included in this research because they did not consistently report high self-control over the life course. A similar issue exists for those classified as low delayers. One might just as easily label these two groups as consistently high versus low in self-reported self-control. From that vantage, it is not nearly so impressive that people who self-classify as being high versus low in self-control perform differently on continuous performance go/no-go-like tasks and that those differences map onto neural processes that have been previously linked to these tasks.

A key focus of the ongoing work with the Bing Longitudinal Study is to examine different life course trajectories of self-control. The full examination of these trajectories will include not only those who remain consistently high or low (an important first step), but also those that change over the life course. It will include, for instance, participants who waited as children but report challenges with self-control later in life and participants who did not wait in the Marshmallow Test but who report adaptive self-regulation as adults. In a full consideration of the different trajectories, we will be better able to isolate which aspects of adult behavioral and neural functioning are uniquely linked to preschool waiting. The substantial costs and time connected with doing this type of investigation led to a focus on just two trajectories in the research of Casey et al. and Berman et al. These promising initial findings suggest that a full exploration of the different life course trajectories is warranted.

The work of Casey et al. and Berman et al. flags another important issue in investigating the behavioral and neural correlates of self-control. This involves the extensive reliance on continuous performance go/no-go-like tasks as the measurement tool for identifying differences in neural processing. Note that both the go/no-go task employed by Casey et al. and the directed forgetting task of Berman et al. are cognitive tasks the involve quick choices among competing options that are presented in a rapidly paced serial decision-making format where target stimuli are interspersed among presumably habituating non-target stimuli. These types of tasks are well suited to fMRI scanning studies and provide a valuable and convenient way to measure one form of impulsive responding, the ability to quickly override a seemingly automatic or habituated response. It is likely that this capacity is implicated and supportive of children's efforts to wait when faced with the Marshmallow Test. But it is important to note that this type of task does not capture the essence of what children appear to be doing while they wait. That behavior is far more deliberate, reasoned, and strategic. Children actively struggle with a decision about what the best course of action might be given what is unfolding in front of them. As such, children are making choices among competing responses, but these choices play out in a manner that appears slow (not quick), singular (not serial), and among two choices where the more immediate option, while tempting, is neither automatic nor habituated.

The findings of Casey et al. and Berman et al. also raise important questions for future work on the neural underpinnings of self-control. For example, Casey et al. document the contextual specificity of go/no-go responding and link this to "hot" responding connected to emotionally laden stimuli. In the original experimental investigations of delay and the conceptual integration provided by Metcalfe and Mischel, "hot" responding made reference to a focus on consummatory and appetitive features of the rewards being pursued. Casey et al. detect individual differences in neural responding by cuing emotion-laden stimuli (happy vs. fearful faces) that do not seem to share this consummatory/appetitive quality. While this is offered as a demonstration of the contextual specificity of the individual difference, it raises critical questions about the generality of "hot" stimuli. Are the cognitive and neural processes connected with a child's desire for a tempting food reward parallel to those engendered by an adult viewing faces that vary in affective tone (hence socially rewarding)? Is the mere "positivity" of the cue sufficient to engage the underlying cognitive processes? These are important questions that speak to the specificity of the neural processes that support self-control.

The work of Berman et al. raises similar important issues. For example, Berman et al. document profound individual differences in the efficiency of engagement of working memory among those labeled as low and high delayers. These differences in neural efficiency do not translate, however, into powerful performance differences in the directed forgetting task that presumably provoked them. This might simply be a reflection of task difficulty, but it raises important questions about the behavioral domain where one might expect observable behavioral differences linked to the efficiency of engagement of working memory. Where and how might these foundational differences in neural functioning play out in the behavior of those labeled as low and high delayers? Would it be evidenced in a more challenging directed forgetting task? More critically, how might these inefficiencies undermine effective self-control in more complex behavioral realms like those involving delay of gratification?

How and Why Children Wait: Lessons from the Marshmallow Test

The research reviewed here provides a critical and comprehensive summary of all findings published to date connected to the original experiments and the ongoing Bing Longitudinal Study. Although the findings reviewed are impressive, they are not as extensive as the exaggerated network of connections often represented in popular portrayals of the work. Caution should be observed when taking such claims at face value. Not everything you read on the Internet is true! Nonetheless, the findings reviewed here do allow some insight into the factors that impact a child's ability to wait. The concluding section of this paper will evaluate the factors that are commonly offered to explain how and why children wait.

Impulsivity and Willpower

As discussed throughout this presentation, the results of the Marshmallow Test and the Bing Longitudinal Study are frequently offered as a marker for the importance of impulse control and willpower over the life course. While it is true that the research documents correlations between preschool waiting and later life outcomes, the attribution of these links to impulse control, while descriptively convenient, appears misplaced. On the one hand, such representations imply that the key to effective waiting lies in a dispositional quality that involves controlling impulses. Children who do not wait are labeled as impulsive. Preschoolers who do wait are suggested to possess willpower. Neither of these dispositional labels fit well with the actual findings of the research.

On the one hand, there are serious questions about whether children's delay of gratification is dispositionally organized at all, regardless of label applied to it. First, the experimental investigations reviewed here demonstrate that the ability to wait is highly contextualized. Subtle changes or shifts in the experimental setting or instructions can change the task from one that is quite challenging for preschoolers to one where children are quite capable of lengthy waits. These findings led Mischel and his students to conclude that delay of gratification is best viewed not as a generalized and decontextualized disposition (like impulsivity or willpower), but as a capability that can be weakened or enhanced by the prevailing circumstances or by the strategies a child is provided to cope with the challenge.

More critically, the documented longitudinal linkages to ego-control and ego-resilience suggest that dispositional impulsivity is not empirically connected to childhood delay. Although often framed as a measure of impulsivity, these findings suggest preschool waiting on the Marshmallow Test is not enduringly related to ego-control and hence dispositional impulsivity. In contrast, the ability to adapt to situational constraints and be flexible does appear to be strongly predicted by preschool delay. Hence, a child's tendency to yield to the temptations, their "impulse" to terminate the wait and take the immediate reward, is far less important than the child's ability to adaptively adjust to the task.

These same findings also call into question the appropriateness of the label willpower. The correlates indicate that the child is not "willing" their way to the end of the wait. They are not "gritting" it out or more generally demonstrating "effortful self-control." They are instead adjusting to the situation as it unfolds, devising strategies to distract from its challenge, and making reasoned choices regarding the values of continuing given their current appraisal of the situation. Hence, the "power" in willpower is far more likely connected to flexibility and strategically deployed distraction than it is to self-control strength or sheer grit. In this manner, the findings of the Bing Longitudinal Study are entirely consistent with recent findings that suggest that the pathway to goal attainment in adults is better served by efforts to avoid temptations than it is to exert willpower over them (Milyavskaya and Inzlicht in press). At the very least, the pattern of findings for this research suggests that it might be time for researchers to find better labels to describe a child's decision to terminate a delay or wait for a desired reward. Impulsivity and willpower convey too much inferential load to be useful descriptions of children's behavior in the Marshmallow Test.

Strategic Attention Deployment

An often unappreciated but central finding of the longitudinal research is that long-term linkages to preschool waiting are almost exclusively limited to those experimental settings where children must face the rewards and are left to their own spontaneous coping strategies during the wait. Longitudinal relations are absent when rewards are not present or if children are provided with instructions on what to do while waiting. The identification of these diagnostic settings illustrates the importance of context not only in explaining variance across experimental conditions but also in organizing individual variation within settings. The significance of this finding cannot be understated. Long-term and consequential individual differences are only revealed when children are tested in settings that are challenging and that require them to rely on their own spontaneous coping strategies to address the challenge. But what are those coping strategies? Since the experimental research strongly suggests that left to their own devices children will tend to focus attention on the consummatory features of rewards, individual differences in waiting in these diagnostic settings may be tied to the child's tendency to spontaneously deploy strategies that distract attention away from the rewards and otherwise reduce the frustration connected to waiting. The longitudinal linkages documented in these diagnostic conditions demonstrate that the oft times cute and captivating activities displayed while waiting are not just happenstance but represent the child's strategic attempts to adapt to the challenge at hand.

Whether children actually strategically deploy attention while waiting, although implied by much of this research, is not addressable directly within the Bing Longitudinal Study sample because no video recordings were made of the original experiments. However, research involving a diverse set of other samples consistently demonstrates linkages between how children deploy attention and their ability to wait. In the most direct and intensive investigation of these attentional strategies, Peake et al. (2002) demonstrated that attention to rewards is detrimental to preschool delay in both waiting and working situations. This research used second-by-second codings of attention deployment to show that when children focus more attention on rewards, delay times are shorter. Conversely, moving attention away from rewards facilitates delay. Peake et al. further demonstrated that one attentional activity, "fixing" attention on rewards at any point during the delay session, is highly predictive of the termination of waiting. A number of investigations using modified assessments of attention deployment have yielded similar results. Rodriguez et al. (1989) showed that attention diversion, measured as the proportion of time children spent looking away from rewards, was highly predictive of waiting time on the Marshmallow Test for older children with social adjustment problems. These researchers also demonstrated that patterns of attention deployment differed substantially near the end of the waiting period, with children who terminate the wait spending significantly more time focusing attention on the rewards. Ayduk et al. (2007) document linkages between attention deployment strategies on the Marshmallow Test and delay time on the task as well as separate measures of verbal and physical aggression in two samples of older children. Sethi et al. (2000) demonstrated that differences in strategic attention deployment recorded in toddlers were subsequently predictive of waiting on the Marshmallow Test when the children were 4 years of age. Most recently, Luerssen et al. (2015) demonstrated that differences in attention deployment strategies during the Marshmallow Test were linked to increased functional coupling between a limbic region (the nucleus accumbens) and cortical structures that foster self-control when children subsequently engaged in a modified Marshmallow Test during fMRI imaging. Taken collectively, these results buttress the notion that children's strategic attention deployment plays a key role in their ability to wait. Several of these studies demonstrate that assessments of attentional strategies might serve as an alternative robust predictor of subsequent life outcomes, perhaps even more robust than the delay time itself. As this work progresses, research energies need to focus on the how to operationalize strategic attention deployment more consistently across studies and to specify the variety of forms these strategies might take as a child engages in goal-directed pursuits.

Tracking children's attention deployment as they wait provides an observable behavioral marker of one strategy that children might be using to adaptively cope while waiting. The early experimental work used instructional sets that directed children toward many other possible strategies: thinking happy thoughts, symbolically representing rewards, focusing on non-consummatory properties of rewards, etc. Mischel (2014) offers these findings as evidence that children can be taught effective self-control strategies. It might be inferred, then, that individual differences in preschool waiting might also be connected to children's spontaneous use of these more complex cognitive strategies. This, of course, is a more challenging empirical question since what children are thinking and how they are representing rewards while they wait are not directly observable. There is an important distinction, however, between what preschoolers can be told to do and what they might actually do spontaneously while they wait. Zimmer-Gembeck and Skinner (2011) present a meta-analysis of children's coping strategies demonstrating that while preschoolers commonly perform simple forms of behavioral distraction and withdrawal, more complex cognitive forms of coping are not typically deployed until middle childhood. Even though preschoolers may successfully follow instructions to execute these cognitive strategies, it is questionable whether they are spontaneously generating these strategies to aid their efforts to wait. It is possible that preschoolers will struggle to learn these more complex strategies.

These questions drive an evolving line of research being conducted by my students at Smith College that focuses on the training of coping strategies in service of facilitating delay of gratification. Our preliminary findings suggest that preschoolers show substantial individual differences in their understanding of strategies for waiting. Preschoolers appear to be capable of acquiring strategies involving simple forms of distraction, and once these are acquired, children wait longer on the Marshmallow Test. These same children show substantially less understanding of more complex cognitive strategies and struggle to acquire those understandings with training. This buttresses the idea that even though preschoolers may be able to be told to use a complex strategy through an experimental instruction, they may not actually be incorporating that strategy into their repertoire of coping techniques. While children appear to be capable of acquiring self-control strategies, intervention directed at training those strategies might need to be keenly sensitive to their natural developmental progression in children.

Executive Functions: Cognitive Control and Working Memory

Attempts to explain why children wait, or even why children might differ behaviorally in how they deploy attention while waiting, increasingly point to the role of the executive functions. Executive functioning is an umbrella label that includes a set of neurocognitive processes implicated in the "conscious control of emotions, thoughts, and behaviors, including working memory, inhibitory control, and set shifting" (Lee and Carlson 2015, p. 1435). Mischel (2014) builds the argument that the Marshmallow Test reveals individual differences in the early development of the executive functions. For Mischel, the executive functions map nicely onto the "cooling" strategies proposed in the hot/cool dual-process system that he uses to understand childhood waiting (Metcalfe and Mischel 1999). The argument that the executive functions may contribute to individual differences in preschool waiting is compelling. First, the Marshmallow Test contains many of the elements of situations where the executive functions are proposed to be engaged (Norman and Shallice 1986). For a preschooler, the delay paradigm is a novel situation that involves planning, decision making, and resisting temptation. Second, the longitudinal correlates documented in the Bing research paint a picture of the children who wait that maps nicely onto the description of adaptive executive functions. Long delaying preschoolers are described later in life as planful, verbally fluent, attentive, responsive to reason, and able to cope with stress, all hallmarks of engaged executive functioning. Third, two specific components of the executive functions, cognitive control and working memory, have been shown empirically to have both behavioral and neural links to waiting in the Marshmallow Test (Ayduk et al. 2008; Berman et al. 2013; Casey et al. 2011; Luerssen et al. 2015).

Despite the compelling and growing argument for the relationship of executive functioning to preschool waiting, the understanding of that linkage is far from complete. The provocative findings of Casey et al. (2011) regarding cognitive control and Berman et al. (2013) regarding working memory both suggest links to the Marshmallow Test but are difficult to interpret due to the grouping criteria that required participants to show lifelong patterns of self-control. That lifelong patterns of self-reported self-control relate to cognitive control and working memory is a significant finding in and of itself, but the direct linkages to preschool waiting are still unclear. Ayduk et al. offer that the ability to wait on the Marshmallow Test is "an early behavioral precursor" of cognitive control in adulthood (2008, p. 151), but then report that empirically these two variables are not correlated. Luerssen et al. (2015) document the most direct and impressive investigation to date of the links between the Marshmallow Test and an aspect of executive functioning (attentional focus away from the rewards). But, even here, the links were documented in older children (aged 7–9) where the functional significance of rewards present seems to have passed, at least with respect to how long children waited. Mean waiting time in the presence of rewards was over 22 min in a paradigm where the maximum wait was 25 min. It is encouraging, nonetheless, that strategic attention deployment (labeled in this study as "cool focus") still demonstrates predictive prowess.

Converging evidence from research not directly connected to the Bing Longitudinal Study also raises important questions about the inferred connection of preschool waiting and executive functioning. Lee and Carlson review findings documenting that "delay of gratification tasks often do not relate to or load on the same factors as typical executive function tasks" (2015, p. 1435). In addition, Diamond and Lee (2011) show that interventions that improve executive functioning in children do not demonstrate corresponding impact on delay of gratification in those same children. Given the expansive scope of definition of executive functioning, there will clearly be some linkages to preschool waiting. However, the specification of which executive functions are involved, how they are involved, and the extent of their impact are questions ripe for further empirical scrutiny. For example, Lee and Carlson (2015) illustrate the importance of "set shifting," the ability to respond adaptively and flexibly to different contexts, for delay choice and savings behavior. That sort of emphasis is entirely consistent with the picture of the effectively delayer that emerges in the current review where the emphasis is placed on the child's ability to rationally adapt and flexibly respond to the changes challenges in the situations they confront.

Trust

Recently, a considerable amount of attention has been given in both academic and popular circles to the role of trust in delay of gratification. Both Kidd et al. (2013) and Michaelson and Munakata (2016) present findings indicating that a child's "trust" that they will receive a promised delayed reward critically impacts waiting in a modified version of the original Marshmallow Test. In Kidd et al., trust was manipulated by having an experimenter either make good or not on the promise to deliver a more desired outcome if the child was willing to wait in two preliminary waiting scenarios. Children then participated in an experimental variation of the Marshmallow Test conducted by the same experimenter. Kidd et al. found that children who worked with a "reliable" experimenter were much more likely to wait than children exposed to an "unreliable" experimenter. Michaelson and Munakata refined this paradigm so that the child observed the experimenter being "untrustworthy" with another adult on a task that did not involve direct delivery of a promise. Children subsequently working with a "trustworthy" experimenter delayed significantly longer than children working with an adult who had been observed to be "untrustworthy." Both sets of researchers suggest that their findings offer an alternative explanation of why children wait, one focused on rational decision making concerning the likelihood of the receipt of the reward, and they raise questions about what might be contributing to the individual differences documented in the Bing Longitudinal Study.

To begin, even the very earliest investigators of delay choice and delay maintenance fully appreciated the important role of children's trust expectations about the delivery of rewards. As reviewed previously, early investigations of delay choice did not conceptualize these choices as the products of some generalized tendency to demonstrate self-control (or impulse control), but contextually driven decisions that children made as they sized up the task they faced. Trust was explicitly manipulated by Mahrer (1956) and implicitly inferred from cultural and familial interactions by Mischel (1958, 1961). Both showed the powerful impact of trust expectations on children's delay choices.

In shifting the research emphasis from delay choice to delay maintenance, the designers of the Marshmallow Test were keenly aware of how trust expectations might influence children's waiting and took steps to explicitly address this in developing the paradigm. Although rarely discussed, experimenters participating in the early Marshmallow studies were required to make repeated visits to the child's classroom for several weeks prior to the beginning of research. Researchers participated in class activities and played with the children in order to build familiarity, rapport, and trust with the children. In designing the task, at least three features of the paradigm were explicitly structured into the task to establish trust. The first of these was the process of having the child ring the bell in order to signal the experimenter to return. It is important to note that this procedure was practiced repeatedly at the outset of the instructions both so the child would understand how to use the signal and so the child would trust the experimenter will actually return. Second, in all experimental settings where rewards were left in the room (except those that were explicitly testing the impact of having either the immediate or delayed reward alone), both rewards were left on the table directly facing the child. In this manner, there was little room for doubt in the child's mind that they would receive the preferred reward if they waited. The desired reward was within their reach the entire time. Finally, the contingencies for waiting were rehearsed repeatedly with the child before the delay period began. Again, the purpose of this rehearsal was to assure that the child understood the contingency and to build trust in what would happen should the child opt to wait or terminate the delay.

As with the early experimental reports from Mischel and his students, it is difficult to discern whether Kidd et al. or Michaelson and Munakata required researchers to spend time establishing rapport with children prior to beginning testing. However, the modified Marshmallow Test used by these researchers systematically eliminated all those procedures that Mischel and his students built into the paradigm to build trust. In the modified paradigm, children were presented with one marshmallow and told that they could either eat it right now or wait for the experimenter to go get more marshmallows. They were promised that if they had not eaten the marshmallow when the experimenter returned, they would get two marshmallows. Missing from this paradigm was the bell and its rehearsal as a signal for the researcher to come back. Kidd et al. acknowledge this was deliberate since the training connected with the bell would "… provide additional information about the experimenter's reliability." That is true, and it is one of the key reasons that the bell and its training were included in the original paradigm. The elimination of the signaling bell also creates a confusing scenario where the child's consumption of the marshmallow means that the child will not get the additional treat but has no particular significance to ending the waiting period. This means that a defining element of the Marshmallow Test, the contingency between opting for the less preferred reward and terminating the wait, is omitted in this revised paradigm. Neither Kidd et al. nor Michaelson and Munakata acknowledge or address the absence of the preferred reward or the rehearsal of contingencies as central features of the Marshmallow Test, but these are likely also important omissions that impact the child's trust. Instead, Kidd et al. claim that all the "major features" of the delay situation they employed were "identical" to those of the original Marshmallow Test and then later suggest that their modified paradigm included only "small procedural differences" (2013, p. 6). Suffice it to say, these small procedural differences fundamentally change the dynamic of waiting situation in many important ways.

If there is a single lesson to be learned from the experiments reviewed previously, it is that small alternations of the experimental setting can have dramatic impact on children's experience of the wait. Those differences can find expression in both group differences across conditions and the meaning of individual differences within settings. Both Mischel and his students were fully aware of the role that trust expectations might play in the Marshmallow Test and took explicit steps to buttress the child's trust and hence reduce individual differences on this variable. There is no doubt that some individual differences in trust were still impacting children's choices, but they should have been small compared to those expressed in the modified paradigm used in the trust research. The findings of Kidd et al. and Michaelson and Munakata provide a useful reminder of the role that trust expectations might play in children's waiting, but they have no bearing on the evaluation of the findings of the Bing Longitudinal Study where children were tested under conditions deliberately structured to minimize the impact of individual differences in trust expectations.

It is interesting to note that the findings of Kidd et al. and Michaelson and Munakata are offered as an example of how children's waiting can be guided by rational decision making, in this case the expectancy that the experimenter will deliver the more desired reward. Both sets of researchers pit this rational decision-making perspective against what appears to be a seemingly irrational, impulsive explanation of children's behavior. For Kidd et al., the contrast is to explanations that invoke children's self-control. For Michaelson and Munakata, the seemingly irrational counterpart are explanations pointing to cognitive control. Such pitting reflects a fundamental misunderstanding of the meaning of findings reviewed in this paper. Far from ascribing children's waiting to irrational and impulsive components, the recurring message throughout this review is that children's behavior, even the decision not to wait, is rational, flexible, adaptive, and responsive to changing circumstances that they face. It is curious that even processes like cognitive control are cast as somehow irrational. If the executive functions are shown to play a substantive role in delay of gratification, the entire of point of those functions is to facilitate better decision making! Far from offering an different view of the factors that impact children's ability to wait, the findings of

Kidd et al. and Michaelson and Munakata buttress the perspective offered here that children in waiting situations are actively processing the contextual cues and strategically adapting their behavior to make choices about whether to continue.

Concluding Comments

The number of seconds a child waits before summoning an experimenter to return during the Marshmallow Test is commonly used a marker of the child's self-control (Duckworth et al. 2013). In both popular and academic treatments, short waits are attached to constructs like impulsivity, while opting to not ring the bell is seen as a sign of the child's willpower. While such ascriptions are descriptively convenient, they carry with them inferential load about how and why children wait that is consequential. In popular treatments, those inferences frequently imply a dispositional tendency toward the control of impulses that is set in place early in life (Goleman 1995). In academic treatments, ascriptions to self-control or more specific processes like cognitive control are taken to imply that the factors driving children's waiting are not "rational" (Kidd et al. 2013; McGuire and Kable 2013; Michaelson and Munakata 2016). The research reviewed here suggests a very different picture of how and why children wait. On the one hand, the experimental studies tell us that children participating in the self-imposed delay of gratification paradigm are keenly responsive to contextual cues and highly adaptive in adopting suggested strategies to facilitate waiting. Individual differences in a narrow range of predictable "diagnostic" experimental settings tap into core psychological processes with enduring longitudinal consequences that are expressed both in direct relations to adaptive functioning and through buffering people from other adult vulnerabilities. Those psychological processes are tied closely to the way children use attention flexibly while waiting and are seen behaviorally in the various coping antics displayed by children as they wait. Collectively, the research points to children differentially and deliberately deploying age-appropriate attentional coping strategies to make a decision about what to do in a novel and continually unfolding situation.

The Marshmallow Test was offered by Mischel and his students as an operationalization of delay of gratification intended to move research in the field beyond the static assessment of delay choices and preferences. The research team sought to devise a paradigm for examining the cognitive and contextual factors that influence the dynamic process of maintaining delay once a preference has been expressed. In its inception, no one knew how the research might unfold or what it might reveal. No one envisioned that this simple framework for engaging preschoolers would evolve into a research program that now spans a half-century. Most certainly, none of the principal researchers anticipated that enormous growth of public interest in the work.

The investigations of children's delay of gratification, conducted by Mischel and his students at the Bing Nursery School nearly 50 years ago, launched a program of research that remains vital to this day. Our current work includes explorations of linkages to economic outcomes in the Bing participants' lives, studies of training children on effective strategies for delay, and examination of different life course self-regulatory trajectories to name just a few. As with any programmatic research, the Bing Longitudinal Study continues to raise challenging questions about the nature of self-regulation as it plays out over the life course. Because the Bing Longitudinal Study was in part accidental in its inception, it was not designed or structured to answer many of the questions that it has raised. It is encouraging to see that active research programs utilizing more tailored designs are emerging to clarify issues raised and lessons learned by this work. The accurate portrayal of what investigations utilizing the Marshmallow Test have revealed to date should assist these continuing efforts to understand how and why children wait and the linkages of early delay of gratification to outcomes over the life course.

References

Abikoye, G. E., & Adekoya, J. A. (2010). Predicting substance abuse in a sample of Nigerian undergraduate students: The role of core self-evaluations and delay of gratification. *Psychological Studies, 55*(4), 299–307. doi:10.1007/s12646-010-0047-9

Addessi, E., Paglieri, F., Beran, M. J., Evans, T. A., Macchitella, L., De Petrillo, F., et al. (2013). Delay choice versus delay maintenance: Different measures of delayed gratification in capuchin monkeys (*Cebus apella*). *Journal of Comparative Psychology, 127*(4), 392–398. doi:10.1037/a0031869

Amelang, M., & Steinmayr, R. (2006). Is there a validity increment for tests of emotional intelligence in explaining the variance of performance criteria? *Intelligence, 34*(5), 459–468. doi:10.1016/j.intell.2006.03.003

Ayduk, O., Mendoza-Denton, R., Mischel, W., Downey, G., Peake, P. K., & Rodriguez, M. (2000). Regulating the interpersonal self: Strategic self-regulation for coping with rejection sensitivity. *Journal of Personality and Social Psychology, 79*(5), 776–792. doi:10.1037/0022-3514.79.5.776

Ayduk, O., Rodriguez, M. L., Mischel, W., Shoda, Y., & Wright, J. (2007). Verbal intelligence and self-regulatory competencies: Joint predictors of boys' aggression. *Journal of Research in Personality, 41*(2), 374–388. doi:10.1016/j.jrp.2006.04.008

Ayduk, O., Zayas, V., Downey, G., Cole, A. B., Shoda, Y., & Mischel, W. (2008). Rejection sensitivity and executive control: Joint predictors of borderline personality features. *Journal of Research in Personality, 42*(1), 151–168. doi:10.1016/j.jrp.2007.04.002

Bandura, A., & Mischel, W. (1965). Modifications of self-imposed delay of reward through exposure to live and symbolic models. *Journal of Personality and Social Psychology, 2*(5), 698–705. doi:10.1037/h0022655

Baumeister, R. F., & Tierney, J. (2011). *Willpower: Rediscovering the greatest human strength.* New York, NY, US: Penguin Press.

Bembenutty, H., & Karabenick, S. A. (2013). Self-regulation, culture, and academic delay of gratification. *Journal of Cognitive Education and Psychology, 12*(3), 323–337. doi:10.1891/1945-8959.12.3.323

Bem, D. J., & Allen, A. (1974). On predicting some of the people some of the time: The search for cross-situational consistencies in behavior. *Psychological Review, 81*(6), 506–520. doi:10.1037/h0037130

Bem, D. J., & Funder, D. C. (1978). Predicting more of the people more of the time: Assessing the personality of situations. *Psychological Review, 85*(6), 485–501. doi:10.1037/0033-295X.85.6.485

Berlyne, D. E. (1960). *Conflict, arousal and curiosity*. New York: McGraw-Hill.

Berman, M. G., Yourganov, G., Askren, M. K., Ayduk, O., Casey, B. J., Gotlib, I. H., et al. (2013). Dimensionality of brain networks linked to life-long individual differences in self-control. *Nature Communications, 4,* 1373. doi:10.1038/ncomms2374

Bindman, S. W., Pomerantz, E. M., & Roisman, G. I. (2015). Do children's executive functions account for associations between early autonomy-supportive parenting and achievement through high school? *Journal of Educational Psychology, 107*(3), 756–770. doi:10.1037/edu0000017

Block, J. (1977). Advancing the psychology of personality: Paradigmatic shift or improving the quality of research. In D. Magnussen & N. S. Endler (Eds.), *Personality at the crossroads; Current issues in interactional psychology*. Hillsdale: Erlbaum.

Block, J. H., & Block, J. (1980). The role of ego-control and ego-resiliency in the organization of behavior. In W. A. Collins (Ed.), *Minnesota symposium on child development* (Vol. 13). Hillsdale: Erlbaum.

Caleza, C., Yãnez-Vico, R. M., Mendoza, A., & Iglesias-Linares, A. (2016). Childhood obesity and delayed gratification behavior: A systematic review of experimental studies. *The Journal of Pediatrics, 169,* 201–207. doi:10.1016/j.jpeds.2015.10.008

Callan, M. J., Shead, N. W., & Olson, J. M. (2011). Personal relative deprivation, delay discounting, and gambling. *Journal of Personality and Social Psychology, 101*(5), 955–973. doi:10.1037/a0024778

Campbell, S. B., & von Stauffenberg, C. (2009). Delay and inhibition as early predictors of ADHD symptoms in third grade. *Journal of Abnormal Child Psychology, 37*(1), 1–15. doi:10.1007/s10802-008-9270-4

Casey, B. J., Somerville, L. H., Gotlib, I. H., Ayduk, O., Franklin, N. T., Askren, M. K., et al. (2011). Behavioral and neural correlates of delay of gratification 40 years later. *Proceedings of the National Academy of Sciences (USA), 108*(36), 14998–15003. doi:10.1073/pnas.1108561108

Diamond, A., & Lee, K. (2011). Interventions shown to aid executive function development in children 4–12 years old. *Science, 333*(6045), 959–964. doi:10.1126/science.1204529

Di Fabio, A., & Palazzeschi, L. (2009). An in-depth look at scholastic success: Fluid intelligence, personality traits or emotional intelligence? *Personality and Individual Differences, 46*(5–6), 581–585. doi:10.1016/j.paid.2008.12.012

Downey, G., & Feldman, S. I. (1996). Implications of rejection sensitivity for intimate relationships. *Journal of Personality and Social Psychology, 70*(6), 1327–1343. doi:10.1037/0022-3514.70.6.1327

Duckworth, A. L., Tsukayama, E., & Kirby, T. A. (2013). Is it really self-control? Examining the predictive power of the delay of gratification task. *Personality and Social Psychology Bulletin, 39*(7), 843–855.

Eigsti, I.-M., Zayas, V., Mischel, W., Shoda, Y., Ayduk, O., Dadlani, M. B., et al. (2006). Predicting cognitive control from preschool to late adolescence and young adulthood. *Psychological Science, 17*(6), 478–484. doi:10.1111/j.1467-9280.2006.01732.x

Estes, W. K. (1972). Reinforcement in human behavior: Reward and punishment influence human actions via informational and cybernetic processes. *American Scientist, 60*(6), 723–729.

Feldman, S., & Downey, G. (1994). Rejection sensitivity as a mediator of the impact of childhood exposure to family violence on adult attachment behavior. *Development and Psychopathology, 6*(01), 231–247. doi:10.1017/S0954579400005976

Fishbein, M., & Ajzen, I. (1972). Attitudes and opinions. *Annual Review of Psychology, 23,* 487–544. doi:10.1146/annurev.ps.23.020172.002415

Freud, S. (1911). Formulations regarding the two principles in mental functioning. In *Collected works* (Vol. 4). New York: Basic Books.

Funder, D. C., Block, J. H., & Block, J. (1983). Delay of gratification: Some longitudinal personality correlates. *Journal of Personality and Social Psychology, 44*(6), 1198–1213. doi:10.1037/0022-3514.44.6.1198

Goleman, D. (1995). *Emotional intelligence: Why it can matter more than IQ (10th Anniversary edition).* New York: Bantam Books.

Green, B. F. (1980). Note on Bem and Funder's scheme for scoring Q sorts. *Psychological Review, 87*(2), 212–214. doi:10.1037/0033-295X.87.2.212

Herman, C. P., & Polivy, J. (2003). Dieting as an exercise in behavioral economics. In G. Loewenstein, D. Read, & R. Baumeister (Eds.), *Time and decision: Economic and psychological perspectives on intertemporal choice* (pp. 459–489). New York, NY, US: Russell Sage Foundation.

Jones, E., & Gerard, H. B. (1967). *Foundations of social psychology*. New York: Wiley.

Kidd, C., Palmeri, H., & Aslin, R. N. (2013). Rational snacking: Young children's decision-making on the marshmallow task is moderated by beliefs about environmental reliability. *Cognition, 126*(1), 109–114. doi:10.1016/j.cognition.2012.08.004

Lee, W. S. C., & Carlson, S. M. (2015). Knowing when to be "rational": Flexible economic decision making and executive function in preschool children. *Child Development, 86*(5), 1434–1448. doi:10.1111/cdev.12401

Luerssen, A., Gyurak, A., Ayduk, O., Wendelken, C., & Bunge, S. A. (2015). Delay of gratification in childhood linked to cortical interactions with the nucleus accumbens. *Social Cognitive and Affective Neuroscience, 10*(12), 1769–1776.

Mahrer, A. R. (1956). The role of expectancy in delayed reinforcement. *Journal of Experimental Psychology, 52*(2), 101–106. doi:10.1037/h0040837

Mayer, J. D., & Salovey, P. (1997). What is emotional intelligence? In P. Salovey & D. J. Sluyter (Eds.), *Emotional development and emotional intelligence: Educational implications* (pp. 3–34). New York, NY: Basic Books.

McGuire, J. T., & Kable, J. W. (2013). Rational temporal predictions can underlie apparent failures to delay gratification. *Psychological Review, 120*(2), 395–410. doi:10.1037/a0031910

Metcalfe, J., & Mischel, W. (1999). A hot/cool-system analysis of delay of gratification: Dynamics of willpower. *Psychological Review, 106*(1), 3–19. doi:10.1037/0033-295X.106.1.3

Michaelson, L. E., & Munakata, Y. (2016). Trust matters: Seeing how an adult treats another person influences preschoolers' willingness to delay gratification. *Developmental Science*. doi:10.1111/desc.12388

Milyavskaya, M., & Inzlicht, M. (in press). What's so great about self control? Examining the importance of effortful self-control and temptation in predicting real-life depletion and goal attainment. *Social Psychology and Personality Science.*

Mischel, H. N., & Mischel, W. (1983). The development of children's knowledge of self-control strategies. *Child Development, 54*(3), 603–619. doi:10.2307/1130047

Mischel, W. (1958). Preference for delayed reinforcement: An experimental study of a cultural observation. *The Journal of Abnormal and Social Psychology, 56*(1), 57–61. doi:10.1037/h0041895

Mischel, W. (1961). Father-absence and delay of gratification. *The Journal of Abnormal and Social Psychology, 63*(1), 116–124. doi:10.1037/h0046877

Mischel, W. (1969). *Personality and assessment*. New York: Wiley.

Mischel, W. (2014). *The Marshmallow test: Mastering self-control*. New York, NY, US: Little, Brown and Co.

Mischel, W., Ayduk, O., Berman, M. G., Casey, B. J., Gotlib, I. H., & Jonides, J. (2011). "Willpower" over the life span: Decomposing self-regulation. *Social Cognitive and Affective Neuroscience, 6*(2), 252–256. doi:10.1093/scan/nsq081

Mischel, W., & Baker, N. (1975). Cognitive appraisals and transformations in delay behavior. *Journal of Personality and Social Psychology, 31*(2), 254–261. doi:10.1037/h0076272

Mischel, W., & Ebbesen, E. B. (1970). Attention in delay of gratification. *Journal of Personality and Social Psychology, 16*(2), 329–337. doi:10.1037/h0029815

Mischel, W., Ebbesen, E. B., & Raskoff Zeiss, A. (1972). Cognitive and attentional mechanisms in delay of gratification. *Journal of Personality and Social Psychology, 21*(2), 204–218. doi:10.1037/h0032198

Mischel, W., & Gilligan, C. (1964). Delay of gratification, motivation for the prohibited gratification, and responses to temptation. *The Journal of Abnormal and Social Psychology, 69*(4), 411–417. doi:10.1037/h0048918

Mischel, W., & Grusec, J. (1967). Waiting for rewards and punishments: Effects of time and probability on choice. *Journal of Personality and Social Psychology, 5*(1), 24–31. doi:10.1037/h0024180

Mischel, W., Grusec, J., & Masters, J. C. (1969). Effects of expected delay time on the subjective value of rewards and punishments. *Journal of Personality and Social Psychology, 11*(4), 363–373. doi:10.1037/h0027265

Mischel, W., & Metzner, R. (1962). Preference for delayed reward as a function of age, intelligence, and length of delay interval. *The Journal of Abnormal and Social Psychology, 64*(6), 425–431. doi:10.1037/h0045046

Mischel, W., & Moore, B. (1973). Effects of attention to symbolically presented rewards on self-control. *Journal of Personality and Social Psychology, 28*(2), 172–179. doi:10.1037/h0035716

Mischel, W., & Moore, B. S. (1980). The role of ideation in voluntary delay for symbolically presented rewards. *Cognitive Therapy and Research, 4*(2), 211–221. doi:10.1007/BF01173652

Mischel, W., & Patterson, C. J. (1976). Substantive and structural elements of effective plans for self-control. *Journal of Personality and Social Psychology, 34*(5), 942–950. doi:10.1037/0022-3514.34.5.942

Mischel, W., & Peake, P. K. (1982). Beyond déjà vu in the search for cross-situational consistency. *Psychological Review, 89*(6), 730–755. doi:10.1037/0033-295X.89.6.730

Mischel, W., & Shoda, Y. (1995). A cognitive-affective system theory of personality: Reconceptualizing situations, dispositions, dynamics, and invariance in personality structure. *Psychological Review, 102*(2), 246–268. doi:10.1037/0033-295X.102.2.246

Mischel, W., Shoda, Y., & Peake, P. K. (1988). The nature of adolescent competencies predicted by preschool delay of gratification. *Journal of Personality and Social Psychology, 54*(4), 687–696. doi:10.1037/0022-3514.54.4.687

Mischel, W., Shoda, Y., & Rodriguez, M. L. (1989). Delay of gratification in children. *Science, 244*(4907), 933–938. doi:10.1126/science.2658056

Mischel, W., & Staub, E. (1965). Effects of expectancy on working and waiting for larger reward. *Journal of Personality and Social Psychology, 2*(5), 625–633. doi:10.1037/h0022677

Mischel, W., & Underwood, B. (1974). Instrumental ideation in delay of gratification. *Child Development, 45*(4), 1083–1088.

Mischel, W., Zeiss, R., & Zeiss, A. (1974). Internal-external control and persistence: Validation and implications of the Stanford preschool internal-external scale. *Journal of Personality and Social Psychology, 29*(2), 265–278. doi:10.1037/h0036020

Moffitt, T. E., Arseneault, L., Belsky, D., Dickson, N., Hancox, R. J., Harrington, H., et al. (2011). A gradient of childhood self-control predicts health, wealth, and public safety. *Proceedings of the National Academy of Sciences (USA), 108*(7), 2693–2698. doi:10.1073/pnas.1010076108

Moore, B., Mischel, W., & Zeiss, A. (1976). Comparative effects of the reward stimulus and its cognitive representation in voluntary delay. *Journal of Personality and Social Psychology, 34*(3), 419–424. doi:10.1037/0022-3514.34.3.419

Norman, D. A., & Shallice, T. (1986). Attention to action: Willed and automatic control of behaviour. In R. J. Davidson, G. E. Schwartz, & D. Shapiro (Eds.), *Consciousness and self-regulation: Advances in research and theory*. New York: Plenum Press.

Patterson, C. J., & Mischel, W. (1976). Effects of temptation-inhibiting and task-facilitating plans on self-control. *Journal of Personality and Social Psychology, 33*(2), 209–217. doi:10.1037/0022-3514.33.2.209

Peake, P. K., Hebl, M., & Mischel, W. (2002). Strategic attention deployment for delay of gratification in working and waiting situations. *Developmental Psychology, 38*(2), 313–326. doi:10.1037/0012-1649.38.2.313

Pietrzak, J., Downey, G., & Ayduk, O. (2005). Rejection sensitivity as an interpersonal vulnerability. In M. W. Baldwin (Ed.), *Interpersonal cognition* (pp. 62–84). New York, NY, US: Guilford Press.

Rappaport, D. (1967). On the psychoanalytic theory of thinking. In M. M. Gill (Ed.), *The collected papers of David Rapaport*. New York: Basic Books.

Reynolds, B., & Schiffbauer, R. (2005). Delay of gratification and delay discounting: A unifying feedback model of delay-related impulsive behavior. *The Psychological Record, 55*(3), 439–460.

Rodriguez, M. L., Mischel, W., & Shoda, Y. (1989). Cognitive person variables in the delay of gratification of older children at risk. *Journal of Personality and Social Psychology, 57*(2), 358–367. doi:10.1037/0022-3514.57.2.358

Rossiter, S., Thompson, J., & Hester, R. (2012). Improving control over the impulse for reward: Sensitivity of harmful alcohol drinkers to delayed reward but not immediate punishment. *Drug and Alcohol Dependence, 125*(1–2), 89–94. doi:10.1016/j.drugalcdep.2012.03.017

Schlam, T. R., Wilson, N. L., Shoda, Y., Mischel, W., & Ayduk, O. (2013). Preschoolers' delay of gratification predicts their body mass 30 years later. *The Journal of Pediatrics, 162*(1), 90–93. doi:10.1016/j.jpeds.2012.06.049

Seeyave, D. M., Coleman, S., Appugliese, D., Corwyn, R. F., Bradley, R. H., Davidson, N. S., et al. (2009). Ability to delay gratification at age 4 years and risk of overweight at age 11 years. *Archives of Pediatrics & Adolescent Medicine, 163*(4), 303–308. doi:10.1001/archpediatrics.2009.12

Sethi, A., Mischel, W., Aber, J. L., Shoda, Y., & Rodriguez, M. L. (2000). The role of strategic attention deployment in development of self-regulation: Predicting preschoolers' delay of gratification from mother–toddler interactions. *Developmental Psychology, 36*(6), 767–777. doi:10.1037/0012-1649.36.6.767

Shoda, Y., Mischel, W., & Peake, P. K. (1990). Predicting adolescent cognitive and self-regulatory competencies from preschool delay of gratification: Identifying diagnostic conditions. *Developmental Psychology, 26*(6), 978–986. doi:10.1037/0012-1649.26.6.978

Shoda, Y., Mischel, W., & Wright, J. C. (1993). Links between personality judgments and contextualized behavior patterns: Situation-behavior profiles of personality prototypes. *Social Cognition, 11*(4), 399–429. doi:10.1521/soco.1993.11.4.399

Shoda, Y., Mischel, W., & Wright, J. C. (1994). Intraindividual stability in the organization and patterning of behavior: Incorporating psychological situations into the idiographic analysis of personality. *Journal of Personality and Social Psychology, 67*(4), 674–687. doi:10.1037/0022-3514.67.4.674

Tobin, R. M., & Graziano, W. G. (2010). Delay of gratification: A review of fifty years of regulation research. In R. H. Hoyle (Ed.), *Handbook of personality and self-regulation* (pp. 47–63). Hoboken: Wiley-Blackwell.

Unkelbach, C., Plessner, H., & Memmert, D. (2009). "Fit" in sports: Self-regulation and athletic performances. In J. P. Forgas, R. F. Baumeister, & D. M. Tice (Eds.), *Psychology of self-regulation: Cognitive, affective, and motivational processes* (Vol. 11, pp. 93–105). New York, NY, US: Psychology Press.

Yates, B. T., & Mischel, W. (1979). Young children's preferred attentional strategies for delaying gratification. *Journal of Personality and Social Psychology, 37*(2), 286–300. doi:10.1037/0022-3514.37.2.286

Young, M. E., & McCoy, A. W. (2015). A delay discounting task produces a greater likelihood of waiting than a deferred gratification task. *Journal of the Experimental Analysis of Behavior, 103*(1), 180–195. doi:10.1002/jeab.119

Zimmer-Gembeck, M. J., & Skinner, E. A. (2011). Review: The development of coping across childhood and adolescence: An integrative review and critique of research. *International Journal of Behavioral Development, 35*(1), 1–17. doi:10.1177/0165025410384923

Chapter 3
From Risk and Time Preferences to Cultural Models of Causality: On the Challenges and Possibilities of Field Experiments, with Examples from Rural Southwestern Madagascar

Bram Tucker

Introduction

In this contribution, I use examples from fieldwork in rural southwestern Madagascar to discuss the limits and possibilities of using choice experiments in field settings to explore how non-Western peoples think about risk and time. My thesis is that it is very challenging to quantitatively measure preferences in any robust (externally and internally valid) or precise way. I argue that we may learn more by using experiments and related methods to interrogate people's shared concepts of risk and time within causal understandings of how the world works. By making this argument, I will address the methodological and epistemological differences between psychology, economics, and anthropology and frame questions about the influence of culture on judgment and decision making.

But first, by way of introduction, I would like to tell a story. This story begins with an academic debate played out in the pages of the journal *Current Anthropology* in 2001–2002 and ends in Madagascar with misfortune, fear, and accusations of sorcery during the rainy months of 2008.

The Kuznar-Henrich and McElreath Debate

The debate that brought risk preference to the attention of many anthropologists was about how to interpret the results of choice experiments conducted among

B. Tucker (✉)
Department of Anthropology, University of Georgia,
250A Baldwin Hall, Jackson Street, Athens, GA 30602, USA
e-mail: bramtuck@uga.edu

J.R. Stevens (ed.), *Impulsivity*, Nebraska Symposium on Motivation 64,
DOI 10.1007/978-3-319-51721-6_3

non-Western peoples. Kuznar (2001) reported the results of a risk preference experiment conducted among Aymara herders in the Peruvian Andes. He had asked a sample of men and women to make a series of hypothetical choices between a smaller number of livestock that they could gain for certain versus a 50% chance to win a larger number of animals. Kuznar argued that herders' choices in this experiment were best explained by their wealth—by the size of their herds outside the experiment. Risk preference bore an inverted U-shaped relationship with herd size (Fig. 3.1a). Moderately wealthy herders were strongly risk averse, while the poorest and the wealthiest herders were only slightly risk averse or even risk prone. Kuznar argued that this result is consistent with the neoclassical economic logic of expected utility theory and a sigmoidal marginal utility curve for wealth (Fig. 3.1b). Poor herders must grow their herds, so they value probable livestock gains more than losses and thus tolerate risk. Moderately wealthy herders want to keep what they have, so they value probable losses more than gains and thus are risk averse. Rich herders have enough livestock to meet their basic needs and so can afford to gamble for the chance to further increase their wealth.

Shortly thereafter, Henrich and McElreath (2002) published the results of two risk choice experiments they had conducted among farmer-herders in Chile and Tanzania and UCLA undergraduates. They found that UCLA students and Chilean Huinca agropastoralists tended to be risk averse, while Mapuche of Chile and Sangu of Tanzania tended to be risk prone. In regression analyses, age, sex, wealth, and income did not explain the variability in risk preferences. The authors concluded that membership within a cultural group (Mapuche, Huinca, Sangu, UCLA student) causally influenced preferences. They argued that what we call preferences are actually socially shared norms governing how to act in risky situations. They linked this interpretation to a version of bounded rationality based on conformist social learning and cultural inheritance (Boyd and Richerson 2001; Henrich and McElreath 2003).

In a series of comments and replies, Henrich (2001) accused Kuznar of circular reasoning, of imputing utility functions from people's choices and then using utility functions that explain those choices. Kuznar (2002) charged that Henrich and McElreath downplay the possibility that intergroup differences in risk preferences may be due to group differences in wealth rather than culture.

Testing Wealth and Group Effects on Risk and Time Preference in Southwestern Madagascar

My field site in southwestern Madagascar seemed the perfect place to evaluate Kuznar's and Henrich and McElreath's claims and to expand the debate to include intertemporal choice. In Madagascar's rural southwest, people make daily choices

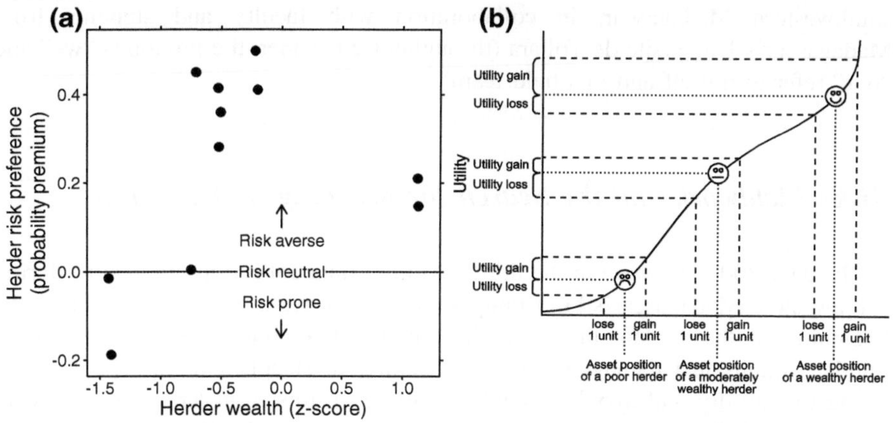

Fig. 3.1 Results and interpretation from Kuznar (2001), illustrating the expected utility model of risk preference. **a** Kuznar found that risk preference among Aymara herders appears to be an inverse U-shaped function of wealth so that risk aversion initially increases and then decreases with increasing wealth. **b** This implies that Aymara herders have an undulating marginal utility function for wealth; poorer herders gamble because they would gain more utility from a win than they might lose from a loss, consistent with increasing marginal utility; moderately wealthy herders are risk averse because they value potential losses over gains (diminishing marginal utility); and wealthy herders gamble because like the poorest herders, they value probable gains for losses (increasing marginal utility). Figures redrawn with permission from the University of Chicago Press

among subsistence options that differ primarily by average reward, risk, and delay, as they choose to spend their time doing agriculture (which is risky with delayed harvests) versus hunting, gathering, and fishing (which are lower risk activities with daily rewards; Tucker et al. 2010).

Pertinent to Henrich and McElreath's (2002) argument that risk preferences are cultural norms, southwestern Malagasy (people of Madagascar) classify themselves into three identity categories which they commonly claim correspond to subsistence modes: To be Masikoro means that one is a savanna farmer-herder, while Mikea are forest foragers and Vezo are marine fishers and sailors (Astuti 1995; Poyer and Kelly 2000; Yount et al. 2001; Tucker 2003), even though in practice people diversify beyond these modes. It could be that these identity groups acculturate their members to specific norms for risk and time, or perhaps one's preferences determine in which group they find membership. Relevant to Kuznar's thesis that risk preference is a function of wealth, farmers, foragers, and fishermen tend to acquire different forms of wealth due to their differing means of production, mainly land and livestock, social capital, and fishing gear (Tucker et al. 2011).

In 2007–2009, I conducted a four-season investigation of the effects of wealth, income, and cultural group membership on risk and time preferences in southwestern Madagascar, in collaboration with faculty and students from Madagascar's Université de Toliara (throughout this paper, the pronouns "we" and "our" refer to myself and this field team).[1]

Risky Fieldwork and the Search for Meaning in Misfortune

By January 2008, we were in the third season of data collection. Fieldwork during southwestern Madagascar's brief rainy season is always a risky venture. From the beginning of the season, the research team felt that things were going wrong. Sudden squalls had damaged our tents, leading to sleepless nights spent vainly trying to stay dry and avoid mosquitos. Failure on this front led to several team members suffering malaria. Most mysteriously, we periodically found our hearts racing with sudden panic triggered by unexpected thunderclaps on sunny days.

One of my Malagasy collaborators, curious as to the cause of our misfortunes, decided to consult a spirit medium (*tromba*) in the small Masikoro village of Antaimbalabo. A forest spirit (*konko*) speaking through the possessed woman told him that our problems had only just begun. The source of our misfortunes was a person known to us, a former coworker with "bad ideas" (*raty hevitse*). We had so enraged him that he had consulted a sorcerer (*mpamorike*) to cast spells to harm us. We knew immediately who the culprit was: a former driver-mechanic, Mr. X as I shall call him here, whom we had recently fired after a dispute.

We returned to the provincial capital of Toliara midseason to repair the tents, service the two field vehicles, and resupply. We brought the truck formerly driven by Mr. X to the neighborhood of Sanfily, where most of the automotive mechanics work. Alongside a street vendor repairing punctured tires and another who performs oil changes, team members found a diviner (*ambiasa*) who specializes in magic related to vehicles and travel. The diviner performed *sikily* divination, in which seeds are cast on the ground and rearranged after precise formulae to gain a vision events in the past, the future, or the spiritual realm. What the diviner saw in the cast seeds confirmed the diagnosis of the spirit medium in Antaimbalabo: Mr. X had indeed hired a sorcerer to cast spells to harm us, and worse yet, Mr. X would not be satisfied until a member of our team died. Mr. X had asked the sorcerer to strike one of us dead with thunder, but the sorcerer had refused, saying that this magic is very old and dangerous. After the divination, the diviner and my colleagues cleaned the truck. Inside, they found three charms, presumably left there by Mr. X, which they interpreted as dangerous magical objects. Finally, they anointed the exterior of the truck with a potion to undo Mr. X's magic.

---

[1]The team included Dr. Tsiazonera, Dr. Jaovola Tombo, Patricia Hajasoa, Mr. Tsimitamby, Charlotte Nagnisaha, Gervais Tantely, Louinaise Rasoanomenjanahary, Miza Razafindravelo, Rolland Lahiniriko, Vorisoa Rene Lahitoka, Jean-Roger Tsikengo, Christian Zahatsy, Amber Huff, Elaina Lill, Jean-Claude Alhayess, Jeannot Olivier Ratsibazafy, Zafimandimby, and Tsitindry Théodore Ramanovontsoa.

Yet, our misfortunes continued. On the Vezo coast, we were continually battered by cyclones. Worse yet, for reasons I still do not understand, I was losing my hearing, first in one ear and then in the other. Two researchers were suffering bad toothaches, in the same tooth. Then, on a rainy day, driving the truck along a narrow road in the dense Mikea Forest, a large tree branch fell unexpectedly on the truck's hood, missing the windshield by a matter of centimeters.

One of my collaborators again consulted a spirit medium. This one was particularly powerful because her possessing spirits (*doany*) included a deceased diviner; she did *sikily* divination while in trance. The divination again implicated Mr. X's "bad ideas" and his intention to magically cause the death of one member of our team. The divination indicated that the fallen tree branch would have killed someone if it were not for the fact that I had good astrological fortune (*andro*) on that particular day. The medium (or rather, the spirit of the dead magician speaking through the medium) gave us a powder of sand and wood to protect us from Mr. X's spells, a pinch of which I have carried on my person ever since. We mixed the powder with water to make a potion that we bathed in, sprinkled on the field vehicles, and anointed our rooms back in Toliara.

A Cultural Perspective on Decision Making Under Risk

A moment's reflection revealed the irony of our situation. The purpose of our fieldwork was to better understand how people value risk and anticipate the future in a non-Western cultural context. Guided by the formal theory of choice under risk dating back to Blaise Pascal, we thought of risk simply as probability-weighted gains (Bernstein 1996). But simultaneous to our posing abstract choices among gambles to our research subjects, through our brush with sorcery we were experiencing risk just as our informants often do, as a series of misfortunes that we causally associated with supernatural powers unleashed by the bad will of a jilted friend.

Around this time, the experimental and behavioral economics literatures filled with articles exploring the effects of culture on decision making. Perhaps the most cited of these is Henrich et al.'s (2010) call for behavioral scholars to go beyond the study of WEIRD people—Western, Educated, Industrialized, Rich, Democratic research subjects, typically undergraduates enrolled in psychology courses. Studies published around that time revealed cross-cultural variability in norms of fairness (Henrich et al. 2005; Chuah et al. 2009; Gächter et al. 2010), naive physics (Beller et al. 2009; Bender and Beller 2011a), folk taxonomies of plants and animals (Atran et al. 2004), spatial cognition (Gaby 2012), quantitative reasoning (Bender et al. 2015), and use of holistic versus analytical reasoning (Nisbett et al. 2001; Uskul et al. 2008).

Some studies, like Henrich and McElreath's risk preference study and Henrich's subsequent cross-cultural ultimatum game studies (Henrich et al. 2005), operationalized culture as residual intergroup variability. Other studies operationalized "culture" around simple binary categories such as tight versus loose or individualist versus collectivist (Nisbett et al. 2001; Uskul et al. 2008). Still others turned culture into a variable, variously called norms (Camerer and Fehr 2004), values (Inglehart and Welzel 2005; Chuah et al. 2009), or preferences (see review below).

Such simplifications may be expedient, for culture is complex and difficult to observe or evaluate. However, after our brush with sorcery, it dawned on me that culture is a deeper thing than is summarized by a simple dichotomy or culture variable. Culture influences decisions because it influences our basic understanding of existential categories and causal relationships (Bender and Beller 2011b; D'Andrade 1992; ojalehto and Medin 2015; Ross 2004). Culture is ontological, and it provides societies with their specific understandings of reality.

The big question then is how much of our understanding of reality is culture-bound and to what degree do different understandings of reality influence choice and behavior (Bender and Beller 2011b)? This is a classic question within the social and behavioral sciences, phrased in nineteenth-century parlance as "psychic unity of humankind" versus "cultural relativism." Cognitive researchers who generalize about human nature from experiments conducted with WEIRD research subjects implicitly assume psychic unity, that all humans basically process information and are motivated to action in the same way. Cross-cultural research that operationalizes culture as norms, values, and preferences similarly assumes that the decisions of all humans may be described with universal formulae in which culture is a variable. For example, risk preference studies assume that all people evaluate risky choices as if they were multiplying the probabilities of different outcomes by the utility value of the probable rewards, where culture is a variable that influences utility. By contrast, anthropologists, particularly denizens of Franz Boas's American school, typically work from the starting assumption that culture encodes very different ways of understanding the world (Sidky 2004), so that culture defines more than just a value to be plugged into a decision-making formula; it changes the formula itself. A culturally relative perspective of choice under risk may ask whether people are concerned with mean and variance at all, or whether risky choices depend on other natural, social, or cosmological uncertainties and anxieties (Tucker et al. 2013).

The notion that humans interpret meaning from misfortune and apply that meaning to understand and predict future events is foundational in anthropological approaches to religion and magic (Frazer 1922 [1890]; Tylor 1958 [1871]). Malinowski (1992 [1948]) famously argued that Trobriand Islanders use more magic before risky deep-sea fishing ventures than before low-risk lagoon fishing and gardening activities, suggesting that magic is an attempt to control risk. Such ways of thinking are neither primitive nor exotic. Educated people with scientific notions of probability and causality frequently invoke magical causal thinking when facing risky prospects in fishing (Poggie and Polnac 1988), sports (Felson and Gmelch 1979), examinations (Rudski et al. 2007), and national politics (Geschiere 1997), and when contemplating the causes of life, disease, and death (Legare et al. 2012).

This introductory narrative outlines the rest of my essay. I begin with a brief review of formal theory of choice under risk and intertemporal choice and explain why researchers have sought to evaluate risk and time preferences in cross-cultural perspectives. Then, I describe seven specific challenges that my Malagasy colleagues and I faced in designing and conducting effective choice experiments, and I summarize what we have learned from this effort. In the final sections of this paper, I discuss my fledgling attempts to explore the cultural models of causality in southwestern Madagascar. I conclude with a summary and a discussion of future research directions.

Choice Under Risk and Intertemporal Choice: Theory and Method

Formal/Normative Models

Formal theory for choice under risk is usually traced to the musings of French mathematician Blaise Pascal, who, interestingly enough considering where this essay is going, developed a theory of risk around the theological question of whether a "rational" person should believe in God (Bernstein 1996). Pascal argued that a rational person should value gambles according to their probability-weighted stakes, what we call today expect value (EV). The expected value of a lottery ticket that offers a 1/100 chance to win \$100 is \$1. Formally,

$$\mathrm{EV} = \sum_{\text{outcomes}} (p_i \times A_i) \tag{3.1}$$

where p_i is the probability of outcome i and A_i is the amount of the reward from outcome i. Pascal argued that according to this calculus, a rational person should believe in God, because even if the probability that he exists approaches zero, the stakes for non-belief approach infinity.

Nearly a century later, Daniel Bernoulli (1738) argued that Pascal's formula cannot apply to all risky decisions, exemplified by the St. Petersburg Paradox, a gamble with infinite expected value. Bernoulli's solution was that different individuals subjectively value probabilistic wins and losses differently, according to their marginal utility for wealth. The expected utility (EU) of a lottery ticket that offers a 1/100 chance to win \$100 is the utility value of winning \$1, where a poor person may perceive greater utility (U) from a win of \$1 than would a rich person.

$$\mathrm{EU} = \sum_{\text{outcomes}} [p_i \times U(A_i)] \tag{3.2}$$

Friedman and Savage (1948) argued that a sigmoidal or undulating marginal utility curve like the one presented previously in Fig. 3.1b could explain why the poor gamble and the rich purchase insurance (as in Fig. 3.1a).

The theoretical roots of intertemporal choice theory may be traced to the writings of John Rae, who speculated that individual variation in self-restraint and desire to bequeath resources to future generations influences individuals' capacity to accumulate wealth, and Eugen Böhm-Bawerk, who theorized about value trade-offs between rewards now versus later (see Frederick et al. 2002). The antecedent to modern modeling attempts is credited to Samuelson (1937), who reasoned that decision makers mentally devalue rewards for which they must wait because of the subjective costs of waiting. Samuelson proposed that the rate at which individuals discount the future may be approximated with an exponential decay function:

$$V_D = Ae^{-kD} \tag{3.3}$$

V_D is the value of the delayed reward at delay D; A is the reward amount at time of receipt; e is the exponential constant 2.71828; and k is the discount parameter.

In recent decades, many cognitive and behavioral researchers have preferred Mazur's (1987) hyperbolic discounting function:

$$V_D = A/(1 + kD) \tag{3.4}$$

The hyperbolic discounting model simulates rapidly increasing value as payday draws nearer. It also accounts for preference reversals as delays are lengthened.[2]

Imagine a wageworker envisioning the value of her next paycheck in 30 days. If her discount parameter were $k = 0$, she would value her delayed \$1000 paycheck at exactly \$1000, as if the waiting time had no effect on her evaluation. Larger k values indicate greater discounting of delayed rewards. Assuming hyperbolic discounting, if our worker discounts the future at $k = 0.001$, she values her delayed paycheck at \$970; at $k = 0.01$, \$770; at $k = 0.1$, \$250; and at $k = 1$, \$32.

How Choice Experiments Work

A risk experiment could start like this. I could ask a research subject, "which option do you prefer: Option A is that I would give you \$10; option B is that I would flip a coin, and if it lands heads I'll give you \$20 and if it lands tails I will give you nothing." Let us imagine that our subject replies that she is indifferent between options A and B (in actual experiments, subjects rarely state that options are of equivalent value, but let us start here for the sake of argument). Indifference between A and B indicates that our subject is risk neutral. To illustrate this, imagine she is presented with this same choice 16 times, and for the first eight tries, she chooses option A and for the second eight, she chooses option B. Imagine further that for option B, she wins exactly four out of eight coin tosses and loses the other four. This is illustrated in Table 3.1. The average payoff from options A and B is the same: \$10; this is the expected value of both options. But option A has no

[2]Imagine, for example, a comparison of Option A, \$100 after 200 days, versus Option B, \$300 after 300 days. Assuming hyperbolic discounting, if the subject discounts both by $k = 0.1$, then the subject prefers B from day 1 until around day 160, when preference switches to option A.

variability (no risk), while option B is variable (risky), with a standard deviation of 10.7. The fact that our participant judges A and B to be the same suggests that she only considers the mean payoff and is ignoring variability; this is risk neutrality. We would assume that she would be equally indifferent to a third option, C, offering a 25% chance to win $40, for this option also averages $10, even though it is even more risky than option B.

Given that options A and B offer the same mean reward but differ only by risk, had our subject chosen option A, this would suggest that she found the extra risk associated with option B to be distasteful; she is risk averse. If she preferred option B, this suggests that the extra risk made this option more appealing; she is risk prone.

Typically, experiments attempt to evaluate not just whether someone is averse, neutral, or prone to risk, but also the degree of aversion or proneness. There are several ways to do this. One is to ask subjects to choose their favorite among a list of gambles (options with different reward amounts and probabilities) spanning a range of preferences (see Binswanger 1980). Another is to offer a list of *n* binary choices between two gambles, A_1 through A_n and B_1 through B_n, where the A gambles graduate from risk averse to risk prone, while the B gambles range from risk prone to risk averse; the point at which preference switches from A to B indicates preference (Holt and Laury 2002). Both of these methods require that subjects are sufficiently literate and numerate to read, remember, and consider lists of quantitative options.

Kuznar (2001) and Henrich and McElreath (2002) used a method called titration, which offers a series of binary choices in which either the reward amount or probability of winning is adjusted in each round contingent on the subject's choice in the previous round. Imagine that when presented with options A ($10 for sure) or B (50% chance to win $20), our decision maker chooses A. In round two, we could offer a choice between option A and a new option D, a 50% chance to win $40. In essence, this asks, would doubling the expected value be enough to compensate for the increased risk? If she now prefers option D, we may then infer that she would be indifferent between option A and a 50% chance to win somewhere between $20 and $40. We might then ask her to choose between A and option E, a 50% chance to win $30. If she chooses E, then her indifference value is between 30 and 40; we could continue with more questions, or simply estimate the indifference value at $35 (EV = $17.5). Contrasted with the riskless option (EV = $10), our subject requires an extra 75% EV to make this gamble worthwhile; we can report the result as a proportional insurance premium of 0.75 (Binswanger and Sillers 1983: 6).

Time preference experiments work similarly. Figure 3.2 presents an example of a time preference experiment that seeks to evaluate the hyperbolic discount parameter, *k*. Our experiment begins with a question like, "which would you prefer: option X is that I give you $10 now; option Y is that I give you $30 in 5 weeks." Imagine that our subject replies that she is indifferent between these options. Mazur's hyperbolic discounting model mathematically relates indifference values (V_i) to discount values, as follows:

Table 3.1 Example gambles

	A. $10 for sure	B. 50% chance to win $20	C. 25% chance to win $40
Try 1	$10	$20	$40
Try 2	$10	$20	$40
Try 3	$10	$20	$0
Try 4	$10	$20	$0
Try 5	$10	$0	$0
Try 6	$10	$0	$0
Try 7	$10	$0	$0
Try 8	$10	$0	$0
Mean (expected value)	$10	$10	$10
SD (risk)	$0	$10.7	$18.5
CV (risk/reward)	$0	1.07	1.85

Note These are three example gambles that yield the same average payoff (the same expected value) but different amounts of risk (standard deviation). A risk-neutral person will judge all three options to be equivalent; a risk-averse person would prefer option A or B over C, and a risk-prone person would prefer option B or C over A

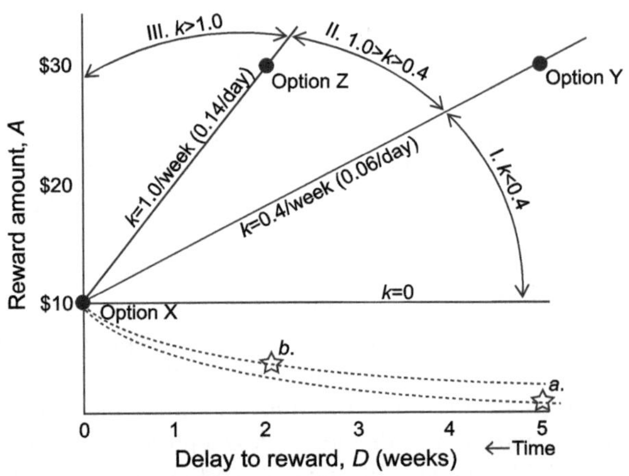

Fig. 3.2 Example of a time preference choice experiment. A subject who is indifferent between option X ($10 now) and $10 in two weeks does not discount the future (k = 0). A subject who is indifferent between options X and Y discounts the future at k = 0.4/week, so that $30 in five weeks is worth $1.67 today (*star a*). A subject indifferent between options X and Z discounts the future at k = 1.0/week, so that $30 in two weeks is worth $3.33 today (*star b*). Preference for Y over X implies that k is in range I. Preference for X over Y indicates that k is in ranges II or III. Preference for Z over X implies that k is in range II. Preference for X over Z places k in range III

$$V_i = A/(1 + kD) \quad (3.5)$$

For a subject indifferent between options X and Y, the value of A is \$10 and the indifference value V_i is \$30 for a delay (D) of 5 weeks. Solving for k,

$$k = [(V_i/A) - 1]/D \quad (3.6)$$

In our example, k is 0.4/week, or 0.06/day. Referring back to Eq. 3.4, this would imply that if our subject had to wait 5 weeks to receive \$10, she would subjectively value the \$10 reward at around \$1.67 relative to options available immediately.

As with risk experiments, experimenters may ask a series of questions in an attempt to titrate the range of possible indifference values. If our subject indicates that she prefers option X over Y, this implies that to switch her choice to a delayed option, this option would have to offer either more reward or a shorter delay. In other words, $k > 0.4$/week. So the next question might be whether she prefers option X (\$10 now) or a new option Z, of \$30 after only two weeks. If she prefers option Z, then k is between 1.0 and 0.4. The researcher might ask further questions, or she might estimate k as the midpoint of this range, $k = 0.70$.

A Brief Review of International and Cross-cultural Risk and Time Experiments

A brief review of international field studies of risk and time choice experiments is presented in Tables 3.2 and 3.3. The majority of the international studies reviewed here were conducted with the goal of exploring the risky or intertemporal judgments of different human populations for the design of effective public interventions such as new credit markets, fishing quotas, or the adoption of new technologies. Excluded from this review are the myriad studies conducted among WEIRD subjects, many of which have sought to reveal deviations from the predictions of formal theory such as loss aversion, preference reversals, and framing effects (for summaries of these studies, see Gigerenzer 1991; Kahneman and Tversky 2000; Frederick et al. 2002; Lichtenstein and Slovic 2006). I include one WEIRD study in each table to represent WEIRD culture.

The tables summarize the experimental designs, evidence for the effects of determinants, and numerical results. The risk studies summarized in Table 3.2 reported various measures of risk (probability premiums, proportional insurance premiums, or coefficients of relative or constant risk aversion). I standardize these by reporting the coefficient of variation (CV, the ratio of standard deviation to mean) for the lowest and highest risk options offered by each experiment and the most common or average choice, where standard deviations are calculated over a representative sample of 100 tries (as demonstrated in Table 3.1) and the mean is the expected value. The review of time preference studies in Table 3.3 reports the range and mean or mode of hyperbolic discount parameters (reported as *k*/day) for each published experiment.[3]

Table 3.2 demonstrates general consistency in mean or modal choices across risk experiments, with most subjects preferring options with a CV between 0.36 and 1.00 (as predicted by Binswanger and Sillers 1983). Henrich and McElreath's risk prone Mapuche and Sangu subjects are clear outliers; 80% of Mapuche said they preferred a 5% chance to win 20,000 pesos over 1000 pesos for sure (CV = 4.4).

In contrast to the general consistency of the risk preference measures, Table 3.3 demonstrates great variability in discount parameters, with mean or modal *k* ranging across orders of magnitude. Frederick et al. (2002) found similar heterogeneity in discount rates in their review of studies with WEIRD subjects.

Tables 3.2 and 3.3 display considerable heterogeneity in support for determinants of risk and time preferences. The most consistent determinant is incentive size; the only study that tested for effects of incentive size and did not find it was Holt and Laury's (2002) laboratory study, and then, only when they offered hypothetical rewards. Evidence for the effects of age, sex, wealth, income, education, and household size is remarkably variable. I discuss the possible explanations for this variability later in this article.

Risk and Time Among Hunter-Gatherers, Farmers, and Fishermen in Southwestern Madagascar

Before describing my attempts to conduct risk and time preference experiments in Madagascar, I think it is necessary to provide a bit more of an anthropological and economic introduction to Mikea hunter-gatherers, Masikoro farmers, and Vezo fishers.

The most basic lesson of modern anthropology is that it is inaccurate to view foraging (hunting and gathering), fishing, and farming lifeways as evolutionary stages. Western social theory has long romanticized hunter-gatherers as relicts of a past way of life that was once the normal state of human affairs (Barnard 1999; Schrire 1984). But there is tremendous diversity among the societies in the hunter-gatherer category, in diet, workload, social organization, gender roles, and market involvement (Kelly 2013), so that any attempt to generalize about a "primitive way of life" is likely to result in paleofantasy (Zuk 2013). Ethnographic and historical information contradicts the notion that contemporary hunter-gatherer populations are pockets of humanity that have remained unchanged since the Stone Age. For example, among Kalahari San, the archetypal "bushmen" of Western

---

[3] I report means when authors clearly state the mean results; otherwise, I report modal choices, the choice that research subjects chose most frequently.

Table 3.2 Review of risk preference studies conducted in international settings

Study	Country, region; subjects (N)	Method	Rewards (Real, hypothetical)	Treatments	Determinants										
					Treatment	Incentive	Age	Female	Income	Wealth	Education	HH size[a]	Other factors tested		
													+	–	ns
Binswanger (1980)	India, Andhra Pradesh; farmers (240)	L	Real, Hyp.	Low incentive		–	ns	+	–	ns	–	ns	SS	AT, LK, RS, SS	GM, RH
				High incentive		+	ns	–	–	ns	ns	ns	SS	LK, SS	AT, RH, RS
Binswanger and Sillers (1983)	India (240 farmers)	L	Real, Hyp.	India	ns	+			ns	ns					
	Philippines (147)			Philippines	ns	+			ns	ns					
	El Salvador (108)			El Salvador	ns	+			ns	ns					
	Thailand (78)			Thailand	ns	+			ns	ns					
Dillon and Scandizzo (1978)	Brazil, Ceará; farmers (130; 64 sharecroppers, 66 farm owners)	T	Hyp.	Sharecroppers	–		+		–			ns			GM
				Owners	+							ns			GM
				Subsistence at risk	+							ns			GM
				Surplus at risk	–							ns			GM
Eggert and Lokina (2007)	Tanzania, Mwanza; fishing boat skippers (473)	R	Hyp.				ns			ns	ns	–	OP	CS	NL, SK, SS
Eggert and Martinsson (2004)	Sweden; commercial fishers (202)	R	Hyp.				ns			ns	ns		LW	FT, IF, QQ	BL
Harrison et al. (2007)	Denmark; representative sample of Danes (268)	S	Real	Incentives		+	U	ns	ns		+	ns		FS,	CH, CP, EX, LA, RT, SS
Henrich and McElreath (2002)	Chile, Mapuche farmers (26) and Huinca farmers (25); Tanzania, Sangu agropastoralists	T, W	Real	Mapuche, Chile	–		ns	ns	ns	ns					
				Huinca, Chile	+										
				Sangu, Tanzania	–		ns	ns	ns	ns					
					+										

(continued)

Table 3.2 (continued)

Study	Country, region; subjects (N)	Method	Rewards (Real, hypothetical)	Treatments	Determinants								Other factors tested		
					Treatment	Incentive	Age	Female	Income	Wealth	Education	HH size[a]	+	–	ns
	(42); UCLA, students (20)			UCLA students											
Holt and Laury (2002), Holt (2006)	USA, Georgia and Florida; students (175)	S	Real	Incentives	+	+		+	–					HI	
			Hyp.	Incentives	ns	ns									
Kuznar (2001)	Peru, highlands; Aymara herders (23)	T	Hyp.	Low altitude	–			ns		∩					
				High altitude	+										
Miyata (2003)	Indonesia, Java; farmers (386)	L	Real	Low incentives	–	+	ns		ns	–	ns	+	LA	RD	AT, OP, SS
				High incentives	+		+		ns	–	–	+		RD	AT, LA, OP, SS
Wik et al. (2004)	Zambia, northern; farmers (110)	L	Real, Hyp.	Incentives	+	+	ns	+	–	ns	ns	–	FS, LX		RH
				Gains losses	ns										

Study	Preferences, CV		
	CV range, choices offered by exp.	Mean (μ)/modal (m) choice	Mean/modal preference
Binswanger (1980)	0–1.00	0.50–0.67[m]	RA
	0–1.00	0.36–0.67[m]	RA
Binswanger and Sillers (1983)	0–1.00	0.36–0.67[m]	RA
	0–1.00	0.36–0.67[m]	RA
	0–1.00	0.36–0.67[m]	RA
	0–1.00	0.36–0.67[m]	RA
Dillon and Scandizzo (1978)			
	0–1.00	0–0.67[mb]	SRA-RA
	0–1.00	0.36–0.67[mb]	RA
Eggert and Lokina (2007)	0.33–0.53	0.34–0.33 (32%)	RA
		0.37–0.35 (34%)	RN
		0.49–0.52 (34%)	RP

(continued)

Table 3.2 (continued)

Study	Preferences, CV		
	CV range, choices offered by exp.	Mean (μ)/modal (m) choice	Mean/modal preference
Eggert and Martinsson (2004)	0.34–0.53	0.34 (26%)	SRA
		0.35–0.36 (26%)	RA
		0.38–0.53 (48%)	RN
Harrison et al. (2007)	0–2.47	0.65^{m}	RA
Henrich and McElreath (2002)	0–4.4	4.4^{m}	RP
			RA
		4.4^{m}	RP
		1.0^{m}	RA
Holt and Laury (2002), Holt (2006)	0–2.47	$0.49–0.95^{m}$	RA
Kuznar (2001)	0–?	0.37^{μ}	RA
		0.60^{μ}	SRA
Miyata (2003)	0–1.00	0^{m}	SRA
	0–1.00	0^{m}	SRA
Wik et al. (2004)	0–1.00	0.5^{m}	RA
		0.35^{m}	RA

Note Methods: *L* list of lotteries, preference indicated by choice of lottery (Binswanger's method); *R* list of binary choices between outcomes with different ranges; mins, means, and maxs (Eggert's method); *S* list of binary choices between lotteries, preference indicated by switchpoint from lottery A to lottery B (Holt and Laury's method); *T* titration; *W* willingness to accept a series of gambles with same EV but different SD; rewards: *H* hypothetical; *R* real; determinants:+ more risk aversion; − less risk aversion; ∩ middle range for this variable is more risk averse than low or high; *U* middle range for this variable is less risk averse than low or high; *ns* not significant; other factors tested: *AT* adopters of new technology; *BL* boat length; *BM* body mass index; *BP* paid high bride price; *CB* carries a balance on credit cards; *CE* consumption expenditure; *CH* has children; *CP* lives in Copenhagen; *CS* crew size; *EB* ethnobotanical knowledge; *UE* unemployed; *EX* experimenter; *FA* is a farmer; *FS* farm size; *FT* trawler only (fishing method); *GH* own good health; *GM* gambler/positive attitude toward gambling; *HI* Hispanic; *IF* income from fishing; *LA* lives alone/single; *LC* poor chance of getting a loan; *LK* luck; *LW* "left-wing" voter; *LX* lost in a previous experiment; *NL* net length (among fishers); *OH* owns own home; *OP* owns means of production (farm, boat, etc.); *QQ* in favor of fishing quotas; *RD* resettled as a result of construction of a dam; *RH* real versus hypothetical rewards; *RS* rented land or sharecropper; *RT* retired; *SD* severity of disease risk; *SK* skills; *SS* site (village, community, county); *WL* engages in wage labor; Preference, *SRA* strongly risk averse; *RA* risk averse; *RN* risk neutral; *RP* risk prone

[a]Household size or number of working age adults; [b]According to Binswanger (1980:402)

Table 3.3 Review of time preference studies conducted in international settings

Study	Country, region; subjects (N)	Method	Rewards (Real, hypothetical)	Treatments	Determinants										
					Treatment	Incentive	Age	Female	Income	Wealth	Education	HH size*	Other factors tested		
													+	–	ns
Anderson et al. (2004)	Vietnam, rural and urban villages near Hanoi (233)	S	Hyp.	Rural village	+			ns	ns						
				Urban village	–										
Harrison et al. (2002)	Denmark, representative sample of Danes (268)	L	Real, Hyp.	Delay	+		ns	ns	ns		–		LC	RT	CB, CH, CP, LA, OH, SK
Kirby and Marakovic (1996)	USA, Massachusetts; students (621)	L	Real	Incentive, mean $30–$35 $55–$65 $70–$85				–							
Kirby et al. (2002), Godoy et al. (2004)	Bolivia, Beni; Tsimane forager-horticulturalists (154)	L	Real	Cash					ns	ns	+			BM, SK	EB
				Candy			U		–	ns	+			SK	BM, EB
Pender (1996)	India, Andhra Pradesh; farmers (96)	L	Real, Hyp.	Delay	+		–	ns		–	ns	ns	RH		
Robberstad (2005)	Tanzania, Hai District; (450)	S	Hyp.	Illness affecting self	ns				ns		–			CE, SD	FA, GH
				Illness affecting others	ns		ns	ns	ns		ns		SS	EX, SD, SS	CE, FA, GH
Salali and Migliano (2015)	Congo, Mbendjele BeYaka hunter-gatherers (111); Bantu farmers (22)	C	Real	Foragers in forest camps	+		ns						WL		BP
				Foragers in town	–										
				Bantu farmers	–										

Study	Hyperbolic discount rate, *k*/day	
	k range, choices offered by exp.	Mean (μ)/modal (m) choice
Anderson et al. (2004)		
Harrison et al. (2002)	0.0000–0.0015	0.0007^{μ}

(continued)

Table 3.3 (continued)

Study	Hyperbolic discount rate, k/day	
	k range, choices offered by exp.	Mean (μ)/modal (m) choice
Kirby and Marakovic (1996)	0.0007–0.0847	0.007[μ] 0.0133[μ] 0.0066[μ] 0.0047[μ]
Kirby et al. (2002), Godoy et al. (2004)	0.0004–0.2488	0.143[μ]
		0.172[μ]
Pender (1996)	−0.0005 to 0.005	0.0012[μ]
Robberstad (2005)		0.071[μ]
		0.068[μ]
Salali and Migliano (2015)	>4.0, <4.0	>4.0[μ]
		<4.0[μ]
		<4.0[μ]

Note. Methods: *C* one-shot choice between one stock (bullion) spice cube now or five tomorrow (Salali and Migliano 2015); *L* choice among list of immediate versus delayed opportunities (similar to Binswanger's 1980 method); *S* state how much you would pay now/have to be paid now to be equivalent to a future payoff (method from Thaler 1981); determinants: + more discounting; − less discounting; ∩ middle range for this variable discounts more than low or high; *U* middle range for this variable discounts less than low or high; *ns* not significant; other abbreviations and notes same as Table 3.2

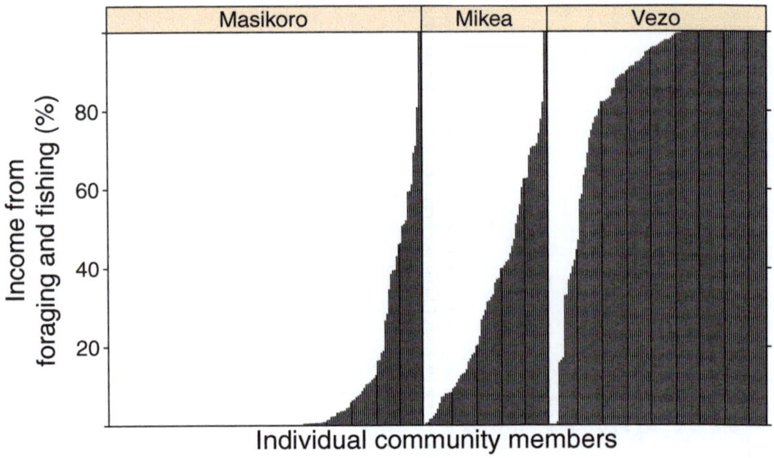

Fig. 3.3 Proportion of total income from foraging and fishing for the 170 Masikoro, 65 Mikea, and 130 Vezo participants in the final rounds of the experiments, Risks 5 and 6 and Times 6 and 7. Each *line* indicates the proportion of an individual's income over nine months from foraging or fishing rather than agriculture, herding, and wages. This graph demonstrates that Masikoro, Mikea, and Vezo do not strictly conform to norms of specialization as farmers, hunter-gatherers, and fishermen, respectively

imagination, some San are descended from farmers, herders, long-distance traders, slaves, and vassals to agropastoral chiefs and states (Wilmsen and Denbow 1990). In Madagascar, Mikea oral historians are unanimous that their ancestors were Masikoro farmers and Vezo fishermen who took refuge in the forest during the past four centuries to escape the tribute demands and slave raids of the Andrevola kings (Tucker 2003). Mikea are not locked into a hunting and gathering evolutionary stage. Rather, for Mikea, hunting and gathering is a choice.

Masikoro, Mikea, and Vezo have a lot of subsistence options from which to choose. Even though the identity terms Masikoro, Mikea, and Vezo are strongly associated with subsistence modes, so that Masikoro are reputed savanna farmers, Mikea are forest foragers, and Vezo are coastal fishers, in practice, most households diversify beyond these modes, practicing a mix of foraging, fishing, farming, herding, and marketing activities. This balance between specialization and diversification is portrayed in Fig. 3.3, which portrays the proportion of individuals' incomes generated from foraging and fishing versus farming, herding, and marketing among 312 Masikoro, Mikea, and Vezo individuals.

I have argued, based on the analyses of production data from Mikea, Masikoro, and Vezo, that the choice between foraging and fishing versus farming reflects some basic trade-offs in reward quantity and quality, and risk and delay (Tucker et al. 2010). Agriculture produces a greater average quantity of food, but the food is of lower quality (in terms of market value, nutrition, and flavor), with high risk and long delays. Foraging and fishing produce smaller quantities of higher quality food with low risk and short delays (see also Winterhalder and Goland 1997; Winterhalder and Kennett 2009; Bowles 2011).

To illustrate these differences, imagine that an individual will spend 100 days doing just one subsistence activity, either cultivating maize or foraging or wild *ovy* tubers. Hundred days of labor spent cultivating maize would result in a 2.3 hectare field and a single harvest averaging 2141 kg, or roughly 7.7 MM calories. Hundred days of labor spent tuber foraging yields up to 100 smaller payoffs that together sum to an average of 957 kg or 1.1 MM calories. The risk of a maize field (CV = 0.57) and a tuber foraging trip (CV = 0.54) is about the same, but one can do 100 tuber foraging trips in the same time that it takes to cultivate one maize field, so that the effective CV for tubers is an order of magnitude lower (0.03). Table 3.4 displays the average payoffs, risk, and delay for a set of important farming, foraging, and fishing activities (see Tucker et al. 2010 for more details).

In colloquial terms, farmers put all their eggs in one basket. The farmer is counting on one field receiving adequate moisture and escaping pests, whereas the tuber forager may move to a fresh patch (or search for alternate prey) depending on daily fortunes. Whereas the farmer returns home from her fields each day with nothing but sweat, blisters, and dreams, the forager or fishermen usually returns from the workday with food. The farmer must strategize how to feed her family during the 100 foodless days before harvest. Anxiety over how to cover costs during the delay to harvest could explain why Masikoro in our study were significantly more food insecure than Mikea or Vezo, despite producing more food on average (Tucker et al. 2010).

When the farmer does harvest maize, she does so simultaneously with her neighbors, so that its market value is very low. Wild foods fetch higher prices in the market due to their rarity and superior flavor. While maize on average produces seven times the number of calories as does tuber foraging, maize produces less than twice the market value of wild tubers due to the lower selling price of maize. This may explain why our analyses found that on average, Masikoro farmers, Mikea foragers, and Vezo fishers produced statistically similar amounts of market-valued production per year (Tucker et al. 2010). Given these trade-offs in risk and delay but the similarity of market-valued incomes, I was eager to learn whether different risk and time preferences might ultimately explain why some people do more foraging, while others do more farming.

Seven Challenges to Designing Effective Experiments for Use in the Field

Overview

In total, we conducted six risk choice experiments and seven time choice experiments during 2003–2008. These are summarized in Tables 3.5 and 3.6. I refer to

Table 3.4 Risk and time in farming, foraging, and fishing activities in southwestern Madagascar

Activity	Mode	Surface area cultivatable given 100 labor days	Mean kcal produced, millions of kcals	Mean market value produced, MGA	Risk (CV)	Time horizon
Maize (*Zea mays*)	Agriculture	2.3 ha	7.7	810,000	0.566	>90 days
Manioc (*Manihot esculenta*)	Agriculture	0.6 ha	2.6	256,000	0.670	90 days to 2 years (average, 10.6 months)
Rice (*Oryza sativa*)	Agriculture	0.9 ha	4.3	962,000	0.715	60 days
Wild *ovy* tubers (*Dioscorea acuminata*)	Forest foraging		1.1	471,000	0.028	Daily
Honey (*Apis melifera*)	Forest foraging		1.7	410,000	0.042	Daily
Snakehead fish (*Channa striata*)	Forest foraging		0.2	282,000	0.029	Daily
Tilapia (*Paratilapia* spp.)	Forest foraging		0.2	152,000	0.048	Daily
Marine finfish (various spp.)	Marine fishing		0.3	259,000	0.053	Daily
Octopus (*Octopus cyanea*)	Marine fishing		0.1	61,000	0.039	Daily
Mud crab (*Scylla serrata*)	Marine fishing		0.1	100,000	0.049	Daily

Note Estimates based on the production data from the region and simulation 100 days of labor spent on one activity (see Tucker et al. 2010 for more details)

Table 3.5 Summary of risk preferences studies in southwestern Madagascar

Experiment	Method	Rewards	Sample	CV range of choices offered by exp.	Modal choice, CV	% choosing mode	X^2 test comparing freq of modal versus non-modal choice by identity group
Risk 1, 2004	One-shot choice among 2 options	Real cups of cooking oil	50 Mikea	0–1.00	0.05-0.13	46	
Risk 2, 2006	One-shot choice among 4 options	Real cups of cooking oil	152 Total 25 Masikoro 47 Mikea 36 Mud-Vezo[b] 44 Vezo	A.0–D.2.60	C. 0.77 C. 0.77 B. 0.37 C. 0.77 B. 0.37	48 44 45 61 47	4.02(3), $p = 0.26$
Risk 3, Jul–Aug 2007	One-shot choice among 5 options	Real cash (or rice if requested)	378 Total 162 Masikoro 82 Mikea 134 Vezo	A.0–E.2.60	B. 0.77 B. 0.77 E. 2.60 B. 0.77	48 53 37 61	30.90(2), $p = 0.00$
Risk 4, Oct–Nov 2007[a]	Titration, 3 binary choices	Real cash (or rice if requested)	440 Total 194 Masikoro 86 Mikea 160 Vezo	0–1.01	1.07 1.07 1.07 1.07	81 81 76 83	NA
Risk 5, Jan–Mar 2008	One-shot choice among 4 options	Real cash (or rice if requested)	440 Total 189 Masikoro 102 Mikea 149 Vezo	A. 0–D. 2.60	C. 1.01 C. 1.01 C. 1.01 C. 1.01	76 78 57 87	30.28(2), $p = 0.00$
Risk 6, May–Jun 2008	One-shot choice among 4 options	Real cash (or rice if requested)	369 Total 172 Masikoro 71 Mikea 126 Vezo	A. 0–D. 2.60	B. 0.37 B&C. 0.37-1.01 B. 0.37 C. 1.01	49 93 61 54	5.24(2), $p = 0.07$

Note The one-shot experiments involved a choice among options A–D or A–E, where A is a riskless choice and D or E is the highest risk choice
[a]Experimental results are obviously unreliable due to methodological inadequacies discussed in the text; [b]"Mud-Vezo" (*Vezompotake*) are coastal Vezo who primarily farm

Table 3.6 Summary of time preferences studies in southwestern Madagascar

Experiment	Method	Rewards	Sample	Range of *k*/day values offered by the experiment	Modal choice, *k*/day	% choosing mode	X^2 test comparing freq of modal versus non-modal choice by identity group
Time 1, 2003, 2004[a]	Titration, 9 binary choices	Hypothetical sacks of maize	79 Mikea	<0.003 to >0.261	bimodal, < 0.003 or	26	
					>0.261	35	
Time 2, 2004	One-shot choice among 2 options	Real cups of cooking oil	49 Mikea	<0.090 to >0.670	0.29–0.67	55	
Time 3, 2006	One-shot choice among 4 options	Real cups of cooking oil	136 Total	D. <0.333 to A. >1.000	D. <0.333	49	1.02(3), $p = 0.80$
			46 Masikoro		D. <0.333	50	
			41 Mikea		D. <0.333	44	
			24 Mud-Vezo[b]		D. <0.333	46	
			25 Vezo		D. <0.333	56	
Time 4, Jul–Aug 2007	One-shot choice among 5 options	Real cash (or rice if requested)	378 Total	E. <0.200 to A. >1.00	E. <0.200	40	9.34(2), $p = 0.01$
			162 Masikoro		E. <0.200	46	
			82 Mikea		A.&E, >1.00–<0.200	26	
			134 Vezo		E. <0.200	41	
Time 5, Oct–Nov 2007[a]	Titration, 3 binary choices	Real cash (or rice if requested)	440 Total	<0.006 to >0.322	<0.006	80	
			194 Masikoro		<0.006	79	
			86 Mikea		<0.006	69	
			160 Vezo		<0.006	85	
Time 6, Jan–Mar 2008	One-shot choice among 4 options	Real cash (or rice if requested)	440 Total	D. <0.009 to A. >0.057	C. 0.013–0.009	47	39.46(2), $p = 0.00$
			189 Masikoro		C. 0.013–0.009	57	
			102 Mikea		A. >0.057	42	
			149 Vezo		C. 0.013–0.009	52	
Time 7, May–Jun 2008	One-shot choice among 4 options	Real cash (or rice if requested)	369 Total	D. <0.009 to A. >0.057	C. 0.013–0.009	47	28.64(2), $p = 0.00$
			172 Masikoro		C. 0.013–0.009	51	
			71 Mikea		A. >0.057	56	
			126 Vezo		C. 0.013–0.009	60	

[a]Experimental results are obviously unreliable due to methodological inadequacies discussed in the text; [b]"Mud-Vezo" (*Vezompotake*) are coastal Vezo who primarily farm

these experiments with the shorthand "Time 1" for our first intertemporal choice experiment in 2003, "Risk 6" for our sixth risky choice experiment in 2008, etc. Here, I describe some of the 13 experiments, and in the process, I discuss seven specific challenges that we faced (many of these challenges are not unique to field experiments, but occur in the laboratory as well). I conclude this section by asking what we have really learned through these attempts to numerically estimate risk preferences and discount rates.

Challenge One: There Are Social and Ethical Concerns Associated with Asking Poor People to Gamble for Food or Money

Each time we designed an experiment, my Malagasy colleagues and I discussed the possible social and ethical risks of asking poor people to gamble for food or money. If we offered some members of a community the chance to win something but we did not offer the same opportunity to others, we risked sparking jealousy, which, within rural communities, can lead to lasting grudges, sorcery accusations, and violence.

Our initial solution to these problems was to offer hypothetical rewards. However, as I discuss below, hypothetical rewards led to hypothetical responses (see discussion in Hertwig and Ortmann 2001). In 2004, we switched to real rewards, but offered cooking oil rather than cash or food because while oil adds flavor and calories to prepared food, it is a dietary supplement rather than a staple, so that winning or losing has little impact on one's food supply. Eventually, for practical reasons, we switched to cash rewards. To limit jealousy and mitigate ethical concerns, we kept rewards rather modest, typically between 200 and 2000 Malagasy Ariary (MGA; \$0.10 to \$1.00 USD; for comparison, a cup of coffee costs 100 MGA and a cup of rice costs 200 MGA; a typical daily wage for a man doing agricultural labor is 5000 MGA, whereas the typical daily wage for women doing laundry is 1000 MGA). These rewards were sufficient to improve a day's meals but not to change one's wealth status. To further reduce the chances of exacerbating jealousy, in 2004 we began sampling exhaustively, allowing all interested individuals to participate in both risk and time experiments. The Institutional Review Board at the University of Georgia approved all research designs. We have heard no complaints about our methods from our research participants. People seemed to enjoy participating.

Challenge Two: There Are Practical Concerns Involving Choice of Reward Currencies, Expressions of Probability, and Paying Out Delayed Rewards

There were some practical disadvantages to using cooking oil as an experimental reward. Oil is heavy and difficult to transport in sufficient quantities. The value of cooking oil may depend on whether the household already has cooking oil in storage. We switched to cash because it is easier to transport, and cash is less likely to have diminishing marginal utility over the modest quantities used in our experiments. However, for cash to have value, one must have a place to spend it. Some of our study sites were 15–20 km distant from the nearest marketplace or shop. In communities where people only had the opportunity to spend money once or twice per month, they could easily wait for larger, delayed options, jeopardizing our time preference experiment. To tackle this issue, we gave all of our subjects the option to receive their winnings in rice rather than cash, at slightly better than market rates.

Another practical concern was how to illustrate probabilities to people who do not have much formal mathematical education. We used two familiar probability idioms, coin flips and a random draw of face-down dominoes (dominoes are a popular game in the region for men and women alike). In doing so, we may have accidentally framed the experiments as recreational rather than economic.

An additional challenge in the time preference experiments involved delivering delayed rewards. In short field seasons, it was impractical to pose delays longer than a few days, because it was impractical to stay longer than a few days. Time experiments also require that subjects trust the researchers to deliver on promised future rewards. We solved these problems with a research design involving multiple rounds of experiments in the same communities.

Challenge Three: Experiments with Hypothetical Rewards May Generate Hypothetical Responses

For the social, ethical, and practical reasons discussed above, in our first experiment, Time 1, we offered hypothetical rewards, in the form of 1–48 imaginary gunnysacks of maize. This was a titration experiment consisting of nine choices among dichotomous options. Delays were six months for the first three choices, 12 months for the next three choices, and one month for the final three choices. Subjects were 79 Mikea adults in three villages. Figure 3.4 displays the experimental design with the frequency of subjects' choices.

If the goal of this experiment was to measure k, this experiment was a failure. Responses were markedly bimodal, suggesting that k is either smaller than 0.08/month (0.003/day) or greater than 47/month (1.57/day). In round three of the experiment, nearly a third of the participants ($n = 22$) said that they would rather

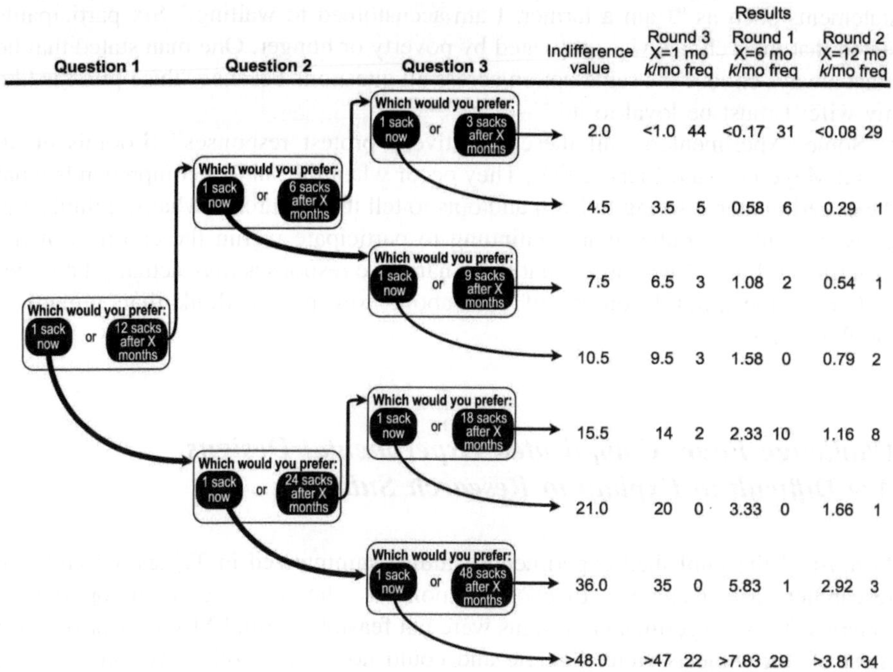

Fig. 3.4 Experimental design and results of Time 1, a failed attempt at titration. Because subjects did not understand the repeated nature of the questions, and because rewards were hypothetical, many subjects consistently chose immediate rewards or delayed rewards as a "protest response."

have one sack of maize now rather than 48 sacks after one month! Six respondents gave inconsistent (or preference reversing) results, saying that they would rather wait a longer time for a smaller reward.

Subjects tended to either always choose the immediate option or always choose the delayed option, either in each round or across all three rounds; nearly two-thirds of the sample (n = 45) always chose the same response across all nine questions. Of these, roughly half (n = 23) always chose the more immediate option, and half (n = 22) always chose the more delayed option. Those who claimed to be primarily foragers (n = 24) were no more likely than those who claimed to be primarily farmers (n = 21) to consistently choose the immediate option ($X^2(1) = 2.7$, $p = 0.10$), nor was there a significant difference by sex ($X^2(1) = 3.15$, $p = 0.08$).

Because the rewards were hypothetical, informants may have treated the entire exercise as hypothetical, as hinted by their narrative responses. After one old man indicated that he would rather have one sack of maize now rather than 48 sacks in one month, I broke script and asked, "Would you prefer one sack of maize now or *2000* sacks in one month?" He replied that he will always prefer the one sack now because "I am a true Mikea, a forager; I will always choose what is in front of me." After this exchange, we ended every experiment by asking informants to explain their choices. Three others said that they could wait for delayed rewards with statements such as "I am a farmer. I am accustomed to waiting." Six participants stated that their choice was motivated by poverty or hunger. One man stated that he must always choose the same option across all questions because "this option is like my wife; I must be loyal to it."[4]

Some experimenters call these narratives "protest responses" (Loomis et al. 2002; Meyerhoff and Liebe 2009). They occur when the subject comprehends what the experimenter is trying to learn and opts to tell the researcher what she thinks the answer should be rather than continuing to participate within the confines of the experiment. Later, I will argue that these narrative responses may actually be richer and more meaningful sources of data about how people think than numerical indifference values.[5]

Challenge Four: Complicated Experimental Designs Are Difficult to Explain to Research Subjects

In most of the published experimental studies summarized in Tables 3.2 and 3.3, researchers asked subjects to choose among a schedule of different options or lotteries. These experimental designs were not feasible in rural Madagascar because most of our subjects were illiterate and could not read or otherwise remember a complicated list of rewards and probabilities or delays. Our research designs had to offer a small set of options that our participants can keep in mind at once.

Following Kuznar (2001) and Henrich and McElreath (2002), many of our first experimental attempts involved titration. The advantage of titration is that it only poses one dichotomous choice at a time, which is easy for research subjects to keep track of without the need for written information. The disadvantage of titration is that it involves a series of such choices, leading to a complicated procedure that may seem dauntingly complex to rural reasoners who are unaccustomed to abstract numerical puzzles.

---

[4]These quotations are translated and paraphrased and not the actual words of my informants.

[5]In an attempt to make the most of these data, a physicist friend of mine, Dr. Daniel Steck at the University of Oregon, performed a bootstrapping procedure to better estimate the discount parameters across the three rounds of the experiment. We classified the Mikea research subjects according to their reaction to recent pressures from conservation organizations to abandon swidden maize agriculture (which was prohibited in 2002) in favor of permanent manioc cultivation. The analyses suggested that Mikea who planned to become manioc farmers had a significantly lower discount parameter (k = 0.05/day) than those who planned to spend more time hunting and gathering (k = 0.13/day). Steck and I cowrote a manuscript with this result that made it through a round a peer review, and I cited this manuscript and described its results in a chapter (Tucker 2006). As I conducted further experiments, it became clearer that the Time 1 experiment probably did not produce numerically valid responses. I abandoned this manuscript, but I still see it cited sometimes—perhaps because it satisfies our preconceived expectations that foragers should discount the future more than farmers. I contradict this conclusion in this article.

I suspect that among the reasons, participants in the Time 1 experiment (introduced above) consistently chose either the immediate or the delayed options was because being unaccustomed to numerical comparisons, they mentally edited out the quantitative information and focused instead on the basic choice between a smaller reward now versus a larger reward later (see Rahimi-Golkhandan et al., this volume). This would explain why, when we asked informants the second or third question in the series, some interjected, "I have already answered this!" A few participants admitted that the experiment was difficult, saying that they had never attended school and did not understand the numbers (although most Mikea do make numerical comparisons in the marketplace).

Two other titration experiments, Risk 4 and Time 5, consisted of one round of three dichotomous choices and, unlike Time 1, offered real cash rewards. In Risk 4, we asked subjects to choose between 400 MGA for sure or a 50% chance (coin flip) of winning a larger reward. In Time 5, we asked subjects to choose between 500 MGA now versus a larger reward after three months. Subjects ($N = 440$) included 194 Masikoro, 86 Mikea, and 160 Vezo adult men and women.

Real rewards are tricky to implement in titration, because subjects' responses to each question must not be influenced by whether they won or lost from the previous question (unless the goal of the experiment is to see how subjects shift choices after wins and losses). In previous studies, researchers told subjects to treat each question as though it involved real rewards, and then, at the end of the experiment, the researcher would randomly select one question as "real." This is a "random round payment mechanism" or RRPM.

These experiments did not go as planned. As with Time 1, it was extremely difficult to explain to subjects why we were offering them a series of choices among similar options. As a result, many participants played the game without fully understanding it, as indicated by their comments in postexperiment debriefings. It was even more challenging to explain the concept of RRPM. We told informants that we would randomly choose one option as the real reward, but because we did not want to spark jealousy, we secretly chose one question ahead of time to serve as the real reward option for all informants. The problem was that this did not remain a secret for long. The combination of the fact that informants did not understand the concept of a series of dichotomous choices and did not understand RRPM plus the fact that our RRPM was not truly random and rumors about the amount of money being offered resulted in almost everyone choosing the option with the greatest rewards: 81% chose the highest risk option and 79% the most delayed option.

Challenge Five: Low Variability in Responses May Limit Analyses

Because a sequence of dichotomous choices made little sense to our informants, the solution was to offer a one-shot choice among multiple options that differed in both reward amount and probability or delay, but to keep the number of options as few and as simple as possible. The 2006 Risk 2 experiment looked like this.

Which would you prefer?

A. one cup of cooking oil for sure (EV = 1, CV = 0);	15
B. a 7/8 chance to win two cups (EV = 1.75, CV = 0.37);	63
C. a 5/8 chance to win three cups (EV = 1.875, CV = 0.77);	73
D. a 1/8 chance to win four cups (EV = 0.5, CV = 2.60);	1

Options A–D represent different trade-offs between mean reward and variation, as measured by the CV. Options A, B, and C represent declining aversion to risk, and option D is risk prone. The numbers after the semicolons are the frequencies of responses. Probabilities are expressed here in eighths and were illustrated in our experiment with a random mix of eight dominoes.

The 2006 Time 3 experiment is below:

Which would you prefer?

A. 1 cup of oil now ($k > 1$);	21
B. 2 cups tomorrow ($1 > k > 0.5$);	39
C. 2.5 cups after 3 days ($0.5 > k > 0.333$);	10
D. 3 cups after 6 days ($0.333 > k > 0$);	66

One hundred and fifty-two people completed the risk exercise, and 136 did the time experiment.

In many respects, these experiments worked well. The experiments were not difficult for the informant to understand. To check for comprehension, after posing the options, we would ask the subject to explain the options back to us, which almost everyone did without problem.

One problem with offering a one-shot choice among four options is that if the reward and probability/delay values offered are not carefully chosen, responses will "bunch" around a single option. Too much bunching makes it difficult to conduct analyses; for example, it is difficult to tell whether men and women make different choices if nearly everyone chooses option C. In the Risk 2 experiment, the bunching around options B and C suggests that a better experiment should explore more options within the range of CV = 0.37–0.77. The bunching in the Time 3 experiment is more serious. Forty-nine percent of participants chose option D, which estimates k as less than 0.333. The experiment cannot say how much less; k could be 0.300 or 0.000003. To better explore this range of discount values would require longer delays, but the 2006 field season was limited to two months, making long delays impractical.

The final two rounds of experiments, Risks 5 and 6 and Times 6 and 7, were designed to reduce bunching and were only partially successful. These are seasonal iterations of the same experiment in the same subject pools, to test for seasonal differences in choices. Again, the numbers after the semicolons are the frequencies that our informants chose each option.

Risks 5 and 6: Which would you prefer?

A. 400 MGA for sure (EV = 400; CV = 0);	13, 5
B. a 7/8 chance to win 800 MGA (EV = 700; CV = 0.37);	59, 179
C. a 4/8 chance to win 2000 MGA (EV = 1000; CV = 1.01);	335, 166
D. a 1/8 chance to win 2400 MGA (EV = 300; CV = 2.60);	33, 19

In Risk 5, there is still considerable bunching around choice C, although the responses are more normally distributed in Risk 6.

Times 6 and 7: Which would you prefer?

A. 1000 MGA now ($k > 0.057$);	91, 140
B. 1400 MGA after 7 days ($0.057 > k > 0.013$);	48, 27
C. 2200 MGA after 90 days ($0.013 > k > 0.009$);	205, 178
D. 2600 MGA after 180 days ($k < 0.009$);	96, 24

Here, we were able to explore a lower range of discount values by offering very long delays, although we still have considerable bunching around option C.

Challenge Six: Absence of Evidence for an Effect Is Not Evidence for Absence of an Effect

To test for the effects of demographic, economic, and cultural determinants on risky and intertemporal choices, starting in 2006, we paired the risk and time experiments with livelihood questionnaires (Tucker et al. 2010, 2015; Tucker 2012).[6] Tables 3.7 and 3.8 report the results of a series of bivariate and multivariate logistic regressions

[6]Age, sex, household size, and years of formal education were self-reported. The material capital score is the sum of the market value of a list of assets, averaged over three seasonal measures. The social capital score is a sum of Likert-scaled responses to questions about how difficult it would be for the informant to achieve a series of favors from non-kin (Cronbach's $\alpha > 0.80$). Income is more than just salary for those who are not entirely market dependent, so our income score is the sum of the market value of all production, whether consumed at home or sold in the market, from foraging, fishing, farming, livestock sales, retailing profits, and wages, based on the three seasonal recalls. The market participation score is the proportion of the total income that was realized in commercial transactions. Percent income from foraging and fishing is the proportion of the income variable gained from foraging and fishing rather than farming, livestock sales, and wages. Food insecurity was evaluated with a modified version of the USDA food insecurity module and is the sum of 11 Likert-scaled questions (Cronbach's $\alpha > 0.80$). Dietary diversity is the sum of "yes" responses to questions whether the informant ate 10 different categories of food in the past week. The food insecurity and dietary diversity scores are three-season averages.

Table 3.7 Logistic regressions predicting the likelihood of choosing more risky options

	Risk exp 2 (2006)		Risk exp 3 (2007)		Risk exp 5 (2007)		Risk exp 6 (2008)	
	Bivariate	Multivariate	Bivariate	Multivariate	Bivariate	Multivariate	Bivariate	Multivariate
LR X^2 (df), p	–	15.77 (10), ns	–	61.54 (12)**	–	41.08 (12)**	–	21.69 (12)*
Pseudo R^2	–	0.07	–	0.20	–	0.14	–	0.04
N	–	107	–	262	–	340	–	365
Sex	ns	ns	0.504**	ns	ns	ns	ns	ns
Household size	ns	0.772**	ns	ns	ns	ns	ns	ns
Education	ns	ns	1.180**	ns	1.131*	ns	ns	ns
Masikoro	ns	ns	0.567**	0.043**	2.395**	ns	ns	ns
Mikea	ns	ns	0.332**	0.025**	0.188**	0.256**	0.469**	ns
Vezo	ns	d	7.835**	d	2.177**	d	ns	d
Income	—	—	ns	ns	ns	ns	ns	ns
Market participation	—	—	1.164**	ns	ns	ns	ns	ns
Foraging and fishing income	—	—	1.096**	ns	ns	ns	ns	ns
Material capital	ns	ns	ns	0.799*	ns	ns	1.233**	1.229**
Social capital	ns	ns	0.833	0.746**	ns	ns	ns	ns
Food insecurity	ns	ns	ns	ns	1.364**	1.328**	ns	ns
Dietary diversity	ns	ns	ns	ns	ns	ns	1.187**	ns

Note Coefficients reported as odds ratios. Continuous variables rescaled to 0–10
ns = not significant, *$p < 0.05$. **$p < 0.01$, – = not applicable, — = did not test, d = dropped due to colinearity

Table 3.8 Logistic regressions predicting the likelihood of choosing more delayed options

	Time exp 3 (2006)		Time exp 4 (2007)		Time exp 6 (2007)		Time exp 7 (2008)	
	Bivariate	Multivariate	Bivariate	Multivariate	Bivariate	Multivariate	Bivariate	Multivariate
LR X^2 (df), p	–	7.00 (10), ns	–	9.08 (12), ns	–	53.39 (12)**	–	43.85 (12)**
Pseudo R^2	–	0.05	–	0.03	–	0.13	–	0.09
N	–	112	–	262	–	340	–	365
Sex	ns	ns	ns	ns	ns	ns	ns	ns
Household size	ns	ns	ns	ns	ns	ns	ns	ns
Education	ns	ns	ns	ns	ns	ns	ns	ns
Masikoro	ns	ns	ns	ns	4.067**	ns	ns	ns
Mikea	ns	ns	0.549*	ns	0.190**	0.298*	0.294**	0.304*
Vezo	ns	d	ns	d	ns	d	2.767**	d
Income	—	—	ns	ns	ns	ns	ns	ns
Market participation	—	—	ns	ns	ns	ns	1.159**	ns
Foraging and fishing income	—	—	0.947*	ns	0.943**	ns	ns	ns
Material capital	ns	ns	ns	ns	ns	ns	ns	ns
Social capital	ns	ns	ns	ns	ns	ns	ns	ns
Food insecurity	ns	ns	ns	ns	1.288**	1.267**	ns	ns
Dietary diversity	ns	ns	ns	ns	ns	ns	ns	ns

Note Coefficients reported as odds ratios. Continuous variables rescaled to 0–10
ns = not significant, *$p < 0.05$. **$p < 0.01$, – = not applicable, — = did not test, d = dropped due to colinearity

predicting whether subjects chose options A or B versus C or D in each experiment. All continuous variables are rescaled to 0–10 (so that effects reflect a 10% change in the independent variable) and coefficients are odds ratios.

The 2006 (Risk 2, Time 3) multivariate models were not significant. One possible reason is we were still in the process of perfecting and validating the livelihood questionnaire. These analyses found no effects because the independent variables were poorly measured and not necessarily because the effects did not exist.

When looking at the heterogeneous evidence for the effects of determinants on preferences in the published studies in Tables 3.2 and 3.3, it is important to realize that these studies measured variables such as income and wealth in many different ways. Unfortunately, few of these studies discuss how they measured or validated their independent variables, so it is difficult to know whether effects are absent because they do not exist or because they were not properly measured. Wealth and income are notoriously challenging to evaluate in societies that are only partially market-integrated and for whom property is communally rather than individually owned (Ellis 2000; Morris et al. 2000; Green and Hulme 2005; Deaton 2010; Tache and Sjaastad 2010; Tucker et al. 2011).

Challenge Seven: Inconsistent Results Are Difficult to Interpret

If my experiments were *internally* valid—if they successfully evaluated the same underlying phenomena (preferences) for all subjects—then we would expect some consistency across the 13 experiments in estimates of risk preferences and discount parameters and in the effects of demographic, cultural, and economic determinants. If my experiments are *externally* valid—if people's choices in experiments predict their choices in real life—then we would expect that preference for low risk and immediate rewards would be associated with an economic emphasis on foraging and fishing rather than farming. Looking across all 13 experiments in Tables 3.5 and 3.6, it is easy to see some consistency and some inconsistency. The big question is, does inconsistency across experiments demonstrate that preferences are flexible, shifting with changing contexts, or does this inconsistency cast doubt on the validity of the experiments?

Consistency in Numerical Estimates of Preferences

There is a reasonable consistency in numerical estimates across the experiments, as demonstrated in the final columns of Tables 3.5 and 3.6. In all of the risk experiments, the most popular choice was CV = 0.10–0.13 with the exception of Risk 4 (the failed titration attempt) and Risk 6. The discount parameters in Times 3, 4, and

5 are bunched at the lowest possible value, less than about 0.2/day. This is consistent with the results of Times 6 and 7, which estimates the range at 0.013–0.009. The results of Time 2 are an outlier. Time 1 and Time 5 are the failed titration attempts explained previously.

Recall that Risk 5 and Risk 6 were seasonal iterations of the same experiment with the same subject pool. What do we make of the fact that in Risk 5, 76% of participants chose option C, whereas in Risk 6, the modal choice (49%) was option B? Two hundred and thirty-five individuals participated in both experiments, of whom 199 (84%) made a different choice in Risk 5 than Risk 6, and 197 (84%) made a different choice in Time 6 than Time 7. A logistic regression model examining the likelihood of shifting to a risker option from Risk 5 to Risk 6 (likelihood ratio $X^2(2) = 24.34$, $p = 0.02$, $R^2 = 0.12$) finds a greater likelihood for Mikea (OR = 16.6) and Masikoro (OR = 7.2) and people with more education (OR = 1.2) and more material capital (OR = 1.4). A similar model examining the likelihood of shifting to a more delayed choice from Time 6 to Time 7 (likelihood ratio $X^2(2) = 28.21$, $p = 0.005$, $R^2 = 0.13$) found an increased likelihood with increased material capital (OR = 1.3). But the fit of these models is rather poor, as indicated by the modest R^2 values. Thus, it is unclear whether this is evidence for seasonal shifts in preference associated with changes of wealth, versus reason to suspect that the experiments do not yield precise and consistent measures.

Consistency in Determinants of Preferences

Tables 3.7 and 3.8 show that different suites of demographic and economic variables predict preferences in different experiments. More social capital predicts a preference for lower risk rewards in Risk 3 but not Risk 5 or 6; greater food insecurity predicts a preference for lower risk in Risk 4 but not Risk 3 or 5. Greater food insecurity predicts a preference for more delayed options in Time 6 but not Time 4 or 7. Material capital predicts a lower likelihood of choosing riskier options in Risk 3, but a greater likelihood of choosing riskier options in Risk 6.

Some of this inconsistency could be caused by multiple collinearities among the predictor variables, which, in the final two rounds of experiments, are up to 46% correlated. A principal component analysis conducted on the demographic and economic variables used in Risk 5 and Risk 6 and Time 6 and Time 7 finds three primary clusters of correlated variables accounting for 52% of this variation. The first component, labeled "income and capitals," consists of positive associations among education, income, market participation, material capital, social capital, and dietary diversity. The second component consists of only one variable, proportion of income from foraging and fishing. A third "needs" component consists of greater household size and greater food insecurity.

I contrast the fit of different logistic regression models testing for the effects of identity (model 1); income and capitals (model 2); proportion of income from foraging and fishing (model 3); needs (model 4); all variables (model 5); and best-fit model (model 6) discovered through backward selection. Model fit was evaluated using Akaike's information criterion (AIC) in Stata 14 (See Appendix).

The most consistent effect is being Mikea, which has the greatest predictive value across all four experiments, predicting a lower likelihood of choosing risky and delayed options. The proportion of income from foraging and fishing models is only significant in the time experiments. The effects are inconsistent; in Time 6, this variable predicts a slightly lower likelihood of choosing delayed rewards, but in Time 7, it predicts a slightly *greater* likelihood of choosing delayed rewards. The proportion of income from foraging and fishing models fits the data less well (lower AIC) than the other models.

Needs predicts choices in both experiments that we did during January–March 2008 (Risk 5 and Time 6), and income and capitals predicts choices in both experiments that we did during May–June 2008 (Risk 6 and Time 7). This consistency within seasons and across experiments suggests a season trend. January–March is the rainy season before the harvest when needs is greatest, and May–June is the harvest season when incomes and capitals is greatest.

External Validity

Are participants in immediate returns economies consistently more likely to prefer lower risk and more immediate rewards? Being Mikea, an identity closely allied with foraging, consistently predicts a preference for lower risk options and more immediate options across all experiments. However, the same is not for Vezo fishers, despite their immediate returns economy.

The variable *percent income from foraging and fishing* best represents each individual's reliance on immediate returns activities. This variable does not consistently predict choices across experiments. In the clustered models just described, this variable has a small effect that is inconsistent across seasons. The external validity of the experiments is unclear.

Were Choice Experiments Worth the Effort?

I began this paper with the debate as to whether wealth and income versus cultural identity best predicts risk preferences. Consistent with Kuznar's (2001) argument, my last four experiments found possible evidence that "needs" predicts choices in the preharvest season, while "income and capitals" does so in the postharvest season, which could be modeled with a sigmoidal utility curve. Consistent with Henrich and McElreath's (2002) argument that preferences are cultural norms, being Mikea is the single best predictor of preferences in all statistical analyses and was generally associated with a preference for less risk and sooner rewards. Yet in some experiments, the majority of Mikea chose the highest risk option (Risk 3) or were split between the most immediate and the most delayed options (Time 4). As I argued in my response to the Kuznar-Henrich and McElreath's debate, strategic and cultural group variables copredict preferences, and this finding is equally consistent with marginal utility and bounded rationality perspectives (Tucker 2012).

But the exercise of numerical evaluation of risk and time preference has told me little that I did not already know. My estimate that southwestern Malagasy prefer risks in the range of CV = 0.37–1.01 compares well with the CV values for actual farming activities in Madagascar, including maize (CV = 0.57), manioc (CV = 0.67), and rice (CV = 0.72; Table 3.4). But, by choosing to plant these crops, my informants are already demonstrating that their risk preferences are in the range of CV = 0.57–0.72. The experiment is unnecessary to arrive at this conclusion.

My estimate that southwestern Malagasy have discounting parameters of $k = 0.013–0.009$ does little to help me understand why southwestern Malagasy mix the delayed rewards of agriculture with the immediate rewards of foraging. For the value of a maize harvest delayed by 100 days to be discounted lower than the value of tuber foraging today, k would have to be an astronomical 6.9/day (contrary to Tucker 2006).

The analyses presented in the Appendix find no clear relationship between reliance on foraging and fishing instead of farming and preference for risk or time, so individuals' preferences do not seem to explain their economic choices. In other words, people's choices (in real life) do not predict their choices (in an experiment). Again, by choosing to forage rather than farm, my informants are demonstrating their preference for low risk and quick returns. The fact that the experiments do not agree with reality casts doubts on the validity of the experiments.

From Preferences to Causal Reasoning

Causality, Epistemology, and Ontology

The problem with risk preference choice experiments is that they seek to evaluate how people subjectively value probability, yet "probability" is not a meaningful causal idiom for many people. Nor are elapsing days necessarily the meaningful component of anticipation of the future. Numerous experiments have documented that probability is non-intuitive. Reasoners judge likelihood based on too few observations, overestimate the frequency of rare and extreme events, and sometimes perceive patterns that do not exist (Tversky and Kahneman 1974; Nisbett and Ross 1980; Chapman and Chapman 1982). These biases facilitate rapid understanding that works pretty well in most ecological circumstances (Gigerenzer 1991, 1996). After all, one need not gather a statistically representative sample of observations of tiger behavior to conclude that tigers are dangerous. The mental search for patterns leads to a human search for meaning behind those patterns (Bloch 2008; Atran and Henrich 2010; Gelman and Legare 2011; Waldmann et al. 2006; see also Rahimi-Golkhandan et al.'s discussion of "gist learning" in this volume).

Economic historian Peter Bernstein (1996) argued that to overcome the limits of human intuition about probability, Arab and European scholars developed formal mathematics, and as a result, scientists have gained better control over their physical and social worlds. Bernstein's narrative describes progress away from reliance on the Gods and toward mastery of the odds, echoing Victorian notions that religion is primitive science that is slowly replaced by modern science as societies "evolve" (Frazer 1922; Tylor 1958 [1871]). Probability theory is certainly an effective epistemology (set of intellectual tools for understanding how the world works) assuming that the future resembles the past. But most people find "randomness" to be an unsatisfying explanation for why crops underproduce, or why illness strikes, because "randomness" is meaning neutral.

All of this is to say that risk and probability, and anticipation of future outcomes, are inherently about causality, whether one is working within a modern scientific or traditional folk scientific epistemology and that WEIRD people and those living in traditional societies are equally interested in understanding both the natural clockwork of the universe and the invisible meaning behind this clockwork. Supernatural causal reasoning is neither primitive nor childish. Legare et al. (2012) find that people invoke natural and supernatural causes at similar frequencies in studies set in the USA, Spain, Madagascar, and South Africa. Contrary to the intuitions of Piaget (1928), Legare et al. found that adults tend to be more likely to endorse supernatural causes than are children.

Theorists initially argued that humans and other organisms judge causality by observing covariation among factors or events. Early experimental studies found that reasoners systematically disregard the frequency of co-non-occurrences and have a difficulty judging trends from serial experiences across time, or when multiple causes have multiple effects (Ward and Jenkins 1965; Kelley 1973; Van Hamme and Wasserman 1994). Thus, we believe that chicken soup cures flu and thunder strikes people dead. Subsequent experimental work argues that we sort correlation from cause by considering base rate frequencies and causal mechanisms (Alloy and Tabachnik 1984; Ahn et al. 1995; Cheng 1997; Griffiths and Tenenbaum 2005). Nisbett and Ross (1980) argued that covariation theories are learned: "Each culture has experts, people of unusual acumen or specialized knowledge, who detect covariations and report them to the culture at large" (p. 111). Over generations, societies probably selectively reteach those causal theories that produce the best results and produce the most meaning.

Anthropologists have long studied non-Western peoples' knowledge of contingency and causality, often termed indigenous knowledge or traditional ecological knowledge (Birkes et al. 2000; Agrawal 2009). Some traditional knowledge consists of illusory correlation: The presence or absence of a groundhog's shadow on February 2 is unlikely to be causally linked to the duration of winter weather. But in other cases, folk knowledge is remarkably accurate. Orlove et al. (2000) demonstrated that Andean farmers can successfully predict annual rainfall based on the number and brightness of stars in the Pleiades on the winter solstice 65% of the time, which is better than predictions based on modern meteorological data.

Anthropologists have studied people's cosmological models of causality (Bird-David 1999; Howell 2012). Evans-Pritchard (1937) explained that Azande agropastoralists of southern Sudan have a perfectly "rational" understanding of why pots break (flaws in their manufacture), livestock die (disease), and aboveground granaries collapse (termites eat their supports), but they answer the question of why such misfortunes happen to harm people at particular moments with witchcraft, the evil thoughts of secret witches. Malinowski (1948) famously argued that magic, as an attempt to control unknown outcomes, is associated with risky and uncertain activities, explaining that Trobrianders have more magical practices associated with highly risky fishing adventures in the open ocean than for the relatively riskless activity of poisoning fish in lagoons. Recently, some ethnographers working with indigenous peoples of the Americas have argued that Native North and South Americans eschew the natural/ supernatural dichotomy entirely and share a view of reality in which humans, animals, and some plants and rocks are all anthropomorphic persons with souls and that the visible world is one of illusions (Vivieros de Castro 2000; Descola 2013; see also Ramos 2012; Graeber 2015).

In a review of experimental work, Legare et al. (2012) offered a typology of coexisting natural and supernatural causal theories. "Target-dependent thinking" describes situations where reasoners maintain multiple natural and supernatural explanations simultaneously without perceiving them to be in conflict and employ different models in different circumstances. Midwestern US schoolchildren easily switch between natural selection and divine creation when explaining the origins of mammals versus humans (Evans et al. 2011), and Vezo in Madagascar are equally capable of explaining death as biologic cessation and as continuity into the afterlife in different circumstances (Astuti and Harris 2008). In "synthetic thinking," natural and supernatural causes are alike and co-influential. Research participants in South Africa told Legare and Gelman (2008) that both unsafe sex and witchcraft may cause AIDS. In "integrative thinking," supernatural forces drive natural forces. Some of Legare's South African informants stated that witchcraft may cause people to have unsafe sex leading to AIDS, echoing Evans-Pritchard's (1937) description of Azande witchcraft.

In the remainder of this paper, I briefly describe some preliminary attempts to explore cultural causal models among Masikoro, Mikea, and Vezo. My goal is to demonstrate the feasibility of exploring mental representations of risk and future anticipation within a rich view of culture and meaning (D'Andrade 1992; Ross 2004; Bender and Beller 2011b; Gelman and Legare 2011; Beller et al. 2012; Legare et al. 2012; ojalehto and Medin 2015). The first study continues to ask how southwestern Malagasy decide which farming, foraging, and fishing activities to practice. The other studies examine when they employ natural versus supernatural causal models.

Risk and Covariation Perception

In 1999, we conducted an historical matrix exercise in 12 Mikea communities and two Masikoro villages (Tucker 2007). The exercise was conducted with mixed-sex groups of participants ranging from 2 to 25 people. The exercise involved laying playing cards on the ground to form a tabular grid in which the rows represent years (1999–1995), the first column represents rainfall, and subsequent columns represent farming, foraging, and fishing activities. Informants were instructed to put a pile of sand on each card representing how much (rain, harvest) there was in each year. Doing the exercise in a group engendered conversation, and we heard some consistent causal narratives across sites, such as "maize loves rain," "manioc hates rain," and "fish drink water, too" (there are more fish in rainy years). Statistical correlations in the order of sand piles across columns supported a regular pattern by which people perceived some activities to covary positively with rainfall and others to covary negatively with rainfall. These results suggest that to reduce risk caused by variable rainfall, southwestern Malagasy choose portfolios of activities that they understand to correlate positively and negatively with rainfall.

Defining Risk and Tolerance of Delay

The local terms for risk are *mirisike* (a Malagasy verb transformation of the French word *risque*) and *kitahitahy* (little blessing), and tolerance of delay is *mahaligny* (able to wait). We asked people to define these terms in 24 sex-segregated focus groups in 12 villages spanning Masikoro, Mikea, Vezo, and Tandroy identities (Tandroy are agropastoralist migrants from southern Madagascar). For a fuller account of these results, see Tucker et al. (2013).

I expected definitions of risk to include statements about both natural and supernatural causality, but much to my surprise they were almost entirely earthly. Of the 46 risk definitions that people voiced, 41% stated that risk describes what one must face in order to gain something, such as livelihood, food, food for hungry children, good things, and wealth; 26% said that risk means you might gain or you might not; and 24% said that risk is something that requires bravery to face (some scholars also define risk this way, as potential danger and source of anxiety; Douglas and Wildavsky 1982; Slovic 1987). Only four people (12% of explanations) made statements combining natural and supernatural causes, such as "risk means something that depends on many factors. Success at fishing depends on whether a funeral has occurred. Honey foraging depends on forest spirits and ancestors. Crops depend on rain and magic."

Informants defined *mahaligny* as suffering in order to gain something good or large (32%); tolerance of pain, suffering, and unpleasant conditions (29%); tolerance of people, especially family, for the benefits of kinship (n = 29%); and having a good heart (*fo*) or soul (*fagnahy*; 14%). Thus, *Mahaligny* (preference for delayed rewards) implies endurance, and patience is a virtue. There were no significant differences in the frequencies of definitions for risk or time by identity group.

Do Southwestern Malagasy Evaluate Risk the Same Way that a Scientist Might?

To explore this question, during the same focus groups described above, we asked informants to list their most significant economic activities, rate them on a four-point scale according to how risky they think each to be, and then explain why they rated each activity as they did (Tucker et al. 2013).

Focus group participants volunteered 53 foraging, fishing, farming, herding, and marketing activities (mean 11.2 activities per group). Groups' ratings were moderately consistent (42.7%) overall and significantly greater than that would be expected by chance (Cohen's $\kappa = 0.18$; $z = 7.70$; $p = 0.00$). While there was disagreement about the risk of particular activities, groups generally agreed that agriculture is riskier than foraging and fishing.

I expected that when asked to explain why each activity was risky, our informants would provide a mix of natural and supernatural causes. Much to my surprise, of the 239 total explanations our informants offered, all but two were natural causes. Explanations for activity risk include loss to pests ($n = 79$), variable climate and ecology ($n = 69$), risk of physical injury or encounters with dangerous animals ($n = 45$), market risks ($n = 24$), and uncertain access to inputs ($N = 20$). Only one Mikea informant offered that success at fishing depended on astrological fortune (*andro*), and another said that honey foraging is risky because one could encounter an undead creature called *tsiboko*.

These findings suggest that southwestern Malagasy generally agree with mean/variance risk measures that find that agriculture is riskier than foraging and fishing. They explain activity risk primarily with natural causes.

The Story of Reolo and Tsiato

In 2014, we conducted a vignette experiment to explore how southwestern Malagasy understand the causes for personal failure and success. Subjects were recruited opportunistically from one Mikea community ($n = 12$) and one Vezo community ($n = 24$). We posed two versions of a vignette about two old friends, Reolo and Tsiato, who discover one day that Reolo consistently harvests more than does his friend. Informants were then asked to explain Reolo's superior success (Tucker et al. 2015).

In an "economic" version of the vignette (administered to half of the participants), Reolo and Tsiato are described as working hard to solve economic problems in their lives, so they often meet in the marketplace. In a "religious" version of the vignette (administered to the other half of the participants), Reolo and Tsiato are described as working hard to solve social problems in their lives, so they often meet at ceremonies.

First, we asked informants to *list* reasons for Reolo's superior success. Then, we posed a list of seven natural causes, three social causes, and eight supernatural causes and asked informants whether they would *endorse* each cause as a potential explanation for Reolo's better harvests.

We expected that informants would provide a mix of natural and supernatural causal explanations and that the economic version of the vignette would elicit more natural causes, while the religious version elicited more supernatural causes. The latter prediction was not supported by analyses, which found that people listed ($t(36) = 0.79$, $p = 0.44$) and endorsed ($t(36) = -1.04$, $p = 0.31$) natural and supernatural causes in similar frequencies across vignette versions.

Table 3.9 summarizes the results. Both Mikea and Vezo primarily listed and endorsed supernatural causes for Reolo's superior success, although some natural

Table 3.9 Frequency that different natural and supernatural factors were listed or endorsed by Mikea and Vezo informants

	Factors listed voluntarily by informants		Factors endorsed by informants when listed by the researcher		Factors listed and endorsed	
	Mikea	Vezo	Mikea	Vezo	Mikea	Vezo
N	12	24	12	24	12	24
Natural factors						
Rainfall	3	0	3	3	6	3
Hard work	5	5	3	9	8	14
Pests^{M}/wind^{V}	0	0	6	3	6	3
Good land^{M}/good canoe^{V}	2	0	1	3	3	3
Weeds^{M}/good nets^{V}	0	0	1	4	1	4
Inherited land^{M}/good swimmer^{V}	1	0	2	1	3	1
Fertilizer^{M}	0	0	0	0	0	0
Social factors						
Age	0	0	2	4	2	4
Poverty	0	0	2	4	2	4
Jealous neighbors	0	0	2	2	2	2
Did not do bad things to others*	0	1	0	0	0	1
Parents*	1	2	0	0	1	2
Supernatural factors						
Ancestors	7	20	2	3	9	23
Possessing spirits	2	1	7	7	9	8
God	11	23	1	1	12	24
Magic	5	4	5	4	10	8
Other people's magical attack	0	0	1	0	1	0
Transgression of taboos	0	0	8	8	8	8

(continued)

Table 3.9 (continued)

	Factors listed voluntarily by informants		Factors endorsed by informants when listed by the researcher		Factors listed and endorsed	
	Mikea	Vezo	Mikea	Vezo	Mikea	Vezo
Astrological destiny	3	0	5	17	8	17
Church attendance	0	0	10	9	10	9
"Anjara" (turn)*	0	10	0	0	0	10
Astrological day*	0	1	0	0	0	1

Note Each informant listed 0–5 causes; when presented with the remaining causes in this list, each endorsed 2–14 additional causes. M = asked to Mikea only; V = asked to Vezo only; * = factors introduced by informants that were not part of our original list

causes were also listed and endorsed. The most frequently listed cause for both groups was the will of God (listed by 7 of 12 Mikea and 23 of 24 Vezo), followed by the blessings of the ancestors (listed by 7 of 12 Mika and 20 of 24 Vezo). Hard work was the most commonly listed and endorsed natural cause. Mikea listed fewer supernatural causes than Vezo, but they endorsed supernatural causes at similar frequencies. There were no significant differences in the frequency of causes listed or endorsed by sex, wealth, or frequency of attendance to a Christian church.

What I Think I Have Learned

These preliminary results suggest that southwestern Malagasy have traditional ecological knowledge of natural covariations between climatic factors and the outcomes of foraging, farming, and fishing activities and that this information leads them to similar conclusions about the level of risk associated with each activity as would mean/variance measures of risk. Southwestern Malagasy primarily think of activity risk in relation to natural causes, while personal risk is understood through persons' relationship with God, ancestors, and other supernatural forces. These results may be consistent with Legare et al.'s (2012) "integrative thinking," where supernatural forces ultimately drive natural forces.

Conclusions

In this article, I have questioned the internal and external validity of risk and time preference choice experiments as tools for understanding how people make choices in non-Western contexts. I have argued that we may learn more about non-Western peoples' risk-sensitive and intertemporal choices by exploring their understandings of causality and meaning. These arguments appear to be about research methods, but at a deeper level, these are conflicts among the epistemological assumptions of economists (formal models generating predictions), psychologists (controlled experiments generating models of thought), anthropologists (culture generating meaning and action), and of course, the epistemological assumptions of the people we are studying (natural and supernatural causes generating real outcomes).

I charge that experimenters have not properly considered the internal and external validity of risk and time choice experiments. Regarding internal validity, we assume that choice experiments evaluate preference, and the concept of "preference" implies at least some consistency in choices over time; yet because few researchers attempt repeated measures, consistency is assumed rather than demonstrated. Thus, researchers risk overgeneralization when they make statements such as "the average Dane is risk-averse" (Harrison et al. 2007: 343) or "Mapuche and Sangu are risk-preferring" (Henrich and McElreath 2002: 172) based on a single experiment.

It is difficult to tell whether inconsistent preferences indicate that preferences shift flexibly or that experimental methods lack internal validity. In large part, this is because it is not clear what preferences are. The concept of preference came into wide use with the birth of neoclassical economics; economists conceptualized "preference" not because of any behavioral evidence for consistency in human decision making, but as a modeling convenience to solve the problem of how to quantify utility (Von Neumann and Morgenstern 1953; Lichtenstein and Slovic 2006). Since then, scholars have argued both that risk and time preferences have some inherited genetic or physiological basis (Zuckerman 1991; Rogers 1994; Daly and Wilson 2001; Reyes-García et al. 2007), or that they are constructed throughout life as we make decisions (Becker and Mulligan 1997; Bowles 1998; Lichtenstein and Slovic 2006), and have argued both that preferences drive behavior (Reyes-García et al. 2007) and behavior drives preferences (Becker and Mulligan 1997).[7]

[7]A major problem with this discussion is that the literature commonly conflates risk preference and time preference with impulsivity and impatience. This was a recurring theme in the 2016 Nebraska Symposium; several presenters found that measures of impulsiveness were not associated with risk preferences and discount rates. Impulsivity may involve "hot cognition" (emotion), whereas economic trade-offs involve "cold cognition" (executive functioning). The structure of experiments may influence which type of reaction is elicited. Contrast, if you will, Slovic's (1966) experimental study of risky choice among boys and girls at a county fair in the USA and Binswanger's (1980) risk preference experiment among farmers in Andhra Pradesh, India. In Slovic's experiment, boys and girls made repeated choices among 10 switches where 9 provided candy and 1 "disaster switch" eliminated previous rewards; children decided how many times to flip switches. I would argue that the rapidness of the task, the sweetness of candy, and the recreational context of the county fair encouraged rapid, emotionally charged, "hot" decisions. In Binswanger's study, farmers were presented with a list of eight gambles to choose from with real monetary rewards that in some treatments were rather large. Participants were given several days to think about their choice and were encouraged to talk it over with other members of their household. This encouraged deliberate and purposive use of "cool cognition."

One possibility is that the experiments capture preferences plus other related thoughts and feelings. Frederick et al. (2002) speculate that discount rates are variable across experiments because they also capture intertemporal arbitrage, uncertainty, inflation, concave utility, habit formation, anticipatory utility, and emotion. Likewise, I offer that risk experiments capture not only probability/reward trade-offs, but also uncertainty, danger, dread, and anxiety (Douglas and Wildavsky 1982; Slovic 1987; Tucker et al. 2013). A second possibility is that experiments do not capture preferences at all, but rather context-specific evaluations within the constraints of the moment. Such on-the-spot judgments may also show some consistency as long as the decision-making environment remains constant.

With regard to external consistency, I question the degree to which we should expect choices in experiments to explain choices in real life and the utility of asking whether foragers prefer less risk and shorter delays than farmers. Salali and Migliano (2015) found that forest-dwelling Congolese BaYaka hunter-gatherers discount stock (bullion) cubes to a greater degree than do BaYaka living in towns who mix foraging with farming and wage labor. I would argue that a BaYaka person's choice to hunt and gather rather than to farm is a better indicator of their preference for immediate rewards than an abstract choice of one stock cube now versus five tomorrow. Experiments offer more controlled choice environments and the chance to manipulate the variance of options while keeping other aspects of the choice constant. This is useful if the purpose of the experiment is to identify decision-making biases, yet as a measurement tool, experimenters may be better off looking at real-life choices.

Thought and choice are meaning rich, and culture is this system of meaning. Meaning clearly influences people's choices; otherwise, framing and priming would not work. Culture is probably the most significant source of frames and primes. In Bickel's contribution to this volume, he shows that meaning-rich narratives may be the only effective way to change the behavior of addicts and others with impulse control problems. For southwestern Malagasy and probably for all humanity, the meaning behind unpredictability and anticipation relates to a clockwork understanding of interacting natural factors that are ultimately influenced by God, ancestors, and other supernatural forces.

Future research into cultural causal models should explore the specific contexts in which people from different cultures invoke natural and supernatural explanations, when they employ Legare et al.'s (2012) target-dependent, synthetic, and integrative thinking, and whether all cultures dichotomize natural and supernatural in the first place (for more on this latter question, see Medin et al. 2014). We also need to know whether and how different cultural understandings of the world influence actual behavior. Such knowledge has the potential to facilitate the greater cross-cultural communication and understanding while celebrating the value of cultural diversity.

Acknowledgements Special thanks to Jeffrey Stevens for inviting me to participate in the 2016 Nebraska Symposium and to Emily Johnson, Juan Duque, and Pamela Waldvogel for making my visit to Lincoln easy and fun. Throughout the process of learning about and conducting choice experiments, I received invaluable advice from many scholars. Thanks to the following people for answering my emails during the past two decades: Lawrence Kuznar, Joseph Henrich, Richard McElreath, Ricardo Godoy, Warren Bickel, Charles Holt, and Kris Kirby. Adam Goodie and Karen Allen provided valuable insights after a practice run of the symposium talk that is the basis of this paper. Dan Steck was a huge help and inspiration early in my experimental career; Dan, sorry our co-authored paper never made it to print. This project has also benefitted from discussions with Victoria Ramenzoni, Jessica Ham, Joseph Lanning, Amber Huff, Elaina Lill, Laura Tilghman, and Aaron Lenihan. For assistance and support in Madagascar, thanks to the National Science Foundation (0650412), the Université de Toliara and its past president Théodoret and current president Alphonse Dina, CeDRATOM and its director Barthélemy Manjakahery, and my Malagasy colleagues and field crew (see Footnote 1). And thanks to the hundreds of Masikoro, Mikea, and Vezo people who tolerated the choice experiments.

Appendix

Results of model fitting of logistic regressions testing for effects of cultural identity and three principal components, "income and capitals," Proportion income from foraging and fishing, and "needs," as well as best fit models, evaluated with Akaike's Information Criterion and revealed through backward selection. (Tables 3.10, 3.11, 3.12 and 3.13).

Table 3.10 Risk 5 (Jan–Mar 2008), predicting likelihood of choosing higher risk options

	Model 1: Identity group effects	Model 2: Capitals	Model 3: Proportion income from foraging	Model 4: Needs	Model 5: All	Model 6: Best fit
Mikea	0.208**				0.274*	0.232**
Masikoro	1.108				1.249	
Vezo	Dropped				Dropped	
Material capital		0.899			0.917	
Income		0.941			1.047	
Market participation		1.070			1.057	
Education		1.077			1.005	
Dietary diversity		1.168			1.013	
Social capital		0.914			0.929	
Proportion income from foraging and farming			1.02		1.022	
Household size				0.950	0.942	
Food insecurity				1.403**	1.323**	1.299**
N	340	340	340	340	340	
Likelihood ratio X^2 R^2	24.88(2)** 0.080	8.21(6) 0.027	0.64(1) 0.000	17.10(2)** 0.057	38.98(11)** 0.130	34.71(2)** 0.115
AIC	282.082	307.279	304.320	289.856	285.982	272.246

Note Likelihood ratio tests demonstrate that model 5 fits similarly well as model 1 (14.10(9), $p = 0.12$) and better than model 2 (30.77(5), $p = 0.00$), model 3 (38.34(10), $p = 0.00$), and model 4 (21.88(9), 0.01)
*$p < 0.05$, **$p < 0.01$

Table 3.11 Risk 6 (May–Jun 2008), predicting likelihood of choosing higher risk options

	Model 1: Identity group effects	Model 2: Capitals	Model 3: Proportion income from foraging	Model 4: Needs	Model 5: All	Model 6: Best fit
Mikea	0.469*				0.940	
Masikoro	0.951				2.029	2.452**
Vezo	Dropped				Dropped	
Material capital		1.198*			1.230*	1.243**
Income		0.963			0.991	
Market participation		0.992			0.987	
Education		1.000			0.990	
Dietary diversity		1.136			1.105	
Social capital		0.998			1.015	
Proportion income from foraging and farming			1.03		1.091	1.099*
Household size				0.991	0.965	
Food insecurity				1.035	1.033	
N	365	365	365	365	365	365
Likelihood ratio X^2 R^2	7.22(2)* 0.010	13.15(6)* 0.026	1.44(1) 0.003	0.39(2) 0.001	21.63(11)* 0.043	18.64(3)** 0.037
AIC	504.705	506.778	508.490	511.5354	508.301	495.292

Note Likelihood ratio tests demonstrate that model 5 fits similarly well as model 1 (14.10(9), $p = 0.12$) and model 2 (8.48(5), 0.13) and better than model 3 (20.19(10), $p = 0.03$) and model 4 (21.23(9), 0.01)

*$p < 0.05$, **$p < 0.01$

Table 3.12 Time 6 (Jan–Mar 2008), predicting likelihood of choosing more delayed options

	Model 1: Identity group effects	Model 2: Capitals	Model 3: Proportion income from foraging	Model 4: Needs	Model 5: All	Model 6: Best fit
Mikea	0.401**				0.298*	0.451*
Masikoro	2.563**				1.985	2.234***
Vezo	Dropped				Dropped	
Material capital		0.953			0.982	
Income		1.117			1.247	
Market participation		0.931			0.953	
Education		1.060			0.993	
Dietary diversity		1.011			0.866	
Social capital		0.841			0.852	0.858*
Proportion income from foraging and farming			0.952		1.003	
Household size				0.997	1.004	
Food insecurity				1.327***	1.269***	1.286***
N	340	340	340	340	340	340
Likelihood ratio X^2 R^2	34.19(2)** 0.085	9.53(6) 0.024	2.71 0.007	18.02(2)** 0.045	53.39(11) ** 0.132	48.48(4)** 0.120
AIC	376.517	409.1829	405.9952	392.6907	375.3191	366.228

Note Likelihood ratio tests demonstrate that model 5 fits better than model 1 (19.20(9), $p = 0.02$), model 2 (43.86(5), 0.00), model 3 (50.86(10), $p = 0.00$), and model 4 (35.37(9), 0.00)

$^*p < 0.05$, $^{**}p < 0.01$

Table 3.13 Time 7 (Jan–Mar 2008), predicting likelihood of choosing more delayed options

	Model 1: Identity group effects	Model 2: Capitals	Model 3: Proportion income from foraging	Model 4: Needs	Model 5: All	Model 6: Best fit
Mikea	0.182***				0.279**	0.183**
Masikoro	0.479***				1.097	0.482**
Vezo	Dropped				Dropped	
Material capital		1.146			1.114	
Income		1.012			1.099	1.054
Market participation		1.134			1.092	
Education		1.004			0.960	
Dietary diversity		1.018			0.909	
Social capital		0.871			0.911	
Proportion income from foraging and farming			1.088***		1.058	
Household size				1.027	1.002	
Food insecurity				1.005	0.973	
N	365	365	365	365	365	365
Likelihood ratio X^2 R^2	30.06(2)** 0.0598	23.76(6)** 0.0473	10.42(1)** 0.0208	0.56(2) 0.0011	42.08(11) ** 0.0838	30.35(3)** 0.0604
AIC	478.1816	492.4789	495.8157	507.6839	484.1634	479.8952

Note Likelihood ratio tests demonstrate that model 5 fits similarly well as model 1 (12.02(9), $p = 0.21$) and better than model 2 (18.32(5), 0.00), model 3 (31.65(10), $p = 0.00$), and model 4 (41.52(9), 0.00)
$^*p < 0.05$, $^{**}p < 0.01$

References

Agrawal, A. (2009). Why "Indigenous" knowledge? *Journal of the Royal Society of New Zealand, 39*(4), 157–158.

Ahn, W. K., Kalish, C. W., Medin, D. L., & Gelman, S. A. (1995). The role of covariation versus mechanism information in causal attribution. *Cognition, 54,* 299–352.

Alloy, L. B., & Tabachnik, N. (1984). Assessment of covariation by humans and animals: The joint influence of prior expectations and current situational information. *Psychological Review, 91*(1), 112–149.

Anderson, C. L., Dietz, M., Gordon, A., & Klawitter, M. (2004). Discount rates in Vietnam. *Economic Development and Cultural Change, 52,* 873–887.

Astuti, R. (1995). 'The Vezo are not a kind of people' Identity, difference, and 'ethnicity' among a fishing people of western Madagascar. *American Ethnologist, 22*(3), 464–482.

Astuti, R., & Harris, P. L. (2008). Understanding mortality and the life of the ancestors in rural Madagascar. *Cognitive Science, 32,* 713–740.

Atran, S., & Henrich, J. (2010). The evolution of religion: How cognitive by-products, adaptive learning heuristics, ritual displays, and group competition generate deep commitments to prosocial religions. *Biological Theory, 5*(1), 18–30.

Atran, S., Medin, D., & Ross, N. (2004). Evolution and devolution of knowledge: A tale of two biologies. *Journal of the Royal Anthropological Institutev, 10,* 395–420.

Barnard, A. (1999). Images of hunters and gatherers in European social thought. In R. B. Lee & R. Daly (Eds.), *The Cambridge encyclopedia of hunters and gatherers* (pp. 375–383). Cambridge: Cambridge University Press.

Becker, G. S., & Mulligan, C. B. (1997). The endogenous determination of time preference. *Quarterly Journal of Economics, 112*(3), 729–758.

Beller, S., Bender, A., & Medin, D. L. (2012). Should anthropology be part of cognitive science? *Topics in Cognitive Science, 4,* 342–353.

Beller, S., Bender, A., & Song, J. (2009). Weighing up physical causes: Effects of culture, linguistic cues, and content. *Joural of Cognition and Culture, 9,* 347–365.

Bender, A., & Beller, S. (2011a). Causal asymmetry across cultures: Assigning causal roles in symmetric physical settings. *Frontiers in Psychology, 2*(231), 1–10.

Bender, A., & Beller, S. (2011b). The cultural constitution of cognition: Taking the anthropological perspective. *Frontiers in Psychology, 2*(67), 1–6.

Bender, A., Schlimm, D., & Beller, S. (2015). The cognitive advantages of counting specifically: A representational analysis of verbal numeration systems in oceanic languages. *Topics in Cognitive Science, 7*(4), 1–18.

Bernoulli, D. (1738). Exposition of a new theory on the measurement of risk. *Econometrica, 22*(1), 23–36.

Bernstein, P. L. (1996). *Against the gods: The remarkable story of risk.* New York: Wiley.

Bird-David, N. (1999). "Animism" revisited: Personhood, environment, and relational epistemology. *Current Anthropology, 40*(S1), S67–S91.

Birkes, F., Colding, J., & Folke, C. (2000). Rediscovery of traditional ecological knowledge as adaptive management. *Ecological Applications, 10,* 1251–1262.

Binswanger, H. P. (1980). Attitudes toward risk: Experimental-measurement in rural India. *American Journal of Agricultural Economics, 62*(3), 395–407.

Binswanger, H. P., & Sillers, D. A. (1983). Risk-aversion and credit constraints in farmers decision-making: A reinterpretation. *Journal of Development Studies, 20*(1), 5–21.

Bloch, M. (2008). Why religion is nothing special but is central. *Philosophical Transactions of the Royal Society B., 363,* 2055–2061.

Bowles, S. (1998). Endogenous preferences: The cultural consequences of markets and other economic institutions. *Journal of Economic Literature, 36,* 75–111.

Bowles, S. (2011). Cultivation of cereals by the first farmers was not more productive than foraging. *Proceedings of the National Academy of Sciences (USA), 108*(12), 4760–4765.

Boyd, R., & Richerson, P. J. (2001). Norms and bounded rationality. In G. Gigerenzer & R. Selten (Eds.), *Bounded rationality: The adaptive toolbox* (pp. 281–296). Cambridge, MA: MIT Press.

Camerer, C., & Fehr, E. (2004). Measuring norms and preferences using experimental games: A guide for social scientists. In J. Henrich, R. Boyd, S. Bowles, C. Camerer, E. Fehr, & H. Gintis (Eds.), *Foundations of human sociality* (pp. 55–95). New York: Oxford University Press.

Chapman, L. J., & Chapman, J. (1982). Test results are what you think they are. In D. Kahneman & A. Tvserksy (Eds.), *Judgment under uncertainty: Heuristics and biases* (pp. 239–248). Cambridge: Cambridge University Press.

Cheng, P. (1997). From covariation to causation: A causal power theory. *Psycholological Review, 104,* 367–405.

Chuah, S.-H., Hoffmann, R., Jones, M., & Williams, G. (2009). An economic anatomy of culture: Attitudes and behaviour in inter- and intra-national ultimatum game experiments. *Journal of Economic Psychology, 30,* 732–744.

D'Andrade, R. G. (1992). *Human motives and cultural models*. New York: Cambridge University Press.

Daly, M., & Wilson, M. (2001). Risk-taking, intrasexual competition, and homicide. In J. A. French, A. C. Kamil, & D. W. Leger (Eds.), *Evolutionary psychology and motivation, Nebraska Symposium on Motivation* (Vol. 47, pp. 1–36). Lincoln, NE: University of Nebraska Press.

Deaton, A. (2010). Price indexes, inequality, and the measurement of world poverty. *American Economic Review, 100*(1), 5–34.

Descola, P. (2013). *Beyond nature and culture*. Chicago: University of Chicago Press.

Dillon, J. L., & Scandizzo, P. L. (1978). Risk attitudes of subsistence farmers in northeast Brazil: A sampling approach. *American Journal of Agricultural Economics, 60,* 425–435.

Douglas, M., & Wildavsky, A. (1982). *Risk and culture: An essay on the selection of technical and environmental dangers*. Berkeley: University of California Press.

Eggert, H. K., & Lokina, R. B. (2007). Small-scale fishermen and risk preferences. *Marine Resource Economics, 22,* 49–67.

Eggert, H. K., & Martinsson, P. (2004). Are commercial fishers risk-lovers? *Land Economics, 80*(4), 550–560.

Ellis, F. (2000). *Rural livelihoods and diversity in developing countries*. Oxford: Oxford University Press.

Evans, E. M., Legare, C. H., & Rosengren, K. (2011). Engaging multiple epistemologies: Implications for science education. In R. Taylor & M. Ferrari (Eds.), *Epistemology and science education: Understanding the evolution versus intelligent design controversy* (pp. 111–139). New York: Routledge.

Evans-Pritchard, E. E. (1937). *Witchcraft, oracles, and magic among the Azande*. Oxford: Clarendon Press.

Felson, R. B., & Gmelch, G. (1979). Uncertainty and the use of magic. *Current Anthropology, 20*(3), 587–589.

Frazer, J. (1922 [1890]). *The golden bough: A study of magic and religion.* New York: Macmillan.

Frederick, S., Loewenstein, G., & O'Donoghue, T. (2002). Time discounting and time preference: A critical review. *Journal of Economic Literature, 40*(2), 351–401.

Friedman, M., & Savage, L. J. (1948). The utility analysis of choices involving risk. *The Journal of Political Economy, 56*(4), 279–304.

Gaby, A. (2012). The Thaayorre think of time like they talk of space. *Frontiers in Psychology, 3,* 1–8.

Gächter, S., Herrmann, B., & Thöni, C. (2010). Culture and cooperation. *Philosophical Transactions of the Royal Society B, 365,* 2651–2661.

Gelman, S. A., & Legare, C. H. (2011). Concepts and folk theories. *Annual Review of Anthropology, 40,* 379–398.

Geschiere, P. (1997). *The modernity of witchcraft: Politics and the occult in postcolonial Africa.* Charlottesville: University of Virginia Press.

Gigerenzer, G. (1991). How to make cognitive illusions disappear: Beyond "heuristics and biases". *European Review of Social Psychology, 2*(1), 83–115.
Gigerenzer, G. (1996). On narrow norms and vague heuristics: A reply to Kahneman and Tversky. *Psychological Review, 103*(3), 592–596.
Godoy, R., Byron, E., Reyes-García, V., Leonard, W. R., Patel, K., Apaza, L., Pérez, E., Vadez, V., & Wilkie, D. (2004). Patience in a foraging-horticultural society: A test of competing hypotheses. *Journal of Anthropological Research, 60*(2), 179–202.
Graeber, D. (2015). Radical alterity is just another way of saying "reality:" A reply to Eduardo Viveiros de Castro. *Hau, 5*(2), 1–41.
Green, M., & Hulme, D. (2005). From correlates and characteristics to causes: Thinking about poverty from a chronic perspective. *World Development, 33*(6), 867–879.
Griffiths, T. L., & Tenenbaum, J. B. (2005). Structure and strength in causal induction. *Cognitive Psychology, 51,* 334–384.
Harrison, G. W., Lau, M. I., & Rutström, E. E. (2007). Estimating risk attitudes in Denmark: A field experiment. *Scandinavian Journal of Economics, 109*(2), 341–368.
Harrison, G. W., Lau, M. I., & Williams, M. B. (2002). Estimating individual discount rates in Denmark: A field experiment. *The American Economic Review, 92,* 1606–1617.
Henrich, J. (2001). On risk preferences and curvilinear utility curves. *Current Anthropology, 42*(5), 711–713.
Henrich, J., Boyd, R., Bowles, S., Camerer, C., Fehr, E., Gintis, H., et al. (2005). Economic man in cross-cultural perspective: Behavioral experiments in 15 small-scale societies. *Behavioral and Brain Sciences, 28*(6), 795–855.
Henrich, J., Heine, S., & Norenzayan, A. (2010). The weirdest people in the world? *Behavioral and Brain Sciences, 33*(2/3), 1–75.
Henrich, J., & McElreath, R. (2002). Are peasants risk-averse decision makers? *Current Anthropology, 43*(1), 172–181.
Henrich, J., & McElreath, R. (2003). The evolution of cultural evolution. *Evolutionary Anthropology, 12*(3), 123–135.
Hertwig, R., & Ortmann, A. (2001). Experimental practices in economics: A methodological challenge for psychologists? *Behavioral and Brain Sciences, 24*(3), 383–451.
Holt, C. A. (2006). *Markets, games, and strategic behavior: Recipes for interactive learning.* Boston: Peaerson Addison Wesley.
Holt, C. A., & Laury, S. K. (2002). Risk aversion and incentive effects. *American Economic Review, 92*(5), 1644–1655.
Howell, S. (2012). Knowledge, morality, and causality in a 'luckless' society: The case of the Chewong in the Malaysian rain forest. *Social Analysis, 56,* 133–147.
Inglehart, R., & Welzel, C. (2005). *Modernization, cultural change and democracy.* Cambridge: Cambridge University Press.
Kahneman, D., & Tversky, A. (Eds.). (2000). *Choices, values, and frames.* Cambridge: Cambridge University Press.
Kelley, H. H. (1973). The processes of causal attribution. *American Psychologist, 28*(2), 107–128.
Kelly, R. L. (2013). *The lifeways of hunter-gatherers: The foraging spectrum.* Cambridge: Cambridge University Press.
Kirby, K. N., Godoy, R., Reyes-García, V., Byron, E., Apaza, L., Leonard, W., et al. (2002). Correlates of delay-discount rates: Evidence from Tsimane' Amerindians of the Bolivian rain forest. *Journal of Economic Psychology, 23*(3), 291–316.
Kirby, K. N., & Marakovic, N. N. (1996). Delay-discounting probabilistic rewards: Rates decrease as amounts increase. *Psychonomic Bulletin & Review, 3*(1), 100–104.
Kuznar, L. A. (2001). Risk sensitivity and value among Andean pastoralists: Measures, models, and empirical tests. *Current Anthropology, 42*(3), 432–440.
Kuznar, L. A. (2002). On risk-prone peasants: Cultural transmission or sigmoid utility maximization? *Current Anthropology, 43*(5), 787–788.
Legare, C. H., Evans, E. M., Rosengren, K. S., & Harris, P. L. (2012). The coexistence of natural and supernatural explanations across cultures and development. *Child Psychology, 83,* 779–793.

Legare, C. H., & Gelman, S. A. (2008). Bewitchment, biology, or both: The co-existence of natural and supernatural explanatory frameworks across development. *Cognitive Science, 32,* 607–642.

Lichtenstein, S., & Slovic, P. (2006). The construction of preference: An overview. In S. Lichtenstein & P. Slovic (Eds.), *The Construction of preference* (pp. 1–40). Cambridge: Cambridge University Press.

Loomis, J. B., Bair, L. S., & González-Cabán, A. (2002). Language-related differences in a contingent valuation study: English versus Spanish. *American Journal of Agricultural Economics, 84*(4), 1091–1102.

Malinowski, B. (1992 [1948]). *Magic, science and religion.* Long Grove, IL: Waveland Press.

Mazur, J. E. (1987). An adjusting procedure for studying delayed reinforcement. In M. Commons, J. E. Mazur, J. A. Nevin, & H. Rachlin (Eds.), *Quantitative analyses of behavior* (pp. 55–73). London: Lawrence Erlbaum Associates, Publishers.

Medin, D. L., ojalehto, b., Marin, A., & Bang, M. (2014). Culture and epistemologies: Putting culture back into the ecosystem. *Advances in Culture and Psychology, 4,* 177–217.

Meyerhoff, J., & Liebe, U. (2009). Status quo effect in choice experiments: Empirical evidence on attitudes and choice task complexity. *Land Economics, 85*(3), 515–528.

Miyata, S. (2003). Household's risk attitudes in Indonesian villages. *Applied Economics, 35,* 573–583.

Morris, S., Carletto, C., Hoddinott, J., & Christiaensen, L. J. M. (2000). Validity of rapid estimates of household wealth and income for health surveys in rural Africa. *Journal of Epidemiology and Community Health, 54,* 381–387.

Nisbett, R., & Ross, L. (1980). *Human inference: Strategies and shortcomings of social judgment.* Englewood Cliffs, NJ: Prentice-Hall Inc.

Nisbett, R. E., Peng, K., Choi, I., & Norenzayan, A. (2001). Culture and systems of thought: Holistic versus analytic cognition. *Psychological Review, 108*(2), 291–310.

ojalehto, b., & Medin, D. (2015). Perspectives on culture and concepts. *Annual Review of Psychology, 66,* 249–275.

Orlove, B., Chiang, J. C. H., & Cane, M. A. (2000). Forecasting Andean rainfall and crop yield from the influence of El Nino on Pleiades visibility. *Nature, 403,* 68–71.

Pender, J. L. (1996). Discount rates and credit markets: Theory and evidence from rural India. *Journal of Development Economics, 50*(2), 257–296.

Piaget, J. (1928). *Judgment and reasoning in the child.* London: Routledge.

Poggie, J. J., & Pollnac, R. B. (1988). Danger and rituals of avoidance among New England fishermen. *Maritime Anthropology Studies, 1,* 66–78.

Poyer, L., & Kelly, R. L. (2000). Mystification of the Mikea: constructions of foraging identity in southwest Madagascar. *Journal of Anthropological Research, 56,* 163–185.

Ramos, A. R. (2012). The politics of perspectivism. *Annual Review of Anthropology, 41,* 481–494.

Reyes-García, V., Godoy, R., Huanca, T., Leonard, W. B., McDade, T., Tanner, S., et al. (2007). The origins of monetary income inequality: Patience, human capital, and division of labor. *Evolution and Human Behavior, 28,* 37–47.

Robberstad, B. (2005). Estimation of private and social time preferences for health in northern Tanzania. *Social Science and Medicine, 61,* 1597–1607.

Rogers, A. R. (1994). Evolution of time preference by natural selection. *American Economic Review, 84*(3), 460–481.

Ross, N. (2004). *Cognition and culture: Implications for theory and method.* Thousand Oaks, CA: Sage Publications Inc.

Rudski, J. M., & Edwards, A. (2007). Malinowski goes to college: Factors influencing students' use of ritual and superstition. *The Journal of General Psychology, 134*(4), 389–403.

Salali, G. D., & Migliano, A. B. (2015). Future discounting in Congo Basin hunter-gatherers declines with socio-economic transitions. *PLoS ONE, 10*(9), e0137806.

Samuelson, P. A. (1937). A note on measurement of utility. *The Review of Economic Studies, 4*(2), 155–161.

Schrire, C. (1984). Wild surmises on savage thoughts. In C. Schrire (Ed.), *Past and present in hunter-gatherer studies* (pp. 1–26). San Diego: Academic Press.

Sidky, H. (2004). *Perspectives on culture: A critical introduction to theory in cultural anthropology*. Upper Saddle River, NJ: Pearson.

Slovic, P. (1966). Risk-taking in children: Age and sex differences. *Child Development, 37*(1), 169–176.

Slovic, P. (1987). Perception of risk. *Science, 236,* 280–285.

Tache, B., & Sjaastad, E. (2010). Pastoralists' conceptions of poverty: An analysis of traditional and conventional indicators from Borana. *Ethiopia. World Development, 38*(8), 1168–1178.

Thaler, R. (1981). Some empirical evidence on dynamic inconsistency. *Economic Letters, 8,* 201–207.

Tucker, B. (2003). Mikea origins: Relicts or refugees? *Michigan Discussions in Anthropology, 14,* 193–215.

Tucker, B. (2006). A future-discounting explanation for the persistence of a mixed foraging/cultivation strategy among the Mikea of Madagascar. In D. Kennett & B. Winterhalder (Eds.), *Behavioral ecology and the transition to agriculture* (pp. 22–40). Berkeley: University of California Press.

Tucker, B. (2007). Perception of interannual covariation and diversification strategies for risk reduction among Mikea of Madagascar: Individual and social learning. *Human Nature, 18*(2), 162–180.

Tucker, B. (2012). Do risk and time experimental choices represent individual strategies for coping with poverty or conformity to social norms? Evidence from rural southwestern Madagascar. *Current Anthropology, 53,* 149–180.

Tucker, B., Huff, A., Tsiazonera, Tombo, J., Hajasoa, P., & Nagnisaha, C. (2011). When the wealthy are poor: Poverty explanations and local perspectives in southwestern Madagascar. *American Anthropologist, 113*(2), 291–305.

Tucker, B., Tombo, J., Tsiazonera, Hajasoa, P., Nagnisaha, C., Lahitoka, V. R., & Zahatsy, C. (2013). Beyond mean and variance: Economic risk versus perceived risk of farming, foraging, and fishing activities in southwestern Madagascar. *Human Ecology*, *41*(3), 393–407.

Tucker, B., Tsiazonera, Tombo, J., Hajasoa, P., & Nagnisaha, C. (2015). Ecological and cosmological coexistence thinking in a hypervariable environment: Causal models of economic success and failure among farmers, foragers, and fishermen of southwestern Madagascar. *Frontiers in Psychology*, *6*, 1–16.

Tucker, B., Tsimitamby, M., Humber, F., Benbow, S., & Iida, T. (2010). Foraging for development: A comparison of food insecurity, production, and risk among farmers, forest foragers, and marine foragers of southwestern Madagascar. *Human Organization*, *69*(4), 375–386.

Tversky, A., & Kahneman, D. (1974). Judgment under uncertainty: Heuristics and biases. *Science, 185*(4157), 1124–1131.

Tylor, E. B. (1958 [1871]). *Primitive culture.* New York: Harper & Row.

Uskul, A. K., Kitayama, S., & Nisbett, R. E. (2008). Ecocultural basis of cognition: Farmers and fishermen are more holistic than herders. *Proceedings of the National Academy of Sciences (USA), 105,* 8552–8556.

Van Hamme, L. J., & Wasserman, E. A. (1994). Cue competition in causality judgments: The role of non presentation of compound stimulus events. *Learning and Motivation, 25,* 127–151.

Vivieros de Castro, E. (2000). Cosmological deixis and Amerindian perspectivism. *Joural of the Royal Anthropological Institute, 4,* 469–488.

Von Neumann, J., & Morgenstern, O. (1953). *Theory of games and economic behavior* (3rd ed.). Princeton, NJ: Princeton University Press.

Waldmann, M. R., Hagmayer, Y., & Blaisdell, A. P. (2006). Beyond the information given: Causal models in learning and reasoning. *Current Directions in Psychological Science, 15,* 307–311.

Ward, W. D., & Jenkins, H. M. (1965). The display of information and the judgment of contingency. *Canadian Journal of Psychology, 19,* 231–241.

Wik, M., Kebede, T. A., Bergland, O., & Holden, S. T. (2004). On the measurement of risk aversion from experimental data. *Applied Economics, 36,* 2443–2451.

Wilmsen, E. N., & Denbow, J. R. (1990). Paradigmatic history of San-speaking peoples and current attempts at revision. *Current Anthropology, 31*(5), 489–524.
Winterhalder, B., & Goland, C. (1997). An evolutionary ecology perspective on diet choice, risk, and plant domestication. In K. J. Gremillion (Ed.), *People, plants and landscapes: Studies in paleoethnobotony* (pp. 123–160). Tuscaloosa: University of Alabama Press.
Winterhalder, B., & Kennett, D. J. (2009). Four neglected concepts with a role to play in explaining the origins of agriculture. *Current Anthropology, 50*(5), 645–648.
Yount, J. W., Tsiazonera, & Tucker, B. (2001). Constructing Mikea identity: Past or present links to forest and foraging. *Ethnohistory*, *48*, 3257–3291.
Zuckerman, M. (1991). *Psychology of personality*. New York: Cambridge University Press.
Zuk, M. (2013). *Paleofantasy: What evolution really teaches us about sex, diet, and how we live*. New York: W.W. Norton & Co.

Chapter 4
A Fuzzy-Trace Theory of Risk and Time Preferences in Decision Making: Integrating Cognition and Motivation

Shahin Rahimi-Golkhandan, David M.N. Garavito, Bertrand B. Reyna-Brainerd and Valerie F. Reyna

Introduction

In this chapter, we provide an overview of fuzzy-trace theory (FTT) and its implications for risk and time preferences. FTT is a dual-process model of reasoning, judgment, and decision making, as well as their development from early childhood to old age. The fuzzy-trace interpretation of risk and time preferences brings together concepts from behavioral economics, psychology, and neuroscience. The most important concept is mental representation, specifically verbatim (literal surface form) and gist (bottom-line meaning) representations. The differences between these types of representation determine risk and time preferences, in combination with social values as well as developmental and individual differences. In particular, sensitivity to rewards and inhibitory control vary across the life span and across people.

FTT's conceptualization of sensitivity to reward and inhibitory control, which contribute to impulsivity, contrasts with that of other dual-process accounts. FTT proposes that gist representations, which support fuzzy yet advanced intuition, are unconscious and automatic, whereas verbatim representations support precise analysis. We begin by introducing the foundations of FTT in economics and prior psychological theories. We then review the basic concepts of the theory, and how they explain risk preferences and time preferences, including delay of gratification. We distinguish risk preference, impulsivity versus intuition, temporal discounting (i.e., delay discounting), and delay of gratification, as well as FTT's approach compared to standard dual-process models of judgment and decision making. As we discuss, there are parallels in FTT's explanations of people's willingness to

S. Rahimi-Golkhandan · D.M.N. Garavito
B.B. Reyna-Brainerd · V.F. Reyna (✉)
Human Neuroscience Institute, Cornell University,
MVR G331, Ithaca, NY 14853, USA
e-mail: vr53@cornell.edu

J.R. Stevens (ed.), *Impulsivity*, Nebraska Symposium on Motivation 64,
DOI 10.1007/978-3-319-51721-6_4

tolerate risk as well as their willingness to wait for future rewards. We conclude that FTT yields qualitatively different interpretations of risk preference and time preference compared to other theories.

Risk Preferences

Economic theories provide a useful framework for quantifying overall value of a course of action, with its roots in mathematics and applications to rational self-interest (von Neumann and Morgenstern 1944; see Tversky and Kahneman 1986). Therefore, we begin with a discussion of core economic principles. Expected value is one of the most well-known antecedents of economic theory, and it describes decision making through the use of two variables: probability and outcome. Probability could be the odds of winning a lottery ticket, and outcome would be the amount of money awarded for winning. These two factors form the core of classical decision theory, and they have been probed for decades by asking people to choose between outcomes that vary in risk. A typical question follows:

(A) Winning $100 for sure
(B) 0.50 probability of winning $200 and a 0.50 probability of winning nothing.

Option B is riskier than Option A because the outcome is more uncertain. That is, following the economic definition of risk, Option B has higher variance in its outcomes (Fox and Tannenbaum 2011). A risk-neutral person would be indifferent between these two options because $0.50 \times \$200 = \$100$. If people interpreted probabilities and outcomes linearly, they would be risk neutral. However, after this initial mathematical formulation, it became obvious that most people are not risk neutral. Instead, they prefer Option A over Option B, demonstrating risk aversion.

In an effort to account for risk aversion among other effects, economists developed the theory of expected utility (EUT). EUT represents outcomes nonlinearly as a negatively accelerated function of objective magnitude. In other words, 50% of $200 is worth *less* than $100. This nonlinearity explains the preference for the sure option (Option A), which is discounted less than the larger value in the risky option. The overall expected utility of an option is then a function of its probability and the subjective value of its outcome. von Neumann and Morgenstern (1944) defined rational decision makers as people who *consistently* choose the option with higher expected utility.

In 1979, Kahneman and Tversky reviewed evidence showing that people did not respond to decisions involving losses in the same way that they did to decisions involving gains. Consider receiving $200, but being required to make the following choice:

(A) Losing $100 for sure
(B) 0.50 probability of losing $200 and 0.50 probability of losing nothing.

For losses, most people prefer the risky option (Option B). Because the same person usually prefers the sure option for gains but the risky option for losses, he or she does not have a consistent risk preference. This shift in risk preferences is called a framing effect, as it is caused by the way in which the options are posed.

Kahneman and Tversky (1979) developed an alternative to EUT called prospect theory to account for several effects including framing. Prospect theory retained the idea of a nonlinear perception of outcomes from EUT, and it added a nonlinear perception of probabilities from subjective expected utility theory (Savage 1954). Ultimately, the theory predicted a fourfold effect such that people were risk seeking for gains with small probabilities and risk averse for losses with small probabilities, in addition to the framing effect described above (Tversky and Kahneman 1992). They described gains and losses as shifts away from a reference point, and these differences were often subjective rather than objective. For example, note that in the examples above, the net outcomes are mathematically identical for gains and losses. However, the outcomes described as losses feel different than those described as gains, and they elicit opposite risk preferences.

FTT was built on the foundation of prospect theory, and it carries the notion of distortions of probabilities and outcomes much further through the concept of gist. Gist incorporates both semantic content and context to represent the overall interpreted meaning of the options of a decision. The concepts of verbatim and gist representations and their application to decision making are discussed in more detail below.

Fuzzy-Trace Theory

According to FTT, when people are presented with information, they will, separately and simultaneously, encode it into both types of representations: verbatim and gist (Reyna and Brainerd 2011; Reyna 2012). Verbatim representations capture surface-level, exact details that were present. In contrast, gist representations encompass the general (or "fuzzy") bottom-line meaning of information. Although both verbatim and gist representations are encoded concurrently, they are independent and stored separately. Furthermore, gist is not extracted from verbatim representations (Reyna 2012). Each of these types of mental representations corresponds to, and supports, a different way of thinking. That is, verbatim representations facilitate precise analysis, representation, and calculation, whereas gist representations facilitate fuzzy, impressionistic thinking.

Fuzzy thinking explains many phenomena involving risk and time preferences. When a person is presented with a gamble and the outcome is not guaranteed, the gist representation that a person extracts as the bottom-line meaning of a gamble may be "there is a chance of winning something or nothing in this gamble." In contrast, the verbatim representation would constitute a much more specific and detailed representation of the presented information (e.g., a "0.50 probability of winning \$200"). In FTT, the same information is encoded at different levels of a continuum that varies from gist to verbatim. One end of the continuum represents the simplest, bottom-line meaning (gist), and the other end represents the most precise and detailed (verbatim) representation (Wilhelms et al. 2014). When people are confronted with a decision, they encode both gist and verbatim representations simultaneously, but, depending on individual differences, they rely more on either the gist or verbatim representations of the information (Reyna and Brainerd 2011).

FTT explains phenomena from the decision-making literature through different means than traditional theories. As discussed, prospect theory differentiates between gains and losses in its predictions about decision making, which depend on how the prospects are *framed*, relative to a reference point (e.g., the status quo). The predictions set forth by FTT go beyond traditional theories by incorporating a decision maker's interpretations and implicit connotations behind the presented options, when making decisions (Kühberger and Tanner 2010; Reyna 2012). In FTT, framing is explained using the ideas that (a) people draw out the gist of the choices present in a decision and (b) subsequently retrieve and apply their values to this gist (Reyna 2008; Wilhelms et al. 2015a).

Consider the gain problem presented earlier (i.e., winning \$100 vs. 0.50 probability of winning \$200; otherwise nothing). Research has shown that the above choice is translated into gist as a choice between "winning some money" versus "winning some money or winning no money" (e.g., Kühberger and Tanner 2010; Reyna 2012; Reyna et al. 2014). Then, in order to make a choice, people apply their values to the decision. In this case, a relevant value is "winning money is good," favoring winning some money over winning nothing and, thus, choosing the sure option. This explains the typical observed preference for risk aversion in the gain frame.

Preference for the sure option in the gain frame contrasts with the previously noted preference for the risky option (Option B) when the question is restated as a loss (losing \$100 for sure versus a 0.50 probability of winning \$200; otherwise nothing). In terms of gist, the choices in the loss frame are interpreted as "losing some money" versus "losing some money or losing no money." Once again, people apply their values, such as "I do not like losing money," to these gist representations of the choices, so now they decide that losing no money, the chance associated with the gamble, is better than losing some money, the guarantee in the sure option, and select the gamble. These gist representations are not arbitrary, but rather capture the simplest distinctions along the dimensions of probability and outcome. Often, multiple gist representations are extracted from the same information. As we discuss below, processing gravitates to the simplest gist representation that accomplishes the task. In this instance, the task is to make a choice between options.

Variations on Framing Effects

According to FTT, decisions can change depending on which values are retrieved and applied to a particular decision, which can be cued by the context (Reyna

2008). This prediction about cued values has been repeatedly demonstrated in both laboratory tasks and in real-life decision making (Mills et al. 2008; Reyna and Mills 2014). There are other differences that can affect risk preferences as in framing effects, too. For example, if both gain and loss frames of identical choices are shown to the same decision maker, the person's decisions and preferences will tend to be more consistent across gain and loss frames. This within-subject consistency reflects metacognitive monitoring and inhibition (Stanovich and West 2008; Liberali et al. 2012). In other words, some people monitor the decisions that are being made and restrain prepotent responses (Reyna and Mills 2007; Stanovich and West 2008; Reyna and Brainerd 2011).

Another variation on framing effects involves truncating the risky option in order to test alternative theories of risk preference (e.g., Reyna and Brainerd 1991, 1995; Reyna et al. 2014). Truncating the risky choice in different ways highlights or de-emphasizes the zero complement. In the previous examples, the zero complements are the 50% chance of gaining $0 in the gain frame and the 50% chance of losing $0 in the loss frame. Truncation is a sensitive theoretical variation of the framing task, which is used to manipulate the type of representation that is relied on. These truncation effects allow for a greater understanding of how framing effects can be altered depending on whether a gist representation is cued or a verbatim representation is cued.

For example, if one were to remove the zero complement from the risky option of the gain frame in a framing task (i.e., leaving only gaining $100 for sure versus a 50% chance of gaining $200), the result would emphasize the trade-offs between probability and outcome and minimize the categorical difference between the choices (winning some money vs. winning some money). Thus, according to FTT, removing the zero complement of the gamble would diminish framing effects. Alternatively, removing the *non*zero complement (i.e., leaving only gaining $100 for sure vs. a 50% chance of gaining $0) highlights the categorical difference between the choices (winning some money vs. winning no money). The theory also predicts that highlighting of a categorical contrast would result in an increase in framing effects. Both of these truncation results have been obtained not only in the context of tests of FTT and prospect theory, but also in independent tests in diverse populations (for a review, see Kühberger and Tanner 2010). All of the experiments on truncation have confirmed predictions of FTT and also disconfirmed predictions of prospect theory (e.g., removing the zero complement eliminates framing effects despite the presence of all theoretically relevant probabilities and outcomes).

Although it may appear that truncation effects are caused or otherwise affected by underlying ambiguity, this is not the case. Chick et al. (2016) conducted a study involving these framing task truncations. In this study, the participants were given clear instructions about how to interpret the omitted portions of the questions. Using our example, these instructions made sure that if participants knew that there was a guarantee of gaining $100 versus a gamble with a 50% chance of gaining $0, the truncated part of this decision must be a 50% chance of gaining $200 and nothing else (i.e., not 50% chance of "about" or "at least" $200). The participants were not only told clear instructions, but they were also quizzed before and after the

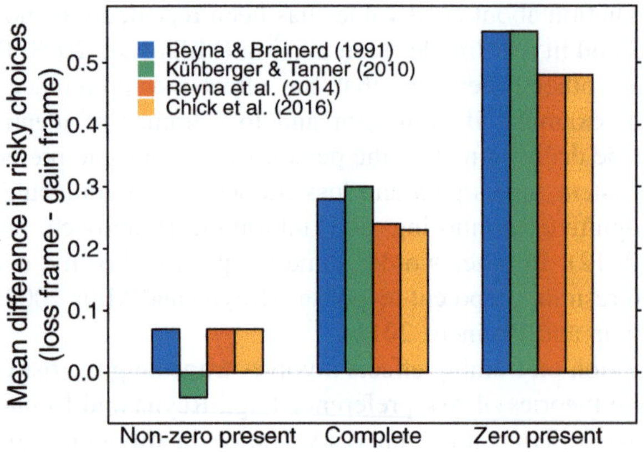

Fig. 4.1 *Bars* represent framing bias yielding a score that could vary from −1.0 (100% risky choices in the gain frame and 0% in the loss frame) to 1.0 (100% risky choices in the loss frame and 0% in the gain frame, standard framing). Framing bias of zero corresponds to no framing effect. Focusing on the nonzero complement (e.g., gain: "1/3 probability that 600 people are saved", loss: "2/3 probability that 600 people die") is presented at the *left*. Both complements are presented (e.g., gain: "1/3 probability that 600 people are saved and 2/3 probability that no one is saved", loss: "2/3 probability that 600 people die and 1/3 probability that no one dies") as shown in the *middle*. Only the zero complement is presented (e.g., gain: "2/3 probability that no one is saved", loss: "1/3 probability that no one dies") at the *right*. Chick et al. (2016) data are for participants who passed the ambiguity quiz

task in order to ensure that they comprehended the choices as the experimenters intended. The participants were also quizzed in order to rule out that filling in the truncated portions of the choices was due to rote memorization of the practice examples rather than true disambiguation of subsequent decisions. The instructions, which were followed by almost all of the participants because they passed the quizzes, controlled for several possible effects of ambiguity and the effects of the truncations remained resilient (Chick et al. 2016). Figure 4.1 shows the average framing effects in four studies on truncation (Reyna and Brainerd 1991; Kühberger and Tanner 2010; Reyna et al. 2014; Chick et al. 2016), all of which show robust effects of truncation as predicted by FTT. In some studies, participants received disambiguation instructions before attempting framing tasks. Presenting the zero risky complement (emphasizing "gist") increased framing, whereas presenting the nonzero risky complement (emphasizing "verbatim") attenuated framing, relative to the standard condition in which both risky complements were presented ("mixed").

Development: Differences and Reversals

FTT posits that both verbatim and gist processing (e.g., through improved analytical and mathematical ability and improved capacity to extract the bottom-line meaning from information, respectively) develop with age. Moreover, the tendency to rely on gist representations increases from childhood to adulthood even when children have the full capacity to extract the bottom-line meaning from information, for example, using child-normed lists of words for recall (Brainerd et al. 2011). Thus, *preference* for gist processing is developmentally advanced, increasing with age and expertise (e.g., Adam and Reyna 2005; Reyna and Lloyd 2006; Brainerd et al. 2008; Reyna et al. 2014).

Applying these developmental tenets, FTT is able to explain certain findings that alternative theories are unable to shed light on. Multiple studies have found that framing effects grow stronger with age and expertise from childhood to adulthood, as initially predicted by FTT (e.g., adults show larger framing effects than adolescents or children; Reyna and Ellis 1994; Reyna et al. 2011). To illustrate, Fig. 4.2 displays data from three studies (Reyna and Ellis 1994; Reyna et al. 2011, 2014) in which participants of different ages and expertise levels completed framing tasks. Reyna et al. (2014), for instance, recruited college students, post-college adults, and intelligence agents—who were trained in risky decision making about national security—to complete 30 gain and loss decisions. Figure 4.2 shows that framing biases are maintained and can grow as people develop across age and expertise: The largest framing effect is observed among intelligence agents who were the most advanced participants in terms of training and experience regarding risky decision making.

Increases in cognitive biases from childhood to adulthood are categorized as developmental reversals. This is called a reversal because there is an *increase* in error rate with increased age and expertise. Framing effects occur despite the fact that children and adults both have the capacity to determine the expected value of

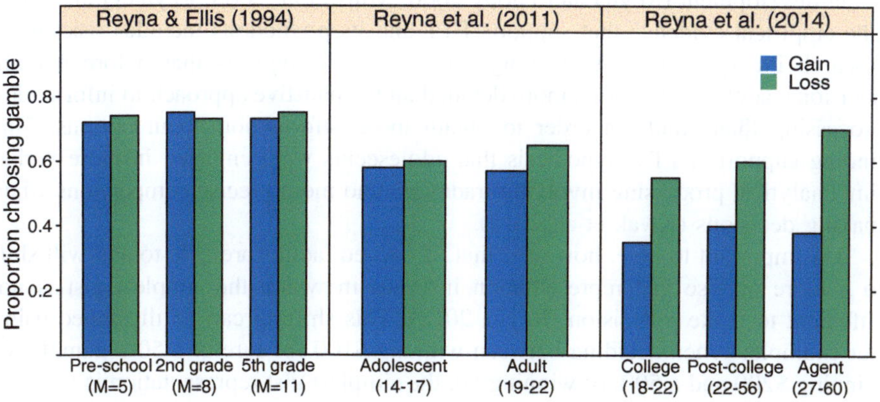

Fig. 4.2 *Bars* represent the proportion of choosing the risky choices in gain and loss frames. The values in *brackets* are either the average age of participants (Reyna and Ellis 1994) or their age range (Reyna et al. 2011, 2014). The values for Reyna and Ellis (1994) are estimated from Figs. 1 and 3 (p. 278) of that article. Reyna et al.'s (2011) values are also estimated from Fig. 2 (p. 1131) of that article

their options by roughly multiplying each outcome by its respective probability (Reyna and Brainerd 1994). In fact, this skill also improves with development from childhood to adulthood (Weller et al. 2011; Corbin et al. 2016). Additionally, older adults and experts show larger framing effects, and they are also more confident in their biased judgments than college students (Reyna et al. 2014). It is apparent, then, that although reliance on gist representations and gist processing is associated with developed reasoning and decision making, this same reliance can facilitate the susceptibility to cognitive biases that are meaning based (Weldon et al. 2013; Reyna et al. 2014). Whereas standard theories would classify these biases as unthinking errors, according to FTT, these biases are expected outcomes caused by an increase in the reliance on the bottom-line meaning, or gist, of information.

The results above, although unexplained by other theories, are consistent with the predictions of FTT. On the one hand, people at more advanced stages of development and expertise (e.g., children vs. adolescents or novices vs. experts) rely more on gist processing, as opposed to verbatim processing. On the other hand, children (and to a lesser extent adolescents) are more likely to rely on precise verbatim details when reasoning or making decisions (Reyna 2011). We are not claiming that children and adolescents are more quantitative when they make decisions (i.e., calculating and using exact probabilities and outcomes; Levin et al. 2007). Computation improves from childhood to adulthood (Reyna and Brainerd 1994). However, less developed individuals are more likely to rely on representations closer to the precise and literal—verbatim—end of a representational continuum. Hence, adults often rely on categorical differences between options in order to make decisions, whereas children make finer distinctions that are within their competence (Reyna and Brainerd 1994, 1995; Reyna and Ellis 1994; Reyna 1996; Reyna and Lloyd 2006; Reyna et al. 2011, 2015a).

Studies on real-life decision making have also supported this theoretical idea about development (Reyna and Farley 2006; Mills et al. 2008; Reyna et al. 2011). The empirical evidence that supports FTT and its predictions includes risk-taking research incorporating eye tracking. This research suggests that before making decisions, adolescents used a more detailed and exhaustive approach to information processing than adults in order to obtain more information about options. This finding supports FTT's hypothesis that adolescents were engaged in more verbatim–analytical processing involving trade-offs and more precise comparisons when making decisions (Kwak et al. 2015).

It is important to note, however, that, if needed, adults are able to and will shift to a more precise gist representation in cases in which the simplest gist is not sufficient to make a decision (Reyna 2012). This shifting can be illustrated using our example: When deciding between winning $100 for sure or a 50% gamble for winning $200 and a 50% of winning $0, the simplest gist representation is winning something versus winning something or winning nothing. A categorical distinction between something and nothing allows a person to make a decision when relying on this representation. In contrast, a choice between a 54% chance of winning $200 and a 46% chance of winning $0 versus a 55% chance of winning $180 and a 45% chance of winning $0 would demand a more precise representation than the previous, categorical gist representation (because both options offer a chance to win something or nothing; see the Allais paradox as discussed in Reyna and Brainerd 2011): Assuming that 54 and 55% are perceived as similar per Stevens (2016), an ordinal representation would distinguish a chance of winning a higher amount (or nothing) versus a chance of winning a lower amount (or nothing), favoring the former.

By acknowledging the role of the reliance on gist representations, FTT is able to illuminate mechanisms behind developmental shifts in decision making (Reyna and Lloyd 2006; Reyna et al. 2014). Specifically, adolescents often appear more logical and calculating, yet take more risks. Similarly, experts are also more likely to rely on gist processing than novices. When it comes to making choices in a person's field of expertise, experts are more likely to rely on their intuition, whereas novices are more likely to rely on more precise and detailed representations and, in some instances, on rote memorization of verbatim details (Reyna and Lloyd 2006).

These FTT tenets imply that for risky decision making, mature qualitative processing which encapsulates the bottom-line gist is gradually given precedence over precise processing of risks and rewards of decision options as age and experience increase. This shift in preference for gist processing, theoretically, results in a protective effect against unnecessary and unhealthy risks and risk taking, as precise comparisons between risks and benefits (or rewards) give way to principles such as "no risk is better than some" (e.g., Mills et al. 2008; Reyna et al. 2011). As decision makers process information less precisely, they rely more on the core gist of the decision, which, in general, reduces risk taking because the risk–reward ratio is often favorable for single instances of risk taking (Reyna and Farley 2006; Reyna and Mills 2014; Wilhelms et al. 2015b). When relying on gist-based representations and processing, decision makers will also apply a number of principles in order to choose between the options that make up a decision. For example, a person relying heavily on gist processing will apply bottom-line gist principles (e.g., "it is better to be safe than sorry") when making a decision. These principles, being less verbatim and more gist-like by definition, ignore specific details about the potential risks or benefits (e.g., probability or magnitude). When relying on and using verbatim processing, conversely, a decision maker trades off risks and benefits. Because the benefits of risky behavior are higher than the corresponding risks more often than not, verbatim representations objectively favor risk taking (Mills et al. 2008).

As an example, the exact (verbatim) probability of contracting HIV from a single act of unprotected sex is very low relative to the potential gains that one may perceive (Wilhelms et al. 2015a, b). This is particularly true when considering the difference in risk between committing one action, such as unprotected sex, versus repeating the same action multiple times (cumulative risk; Mills et al. 2008). These precise, verbatim comparisons and the associated trading-off between risks and rewards stand in stark contrast to the gist representation of the situation, however. The gist of this decision whether or not to take the risk associated with this one act would be that there is some chance of HIV versus no chance of HIV. Most people would categorize this risk as "bad" and a related gist principle might be "it only takes once to get HIV," indicating that unprotected sex (and the extreme risk associated) should be avoided categorically (Reyna 2008; Wilhelms et al. 2014). The connection between risk taking and the reliance on gist processing and gist principles has been supported by empirical findings which have shown that increases with age are associated with increased reliance on gist processing, more frequent agreement with and use of gist principles, and that risk preference decreases from childhood to adulthood (Reyna and Ellis 1994; Rivers et al. 2008; Defoe et al. 2015). We will delve deeper into developmental differences and FTT's explanation for these differences (compared to standard theories) in the following section on impulsivity and intuition.

Intuition and Impulsivity: FTT Versus Standard Dual-Process Theories

A major difference between FTT and standard dual-process theories is the distinction between intuition and impulsivity. In FTT, intuition and impulsivity, the latter operationalized as the failure of self-control or inhibition (Reyna and Mills 2007), are seen as separate and distinct from one another. Instead of being collapsed with an array of evolutionarily primitive System 1 processes, intuition is considered an unconscious, parallel, and impressionistic kind of processing that relies on gist representations, which is developmentally advanced.

In standard dual-process theories of risk taking, there is an emphasis on the conflict between impulsive and deliberative thinking (see Cokely and Kelley, 2009; Reyna and Rivers 2008). This emphasis is within the context of a dual-systems account that discriminates between two types of processes. System 1 processes are quick and general, whereas System 2 processes are deliberative and logical (Epstein 1994; Steinberg 2008; Kahneman 2011; Casey and Caudle 2013; see also Type 1 and 2 processes in Evans and Stanovich 2013). Intuitive and impulsive thinking (as these concepts are collapsed in standard theories) is often considered less advanced, attributed to children and traditionally linked to errors in judgment and decision making, and generally giving way to complex and analytical processing in adulthood. In other words, the deliberative, calculating thinking found in System 2 processes is analytical and can correct for the errors made by intuitive thinking and is associated with more advanced reasoning (see also Peters et al. 2006). This analytical thinking is also the type that, according to standard theories, develops with age and expertise. More recently, standard dual-process theories have also classified a third kind of processing, which is associated with reflection and inhibition (i.e., "the reflective mind"; Evans and Stanovich 2013). It is also important to note that these systems in standard dual-process theories are default interventionist (see De Neys and Vanderputte, 2011). This means that System 2 processes, and the thinking associated with them, are invoked if an anomaly is detected (i.e., when System 1 thinking requires overriding; Kahneman 2011; Evans and Stanovich 2013). Developmental dual-process theories similarly assume that impulsivity is the source of unhealthy risks in adolescence. Thus, standard dual-process approaches attribute age-related differences in decisions to adolescents' heightened levels of sensation seeking, impulsivity, and lack of self-control (Wilhelms and Reyna 2013).

In FTT, risk taking concerns more than simply System 1 and System 2 thinking. Although standard dual-process theories have described the analytical thinking present in System 2 as advanced reasoning, FTT also incorporates intuitive reasoning using gist representations in its predictions. As gist-based processing is fuzzy and qualitative rather than exact and analytical, it is discussed in terms of intuition. This type of reasoning based on intuition is not categorized as impulsivity; however, gist-based intuition *is* developmentally superior, as reliance on gist processing increases from youth to adulthood and from inexperience to expertise. This shift facilitates making healthy decisions and avoiding unnecessary risks. FTT posits that it is this type of reasoning that most adults use when making judgments, inferences, and decisions about risk. Reliance on gist and gist-based processes and intuition is an advanced mode of thinking based on the underlying meaning of data and information instead of literal details (Adam and Reyna 2005; Reyna and Lloyd 2006).

Because reliance on qualitative, intuitive decision making is associated with impulsive decision making and risk taking in standard dual-process theories, FTT's predictions may be seen as counterintuitive. In other words, the idea that intuitive processing develops with age and expertise and is the foundation for higher-level cognition, as opposed to more deliberative processing, may seem somewhat improbable. Yet, empirical evidence and laboratory tasks support this prediction and highlight the advantages of intuition. This idea that gist-based intuition is developmentally advanced and cognitively superior has been supported by research showing that not only does reliance on gist-based processing encourage accurate decision making in realistic scenarios (Reyna and Lloyd 2006), but gist-based intuition underlies sophisticated and accurate cognition (Usher et al. 2011; Rusou et al. 2013). In contrast to standard dual-process theory, FTT would not classify the intuitions of experts with impulsivity found in children as the same type or system of reasoning (Reyna et al. 2015a). Thus, according to FTT, experts rely on educated intuition, which has been linked to superior decision-making behavior as assessed by agreement with practice guidelines and other evaluation rubrics (Reyna and Lloyd 2006; Reyna et al. 2015a). More generally, gist-based intuition has been associated with healthier decisions, and as assessed in randomized experiments, inducing such intuition improves the quality of decision making and reduces unhealthy choices (e.g., Reyna and Mills 2014; Fraenkel et al. 2015; Wolfe et al. 2015).

In sum, by distinguishing between intuition and impulsivity, as well as taking into account the distinct role of cognitive representations, FTT sheds light on the increase in risk taking that occurs during adolescence despite a decrease in risk preferences. This theory both predicts and rationalizes counterintuitive observations, for example, that children make risky choices more than adolescents under controlled conditions in the laboratory, contradicting standard dual-process theory.

In standard dual-process theory, impulsivity and intuition are collapsed into System 1 processes (e.g., Steinberg 2008; Casey and Caudle 2013), but research shows they diverge predictably. FTT conceptualizes impulsivity and intuition as divergent processes that develop independently and affect behavior differently (Reyna 2013; Reyna et al. 2015b). According to FTT, developmental trajectories of impulsivity and intuition proceed in opposite directions: Impulsivity decreases from childhood to adulthood, whereas cumulative experience in life—either as people age or progress from being a novice to an expert—enhances gist-based intuition (Reyna and Lloyd 2006; Reyna and Rivers 2008; Reyna and Brainerd 2011). Thus, research not only refutes the view that intuition is a developmentally primitive process (Barrouillet 2011), but it shows that gist-based intuition underlies developmentally advanced thinking.

Time Preferences

Armed with our distinctions grounded in research on risk preferences, we now apply these to time preferences. Time preferences involve preferences for immediate versus later rewards, and, more generally, future orientation (Frederick et al. 2002; Stevens 2016). In this context, impulsivity refers to the inability to wait for greater rewards, succumbing instead to immediate pleasures. As we discussed, the literature on risk preferences shows that different presentations of the same information (i.e., information that describes the same objective consequences, such as winning $100) elicit different mental representations, which in turn modulates risky choices. We argue that similar factors are at work in time preferences. Thus, cueing different mental representations of rewards by presenting the reward in different ways (e.g., *a delicious salad* instead of a *low-calorie salad*) would be expected to shape the gist of rewards, effectively mediating the relationship between reward sensitivity and unhealthy choices by changing the meaning of options (see also Ochsner and Gross 2008; Zayas et al. 2014). Moreover, as discussed in detail below, different levels of representation would be expected to influence time preferences by focusing processing on simple gist distinctions that promote insightful intuition.

FTT proposes two distinct routes to risky decision making and unhealthy behavior: One is deliberative, analytical reasoning that we have discussed, which relies on superficial, verbatim mental representations of choices that emphasize trading-off risk for reward. The second route to unhealthy choices is impulsive reactivity that accompanies a dopaminergic response to reward (e.g., food or alcohol; Reyna and Farley 2006). Impulsivity has been implicated in a range of health outcomes, including sexual health, substance abuse, and obesity (Metcalfe and Mischel 1999; Reyna and Farley 2006; Weller et al. 2008).

With regard to time preferences, impulsivity, as a multifaceted construct, has been operationalized as both a preference for smaller, immediate rewards over larger, delayed rewards and a tendency to take risks (Dalley et al. 2011). However, correlations are negligible or nonexistent between risky decision making and choices between immediate and delayed reward (de Water et al. 2014). In spite of the partial overlap between the neural correlates of temporal discounting and risk preference, distinct neural systems are involved (see Robbins and Dalley, this volume). The regions showing more activity during risky choices, relative to those between immediate and delayed rewards, are the lateral prefrontal cortex (PFC) and the parietal cortex (Weber and Huettel 2008). In contrast, the activity of posterior cingulate cortex (Weber and Huettel 2008) and the middle occipital areas (Peters and Buchel 2009) is higher for choices between immediate and delayed rewards than for risky choices. However, neural correlates are not definitive evidence for distinct processing. Instead, empirically supported theoretical distinctions are needed in order to interpret neural activity. Therefore, we discuss the theoretical underpinnings of time preferences.

First, we compare and contrast temporal discounting with delay of gratification. Then, we discuss the implications of steep discounting and evaluate the evidence on the malleability of discounting tendencies. This discussion is followed by an in-depth review of FTT's predictions regarding the manipulation of temporal discounting. We show how standard dual-process models fail to capture the whole picture about the mechanisms involved in the manipulation of temporal discounting. More specifically, we discuss the role of cueing gist principles and, consequently, gist-based processing on altering temporal discounting and present specific hypotheses based on FTT. We wrap up with a review of recent findings that show qualitative, gist mental representations of core social and moral values (i.e., gist principles) are stronger predictors of delay of gratification than verbatim, analytical processing.

Temporal Discounting Versus Delay of Gratification

Although the operationalization of temporal discounting and delay of gratification and the tasks used to measure them are superficially similar, they do not measure the same thing. To illustrate, delay of gratification is often defined as the extent to which one can wait for a larger reward, which is distinct from preference for it (Peake, this volume), whereas temporal discounting, defined as the tendency to weigh delayed rewards with less subjective value than immediate rewards, characterizes the degree to which later rewards are preferred to sooner ones (Frederick et al. 2002; Zayas et al. 2014). Thus, temporal discounting is traditionally conceptualized as a continuous trade-off between different quantities of reward and time (Doyle 2013) that reflects the degree to which the magnitude of delayed rewards compensates for the time until their delivery (Prelec and Loewenstein 1998; Zimbardo and Boyd 1999; Dai et al. 2014). Therefore, whereas temporal discounting tasks measure time preferences using a series of choices between immediate rewards and larger delayed rewards, delay-of-gratification tasks measure the ability to sustain an initial choice and resist temptations over time in order to obtain a larger reward (Reynolds and Schiffbauer 2005).

Discount Rate as an Index of Impulsivity

The main index of temporal discounting, which is argued to be a stable individual difference (Kirby 2009), is called *the discount rate*, which measures the rate of discounting over time. Participants respond to a series of questions in which they choose between an immediate reward (e.g., \$100 now) and a larger delayed reward (e.g., \$200 in 30 days). Modeling techniques use these choices to calculate an indifference point at which certain magnitudes of time and delayed reward induce indifference between the immediate and delayed options. Different mathematical models have been put forward that quantify the relationship between the delay to the receipt of some reward and its present value (Koffarnus et al. 2013). The most popular of these is the hyperbolic model (Mazur 1987) in which the discount parameter (k) is calculated using the following formula: $V = A/(1 + kD)$. V is the subjective value of reward A at the delay of D, and k is a free parameter related to the rate at which later rewards are devalued as a function of delay (Koffarnus et al. 2013). Discounting rates systematically decrease as a function of development (Green et al. 1994), with the most notable drop being between the ages of 20–30 years, after which the discount rate remains relatively stable (Green et al. 1996). Given that a high discount rate indicates a preference for smaller, immediate rewards, the age-related decrease of discount rate is taken to reflect changes in overall impulsivity.

Heightened discount rates have been linked to a range of unhealthy behaviors including tobacco, drug and alcohol abuse, obesity, as well as gambling problems, and low academic achievement (Petry and Casarella 1999; Weller et al. 2008; Bickel and Mueller 2009; Bickel et al. 2012, this volume; Johnson and Bruner 2011). Steep discounting, which acts as a trans-disease process and operates as a biomarker across a range of clinical conditions (Rachlin et al. 1991; Bickel and Mueller 2009; Bickel 2012), is linked to many modifiable health-related behaviors that contribute to major causes of preventable death and disease (Sheffer et al. 2016). Given that excessive discounting underlies choices that lead to negative health conditions (Koffarnus et al. 2013), it is important to question whether discount rates are modifiable, in order to improve choice behavior, which, in turn, would enhance health and quality of life. The traditional view is that such rates are not modifiable because they represent traits that distinguish types of people, although they vary across development.

Malleability of Discount Rate

Temporal discounting has been linked to various social and cultural factors including attitudes toward time (Hsee 1999; Weber and Hsee 1999), socioeconomic status (Sweitzer et al. 2008; Griskevicius et al. 2011; Sweitzer et al. 2012), age (Green et al. 1999; Steinberg et al. 2009), and education (Jaroni et al. 2004). Thus, an important question is whether discounting is a result of the current environment and a stable trait or is a modifiable pattern of behavior, one which can be regarded as a state variable (Odum 2011). Existing literature suggests that temporal discounting may indeed be a stable trait due to the fact that discount rate has a high test–retest reliability for periods of up to one year (Simpson and Vuchinich 2000; Baker et al. 2003; Ohmura et al. 2006; Takahashi et al. 2007; Beck and Triplett 2009; Kirby 2009; Black and Rosen 2011) and that discount rates of different commodities are highly correlated (Bickel et al. 2011b; Odum 2011).

However, certain interventions and environmental manipulations have been successful in altering patterns of discounting (for a review see Koffarnus et al. 2013). Among these are intensive therapeutic interventions such as working memory training (Bickel et al. 2011b) and stimulations of dorsolateral PFC (Cho et al. 2010; Sheffer et al. 2013). Less intensive interventions include those that cue future thinking by evoking future events specific to each participant (Peters and Buchel 2009), align delayed reward to a specific date (e.g., "15th of July" instead of "in 30 days") (Read et al. 2005), as well as reframing choices to emphasize the "hidden zero" in the traditional format of temporal discounting choices (Magen et al. 2008; Radu et al. 2011; Magen et al. 2014). The latter manipulation of the hidden zero in temporal discounting problems is the most obviously connected to the tenets of FTT. FTT offers the promise of changing attitudes and behaviors by changing mental representations of choices (Reyna et al. 2015a).

Specifically, Magen et al. (2008) first demonstrated that adding the hidden zero into the choice task (e.g., "$100 today and $0 in 30 days or $0 today and $200 in 30 days" instead of "$100 today or $200 in 30 days") significantly reduced discount rates in their sample. From the perspective of FTT, adding hidden zeros to both parts of the problem emphasizes good and bad categorical distinctions for immediate and delayed choices—that is, this manipulation facilitates categorical distinctions between *some now but none later* versus *none now but some later* using gist representations of choice options. The reframing effect of adding the hidden zero into the temporal discounting choice task is similar to that of Allais paradox in which adding a win of $0 to the two choice options results in strikingly different risk preferences compared to having a win of $0 in one choice option (Reyna and Brainerd 2011). That is, the Allais paradox involves two choices, one between A and B and another between C and D:

A. A sure win of $1 million,
B. 89% chance of $1 million, 10% chance of $5 million, and 1% chance of $0,
C. 11% chance of $1 million and 89% chance of $0, and
D. 10% chance of $5 million and 90% chance of $0.

Many people choose A over B but also choose D over C, reflecting inconsistent risk preferences (e.g., see Tversky and Kahneman 1986). Note that the choice between A and B is explained by FTT just as risky choices in the gain frame are by assuming that the simplest gist guides preferences: winning some money versus winning some money or winning nothing. However, the choice between C and D cannot be resolved with the simplest gist; both options boil down to winning some money or winning nothing. Therefore, based on similarity (Rubinstein 1988; Leland 1994; Stevens 2016), probabilities are assimilated but outcomes are distinguished at the ordinal level; the choices become a low chance of less money (or nothing) versus a low chance of more money (or nothing), favoring D. As we discuss below, the hidden zero operates analogously to the zeros in risky choice problems. Additionally, the hidden-zero effect is also analogous to the truncation effect seen in risky choice framing tasks, linking the two types of impulsivity (risk preference and time preference) through similar qualitative manipulations.

Given the widespread effect of steep discounting on problem behaviors, even small increases in the valuation of delayed rewards could have a significant clinical impact (Sheffer et al. 2016). Indeed, the association between discount rate and health-related choices is incremental, in that small changes in discounting are linked to a greater likelihood of successful treatments and lower frequency of behaviors that put one's well-being at risk (Yoon et al. 2007; Sheffer et al. 2012; Stanger et al. 2012; Bickel et al. 2015). Therefore, it is of crucial importance to understand the mechanisms through which interventions may alter discounting because such knowledge facilitates the design of more effective interventions or the improvement of existing ones. Next, we will compare and contrast interpretations of discounting mechanisms from the perspectives of standard dual-process theories and FTT and demonstrate how the explanations based on standard models do not tell the whole story about how discount rate may be manipulated.

FTT Versus Standard Dual-Process Theories: Different Takes on the Underlying Mechanisms of Discounting

McClure et al. (2004) used a temporal discounting task in which rewards of different magnitude ($5–$40) were presented using different levels of immediacy (i.e., from *today* to *6 weeks*). People's choices for immediate rewards on this task were linked to activity in limbic and paralimbic areas (i.e., the ventral striatum, the medial orbitofrontal cortex [OFC], medial PFC, and posterior cingulate cortex), whereas choices for delayed rewards were associated with the activation of lateral prefrontal regions (i.e., the dorsolateral PFC, the ventrolateral PFC, and the lateral OFC). This finding is similar to that of other functional magnetic resonance imaging (fMRI) studies of delay discounting in which (a) the *impulsive* system showed higher levels of activity during the choice of immediate rewards (Kable and Glimcher 2007, 2010; McClure et al. 2007; Monterosso et al. 2007; Bickel et al. 2009b; Xu et al. 2009) and (b) the *executive/control* system showed more activity for the choice of delayed rewards (e.g., McClure et al. 2007; Monterosso et al. 2007; Hoffman et al. 2008; Bickel et al. 2009a; Xu et al. 2009; Meade et al. 2011).

In a similar vein, Knutson and others (Knutson et al. 2005; Ballard and Knutson 2009) demonstrated that when delay and reward amounts are presented at separate times, activity in the limbic and paralimbic regions is associated with the magnitude of reward, whereas activity in the lateral prefrontal regions is associated with the magnitude of delay. Knutson and colleagues argued that these two distinct neural systems affect choice behavior by influencing the attribution of value of choice options in a temporal discounting scenario. This explanation and the results of the aforementioned fMRI studies are in line with the standard dual-process models of decision making (Jentsch and Taylor 1999; Bechara 2005; Bickel et al. 2011a; Kahneman 2011; but see Wood and Bechara 2014) in that delay discounting is linked to the relative activation of two distinct neural systems, the *impulsive* and the *controlling* (see Bickel et al., this volume).

FTT incorporates the aforementioned cognitive and socioemotional factors (e.g., self-control, impulsivity, and planning), but it predicts that meaningful gist-based intuition also enhances the ability to refrain from unhealthy risky choices (Reyna et al. 2015a) and delay immediate gratification (Reyna and Wilhelms, 2016). As we have noted, this view is in direct contrast with that of standard dual-process models that consider both intuition and impulsivity as dimensions of System 1 or Type 1 processes (Evans and Stanovich 2013). Based on FTT, meaningful, intuitive understanding associated with gist representations of response options influences mental representations of choices, which in turn affect behavior in a risky decision making or a temporal discounting/delay-of-gratification task. Therefore, gist-based intuition, as opposed to verbatim-based processing and deliberative analysis, which is the ideal of dual-process models, can act as a protective mechanism which increases the likelihood of healthier choices. However, the protective effect of gist-based processing relies on one's ability to accurately understand and encode the advanced gist of choices and be able to retrieve and process that gist at the moment of deciding (Wilhelms and Reyna 2013). Next, we will discuss how an understanding of the gist of response options or cueing such gist-based processing may predict and alter one's discounting tendencies.

The Effects of Gist-Based Processing on Temporal Discounting

According to FTT, core social and cultural values (e.g., "sacrifice now, enjoy later") are represented in the form of fuzzy, yet meaningful long-term memories. However, these gist representations are not mindless memorized rules applied universally. Rather, they are fuzzy guidelines that reflect a construal or interpretation of choice options (Reyna and Wilhelms, 2016). Evoking these gist principles, via meaningful cues in a context, may reduce arousal, and consequently impulsivity, by altering one's interpretation of a situation (Reyna and Brainerd 1991). Although people encode both verbatim and gist representations in parallel (Reyna et al. 2012), as development progresses and people gain experience, gist representations become more influential in decision making than precise, analytical processing associated with verbatim representations (Reyna and Farley 2006; Reyna and Lloyd 2006; Reyna et al. 2011, 2014). Gist representations are encoded along a hierarchy ranging from the simplest possible gist denoting categorical distinctions (e.g., "some money now" versus "no money later"), through ordinal distinctions (e.g., "less money now" versus "more money later"), and on through more finely grained distinction (e.g., "$100 now vs. $200 in 30 days"). If a decision can be made by relying on the simplest gist, mature adults rely on this categorical distinction and only proceed to more precise higher levels of the hierarchy if lower levels prevent them from making a decision between two or more choices. This reliance on the simplest gist increases from childhood to adulthood (Reyna and Brainerd 2011).

According to FTT, enabling one to focus on the simple gist of a decision facilitates the retrieval of gist principles (i.e., representations of relevant social and moral values such as "sacrifice now, enjoy later"), which in turn affect behavior choices (Fujita and Han 2009; Reyna and Wilhelms, 2016). Given that gist representations are more resistant than verbatim ones to interference (e.g., high arousal), and have been shown to endure over time (Rivers et al. 2008), cueing gist-based intuition may counter the negative effects of impulsivity. Therefore, similar to the predictions of FTT for risky decision making (e.g., Kühberger and Tanner 2010; Reyna et al. 2014), advanced thinking about temporal discounting or delay of gratification is not trading off exact quantities (e.g., "$100 now vs. $200 in a 30 days"), but understanding the simple bottom line of core social and moral values (e.g., "sacrifice now, enjoy later") and how they apply to different situations (Reyna and Wilhelms, 2016). In other words, gist-based thinking, which focuses on the qualitative meaning or bottom line of choices, promotes better decision making by decreasing unhealthy choices such as risk taking or opting for smaller, immediate rewards (Mills et al. 2008; Fukukura et al. 2013; Reyna and Mills 2014). Indeed, the gist of many economic and health-related decisions is that it is advantageous to sacrifice now and reap the benefits later.

Given that people—particularly mature adults—rely on the simplest possible gist in different situations to make decisions, FTT proposes that emphasizing gist-based processing, and more specifically cueing categorical gist about the choice options in a temporal discounting task, may alter discounting behavior. People generally prefer to rely on the simplest, least precise gist; that is, if both categorical and ordinal gists apply to a choice, the categorical gist is relied on to make a decision (Wilhelms and Reyna 2013). The traditional format in which temporal discounting choices are presented (i.e., "$100 now vs. $200 in 30 days") does not enable one to make clear categorical distinctions between the response options as the two choices are viewed as "some money now versus some more later." However, the inclusion of a hidden zero in either part of the choice facilitates the ability to easily extract the categorical gist of the decision. To illustrate, the question of whether one wants "$100 now and $0 in 30 days, or $200 in 30 days" draws attention away from "now" and cues categorical thinking about the consequences of choice for future—that is, "nothing later versus something later." The very simple fact that having some money is better than having none could encourage people to choose the latter option. Likewise, including a zero in the second part of the question (i.e., "$100 now, or $0 now and $200 in 30 days") draws attention away from "future" and cues the following categorical gist: "something now versus nothing now." Once more, given that having something good is qualitatively better than having nothing, one would assume that people will be more inclined to choose the former option (i.e., "$100 now").

It is worth noting that these proposed changes in discounting behavior indicate that gist-based processing does not necessarily always lead to a healthier choice. On the other hand, including a hidden zero in both parts of the choice (i.e., "$100 now and $0 in 30 days vs. $0 now and $200 in 30 days") may not be as effective as having zero in either part of the problem because this manipulation does not cue clear categorical distinctions—that can sway people's response to either immediate or delayed reward—because the gist of the choice is narrowed down to "some now and nothing later versus nothing now and some more later." Given that temporal discounting is traditionally perceived as trading-off magnitudes of reward with magnitudes of time (verbatim processing of trade-offs), one would not expect to observe changes in discounting rate as a result of adding hidden zero because the choices are still mathematically the same. However, FTT predicts that the aforementioned manipulations (i.e., adding zero to either part of the problem) modify discounting tendencies by facilitating the comparison of qualitative categories (gist processing).

The proposed changes in the presentation of temporal discounting choices suggest that cueing simple categorical gist of options may change people's preferences due to modifying their mental representations of the options which in turn facilitates the ability to apply gist values and principles to the response options. The impact of this modification is similar to the omitting of (or including) mathematically uninformative zero complements from the risky choice options in loss and gain frames which either emphasizes or de-emphasizes focus on categorical gist of decision and alters framing effects (e.g., Reyna et al. 2014). The observed changes in risky decision making and the hypothesized manipulation of temporal discounting choices—based on specific FTT predictions—cannot be explained by standard dual-process models because the options are mathematically equivalent with and without the zero. *Eliminating* the hidden zero from the temporal discounting choice in one option or including the hidden zero in both response options simulates what FTT predicts children (and to a lesser extent adolescents) would do —that is, it encourages a more precise processing of response options (toward the verbatim end of the cognitive continuum) and minimizes the likelihood of retrieving the relevant gist principles and relying on gist-based intuition, thereby increasing proneness to the interference of arousal and impulsivity. Thus, unlike standard dual-process theories, FTT emphasizes the power of gist representations to alter the salience of either immediate or delayed rewards, which modifies people's apparent discount rate. In other words, cueing the categorical gist of response options in a temporal discounting task facilitates the reinterpretation of the gist of choices through cognitive reframing (Zayas et al. 2014). Next, we will review recent findings that show how qualitative, gist representations of delay of gratification influence decisions.

The Gist of Delay of Gratification

Just as in any other scenario, people encode both the verbatim (e.g., "one marshmallow now versus two marshmallows in an hour") and gist (e.g., "some food now versus some more food later") representations of options in delay-of-gratification tasks. Given that people—especially adults—tend to retrieve the simplest relevant gist required to attempt a task, FTT suggests that qualitative, gist distinctions in choice options tend to have a greater influence on decisions than quantitative, verbatim ones. One hypothesis is that the qualitative distinction or gist of options in a delay-of-gratification task has a greater predictive validity for unhealthy behaviors than precise, elaborate, and mathematical processing because the underlying gist of delay-of-gratification situations is more likely to be relevant to other decisions (e.g., monetary, health-related) in everyday life. Thus, according to FTT, the predictive validity of measures that are based on gist principles and cue gist-based intuition is higher than that of measures relying on verbatim processing.

To test this hypothesis, Reyna and Wilhelms (2016) compared the predictive validity of a measure—called Delay-of-Gratification Gist scale (DG-Gist)—that directly assesses people's beliefs about the qualitative gist of delay of gratification, with the predictive validity of traditional measures of temporal discounting and impulsivity that are based on verbatim processing. DG-Gist is a new 12-item FTT measure that captures a single dimension of delay of gratification. Items (e.g., "I spend more money on having fun today and don't worry about tomorrow") do not involve quantitative trade-offs and are scored on 5-point Likert scale ranging from "strongly disagree" to "strongly agree." A lower score indicates a better ability to delay gratification. Reyna and Wilhelms examined the convergent and divergent validity of DG-Gist with other potentially related scales such as Future Orientation, Propensity to Plan, Time Perspectives Inventory, Spendthrift–Tightwad, Sensation Seeking, Cognitive Reflection, Barratt Impulsiveness, and the Monetary Choice Questionnaire (temporal discounting). Although DG-Gist was correlated with the aforementioned scales, it explained unique variance—in predicting self-reported problem behaviors such as overdrawing bank accounts and substance abuse—beyond sensation seeking and inhibition (see Fig. 4.3). This finding indicates that the qualitative gist of delay of gratification, as a social and moral value, cannot be reduced to either a dualist distinction—between reward-related approach motivation, including sensation seeking, and inhibitory faculties, including cognitive reflection—or quantitative conceptions of temporal discounting (Reyna and Wilhelms, 2016).

Cueing gist-based intuition and expressing delay of gratification in the form of gist principles—as opposed to verbatim analyses of precise numbers—provided new evidence for the role of long-term, fuzzy mental representation of social and

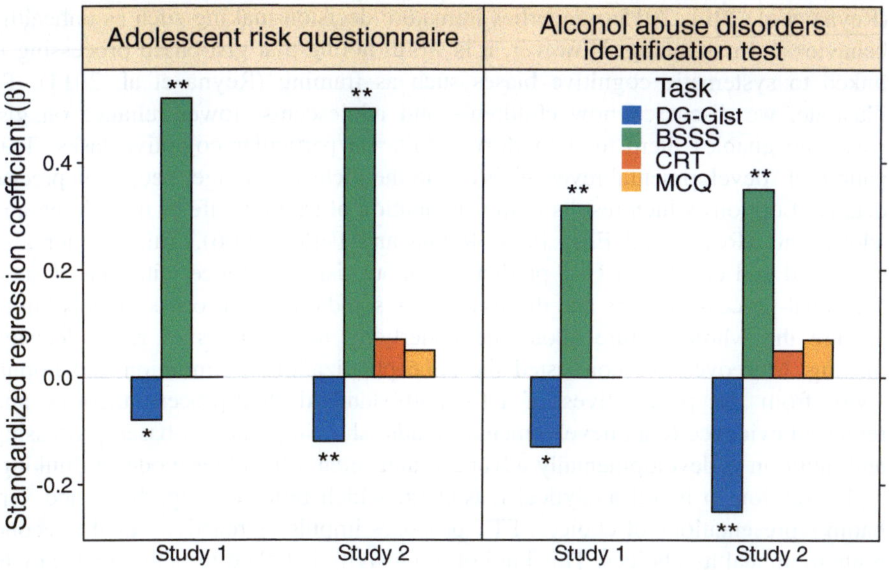

Fig. 4.3 Standardized regression coefficients showing DG-Gist accounted for unique variance in risky behaviors beyond measures of sensation seeking (BSSS), inhibition (CRT), and temporal discounting (MCQ). The measures of risky behavior were the Adolescent Risk Questionnaire (ARQ; Gullone et al. 2000), which records the frequency of engaging in 22 activities (e.g., drinking and driving, unprotected sex, and drug use), and the Alcohol Use Disorders Identification Test (AUDIT; Babor et al. 2001), which is a 10-item survey of alcohol use and dependency. *DV* Dependent variable; *DG-Gist* Delay-of-gratification Gist; *BSSS* Brief Sensation Seeking Scale; *CRT* Cognitive Reflection Test; *MCQ* Money Choice Questionnaire. $*p < 0.05$, $**p < 0.01$

moral values in deferring gratification and resisting risky behavior. Thus, unlike the predictions of standard dual-process models, empirical evidence (e.g., Mills et al. 2008; Reyna and Wilhelms, 2016) has shown that making finer distinctions (i.e., verbatim, analytical processing) is not necessarily associated with better, healthier outcomes. On the contrary, it is the gist-based intuition which is linked to fewer risky behaviors and an enhanced ability to delay gratification.

Conclusion

The evidence reviewed in this chapter shows how FTT—as an integrative framework—facilitates the understanding and prediction of risky behavior. One of the basic tenets of FTT, which is a theory of reasoning, judgment, and decision making, is that gist-based processing and reliance on bottom-line meaning of choices support advanced cognition. A recurrent finding is that as people age, they rely more and more on bottom-line intuition. The reliance of children and, to a lesser extent, adolescents on literal, surface, and verbatim representations of choices

(Reyna et al. 2011, 2015a) underlies immature decision making such as unhealthy behavior and risk taking. However, it is worth noting that gist-based processing is linked to systematic cognitive biases such as framing (Reyna et al. 2014). To illustrate, we discussed how children's and adolescents' lower reliance on gist reasoning enables them to outperform adults on particular cognitive tasks. This pattern of "developmental reversal" is due to the focus of younger people on precise details of options which results in the attenuation of framing effects in children and adolescents (Reyna and Ellis 1994; Reyna and Farley 2006). This chapter also compared and contrasted FTT predictions about risk preference with that of standard dual-process theories and discussed how standard dual-process models fail to capture the whole picture about the underlying mechanisms of risky decision making. Moreover, we contrasted the conceptualizations of intuition and impulsivity from the perspectives of FTT and standard dual-process theories and reviewed evidence (e.g., developmental trends) showing that gist-based processing and intuition is developmentally advanced and often a healthier mode of thinking.

In addition to literal analytical reasoning, which relies on superficial and verbatim representations of choices, FTT proposes impulsive reactivity as the second route to unhealthy choices. This kind of impulsivity is linked to both a tendency to take risks and a tendency to choose smaller, immediate rewards over larger, delayed ones. After a discussion of risk preferences, our chapter turned to this latter aspect of impulsivity that involves time preferences. We distinguished temporal discounting from delay of gratification, described how discount rate is often assumed to index impulsivity, discussed the implications of steep temporal discounting, and evaluated evidence supporting the claim that discount rate is a stable trait. However, research suggests that discounting is indeed malleable and that particular interventions and manipulations have been successful in altering patterns of discounting.

Our focus then turned to the underlying mechanisms of temporal discounting from the perspective of FTT and, more specifically, the impact of cueing gist principles and gist-based processing via truncating the choices in temporal discounting problems. We discussed how the inclusion of a hidden zero in either part of a temporal discounting problem theoretically modulates discounting by modifying a decision maker's mental representation of the options. When they emphasize categorical gist contrasts with receiving no reward ($0), these hidden-zero manipulations facilitate the ability to apply gist values and principles to the response options, thus evoking less impulsive choices. When zeros are in both options, they facilitate a more evenhanded approach to immediate versus delayed rewards, which can increase or decrease impulsivity relative to a no-zero baseline, depending on individual and developmental differences. In other words, if people are highly impulsive, emphasizing good and bad in each option can reduce impulsivity and conversely.

Finally, we presented recent evidence (Reyna and Wilhelms, 2016) on the role of long-term, fuzzy mental representations of social and moral values in deferring gratification and resisting risky behavior. To illustrate, DG-Gist, which is a 12-item self-report measure of people's agreement with the qualitative gist of delay of gratification, explained unique variance in problem behaviors over and above standard measures of impulsivity and delay discounting that are based on verbatim processing. We conclude that the qualitative gist of delay of gratification, as a social and moral value, cannot be reduced to either a dualist distinction—between reward-related approach motivation and inhibitory faculties—or quantitative conceptions of delay discounting.

In sum, FTT's explanations for the role of gist and verbatim mental representations in reasoning, judgment, and decision making account for a wide range of phenomena (e.g., framing effects, reverse framing, truncation effects including framing problems, and the hidden zero in temporal discounting and delay of gratification) that other theories fail to fully account for. The examination of the neural underpinnings of reward sensitivity, subjective value, numeracy, risky choice, and mental representations not only enhances our understanding of the underlying mechanisms of judgment and decision making, but also facilitates the design of interventions that reduce unhealthy behavior.

Acknowledgements The preparation of this manuscript was supported in part by the National Institutes of Health (National Institute of Nursing Research award RO1NR014368-01), National Science Foundation (award 1536238), and the National Institute of Food and Agriculture, United States Department of Agriculture (federal formula funds awards NYC-321423 and NYC-321436) to the last author. The content is solely the responsibility of the authors and does not necessarily represent the official views of the granting agencies.

References

Adam, M. B., & Reyna, V. F. (2005). Coherence and correspondence criteria for rationality: Experts' estimation of risks of sexually transmitted infections. *Journal of Behavioral Decision Making, 18*(3), 169–186. doi:10.1002/bdm.493

Babor, T. F., Higgins-Biddle, J. C., Saunders, J. B., & Monteiro, M. G. (2001). *The alcohol use disorders identification test. Guidelines for use in primary care* (2nd ed.). Geneva, Switzerland: World Health Organization.

Baker, F., Johnson, M. W., & Bickel, W. K. (2003). Delay discounting in current and never before cigarette smokers: Similarities and differences across commodity, sign, and magnitude. *Journal of Abnormal Psychology, 112*(3), 382–392. doi:10.1037/0021-843X.112.3.382

Ballard, K., & Knutson, B. (2009). Dissociable neural representations of future reward magnitude and delay during temporal discounting. *Neuroimage, 45,* 143–150.

Barrouillet, P. (2011). Dual-process theories and cognitive development: Advances and challenges. *Developmental Review, 31,* 79–85.

Bechara, A. (2005). Decision making, impulse control and loss of willpower to resist drugs: A neurocognitive perspective. *Nature Neuroscience, 8*(11), 1458–1463. doi:10.1038/nn1584

Beck, R. C., & Triplett, M. F. (2009). Test-retest reliability of a group-administered paper-pencil measure of delay discounting. *Experimental and Clinical Psychopharmacology, 17*(5), 345–355. doi:10.1037/a0017078

Bickel, W. K. (2012). The emerging new science of psychopathology. *Addiction, 107*(10), 1738–1739. doi:10.1111/j.1360-0443.2012.03968

Bickel, W. K., & Mueller, E. T. (2009). Toward the study of trans-disease processes: A novel approach with special reference to the study of co-morbidity. *Journal of Dual Diagnosis, 5*(2), 131–138.

Bickel, W. K., Pitcock, J. A., Yi, R., & Angtuaco, E. J. (2009a). Equivalent neural correlates across intertemporal choice conditions. *NeuroImage, 47*(Supplement 1), S39–S41.

Bickel, W. K., Pitcock, J. A., Yi, R., & Angtuaco, E. J. C. (2009b). Congruence of BOLD response across intertemporal choice conditions: Fictive and real money gains and losses. *Journal of Neuroscience, 29*(27), 8839–8846. doi:10.1523/jneurosci.5319-08.2009

Bickel, W. K., Jarmolowicz, D. P., Mueller, E. T., & Gatchalian, K. M. (2011a). The behavioral economics and neuroeconomics of reinforcer pathologies: Implications for etiology and treatment of addiction. *Current Psychiatry Reports, 13*(5), 406–415. doi:10.1007/s11920-011-0215-1

Bickel, W. K., Landes, R. D., Christensen, D. R., Jackson, L., Jones, B. A., Kurth-Nelson, Z., et al. (2011b). Single- and cross-commodity discounting among cocaine addicts: The commodity and its temporal location determine discounting rate. *Psychopharmacology (Berlin), 217*(2), 177–187. doi:10.1007/s00213-011-2272-x

Bickel, W. K., Jarmolowicz, D. P., Mueller, E. T., Franck, C. T., Carrin, C., & Gatchalian, K. M. (2012). Altruism in time: Social temporal discounting differentiates smokers from problem drinkers. *Psychopharmacology (Berlin), 224,* 109–120. doi:10.1007/s00213-012-2745-6

Bickel, W. K., Quisenberry, A. J., Moody, L., & Wilson, A. G. (2015). Therapeutic opportunities for self-control repair in addiction and related disorders: Change and the limits of change in trans-disease processes. *Clinical Psychological Science, 3*(1), 140–153. doi:10.1177/2167702614541260

Black, A. C., & Rosen, M. I. (2011). A money management-based substance use treatment increases valuation of future rewards. *Addictive Behaviors, 36*(1–2), 125–128. doi:10.1016/j.addbeh.2010.08.014

Brainerd, C. J., Reyna, V. F., & Ceci, S. J. (2008). Developmental reversals in false memory: A review of data and theory. *Psychological Bulletin, 134*(3), 343–382.

Brainerd, C. J., Reyna, V. F., & Zember, E. (2011). Theoretical and forensic implications of developmental studies of the DRM illusion. *Memory & Cognition, 39*(3), 365–380.

Casey, B. J., & Caudle, K. (2013). The teenage brain. Self-control. *Current Directions in Psychological Science, 22*(2), 82–87. doi:10.1177/0963721413480170

Chick, C. F., Reyna, V. F., & Corbin, J. C. (2016). Framing effects are robust to linguistic disambiguation: A critical test of contemporary theory. *Journal of Experimental Psychology. Learning, Memory, and Cognition, 42*(2), 238–256. doi:10.1037/xlm0000158

Cho, S. S., Ko, J. H., Pellecchia, G., Van Eimeren, T., Cilia, R., & Strafella, A. P. (2010). Continuous theta burst stimulation of right dorsolateral prefrontal cortex induces changes in impulsivity level. *Brain Stimulation, 3*(3), 170–176. doi:10.1016/j.brs.2009.10.002

Cokely, E. T., & Kelley, C. M. (2009). Cognitive abilities and superior decision making under risk: A protocol analysis and process model evaluation. *Judgment and Decision Making, 4*(1), 20–33.

Corbin, J. C., Reyna, V. F., Weldon, R. B., & Brainerd, C. J. (2016). How reasoning, judgment, and decision making are colored by gist-based intuition: A fuzzy-trace theory approach. *Journal of Applied Research in Memory and Cognition, 4,* 344–355. doi:10.1016/j.jarmac.2015.09.001

Dai, H., Milkman, K. L., & Riis, J. (2014). The fresh start effect: Temporal landmarks motivate aspirational behavior. *Management Science, 60*(10), 2563–2582. doi:10.1287/mnsc.2014.1901

Dalley, J. W., Everitt, B. J., & Robbins, T. W. (2011). Impulsivity, compulsivity, and top down cognitive control. *Neuron, 69,* 680–694.

De Neys, W., & Vanderputte, K. (2011). When less is not always more: Stereotype knowledge and reasoning development. *Developmental Psychology, 47*(2), 432–441.

De Water, E., Cillessen, A., & Scheres, A. (2014). Distinct age-related differences in temporal discounting and risk taking in adolescents and young adults. *Child Development, 85,* 1881–1897. doi:10.1111/cdev.12245

Defoe, I. N., Dubas, J. S., Figner, B., & Van Aken, M. A. (2015). A meta-analysis on age differences in risky decision making: Adolescents versus children and adults. *Psychological Bulletin, 141*(1), 48–84. doi:10.1037/a0038088

Doyle, J. R. (2013). Survey of time preference, delay discounting models. *Judgment and Decision Making, 8,* 116–135.

Epstein, S. (1994). Integration of the cognitive and the psychodynamic unconscious. *American Psychologist, 49*(8), 709–724. doi:10.1037/0003-066X.49.8.709

Evans, J. S. B. T., & Stanovich, K. E. (2013). Dual-process theories of higher cognition: Advancing the debate. *Perspectives on Psychological Science, 8*(3), 223–241. doi:10.1177/1745691612460685

Fox, C. R., & Tannenbaum, D. (2011). The elusive search for stable risk preferences. *Frontiers in Psychology, 2,* 298. doi:10.3389/fpsyg.2011.00298

Fraenkel, L., Matzko, C. K., Webb, D. E., Oppermann, B., Charpentier, P., Peters, E., et al. (2015). Use of decision support for improved knowledge, values clarification, and informed choice in patients with rheumatoid arthritis. *Arthritis Care & Research, 67*(11), 1496–1502. doi:10.1002/acr.22659

Frederick, S., Loewenstein, G., & O'Donoghue, T. (2002). Time discounting and time preference: A critical review. *Journal of Economic Literature, 40,* 351–401. doi:10.1257/jel.40.2.351

Fujita, K., & Han, H. A. (2009). Moving beyond deliberative control of impulses: The effects of construal levels on evaluative associations in self-control. *Psychological Science, 20,* 799–804.

Fukukura, J., Ferguson, M. J., & Fujita, K. (2013). Psychological distance can improve decision making under information overload via gist memory. *Journal of Experimental Psychology: General, 142*(3), 658–665. doi:10.1037/a0030730

Green, L., Fry, A., & Myerson, J. (1994). Discounting of delayed rewards: A life-span comparison. *Psychological Science, 5*(1), 33–36.

Green, L., Myerson, J., Lichtman, D., Rosen, S., & Fry, A. (1996). Temporal discounting in choice between delayed rewards; The role of age and income. *Psychology and Aging, 11,* 79–84.

Green, L., Myerson, J., & Ostaszewski, P. (1999). Discounting of delayed rewards across the life span: Age differences in individual discounting functions. *Behavioural Processes, 46,* 89–96.

Griskevicius, V., Tybur, J. M., Delton, A. W., & Robertson, T. E. (2011). The influence of mortality and socioeconomic status on risk and delayed rewards: A life history theory approach. *Journal of Personality and Social Psychology, 100,* 1015–1026. doi:10.1037/a0022403

Gullone, E., Moore, S., Moss, S., & Boyd, C. (2000). The adolescent risk-taking questionnaire: Development and psychometric evaluation. *Journal of Adolescent Research, 15*(2), 231–250.

Hoffman, W. F., Schwartz, D. L., Huckans, M. S., McFarland, B. H., Meiri, G., Stevens, A. A., et al. (2008). Cortical activation during delay discounting in abstinent meth- amphetamine dependent individuals. *Psychopharmacology (Berlin), 201*(2), 183–193. doi:10.1007/s00213-008-1261-1

Hsee, C. K. (1999). Value seeking and prediction decision inconsistency: Why don't people take what they predict they'll like the most? *Psychonomic Bulletin & Review, 6,* 555–561.

Jaroni, J. L., Wright, S. M., Lerman, C., & Epstein, L. H. (2004). Relationship between education and delay discounting in smokers. *Addictive Behavior, 29,* 1171–1175.

Jentsch, J. D., & Taylor, J. R. (1999). Impulsivity resulting from frontostriatal dysfunction in drug abuse: Implications for the control of behavior by reward-related stimuli. *Psychopharmacology (Berlin), 146,* 373–390.

Johnson, M. W., & Bruner, N. R. (2011). The sexual discounting task: HIV risk behavior and the discounting of delayed sexual rewards in cocaine dependence. *Drug and Alcohol Dependence, 123,* 15–21.

Kable, J. W., & Glimcher, P. W. (2007). The neural correlates of subjective value during intertemporal choice. *Nature Neuroscience, 10,* 1625–1633. doi:10.1038/nn2007

Kable, J. W., & Glimcher, P. W. (2010). An "as soon as possible" effect in human intertemporal decision making: Behavioral evidence and neural mechanisms. *Journal of Neurophysiology, 103*(5), 2513–2531. doi:10.1152/jn.00177.2009

Kahneman, D. (2011). *Thinking fast and slow*. London, UK: Penguin.

Kahneman, D., & Tversky, A. (1979). Prospect theory: An analysis of decision under risk. *Econometrica, 47,* 263–291. doi:10.2307/1914185

Kirby, K. N. (2009). One-year temporal stability of delay-discount rates. *Psychonomic Bulletin & Review, 16,* 457–462.

Knutson, B., Taylor, J., Kaufman, M., Peterson, R., & Glover, G. (2005). Distributed neural representation of expected value. *Journal of Neuroscience, 25,* 4806–4812.

Koffarnus, M. N., Jarmolowicz, D. P., Mueller, E. T., & Bickel, W. K. (2013). Changing delay discounting in the light of the competing neurobehavioral decision systems theory: A review. *Journal of Experimental Analysis of Behavior, 99,* 32–57. doi:10.1002/jeab.2

Kühberger, A., & Tanner, C. (2010). Risky choice framing: Task versions and a comparison of prospect theory and fuzzy-trace theory. *Journal of Behavioral Decision Making, 23*(3), 314–329. doi:10.1002/bdm.656

Kwak, Y., Payne, J. W., Cohen, A. L., & Huettel, S. A. (2015). The rational adolescent: Strategic information processing during decision making revealed by eye tracking. *Cognitive Development, 36,* 20–30. doi:10.1016/j.cogdev.2015.08.001

Leland, J. W. (1994). Generalized similarity judgments: An alternative explanation for choice anomalies. *Journal of Risk and Uncertainty, 9*(2), 151–172.

Levin, I. P., Weller, J. A., Pederson, A. A., & Harshman, L. A. (2007). Age-related differences in adaptive decision making: Sensitivity to expected value in risky choice. *Judgment and Decision Making, 2*(4), 225–233.

Liberali, J. M., Reyna, V. F., Furlan, S., Stein, L. M., & Pardo, S. T. (2012). Individual differences in numeracy and cognitive reflection, with implications for biases and fallacies in probability judgment. *Journal of Behavioral Decision Making, 25*(4), 361–381.

Magen, E., Dweck, C. S., & Gross, J. J. (2008). The hidden-zero effect: Representing a single choice as an extended sequence reduces impulsive choice. *Psychological Science, 19,* 648–649. doi:10.1111/j.1467-9280.2008.02137.x

Magen, E., Kim, B., Dweck, C. S., Gross, J. J., & McClure, S. M. (2014). Behavioral and neural correlates of increased self-control in the absence of increased willpower. *Proceedings of the National Academy of Sciences (USA), 111,* 9786–9791. doi:10.1073/pnas.1408991111

Mazur, James E. (1987). An adjustment procedure for studying delayed reinforcement. In M. L. Commons, J. E. Mazur, J. A. Nevin, & H. Rachlin (Eds.), *Quantitative analysis of behavior: The effect of delay and intervening events on reinforcement value*. Hillsdale, NJ: Erlbaum.

McClure, S. M., Laibson, D. I., Loewenstein, G., & Cohen, J. D. (2004). Separate neural systems value immediate and delayed monetary rewards. *Science, 306,* 503–507.

McClure, S. M., Ericson, K. M., Laibson, D. I., Loewenstein, G., & Cohen, J. D. (2007). Time discounting for primary rewards. *Journal of Neuroscience, 27,* 5796–5804.

Meade, C. S., Lowen, S. B., Maclean, R. R., Key, M. D., & Lukas, S. E. (2011). fMRI brain activation during a delay discounting task in HIV-positive adults with and without cocaine dependence. *Psychiatry Research, 192*(3), 167–175. doi:10.1016/j.pscychresns.2010.12.011

Metcalfe, J., & Mischel, W. (1999). A hot/cool-system analysis of delay of gratification: Dynamics of willpower. *Psychological Review, 106*(1), 3–19. doi:10.1037/0033-295X.106.1.3

Mills, B., Reyna, V. F., & Estrada, S. (2008). Explaining contradictory relations between risk perception and risk taking. *Psychological Science, 19*(5), 429–433. doi:10.1111/j.1467-9280.2008.02104.x

Monterosso, J. R., Ainslie, G., Xu, J., Cordova, X., Domier, C. P., & London, E. D. (2007). Frontoparietal cortical activity of methamphetamine-dependent and comparison subjects performing a delay discounting task. *Human Brain Mapping, 28,* 383–393.

Ochsner, K. N., & Gross, J. J. (2008). Cognitive emotion regulation: Insights from social cognitive and affective neuroscience. *Current Directions in Psychological Science, 17*(2), 153–158. doi:10.1111/j.1467-8721.2008.00566.x

Odum, A. L. (2011). Delay discounting: Trait variable? *Behavioural Processes, 87,* 1–9. doi:10.1016/j.beproc.2011.02.007

Ohmura, Y., Takahashi, T., Kitamura, N., & Wehr, P. (2006). Three-month stability of delay and probability discounting measures. *Experimental and Clinical Psychopharmacology, 14*(3), 318–328. doi:10.1037/1064-1297.14.3.318

Peters, J., & Buchel, C. (2009). Overlapping and distinct neural systems code for subjective value during intertemporal and risky decision making. *The Journal of Neuroscience, 29,* 15727–15734.

Peters, E., Västfjäll, D., Slovic, P., Mertz, C. K., Mazzocco, K., & Dickert, S. (2006). Numeracy and decision making. *Psychological Science, 17*(5), 407–413.

Petry, N. M., & Casarella, T. (1999). Excessive discounting of delayed rewards in substance abusers with gambling problems. *Drug and Alcohol Dependence, 56,* 25–32.

Prelec, D., & Loewenstein, G. (1998). The red and the black: Mental accounting of savings and debt. *Marketing Science, 17*(1), 4–28. doi:10.1287/mksc.17.1.4

Rachlin, H., Raineri, A., & Cross, D. (1991). Subjective probability and delay. *Journal of Experimental Analysis of Behavior, 55,* 233–244.

Radu, P. T., Yi, R., Bickel, W. K., Gross, J. J., & McClure, S. M. (2011). A mechanism for reducing delay discounting by altering temporal attention. *Journal of the Experimental Analysis of Behavior, 96,* 363–385. doi:10.1901/jeab.2011.96-363

Read, D., Frederick, S., Orsel, B., & Rahman, J. (2005). Four score and seven years from now: The date/delay effect in temporal discounting. *Management Science, 51*(9), 1326–1335. doi:10.1287/mnsc.1050.0412

Reyna, V. F. (1996). Conceptions of memory development with implications for reasoning and decision making. *Annals of Child Development, 12,* 87–118.

Reyna, V. F. (2008). A theory of medical decision making and health: Fuzzy-trace theory. *Medical Decision Making, 28,* 829–833. doi: 10.1177/0272989X08327069

Reyna, V. F. (2011). Across the lifespan. In B. Fischhoff, N. T.Brewer & J. S. Downs (Eds.), *Communicating risks and benefits: An evidence-based user's guide* (pp. 111–119). U.S. Department of Health and Human Services, Food and Drug Administration. Retrieved from http://www.fda.gov/ScienceResearch/SpecialTopics/RiskCommunication/default.htm

Reyna, V. F. (2012). A new intuitionism: Meaning, memory, and development in fuzzy-trace theory. *Judgment and Decision Making, 7*(3), 332–359.

Reyna, V. F. (2013). Intuition, reasoning, and development: A fuzzy-trace theory approach. In P. Barrouillet & C. Gauffroy (Eds.), *The development of thinking and reasoning* (pp. 193–220). Hove, UK: Psychology Press.

Reyna, V. F., & Brainerd, C. J. (1991). Fuzzy-trace theory and children's acquisition of scientific and mathematical concepts. *Learning and Individual Differences, 3*(1), 27–59. doi:10.1016/1041-6080(91)90003-J

Reyna, V. F., & Brainerd, C. J. (1994). The origins of probability judgment: A review of data and theories. In G. Wright & P. Ayton (Eds.), *Subjective probability* (pp. 239–272). New York, NY: Wiley.

Reyna, V. F., & Brainerd, C. J. (1995). Fuzzy-trace theory: An interim synthesis. *Learning and Individual Differences, 7*(1), 1–75. doi:10.1016/1041-6080(95)90031-4

Reyna, V. F., & Brainerd, C. J. (2011). Dual processes in decision making and developmental neuroscience: A fuzzy-trace model. *Developmental Review, 31,* 180–206. doi:10.1016/j.dr.2011.07.004

Reyna, V. F., & Ellis, S. C. (1994). Fuzzy-trace theory and framing effects in children's risky decision making. *Psychological Science, 5,* 275–279. doi:10.1111/j.1467-9280.1994.tb00625.x

Reyna, V. F., & Farley, F. (2006). Risk and rationality in adolescent decision making. *Psychological Science in the Public Interest, 7*(1), 1–44. doi:10.1111/j.1529-1006.2006.00026.x

Reyna, V. F., & Lloyd, F. J. (2006). Physician decision making and cardiac risk: Effects of knowledge, risk perception, risk tolerance, and fuzzy processing. *Journal of Experimental Psychology: Applied, 12*(3), 179–195. doi:10.1037/1076-898X.12.3.179

Reyna, V. F., & Mills, B. A. (2007). Interference processes in fuzzy-trace theory: Aging, Alzheimer's disease, and development. In D. Gorfein & C. MacLeod (Eds.), *Inhibition in cognition* (pp. 185–210). Washington: APA Press.

Reyna, V. F., & Mills, B. A. (2014). Theoretically motivated interventions for reducing sexual risk taking in adolescence: A randomized controlled experiment applying fuzzy-trace theory. *Journal of Experimental Psychology: General, 143*(4), 1627–1648. doi:10.1037/a0036717

Reyna, V. F., & Rivers, S. E. (2008). Current theories of risk and rational decision making. *Developmental Review, 28*(1), 1–11. doi:10.1016/j.dr.2008.01.002

Reyna, V. F., & Wilhelms, E. A. (2016). The gist of delay of gratification: Understanding and predicting problem behaviors. *Journal of Behavioral Decision Making. Advance online publication.* doi: 10.1002/bdm.1977

Reyna, V. F., Estrada, S. M., DeMarinis, J. A., Myers, R. M., Stanisz, J. M., & Mills, B. A. (2011). Neurobiological and memory models of risky decision making in adolescents versus young adults. *Journal of Experimental Psychology. Learning, Memory, and Cognition, 37*(5), 1125–1142. doi:10.1037/a0023943

Reyna, V. F., Chapman, S. B., Dougherty, M. R., & Confrey, J. E. (Eds.). (2012). *The adolescent brain: Learning, reasoning, and decision making*. Washington, DC: American Psychological Association.

Reyna, V. F., Chick, C. F., Corbin, J. C., & Hsia, A. N. (2014). Developmental reversals in risky decision making: Intelligence agents show larger decision biases than college students. *Psychological Science, 25*(1), 76–84. doi:10.1177/0956797613497022

Reyna, V. F., Weldon, R. B., & McCormick, M. J. (2015a). Educating intuition: Reducing risky decisions using fuzzy-trace theory. *Current Directions in Psychological Science, 24*(5), 392–398. doi:10.1177/0963721415588081

Reyna, V. F., Wilhelms, E. A., McCormick, M. J., & Weldon, R. B. (2015b). Development of risky decision making: Fuzzy-trace theory and neurobiological perspectives. *Child Development Perspectives, 9*(2), 122–127. doi:10.1111/cdep.12117

Reynolds, B., & Schiffbauer, R. (2005). Delay of gratification and delay discounting: A unifying feedback model of delay-related impulsive behavior. *Psychological Record, 55,* 439–460.

Rivers, S. E., Reyna, V. F., & Mills, B. A. (2008). Risk taking under the influence: A fuzzy-trace theory of emotion in adolescence. *Developmental Review, 28*(1), 107–144. doi:10.1016/j.dr.2007.11.002

Rubinstein, A. (1988). Similarity and decision-making under risk (Is there a utility theory resolution to the Allais paradox?). *Journal of Economic Theory, 46*(1), 145–153.

Rusou, Z., Zakay, D., & Usher, M. (2013). Pitting intuitive and analytical thinking against each other: The case of transivity. *Psychological Bulletin & Review, 20*(3), 608–614. doi:10.3758/s13423-013-0382-7

Savage, L. J. (1954). *The foundations of statistics*. New York: Wiley.

Sheffer, C. E., Mackillop, J., McGeary, J., Landes, R., Carter, L., Yi, R., et al. (2012). Delay discounting, locus of control, and cognitive impulsiveness independently predict tobacco dependence treatment outcomes in a highly dependent, lower socioeconomic group of smokers. *The American Journal on Addictions, 21,* 221–232. doi:10.1111/j.1521-0391,2012.00224

Sheffer, C. E., Mennemeier, M., Landes, R. D., Bickel, W. K., Brackman, S., Dornhoffer, J., et al. (2013). Neuromodulation of delay discounting, the reflection effect, and cigarette consumption. *Journal of Substance Abuse Treatment, 45*(2), 206–214. doi:10.1016/j.jsat.2013.01.012

Sheffer, C. E., Mackillop, J., Fernandez, A., Christensen, D., Bickel, W. K., Johnson, M. W., et al. (2016). Initial examination of priming tasks to decrease delay discounting. *Behavioural Processes, 128,* 144–152.

Simpson, C. A., & Vuchinich, R. E. (2000). Reliability of a measure of temporal discounting. *Psychological Records, 50*(1), 3–16.

Stanger, C., Ryan, S. R., Fu, H., Landes, R. D., Jones, B. A., Bickel, W. K., et al. (2012). Delay discounting predicts adolescent substance abuse treatment outcome. *Experimental and Clinical Psychopharmacology, 20*(3), 205–212. doi:10.1037/a0026543

Stanovich, K. E., & West, R. F. (2008). On the relative independence of thinking biases and cognitive ability. *Journal of Personality and Social Psychology, 94*(4), 672–695. doi:10.1037/0022-3514.94.4.672

Steinberg, L. (2008). A social neuroscience perspective on adolescent risk taking. *Developmental Review, 28*(1), 78–106. doi:10.1111/j.1467-8721.2007.00475.x

Steinberg, L., Cauffman, E., Woolard, J., Graham, S., & Banich, M. (2009). Are adolescents less mature than adults? Minors' access to abortion, the juvenile death penalty, and the alleged APA 'flip-flop'. *American Psychologist, 64*(7), 583–594.

Stevens, J. R. (2016). Intertemporal similarity: Discounting as a last resort. *Journal of Behavioral Decision Making, 29,* 12–24. doi:10.1002/bdm.1870

Sweitzer, M. M., Donny, E. C., Dierker, L. C., Flory, J. D., & Manuck, S. B. (2008). Delay discounting and smoking: Association with the Fagerstrom test for nicotine dependence but not cigarettes smoked per day. *Nicotine & Tobacco Research, 10*(10), 1571–1575. doi:10.1080/14622200802323274

Sweitzer, M. M., Donny, E. C., & Hariri, A. R. (2012). Imaging genetics and the neurobiological basis of individual differences in vulnerability to addiction. *Drug and Alcohol Dependence, 123*(Suppl 1), S59–S71.

Takahashi, T., Furukawa, A., Miyakawa, T., Maesato, H., & Higuchi, S. (2007). Two-month stability of hyperbolic discount rates for delayed monetary gains in abstinent inpatient alcoholics. *Neuroendocrinology Letters, 28*(2), 131–136.

Tversky, A., & Kahneman, D. (1986). Rational choice and the framing of decisions. *Journal of Business, 59*(4), S251–S278.

Tversky, A., & Kahneman, D. (1992). Advances in prospect theory: cumulative representation of uncertainty. *Journal of Risk and Uncertainty, 5*(4), 297–323.

Usher, M., Russo, Z., Weyers, M., Brauner, R., & Zakay, D. (2011). The impact of the mode of thought in complex decisions: Intuitive decisions are better. *Frontiers in Psychology, 2,* 37. doi:10.3389/fpsyg.2011.00037

Von Neumann, J., & Morgenstern, O. (1944). *Theory of games and economic behavior*. Princeton, NJ: Princeton University Press.

Weber, E. U., & Hsee, C. K. (1999). Models and mosaics: Investigating cross-cultural differences in risk perception and risk preference. *Psychonomic Bulletin & Review, 6,* 611–617.

Weber, B. J., & Huettel, S. A. (2008). The neural substrates of probabilistic and intertemporal decision making. *Brain Research, 1234,* 104–115.

Weldon, R. B., Corbin, J. C., & Reyna, V. F. (2013). Gist processing in judgment and decision making: Developmental reversals predicted by fuzzy-trace theory. In H. Markovits (Ed.), *The developmental psychology of reasoning and decision-making* (pp. 36–62). New York: Psychology Press.

Weller, R. E., Cook, E. W., 3rd, Avsar, K. B., & Cox, J. E. (2008). Obese women show greater delay discounting than healthy-weight women. *Appetite, 51,* 563–569.

Weller, J. A., Levin, I. P., & Denburg, N. L. (2011). Trajectory of risky decision making for potential gains and losses from ages 5 to 85. *Journal of Behavioral Decision Making, 24,* 331–344. doi:10.1002/bdm.690

Wilhelms, E. A., & Reyna, V. F. (2013). Fuzzy trace theory and medical decisions by minors: Differences in reasoning between adolescents and adults. *Journal of Medicine and Philosophy, 38,* 268–282.

Wilhelms, E. A., Helm, R. K., Setton, R. A., & Reyna, V. F. (2014). Fuzzy trace theory explains paradoxical dissociations in affective forecasting. In E. A. Wilhelms & V. F. Reyna (Eds.), *Neuroeconomics, judgment, and decision making* (pp. 49–73). New York, NY: Psychology Press.

Wilhelms, E. A., Corbin, J. C., & Reyna, V. F. (2015a). Gist memory in reasoning and decision making. In A. Feeney & V. Thompson (Eds.), *Reasoning as memory* (pp. 93–109). New York, NY: Psychology Press.

Wilhelms, E. A., Reyna, V. F., Brust-Renck, P. G., Weldon, R. B., & Corbin, J. C. (2015b). Gist representations and communications of risks about HIV-AIDS: A fuzzy-trace theory approach. *Current HIV Research, 13*(5), 399–407. doi:10.2174/1570162X13666150511142748

Wolfe, C. R., Reyna, V. F., Widmer, C. L., Cedillos, E. M., Fisher, C. R., Brust-Renck, P. G., et al. (2015). Efficacy of a web-based intelligent tutoring system for communicating genetic risk of breast cancer: A fuzzy-trace theory approach. *Medical Decision Making, 35,* 46–59. doi:10.1177/0272989X14535983

Wood, S. M. W., & Bechara, A. (2014). The neuroscience of dual (and triple) systems in decision making. In V. F. Reyna & V. Zayas (Eds.), *The neuroscience of risky decision making*. Washington, DC: American Psychological Association.

Xu, L., Liang, Z. Y., Wang, K., Li, S., & Jiang, T. (2009). Neural mechanism of intertemporal choice: From discounting future gains to future losses. *Brain Research, 1261,* 65–74.

Yoon, J. H., Higgins, S. T., Heil, S. H., Sugarbaker, R. J., Thomas, C. S., & Badger, G. J. (2007). Delay discounting predicts postpartum relapse to cigarette smoking among pregnant women. *Experimental Clinical Psychopharmacology, 15*(2), 176–186. doi:10.1037/1064-1297.15.2.186

Zayas, V., Mischel, W., & Pandey, G. (2014). Mind and brain in delay of gratification. In V. F. Reyna & V. Zayas (Eds.), *The neuroscience of risky decision making* (pp. 145–176). Washington, DC: American Psychological Association.

Zimbardo, P. G., & Boyd, J. N. (1999). Putting time in perspective: A valid, reliable, individual differences metric. *Journal of Personality and Social Psychology, 77,* 1271–1288.

Chapter 5
Devaluation of Outcomes Due to Their Cost: Extending Discounting Models Beyond Delay

Suzanne H. Mitchell

Introduction

Many health issues develop because people engage in behaviors that are ultimately unhealthy. For example, the link between drinking significant amounts of alcohol for a prolonged period and developing cirrhosis of the liver is well established. Similar causal links have been shown between diet and diabetes and, more recently, dental hygiene and cardiovascular disease; and there are many additional examples. This observation does not negate the importance of other factors, such as genotype, which may confer a heightened risk that specific behaviors will lead to illnesses, or influence the progression and treatment of disease after its onset. However, following from the idea that behavior plays an important role in illness, an obvious next step to increase public health is to reduce the likelihood or frequency with which people engage in problematic behaviors. One basic approach involves examining why these behaviors, such as "drink alcohol," are more attractive than the alternatives, such as "do not drink alcohol" or "drink a nonalcoholic beverage." Reinforcement theory would suggest that repeated alcohol drinking is due to the consequences of drinking alcohol being more rewarding or valuable than the consequences of not drinking (Skinner 1969; de Villiers 1977). However, the consequences of drinking are complex and occur at different times. For example, the action of alcohol as a social lubricant and other, positive subjective effects are more proximate to drinking than the depressant effects of alcohol, subsequent hangover or the development of any alcohol-associated disease. Recognizing the potential importance of the immediate and delayed consequences of problematic behaviors has prompted researchers to frame this situation as one in which an individual is choosing between a behavior with a relatively immediate positive

S.H. Mitchell (✉)
Departments of Behavioral Neuroscience and Psychiatry, Oregon Health & Science University, 3181 SW Sam Jackson Park Road, L470, Portland, OR 97239, USA
e-mail: mitchesu@ohsu.edu

J.R. Stevens (ed.), *Impulsivity*, Nebraska Symposium on Motivation 64,
DOI 10.1007/978-3-319-51721-6_5

consequence and a behavior that will only pay off in the distant future. In the laboratory, choices between small, immediate monetary rewards and larger, delayed monetary rewards are often used for human studies of this choice problem, while animal studies use small, immediate, and larger, later food rewards.

Inherent in this conceptualization is the idea that delayed consequences are devalued, making the option to engage in a problematic behavior more valuable than the alternative because the positive health consequences of not drinking, while large, are substantially delayed. This process of devaluing or discounting delayed consequences has been the focus of intense laboratory study beginning in the mid-1980s. The hope being that, by understanding the neural, genetic, and psychological foundations of the discounting process, it will be possible to identify individuals at-risk for engaging in unhealthy behaviors and identify ways to manipulate the process to reduce the frequency of these ill-considered behaviors. This chapter examines conceptual and practical issues associated with assessing temporal or delay discounting in the laboratory, before reviewing the literature on a less-examined discounting process: effort discounting. This review will highlight best practices in effort discounting research and identify knowledge gaps that suggest avenues for additional research.

Temporal Discounting

A typical question in a temporal discounting assessment for human participants is: Would you prefer $95 right now or $100 in a month? Most of us would prefer $95 immediately rather than waiting for a month for an additional $5. Objectively, this preference is economically irrational if we assume that people's choices should maximize their monetary gains. However, we assume that the delayed delivery is what has reduced the subjective value of the $100 to a level at which $95 is more preferred. In other words, the objective value of the $100 has been discounted due to its delayed delivery. To obtain the precise assessment of an individual's degree of temporal discounting, we can reduce the amount of reward offered immediately until preference switches from the immediate reward to waiting for the $100 in 1 month. If this was done in $5 steps, perhaps at $70 immediately, our hypothetical participant might switch their preference to the larger, later alternative. Traditionally, the midpoint between the lowest immediate amount preferred ($75 in this example) and the largest amount rejected ($70) is defined as the indifference point. A similar adjustment strategy can be used to identify indifference points associated with other delays, e.g., 6 months and 1 year. As might be expected, as the delay lengthens, the value of the delayed reward declines. This phenomenon is often called temporal discounting; but in different academic disciplines, it is also referred to as delay discounting, intertemporal choice, delay aversion, and an inability to delay gratification. Between these disciplines, there are some subtle differences in the theoretical and experimental protocols used to explore this phenomenon, but the basic similarities in procedures and findings suggest that researchers interested in this discounting area should explore literature across a number of academic domains. For convenience, I will use temporal discounting here and will focus on temporal discounting of rewards/gains, as illustrated in the receiving-$100-in-a-month example, rather than losses in which participants are asked how much they would prefer to pay: a small amount now or larger amount later. While there are studies of temporal discounting for losses (e.g., Baker et al. 2003; Takahashi et al. 2009; Appelt et al. 2011), this field is less developed than that of delayed gain discounting. But interestingly, early studies suggest that factors affecting gain discounting do not necessarily affect loss discounting in the same way (e.g., Estle et al. 2006; Mitchell and Wilson 2010). Further, this discussion of temporal discounting will draw examples primarily from the literature focused on human participants. However, there is a robust and vibrant literature examining temporal discounting in nonhuman animal models including mice (e.g., Helms et al. 2008; Oberlin and Grahame 2009), rats (e.g., Evenden and Ryan 1996; Pattij et al. 2009), and nonhuman primates (e.g., Woolverton et al. 2007; Maguire et al. 2013; Barack and Platt, this volume). Many of the issues to be raised can also be applied to those studies.

From a psychological standpoint, it is not clear what processes are responsible for temporal discounting. Some have suggested that individuals may view delays negatively because it is possible that during the delay period something might happen that makes the delayed outcome unavailable (e.g., Sozou 1998). However, experimental evidence from Takahashi et al. (2007), suggests that while this factor may play a role, the extent to which rewards are discounted cannot be fully accounted for by decreases in the perceived likelihood of receiving the reward and that there is an individual "time preference factor" related to aversion to waiting. As anyone who has waited for something to be delivered knows, waiting can be highly aversive. However, in virtually all tasks used to assess temporal discounting with human participants, the delays and the rewards are hypothetical or, in cases when the rewards are real, people are not actively waiting during the delay but leave the laboratory to engage in everyday activities until the reward is delivered (but see Mischel et al. 1989; Reynolds and Schiffbauer 2004; Schweighofer et al. 2006 for examples of research tasks for humans that impose real-time waiting). Thus, temporal discounting in human participants does not seem, logically, to be assessing aversion to the waiting per se, but may still represent an aversion to the temporary unavailability of one reward, when there is a simultaneously available but less valuable reward. In other words, temporal discounting may reflect, in colloquial terms, willingness to settle for what is currently available. Studies using nonhuman animals, in contrast, do impose actual delays before the larger, later reward is delivered, opening up an avenue for processes involved in temporal discounting to differ between the human and animal models.

The idea that temporal discounting is critically bound to the value of the immediately available reward has resulted in discounting being equated with the personality trait of impulsivity, and indeed some literature refers to temporal discounting as impulsive choice (e.g., Cardinal et al. 2001; Robbins and Dalley, this volume) or waiting impulsivity (e.g., Robbins and Dalley, this volume). Numerous questionnaire measures have been developed to assess impulsivity as a personality trait, for example, the Barratt Impulsiveness Scale (Patton et al. 1995), the Impulsivity Inventory (Dickman 1990), the Impulsiveness, Venturesome and Empathy Scale (Eysenck and Eysenck 1991), and the UPPS-P Impulsive Behavior Scale (Whiteside and Lyman 2003 with additions from Cyders et al. 2007). These questionnaires usually focus on whether individuals engage in behaviors with a potential for negative outcomes ("I do things without thinking": an item from the Barratt Impulsiveness Scale), based on the idea that impulsivity involves a lack of forethought, inappropriateness, and possibly negative outcomes (Evenden 1999). Given the wide-ranging scope for questionnaire measures versus the circumscribed focus of temporal discounting, it is unsurprising that correlations between temporal discounting and impulsivity measures derived from these questionnaires are often low (e.g., Mitchell 1999), even though stability data suggest that temporal discounting has trait-associated components (Odum 2011). Consequently, if temporal discounting is to be thought of as a measure of impulsivity, we should recognize that it encompasses only a fraction of the conceptual aspects of more personality-focused measures of impulsivity.

As indicated in the Introduction, researchers are interested in temporal discounting because numerous studies have indicated that temporal discounting is more pronounced in individuals who engage in behaviors associated with ill health. For example, those who have been diagnosed with some type of psychopathology compared to those who have not. These psychopathologies include substance use disorders (see MacKillop and Tidey 2011 for a meta-analysis; also Bickel et al., this volume), and neurodevelopmental disorders like attention-deficit/hyperactivity disorder (Scheres et al. 2010; Robbins and Dalley, this volume) and schizophrenia (Wing et al. 2012). Also, obese individuals show more discounting than healthy weight individuals (e.g., Jarmolowicz et al. 2014), and people who do not perform preventative health activities such as scheduling regular dental appointments show more discounting than those who do (e.g., Story et al. 2014). In virtually all of these studies, temporal discounting has been assessed by offering participants a choice between a smaller, *immediate* reward and a larger, later reward. The use of immediate rewards creates the possibility that group differences in these studies are due to differential responses to immediate rewards rather than higher levels of devaluation of the delayed reward. Addressing this issue, Mitchell and Wilson (2012) examined whether more pronounced temporal discounting in cigarette smokers compared to never smokers remained when both rewards were delayed. They found that group differences were still seen but to a much lower degree than would be predicted based on discounting when the smaller reward was immediate. This led them to conclude that the steeper discounting observed in numerous studies (e.g., Bickel et al. 1999, 2008; Mitchell 1999; MacKillop and Tidey 2011; Friedel et al. 2014) was probably due both to a relative heightened sensitivity to the availability of the immediate, smaller reward by smokers, as well as heightened aversion to the delay associated with the larger, later reward. However, such a conclusion requires additional studies to replicate these effects, and possibly to extend this observation to other populations who engage in behaviors associated with ill health.

In the majority of studies using human and nonhuman animal models, temporal discounting is examined using choice paradigms. An excellent discussion of the currently used variants for human and nonhuman research, as well as their positive and negative features, is provided by Madden et al. (2010). As pointed out by Richards et al. (1997), all are examples of psychophysical procedures. Many research groups use procedures based on the method of adjustment, which varies the amounts or delays presented to participants based on responses to earlier choices (e.g., Richards et al. 1997; Johnson and Bickel 2008; Koffarnus and Bickel 2014); for example, increasing the size of the smaller, immediate reward following a choice in which the participant preferred the larger, later alternative. Less frequently used are tasks, such as the Monetary Choice Questionnaire (Kirby et al. 1999), which rely on the method of constant stimuli. This method presents smaller, sooner and larger, later rewards in an order that is independent of participants' choices. In principle, this type of procedure permits researchers to assess whether preference switches are "clean," such that all values above the indifference point are for the smaller, immediate alternative and all values below are for the larger, later alternative, or show some inconsistencies around the threshold. Several authors have remarked that this type of measure might provide some interpretational nuances that can supplement the use of discount functions and area-under-the-curve analyses (e.g., Luo et al. 2012). However, this remains an unanswered empirical question.

While the temporal discounting literature is dominated by studies using choice procedures, it is worthwhile remembering that choice is not the only way to assess subjective value. As elegantly discussed by Grace and Nevin (1997), subjective value can be estimated in multiple ways, all of which should show some convergence, as indicated by correlations. One way is to ask how much participants would "pay" to remove the delay to the larger, later reward or the degree of compensation needed for an immediate reward to be acceptable after a delay. The former procedure is analogous to selecting the delivery options offered to customers of some mail-order businesses in which customers can pay to have items delivered the next day rather than in, for example, 5–7 days. Weber et al. (2007) used a variant of this accelerating-delivery approach to investigate the effect of manipulating thoughts or "queries" about consumption of the delayed reward on the willingness to tolerate delays. Scholten and Read (2010, 2013) have also examined these types of procedures and demonstrated that people will pay less for delays to be removed than the compensation that they require to accept a delay of the same length. These authors suggest that this is consistent with the well-accepted distinction in the judgment and decision-making literature on willingness-to-pay/willingness-to-accept; that is, individuals tend to understate the amount they will pay for a desirable change (receiving a reward earlier) and overstate the amount they need to receive to accept an undesirable change (receiving a reward later). Whether these procedures are sensitive to factors shown to affect temporal discounting assessed using choice procedures, such as cigarette smoking or the use of nonmonetary rewards, is as yet an open question.

Effort Discounting

Delay and likelihood of nonreward (probability) can be viewed as costs that result in the devaluation of rewards. However, it has long been recognized that the "effort," to use the term introduced by Tolman (1932), expended to earn rewards also affects their selection. In the early part of the twentieth century, numerous studies demonstrated that when offered equal-sized rewards, nonhuman animals would select the alternative associated with the smaller effort requirement, whether that be traversing the shortest runway (DeCamp 1920; Kuo 1922; Grice 1942), pushing the door with the least resistance (Tsai 1932), pulling the lightest tray (McCulloch 1934), or pressing the lever with the least weighted resistance (Thompson 1944). These results are embodied in the Principle of Least Effort (Hull 1943), which states that "If two or more behavior sequences, each involving a different amount of energy consumption or work (W) have been equally well reinforced an equal number of times, the organism will gradually learn to choose the less laborious behavior sequence leading to the attainment of the reinforcing state of affairs" (p. 294). Others have suggested alternative wording but with the same basic message (e.g., Mackintosh 1974).

For researchers presenting human and nonhuman subjects with consumable rewards, such as cigarettes or food, the concept of the Principle of Least Effort fits well with the ideas about relative cost from behavioral economics. In that area of study, demand for a commodity is a function of its unit price, that is, the amount of a commodity divided by the cost of obtaining it. While most recent studies use the number of responses required to obtain a reward to represent unit price in the laboratory, the original formulation provided by Hursh et al. (1988) explicitly included both number of responses and the force required to complete the response. For studies using operant chambers, this force would be the weight required to close the microswitches of response levers in rodent operant chambers. The Principle of Least Effort also fits well with the tenets of foraging theory (Stephens and Krebs 1986), where evolution is assumed to have selected organisms that will maximize their net rate of energy gain. Of note, this metric, unlike the unit price formulation, includes both the temporal aspects of reward delivery as well as considerations about energy expenditure. However, few experimental studies have actually assessed energy expenditure directly and usually use a proxy measure such as lever presses, or distance travelled during specific periods. While these proxies probably provide good approximations of the rate of energy expenditure under many circumstances, Brener and Mitchell (1989) demonstrated that during rats' acquisition of lever pressing in an operant chamber, work rate on the lever increased because lever pressing rate increased. However, rate of overall energy expenditure, measured using oxygen consumption, declined reflecting the refinement of responses to more closely approximate the forces required to be classified as a response, concurrent with reductions in activity extraneous to lever pressing while in the operant chamber.

While energy expenditure might be the ultimate currency evaluated by participants during effort discounting tasks, studies of effort discounting have taken a simpler approach to manipulating effort. These manipulations have included squeezing hand grips to some percentage of a previously determined maximum for that individual (Mitchell 1999, 2004; Hartmann et al. 2013) or climbing different numbers of flights of stairs (Ostaszewski et al. 2013) or making different numbers of button presses (Treadway et al. 2009) in studies using human participants. For rodents and nonhuman primates, manipulations have included varying the number of responses required on a lever (Floresco et al. 2008; Farrar et al. 2010), requiring rats to climb barriers of different heights (Denk et al. 2005; Kosheleff et al. 2012) or varying the trail that has to be navigated using a joystick (Evans and Krueger 2014). The latter type of manipulation has been examined in a parallel literature focused on spatial discounting, which has focused on the distribution and distance required to travel between food rewards and how that influences choices between closer, but less preferred items (e.g., Stevens et al. 2005; Mühlhoff et al. 2011). Interestingly, in addition to these physical effort manipulation procedures, there has been recent attempt to develop tasks to manipulate cognitive effort. As might be anticipated, most of these attempts have been directed toward human participants. Thus, Botvinick et al. (2009) required participants to choose between blocks of trials in which there would be a low- or high-cognitive effort demand, where demand varied by requiring more frequent shifting between performing a magnitude judgment task and an ink color identification (Stroop) task. Westbrook et al. (2013) developed a task in which individuals performed an N-back memory task, and then made choices between small and large rewards each associated with different N-back memory requirements. Ostaszewski et al. (2013) required people to choose between an effortless reward and a reward requiring that they read different lengths of text and create a presentation for a class on that text. Schouppe et al. (2014) varied the number of trials with consistent or inconsistent stimuli in a task requiring participants identify the direction of only the center arrow (Flanker task) to vary the attentional requirements. Data presented from each of these tasks indicated that the value of the larger, more effort-requiring reward was reduced systematically as the cognitive effort required increased. In other words, cognitive effort discounting occurred. In addition to these human-focused tasks, a single task for rodents has been developed by Catherine Winstanley (Cocker et al. 2012; Hosking et al. 2014, 2015). This task requires rodents to perform an attentional task where the duration of the stimulus signaling the location of the nose poke required for reward varies making it easy or difficult to detect the signal.

As might be expected, and similar to temporal discounting research, studies using rodents and monkeys have required that the physical and cognitive effort be completed prior to earning a reward, while studies using human participants have used hypothetical effort requirements in many instances of physical and cognitive effort. Unlike the temporal discounting literature, in which studies have suggested similar discounting functions are obtained with real and hypothetical rewards (e.g., Madden et al. 2004), there is reason to believe that real and hypothetical studies may result in significantly different functions for effort discounting. Research to confirm this is required, but two sets of findings from my laboratory are pertinent. First, in an attempt to create a task similar to that used in nonhuman animals, my laboratory experimented with a real-time experiential effort discounting task, in which participants had to complete the effort associated with their chosen alternative following each choice. It rapidly became apparent that unlike studies using rodents, indifference points could not be identified easily. Participants reported that they would select the no-effort alternative to "have a rest" following a prior, high-effort choice, rather than selecting based on the values of the alternatives being offered. Similarly, they reported selecting the no-effort alternative to "gather my strength" in case an attractive large-reward, high-exertion option was presented next. Thus, choices were not independent of one another, and the resulting discounting function was driven by the order of the questions presented. These would not be considerations if requirements were hypothetical. Second, my laboratory has published several studies using a handgrip to examine physical effort discounting (Mitchell 1999,2003, 2004). During the research process, several experimental considerations became apparent. The protocol required participants to squeeze a handgrip "as hard as they could" during screening to identify the maximum force that an individual could generate (maximum voluntary contraction [MVC]). Following this screening, participants chose between a small amount of money available for exerting minimal effort and $10 available after successful completion of a squeeze with some percentage of the MVC. One choice question was selected at random after the task was completed and participants completed the requirements associated with that question. Participants almost always selected the larger, harder alternative when the MVC was 100% or lower but, surprisingly, continued to sometimes select the larger, harder alternative when MVC values were larger than what they had completed during screening, although participants' ratings of their confidence of successfully completing the requirement fell from 100 (completely confident of completing the requirement) toward 0 (completely confident of not completing the requirement). As described in (Mitchell 2003), indifference point-MVC percent function looked highly unlike discount functions seen in temporal discounting studies (Fig. 5.1a). However, using the procedure developed by Rachlin et al. (1991) to convert probability to odds against, the confidence ratings obtained for the different MVC requirements (Fig. 5.1b) were transformed to perceived odds-against scores. Creating a discounting function by plotting the indifference points against these transformed ratios resulted in the effort discounting function looking identical to temporal discounting functions, as can be seen by fitting a hyperbolic function to these data (Fig. 5.1c). The ability of this transformation to create systematic functions underscores the importance to human participants of the participant's perception that the larger reward might not be received. Conceivably, this could be an important consideration for participants in cognitive effort discounting tasks, as well as the physical effort tasks, again illustrating a consideration associated with the use of real rather than hypothetical choices. Another feature of this analysis is important. Some might assert that the purpose of effort discounting assessments is to determine devaluation of the value of the large reward due to participants not being willing to accept the cost. This is not being

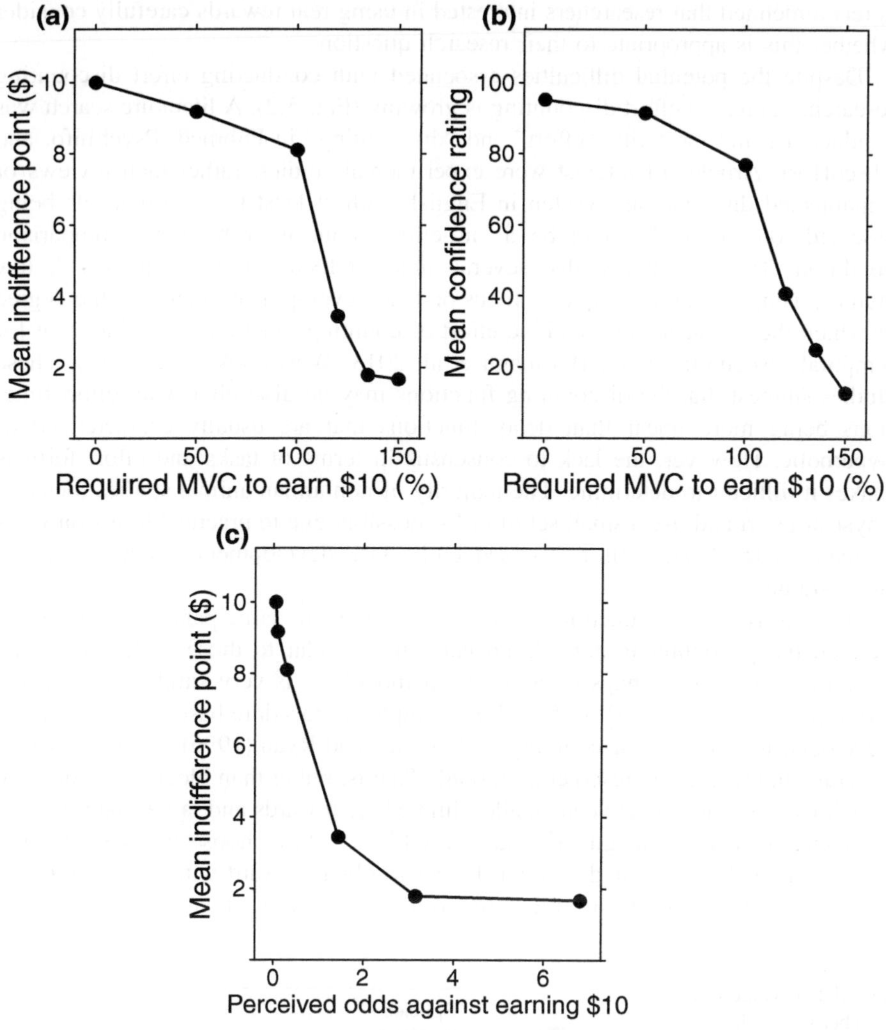

Fig. 5.1 Effort discounting data. Each participant squeezed a handgrip as hard as they could during screening and that was defined as an individual's maximum voluntary contraction (100% MVC). **a** Mean indifference points for 20 participants as a function of the MVC required to earn $10 (0, 50, 100, 125, 135, 150%). **b** Mean confidence rating for the ability to complete the MVC requirement successfully (0–100% confident). **c** Confident rating was converted to a perceived odds against receiving $10 index (100/rating − 1) and mean indifference points were plotted as a function of perceived odds against

accomplished if the choices in the effort discounting are driven by the possibility of failure to successfully complete the effort requirement. In other words, if participants believe that they may be unable to successfully complete the physical or cognitive effort requirement, discounting might not be relevant to differences in reward valuation associated with apathy and conditions characterized by apathy. It is recommended that researchers interested in using real rewards carefully consider whether this is appropriate to their research question.

Despite the potential difficulties associated with conducting effort discounting research, interest in effort discounting is growing (Fig. 5.2). A literature search was conducted using the terms "effort" and "discounting" in Pubmed, PsychInfo, and EbscoHost. Articles of interest were experimental studies, rather than reviews or unpublished dissertations, written in English with at least two effort levels being assessed, on of which could be a "no-effort" control or baseline, comparison condition. This search revealed several areas of focus in these studies. A few studies, using human participants, focus on task development, including the degree to which the physical and cognitive effort discounting functions resembles that for temporal discounting (e.g., Hartmann et al. 2013; Westbrook et al. 2013). These studies suggest that the discounting functions may be dissimilar, with effort functions being more linear than delay functions that are usually characterized as hyperbolic. However, the lack to consensus in terms of tasks and effort formats makes it difficult to determine. The majority of nonhuman animal studies focus on physical effort and use a small set of tasks, possibly due to practical limits on ways to manipulate physical effort. Consequently, task development is not a focus of these studies.

In contrast to the functions derived from human participants, the functions derived using nonhuman animals appear fairly similar to those of temporal discounting functions, perhaps because the methodology is very similar between the two types of discounting (Fig. 5.3). For example, a procedure based directly on that developed for temporal discounting by Evenden and Ryan (1996) has been used in several studies, e.g., Floresco et al. (2008). That is, rather than blocks of choices in which rodents choose between smaller, immediate rewards and larger, later reward with increases in the length of delay over blocks, they choose between smaller, easily obtained rewards and a larger, harder to obtain reward with increases in the difficulty over blocks. One useful feature of this procedure is that it is easy to create

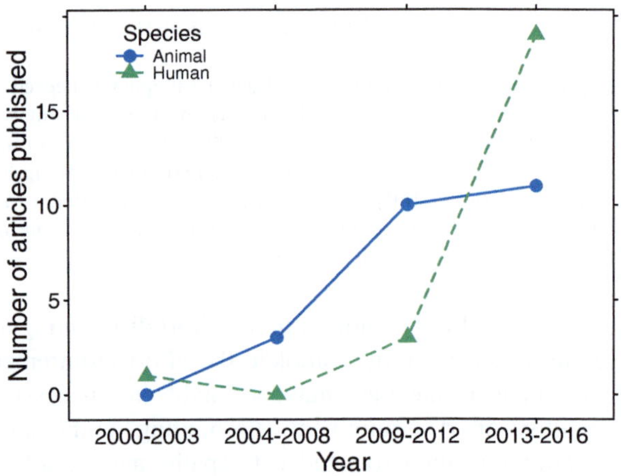

Fig. 5.2 Change in the number of articles investigating effort discounting with humans and animals based on a search of PubMed, PsychInfo, and Ebscohost using the search terms "effort" and "discounting." See text for additional details about inclusions and exclusions

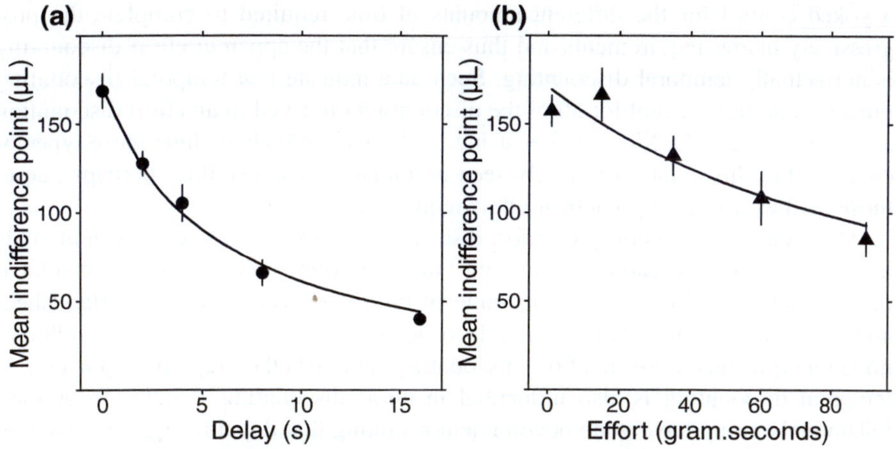

Fig. 5.3 Plots of the median indifference points as a function of delay (**a**) or effort (**b**) to a 150 μl sucrose solution reward obtained from the same 27 male Long Evans rats. Rats experienced all five delay values (0, 2, 4, 8, 16 s) in a random order over five sessions, then all five effort values (0, 15, 35, 60, 90 g s) in a random order over five sessions. This delay–effort alternation occurred five times, and presented data are means of these five exposures. Gram seconds refers to the amount of gram force exerted on the response lever integrated over time; thus, 1 g s could be 1 g force exerted for a second, 2 g force exerted over 0.5 s, etc. Error bars are standard errors of the mean

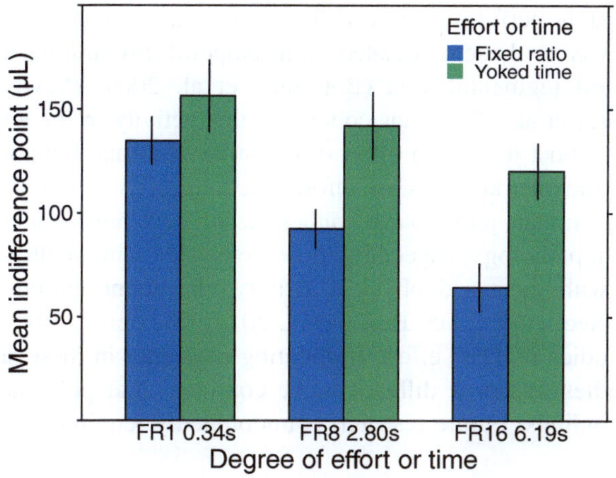

Fig. 5.4 Indifference points from an effort discounting procedure in which food-restricted rats received 150 μl sucrose solution for completing a fixed ratio schedule requirement (FR1, 8, 16) versus an FR1 with an adjusting amount of sucrose solution (Fixed ratio), and indifference points for completing and FR1 coupled with a delay derived from the times to complete each of the fixed ratios versus an FR1 with an adjusting amount of sucrose solution (Yoked time). Error bars are standard errors of the mean

a yoked control for the different amounts of time required to complete the progressively harder requirements and thus ensure that the apparent effort discounting is not actually temporal discounting. Such data indicate that temporal discounting processes do not account for all of the discounting observed in an effort discounting study (e.g., Fig. 5.4). Most studies using nonhuman animals include these types of controls, but this is far more rarely seen in human-focused studies, perhaps due to those studies use of hypothetical effort requirements.

The focus of the majority of effort discounting studies using nonhuman animals is neuroscience research examining the neurophysiology of effort-related decision-making. The role of dopamine in the motor system is well established, and so many studies have worked to identify the contribution of different dopaminergic receptors in effort discounting, and whether region implicated in temporal discounting is also influential in effort discounting. Studies from John Salamone's group have gone beyond demonstrating that dopaminergic blockage in the nucleus accumbens reduces willingness to exert effort and have established interactions with adrenergic 2A receptors and the acetylcholine system (see Nunes et al. 2013 for review). In addition to this research, other studies have examined the role of particular anatomical regions in the effort discounting decision-making process. Critical areas that have been identified using inactivation of GABAergic neurons are similar to those identified in the studies of temporal discounting and other studies of decision-making: the nucleus accumbens, and the basolateral amygdala (Ghods-Sharifi et al. 2009; Ghods-Sharifi and Floresco 2010), prefrontal cortex (Piantadosi et al. 2016). Functional magnetic resonance imaging (fMRI) in human participants performing effort discounting has also identified overlapping regions of activity to those associated with temporal discounting: nucleus accumbens and ventral tegmental area (Botvinick et al. 2009; Prevost et al. 2010). However, Massar et al. (2015) has concluded that activity in the anterior cingulate cortex is more robust during an effort discounting task than temporal discounting. The focus on the neural bases of effort discounting is less pronounced in the literature using human participants, rather researchers have concentrated on the effects of psychopathology, especially those associated with apathy-like depression or associated with increased physical activity like attention-deficit/hyperactivity disorder (e.g., Neef et al. 2005; Burke et al. 2013; Docx et al. 2015; Culbreth et al. 2016). Such studies indicate effort discounting is steeper in these samples, but the number of studies makes it difficult to be confident that publication bias is not driving these findings. Future research is undoubtedly required.

Conclusion

Effort discounting is an exciting, emerging area of research. While there are some methodological and neurobiological commonalities with temporal discounting, and also probability discounting, studies demonstrate that effort discounting is a distinct process behaviorally and neurologically. The extent to which variables that affect temporal and probability discounting also influence effort discounting, such as intellectual functioning (Shamosh and Gray 2008), remains to be determined, and research linking effort discounting to psychopathology is in its infancy. For researchers working with human participants, some important methodological details are unresolved, such as the differences between discounting when participants know that they can complete the hard requirements successfully and discounting under conditions when success is not a given. Cognitive effort discounting procedures are especially interesting in this regard because discounting when participants know the effort can be completed may cast light on apathy, and permit researchers to better understand and model this prevalent characteristic of multiple psychiatric and neuroinflammatory disorders.

Acknowledgements SHM was supported by NIH grants P60 AA010760 and R03 DA040854 and would like to thank Darby Dyar, Alyssa Moore, Austin Phanouvong, and Vanessa Wilson for assisting with the preparation of material in this manuscript.

References

Appelt, K. C., Hardisty, D. J., & Weber, E. U. (2011). Asymmetric discounting of gains and losses: A query theory account. *Journal of Risk and Uncertainty, 43*(2), 107–126.

Baker, F., Johnson, M. W., & Bickel, W. K. (2003). Delay discounting in current and never-before cigarette smokers: Similarities and differences across commodity, sign, and magnitude. *Journal of Abnormal Psychology, 112*(3), 382–392.

Bickel, W. K., Odum, A. L., & Madden, G. J. (1999). Impulsivity and cigarette smoking: Delay discounting in current, never, and ex-smokers. *Psychopharmacology (Berl), 146*(4), 447–454.

Bickel, W. K., Yi, R., Kowal, B. P., & Gatchalian, K. M. (2008). Cigarette smokers discount past and future rewards symmetrically and more than controls: Is discounting a measure of impulsivity? *Drug and Alcohol Dependence, 96*(3), 256–262.

Botvinick, M. M., Huffstetler, S., & McGuire, J. T. (2009). Effort discounting in human nucleus accumbens. *Cognitive, Affective & Behavioral Neuroscience, 9*(1), 16–27.

Brener, J., & Mitchell, S. (1989). Changes in energy expenditure and work during response acquisition in rats. *Journal of Experimental Psychology: Animal Behavior Processes, 15*(2), 166–175.

Burke, C. J., Brunger, C., Kahnt, T., Park, S. Q., & Tobler, P. N. (2013). Neural integration of risk and effort costs by the frontal pole: Only upon request. *Journal of Neuroscience, 33*(4), 1706–1713a.

Cardinal, R. N., Pennicott, D. R., Sugathapala, C. L., Robbins, T. W., & Everitt, B. J. (2001). Impulsive choice induced in rats by lesions of the nucleus accumbens core. *Science, 292,* 2499–2501.

Cocker, P. J., Hosking, J. G., Benoit, J., & Winstanley, C. A. (2012). Sensitivity to cognitive effort mediates psychostimulant effects on a novel rodent cost/benefit decision-making task. *Neuropsychopharmacology, 37*(8), 1825–1837.

Culbreth, A., Westbrook, A., & Barch, D. (2016). Negative symptoms are associated with an increased subjective cost of cognitive effort. *Journal of Abnormal Psychology, 125*(4), 528–536.

Cyders, M. A., Smith, G. T., Spillane, N. S., Fischer, S., Annus, A. M., & Peterson, C. (2007). Integration of impulsivity and positive mood to predict risky behavior: Development and validation of a measure of positive urgency. *Psychological Assessment, 19*(1), 107–118.

DeCamp, J. E. (1920). Relative distance as a factor in the white rat's selection of a path. *Psychobiology, 2,* 245–253.

Denk, F., Walton, M. E., Jennings, K. A., Sharp, T., Rushworth, M. F. S., & Bannerman, D. M. (2005). Differential involvement of serotonin and dopamine systems in cost-benefit decisions about delay or effort. *Psychopharmacology (Berl), 179,* 587–596.

de Villiers, P. A. (1977). Choice in concurrent schedules and a quantitative formulation of the Law of Effect. In W. K. Honig & J. E. R. Staddon (Eds.), *Handbook of operant behavior*. Englewood Cliffs, N.J.: Prentice-Hall.

Docx, L., de la Asuncion, J., Sabbe, B., Hoste, L., Baeten, R., Warnaerts, N., et al. (2015). Effort discounting and its association with negative symptoms in schizophrenia. *Cognitive Neuropsychiatry, 20*(2), 172–185.

Dickman, S. J. (1990). Functional and dysfunctional impulsivity: Personality and cognitive correlates. *Journal of Personality and Social Psychology, 58*(1), 95–102.

Estle, S. J., Green, L., Myerson, J., & Holt, D. D. (2006). Differential effects of amount on temporal and probability discounting of gains and losses. *Memory and Cognition, 34*(4), 914–928.

Evenden, J. L. (1999). Varieties of impulsivity. *Psychopharmacology (Berl), 146*(4), 348–361.

Evenden, J. L., & Ryan, C. N. (1996). The pharmacology of impulsive behaviour in rats: The effects of drugs on response choice with varying delays of reinforcement. *Psychopharmacology (Berl), 128*(2), 161–170.

Evans, A. M., & Krueger, J. I. (2014). Outcomes and expectations in dilemmas of trust. *Judgment and Decision Making, 9*(2), 90–103.

Eysenck, H. J., & Eysenck, S. B. G. (1991). *Manual of Eysenck personality scales (EPS adult): Comprising the EPQ-Revised (EPQ-R)*. EPQ-R short scale, Impulsiveness (IVE) questionnaire: Hodder & Stoughton.

Farrar, A. M., Segovia, K. N., Randall, P. A., Nunes, E. J., Collins, L. E., Stopper, C. M., et al. (2010). Nucleus accumbens and effort-related functions: Behavioral and neural markers of the interactions between adenosine A2A and dopamine D2 receptors. *Neuroscience, 166*(4), 1056–1067.

Floresco, S. B., Tse, M. T., & Ghods-Sharifi, S. (2008). Dopaminergic and glutamatergic regulation of effort- and delay-based decision making. *Neuropsychopharmacology, 33*(8), 1966–1979.

Friedel, J. E., DeHart, W. B., Madden, G. J., & Odum, A. L. (2014). Impulsivity and cigarette smoking: Discounting of monetary and consumable outcomes in current and non-smokers. *Psychopharmacology (Berl), 231*(23), 4517–4526.

Ghods-Sharifi, S., & Floresco, S. B. (2010). Differential effects on effort discounting induced by inactivations of the nucleus accumbens core or shell. *Behavioral Neuroscience, 124*(2), 179–191.

Ghods-Sharifi, S., St Onge, J. R., & Floresco, S. B. (2009). Fundamental contribution by the basolateral amygdala to different forms of decision making. *Journal of Neuroscience, 29*(16), 5251–5259.

Grace, R. C., & Nevin, J. A. (1997). On the relation between preference and resistance to change. *Journal of the Experimental Analysis of Behavior, 67*(1), 43–65.

Grice, G. R. (1942). An experimental study of the gradient of reinforcement in maze learning. *Journal of Experimental Psychology, 30,* 475–489.

Hartmann, M. N., Hager, O. M., Tobler, P. N., & Kaiser, S. (2013). Parabolic discounting of monetary rewards by physical effort. *Behavioral Processes, 100,* 192–196.

Helms, C. M., Gubner, N. R., Wilhelm, C. J., Mitchell, S. H., & Grandy, D. K. (2008). D_4 receptor deficiency in mice has limited effects on impulsivity and novelty seeking. *Pharmacology, Biochemistry and Behavior, 90,* 393–397.

Hosking, J. G., Cocker, P. J., & Winstanley, C. A. (2014). Dissociable contributions of anterior cingulate cortex and basolateral amygdala on a rodent cost/benefit decision-making task of cognitive effort. *Neuropsychopharmacology, 39*(7), 1558–1567.

Hosking, J. G., Floresco, S. B., & Winstanley, C. A. (2015). Dopamine antagonism decreases willingness to expend physical, but not cognitive, effort: A comparison of two rodent cost/benefit decision-making tasks. *Neuropsychopharmacology, 40*(4), 1005–1015. doi:10.1038/npp.2014.285

Hull, C. L. (1943). *Principles of behavior*. New York: Appleton Century.

Hursh, S. R., Raslear, T. G., Shurtleff, D., Bauman, R., & Simmons, L. (1988). A cost-benefit analysis of demand for food. *Journal of the Experimental Analysis of Behavior, 50*(3), 419–440.

Jarmolowicz, D. P., Cherry, J. B., Reed, D. D., Bruce, J. M., Crespi, J. M., Lusk, J. L., et al. (2014). Robust relation between temporal discounting rates and body mass. *Appetite, 78,* 63–67.

Johnson, M. W., & Bickel, W. K. (2008). An algorithm for identifying nonsystematic delay-discounting data. *Experimental and Clinical Psychopharmacology, 16*(3), 264–274.

Kirby, K. N., Petry, N. M., & Bickel, W. K. (1999). Heroin addicts have higher discount rates for delayed rewards than non-drug-using controls. *Journal of Experimental Psychology: General, 128*(1), 78–87.

Koffarnus, M. N., & Bickel, W. K. (2014). A 5-trial adjusting delay discounting task: Accurate discount rates in less than one minute. *Experimental and Clinical Psychopharmacology, 22*(3), 222–228.

Kosheleff, A. R., Grimes, M., O'Dell, S. J., Marshall, J. F., & Izquierdo, A. (2012). Work aversion and associated changes in dopamine and serotonin transporter after methamphetamine exposure in rats. *Psychopharmacology (Berl), 219*(2), 411–420. doi:10.1007/s00213-011-2367-4

Kuo, Z. Y. (1922). The nature of unsuccessful acts and their order of elimination in animal learning. *Journal of Comparative Psychology, 2,* 1–27.

Luo, S., Ainslie, G., Pollini, D., Giragosian, L., & Monterosso, J. R. (2012). Moderators of the association between brain activation and farsighted choice. *Neuroimage, 59*(2), 1469–1477.

MacKillop, J., & Tidey, J. W. (2011). Cigarette demand and delayed reward discounting in nicotine-dependent individuals with schizophrenia and controls: An initial study. *Psychopharmacology (Berl), 216*(1), 91–99.

MacKintosh, N. J. (1974). *The psychology of animal learning*. London: Academic Press.

Madden, G. J., Johnson, P. S., Brewer, A. T., Pinkston, J. W., & Fowler, S. C. (2010). Effects of pramipexole on impulsive choice in male Wistar rats. *Experimental and Clinical Psychopharmacology, 18*(3), 267–276.

Madden, G. J., Raiff, B. R., Lagorio, C. H., Begotka, A. M., Mueller, A. M., Hehli, D. J., et al. (2004). Delay discounting of potentially real and hypothetical rewards: II. Between- and within-subject comparisons. *Experimental and Clinical Psychopharmacology, 12*(4), 251–261.

Maguire, D. R., Gerak, L. R., & France, C. P. (2013). Delay discounting of food and remifentanil in rhesus monkeys. *Psychopharmacology (Berl), 229*(2), 323–330.

Massar, S. A., Libedinsky, C., Weiyan, C., Huettel, S. A., & Chee, M. W. (2015). Separate and overlapping brain areas encode subjective value during delay and effort discounting. *Neuroimage, 120,* 104–113.

McCulloch, T. L. (1934). Optimization theory in evolution. *Annual Review of Ecology and Systematics, 9,* 31–56.

Mischel, W., Shoda, Y., & Rodriguez, M. I. (1989). Delay of gratification in children. *Science, 244* (4907), 933–938.

Mitchell, S. H. (1999). Measures of impulsivity in cigarette smokers and non-smokers. *Psychopharmacology (Berl), 146*(4), 455–464.

Mitchell, S. H. (2003). Discounting the value of commodities according to different types of cost In: N. Heather and R. E. Vuchinich (Eds.), *Choice, behavioral economics and addiction: Theory, evidence and applications.*New York: Elsevier. (pp. 339–357).

Mitchell, S. H. (2004). Effects of short-term nicotine deprivation on decision-making: Delay, uncertainty and effort discounting. *Nicotine & Tobacco Research, 6*(5), 819–828.

Mitchell, S. H., & Wilson, V. B. (2010). The subjective value of delayed and probabilistic outcomes: Outcome size matters for gains but not for losses. *Behavioral Processes, 83*(1), 36–40.

Mitchell, S. H., & Wilson, V. B. (2012). Differences in delay discounting between smokers and nonsmokers remain when both rewards are delayed. *Psychopharmacology (Berl), 219*(2), 549–562.

Mühlhoff, N., Stevens, J. R., & Reader, S. M. (2011). Spatial discounting of food and social rewards in guppies (*Poecilia reticulata*). *Frontiers in Psychology, 2,* 68.

Neef, N. A., Marckel, J., Ferreri, S. J., Bicard, D. F., Endo, S., Aman, M. G., et al. (2005). Behavioral assessment of impulsivity: A comparison of children with and without attention deficit hyperactivity disorder. *Journal of Applied Behavior Analysis, 38*(1), 23–37.

Nunes, E. J., Randall, P. A., Podurgiel, S., Correa, M., & Salamone, J. D. (2013). Nucleus accumbens neurotransmission and effort-related choice behavior in food motivation: Effects of drugs acting on dopamine, adenosine, and muscarinic acetylcholine receptors. *Neuroscience and Biobehavioral Reviews*, 37(9 Pt A), 2015–2025.

Oberlin, B. G., & Grahame, N. J. (2009). High-alcohol preferring mice are more impulsive than low-alcohol preferring mice as measured in the delay discounting task. *Alcoholism, Clinical and Experimental Research, 33,* 1–10.

Odum, A. L. (2011). Delay discounting: Trait variable? *Behavioral Processes, 87*(1), 1–9.

Ostaszewski, P., Bąbel, P., & Swebodziński, B. (2013). Physical and cognitive effort discounting of hypothetical monetary rewards. *Japanese Psychological Research, 55*(4), 329–337.

Pattij, T., Schetters, D., Janssen, M. C., Wiskerke, J., & Schoffelmeer, A. N. (2009). Acute effects of morphine on distinct forms of impulsive behavior in rats. *Psychopharmacology (Berl), 205* (3), 489–502.

Patton, J. H., Stanford, M. S., & Barratt, E. S. (1995). Factor structure of the Barratt Impulsiveness Scale. *Journal of Clinical Psychology, 51*(6), 768–774.

Piantadosi, P. T., Khayambashi, S., Schluter, M. G., Kutarna, A., & Floresco, S. B. (2016). Perturbations in reward-related decision-making induced by reduced prefrontal cortical GABA transmission: Relevance for psychiatric disorders. *Neuropharmacology, 101,* 279–290.

Prevost, C., Pessiglione, M., Metereau, E., Clery-Melin, M. L., & Dreher, J. C. (2010). Separate valuation subsystems for delay and effort decision costs. *Journal of Neuroscience, 30*(42), 14080–14090.

Rachlin, H., Raineri, A., & Cross, D. (1991). Subjective probability and delay. *Journal of the experimental analysis of behavior*, *55*(2), 233–244.

Reynolds, B., & Schiffbauer, R. (2004). Measuring state changes in human delay discounting: An experiential discounting task. *Behavioral Processes, 67*(3), 343–356.

Richards, J. B., Mitchell, S. H., de Wit, H., & Seiden, L. S. (1997). Determination of discount functions in rats with an adjusting-amount procedure. *Journal of the Experimental Analysis of Behavior, 67*(3), 353–366.

Scheres, A., Sumiya, M., & Thoeny, A. L. (2010). Studying the relation between temporal reward discounting tasks used in populations with ADHD: A factor analysis. *International Journal of Methods in Psychiatric Research, 19*(3), 167–176.

Scholten, M., & Read, D. (2010). The psychology of intertemporal tradeoffs. *Psychological Review, 117*(3), 925–944.

Scholten, M., & Read, D. (2013). Time and outcome framing in intertemporal tradeoffs. *Journal of Experimental Psychology. Learning, Memory, and Cognition, 39*(4), 1192–1212.

Schouppe, N., Demanet, J., Boehler, C. N., Ridderinkhof, K. R., & Notebaert, W. (2014). The role of the striatum in effort-based decision-making in the absence of reward. *Journal of Neuroscience, 34*(6), 2148–2154.

Schweighofer, N., Shishida, K., Han, C. E., Okamoto, Y., Tanaka, S. C., Yamawaki, S., et al. (2006). Humans can adopt optimal discounting strategy under real-time constraints. *PLoS Computational Biology, 2*(11), e152.

Shamosh, N. A., & Gray, J. R. (2008). Delay discounting and intelligence: A meta-analysis. *Intelligence, 36,* 289–305.

Skinner, B. F. (1969). *Contingencies of reinforcement: A theoretical analysis*. Englewood Cliffs, N.J: Prentice Hall.

Sozou, P. D. (1998). On hyperbolic discounting and uncertain hazard rates. *Proceedings of the Royal Society of London, B, 265,* 2015–2020.

Stephens, D. W., & Krebs, J. R. (1986). *Foraging theory*. Princeton, N.J.: Princeton University Press.

Stevens, J. R., Rosati, A. G., Ross, K. R., & Hauser, M. D. (2005). Will travel for food: Spatial discounting and reward magnitude in two New World monkeys. *Current Biology, 15,* 1855–1860.

Story, G. W., Vlaev, I., Seymour, B., Darzi, A., & Dolan, R. J. (2014). Does temporal discounting explain unhealthy behavior? A systematic review and reinforcement learning perspective. *Frontiers in Behavioral Neuroscience, 8,* 76.

Takahashi, T., Ikeda, K., & Hasegawa, T. (2007). A hyperbolic decay of subjective probability of obtaining delayed rewards. *Behavioral and Brain Functions, 3,* 52.

Takahashi, T., Ohmura, Y., Oono, H., & Radford, M. (2009). Alcohol use and discounting of delayed and probabilistic gain and loss. *Neuro Endocrinology Letters, 30*(6), 749–752.

Thompson, M. E. (1944). An experimental investigation of the gradient of reinforcement in maze learning. *Journal of Experimental Psychology, 34,* 390–403.

Tolman, E. C. (1932). *Purposive behavior in animals and in man*. New York: Century Company.

Treadway, M. T., Buckholtz, J. W., Schwartzman, A. N., Lambert, W. E., & Zald, D. H. (2009). Worth the 'EEfRT'? The effort expenditure for rewards task as an objective measure of motivation and anhedonia. *PLoS ONE, 4*(8), e6598.

Tsai, L.S. (1932). *The laws of minimum effort and maximum satisfaction in animal behavior.* Monograph of the National Research Institute of Psychology (Peiping, China), 1, 1932. (From *Psychological Abstracts,* 1932, 6, Abstract No. 4329).

Weber, E. U., Johnson, E. J., Milch, K. F., Chang, H., Brodscholl, J. C., & Goldstein, D. G. (2007). Asymmetric discounting in intertemporal choice: A query-theory account. *Psychological Science, 18*(6), 516–523.

Westbrook, A., Kester, D., & Braver, T. S. (2013). What is the subjective cost of cognitive effort? Load, trait, and aging effects revealed by economic preference. *PLoS ONE, 8*(7), e68210.

Whiteside, S. P., & Lynam, D. R. (2003). Understanding the role of impulsivity and externalizing psychopathology in alcohol abuse: Application of the UPPS impulsive behavior scale. *Experimental and Clinical Psychopharmacology, 11,* 210–217.

Wing, V. C., Moss, T. G., Rabin, R. A., & George, T. P. (2012). Effects of cigarette smoking status on delay discounting in schizophrenia and healthy controls. *Addictive Behaviors, 37*(1), 67–72.

Woolverton, W. L., Myerson, J., & Green, L. (2007). Delay discounting of cocaine by rhesus monkeys. *Experimental and Clinical Psychopharmacology, 15*(3), 238–244.

Chapter 6
Engaging and Exploring: Cortical Circuits for Adaptive Foraging Decisions

David L. Barack and Michael L. Platt

Introduction

Impulsive decisions often have unforeseen and regrettable outcomes. By choosing in the heat of the moment, the longer-term consequences that result from our decisions are often overlooked in favor of the ephemeral but seductive present (Loewenstein 1996; Bickel and Marsch 2001; Frederick et al. 2002; Bickel et al. 2007; Glimcher et al. 2007). By choosing to have that last round, clicking on that tempting link, or taking the plunge on the big buy, we commit ourselves to immediate gratification at the expense of potentially better long-term outcomes. The evolutionary contexts within which our decision circuits evolved reflect these so-called intertemporal choices. The primary adaptive function of our decision circuitry lies in maximizing fitness over the longer term (Hamilton 1964; Williams 1966; Trivers 1971, 1972; Charnov 1976; Krebs et al. 1978). Those long-term consequences are driven by how efficiently we gather resources over multiple decisions. Understanding how we make choices in time thus requires that we first understand how decision circuits function in their adaptive context. Perhaps the most fundamental of these is the context of foraging decisions (Stephens and Krebs 1986).

Foraging describes the process by which animals actively search for and harvest resources (Stephens and Krebs 1986). Two broad classes of foraging decisions are generally recognized: choosing whether to accept or reject a particular item upon encounter and choosing when to leave a depleting patch of resources to search for a

D.L. Barack
Department of Philosophy, Department of Neuroscience, Department of Economics, and Center for Science and Society, Columbia University, New York, NY, USA

M.L. Platt (✉)
Department of Neuroscience, University of Pennsylvania, Clinical Research Building, 411 Curie Blvd., Philadelphia, PA 19104, USA
e-mail: mplatt@mail.med.upenn.edu

J.R. Stevens (ed.), *Impulsivity*, Nebraska Symposium on Motivation 64,
DOI 10.1007/978-3-319-51721-6_6

better one. The ubiquity of such decisions makes foraging fundamental to decision making (Real 1991; Stephens 2008). Building upon this prior work, here we provide an analysis of foraging choice contexts and survey the neural mechanisms mediating foraging behavior with a special focus on how foraging strategies are regulated to meet the demands of volatile and stochastic environments.

Neurobiological studies of foraging have focused on sequential, non-exclusive, accept-or-reject decisions in iterated choice contexts in which choosing to accept or reject an option now does not forego returning to the alternative at a later time, and the choice facing the organism occurs repeatedly, with different options presented in sequence (Stephens 2008; Calhoun and Hayden 2015). For example, organisms foraging for food distributed in patches repeatedly choose whether to continue harvesting from the same patch or leave to search for a new, potentially better alternative (Charnov 1976; Stephens and Krebs 1986). Likewise, organisms traveling along a well-worn foraging path repeatedly decide whether to visit their habitual haunts or to explore new ones (Berger-Tal and Bar-David 2015). Finally, organisms in dynamic environments must continuously compare the probability that the world has changed against the relative noisiness in the pattern of rewards and adjust their behavior accordingly (Nassar et al. 2010).

Primates, who have diverse diets (Harding and Teleki 1981), exhibit especially complex and flexible foraging behavior. The need to remember the types, locations, and renewal times of many food resources requires spatial memory, and efficiently harvesting these resources requires strategic planning (Clutton-Brock and Harvey 1980; Milton 1981). Indeed, the complexity of such foraging has been hypothesized as a major selective pressure driving the expansion of the neocortex in primates (Milton 1988; Passingham and Wise 2012; Genovesio et al. 2014). The foraging hypothesis explicitly proposes that primate dietary diversity placed selective pressure on our forebears for larger and more complex brains.

Besides food, organisms forage for a wide range of resources, including water, minerals, sexual opportunities, social encounters, and other biologically relevant resources (Stephens and Krebs 1986) like information (Dukas 2002; Fu and Pirolli 2007; Pirolli 2007; Dukas and Jim 2009). Though foraging in external spaces stands as a basic ability of cognitive systems, the mechanisms used for foraging and the formal models describing foraging behavior can be extended to the search and exploration of mental space. Foraging models have been applied to complex cognitive activity, including visual search (Cain et al. 2012; Anderson et al. 2013, Wolfe 2013), free recall (Hills et al. 2012, 2013, 2015; though for a dissenting view, see Abbott et al. 2015), planning (Wilke et al. 2009), task-switching (Payne et al. 2007; Farmer et al. 2011; Janssen et al. 2011), studying (Metcalfe and Jacobs 2010), social processing (Hills and Pachur 2012), and problem solving (Hills 2010; Hills et al. 2010, Payne and Duggan 2011).

The capacity to forage through internal spaces is hypothesized to be one of, if not the, most central cognitive skills (Newell 1994, Hills et al. 2010). Understanding how organisms forage thus illuminates a range of both fundamental and complex cognitive behaviors. Whether searching for food, social encounters, information, items in memory, or concepts, organisms must navigate a rich array of possibilities, deciding which opportunities to pursue and which to forego. Only recently, however, have the neural circuits mediating foraging in humans (Kolling et al. 2012; Shenhav et al. 2014), nonhuman primates (Hayden et al. 2011), and other animals (Bendesky et al. 2011; Ranade et al. 2013) begun to be described.

In this review, we describe in detail a circuit for foraging decisions (Kolling et al. 2012; Calhoun and Hayden 2015), the set of brain regions and neural computations underlying the ability to forage efficiently. Malfunction in this set of regions can result in impulsive and risky choices that fail to adequately account for the long-term consequences of our actions. This network of areas is modulated by two catecholamines, dopamine and norepinephrine, originating in subcortical nuclei and playing key roles during foraging. Here, we focus on an interconnected network of cortical areas, composed of the anterior cingulate, medial prefrontal, and posterior cingulate cortices. Efficient foraging behavior requires not only keeping track of foregone opportunities, a function we ascribe to the dorsal bank of the anterior cingulate sulcus (dACC), but also computing the value of current options by integrating over various environmental properties, a function of prefrontal cortical regions including the medial orbitofrontal cortex (mOFC) and ventromedial prefrontal cortex (vmPFC) with inputs from subcortical dopaminergic pathways, and non-specific optimization computations that shift behaviors into an exploratory regime, a function that we ascribe to the posterior cingulate cortex (PCC). While these areas may execute the same computations to organize other kinds of behavior, such as simultaneous, value-based decision making (Shenhav et al. 2014, 2016), we argue that this interconnected network of areas (Vogt et al. 1979; Heilbronner and Haber 2014) comprises a foraging circuit that regulates adaptive decisions to engage or to explore, the fulcrum of foraging behavior.

Foraging and Decision Making

Imagine you are a monkey, and you are foraging in a berry patch. As you forage, you gather berries, which take time and energy to find and consume. Other members of the troop are also gathering food, and there is the ever-present danger of predation. Some of these competitors and dangers you can see, and some you can't. The decline in the available resources, the competition from other foragers, and the dangers posed by predators continually force the decision to choose between continuing to forage at the same location and abandoning the current patch for newer, potentially more rewarding grounds.

This hypothetical situation highlights some of the prominent features of foraging (Fig. 6.1a, left panel). Such choices are iterated, recurring again and again in a particular context, and non-exclusive, where choosing one option does not prevent choosing other options at a later time (Stephens 2008; Stephens et al. 2012). When foraging within a patch of resources, organisms repeatedly decide to continue harvesting reward or to search for new resources. Deciding to continue foraging in a patch does not commit an organism to staying within that patch beyond the current

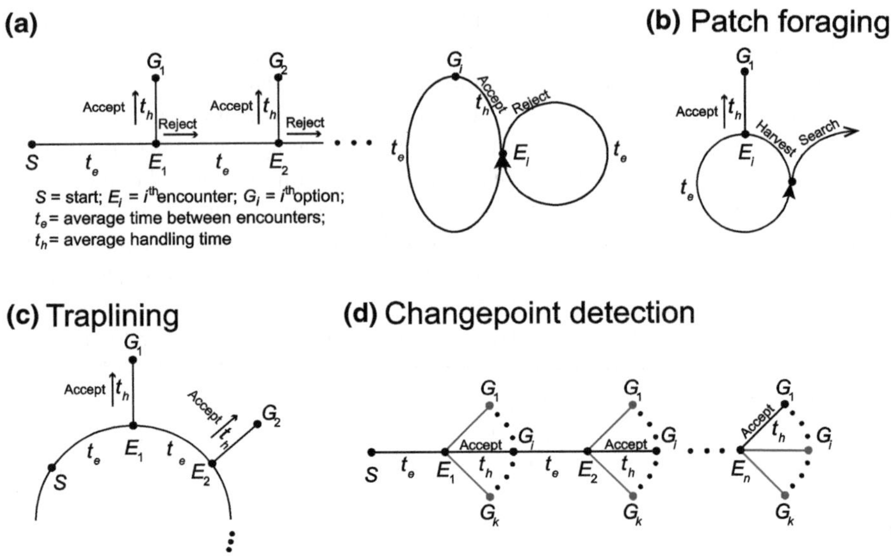

Fig. 6.1 **a** Schematic for foraging problems. (*Left panel*) Successive encounters result in a series of accept-or-reject decisions by the forager. (*Right panel*) Foraging is often a recursive series of such decisions. **b** Patch-leaving decisions exemplify this basic structure. As the organism forages in a patch, they can choose to continue to harvest reward from the patch or to search for a new one, often at unknown locations and for unknown costs. **c** Traplining also illustrates the basic foraging structure, as organisms make a series of accept-or-reject decisions along a preset pathway. **d** Changepoint detection poses a multi-alternative foraging problem for organisms, who must integrate information over multiple choices about which foreground option is the best, akin to sampling from a patch over time in order to decide when to switch, albeit to a known location whose value may have changed

choice. Even within a patch, decisions to continue to search or feed at one within-patch resource are often made repeatedly, as many patches contain multiple exploitable resources. And, choosing to forego eating a food item, perhaps because it is less desirable now, does not prevent choosing to eat it later, perhaps because it has become more desirable. The non-exclusive nature of such choices implies that foregone options can be returned to at a later time, but only if the organism can recall the location and value of these options.

Foraging contexts typically involve so-called foreground and background options, with organisms making an accept-or-reject decision about the foreground option (Stephens 2008; Kacelnik et al. 2011; Calhoun and Hayden 2015). Coming across a less desirable berry may result in a monkey rejecting it and continuing to search for a better one. A larger, riper berry may elicit an accept response. Likewise, the foreground choice may be to begin foraging in a patch, whereas the background choice is to continue searching. Foreground/background options can also be framed as continuing with a plan or diverting from it, as occurs in planned foraging routines. The foreground and background options establish the decision context for the foreground choices.

Sometimes, foraging decisions are framed in terms of default and non-default choices (Kolling et al. 2012, 2016; Shenhav et al. 2014). Default options are ones that are chosen more often in a decision context, whereas non-default options are chosen less often. Whether the foreground option is a default one depends on the choice context. The foreground option can be the non-default option when foreground options are often rejected, or the default option when such options are usually accepted. Whether the foreground option is default depends on the relative probability of accepting that option.

In general, the decision to accept or reject the foreground option is governed by the average reward rate over a period of time (Charnov 1976). Average reward rate has been conceived of as the opportunity cost of time (Niv et al. 2005, 2007; Constantino and Daw 2015) and proposed as a unifying variable underlying response vigor (Guitart-Masip et al. 2011; Beierholm et al. 2013), exploration/exploitation trade-offs (Aston-Jones and Cohen 2005; Gilzenrat et al. 2010), temporal discounting (Kacelnik 1997; Gallistel and Gibbon 2000), as well as risk sensitivity and self-control (Constantino and Daw 2015), thus highlighting the relevance of foraging to a diverse array of behaviors and cognitive processes.

Choices between options are typically sequential, not simultaneous, and recur over and over (Fig. 6.1a, right panel) (Freidin et al. 2009; Kacelnik et al. 2011). Within a patch, an organism may make repeated selections from the array of food options, sequentially encountering possible prey items and choosing which to consume. In deciding when to leave the patch, the organism may make a sequence of stay in patch decisions before finally deciding to depart.

Foraging often occurs within changing environments or against a background of new information gained over multiple choices (Calhoun and Hayden 2015). As organisms forage within a patch, they decrease the overall quality of the patch by consuming resources, thus changing the prospects for the present patch. Or, similarly, as they explore the local environment for a new patch, organisms learn about the distribution of patches in the environment, how far apart and rich they are, changing their expectations and hence their decision computations. Organisms must integrate this information and subsequently adjust both their estimates of the local and global reward rates and their foraging strategy to take into account this new information. Foragers can also actively explore their environments to improve the set of foraging opportunities, either for present consumption or for future planning of foraging routes.

A Process Model of Foraging

Our process model of foraging computations includes a basic value-guided threshold decision circuit assisted by a set of behavior optimization routines (Fig. 6.2). The basic choice mechanism includes a running assessment of the value of the background option (typically the average reward rate for the current environment), the assignment of a value for the current foreground option, and

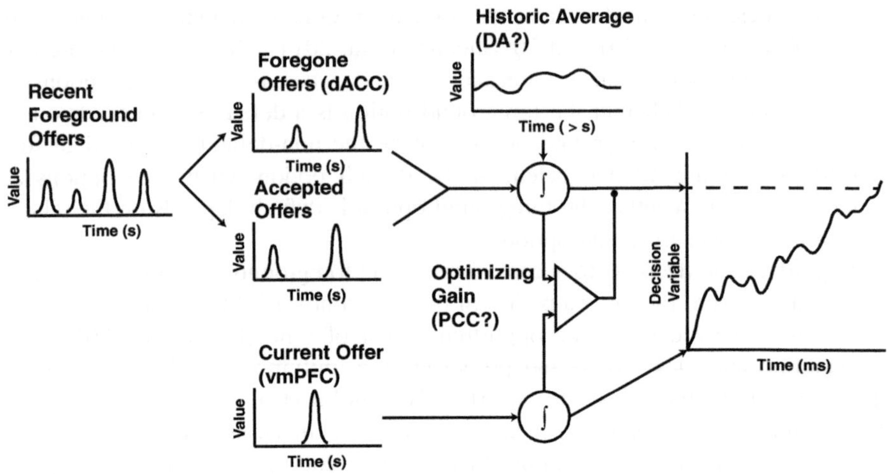

Fig. 6.2 The proposed process model and speculation about the areas executing the relevant computations. Foragers make accept-or-reject decisions about foreground offers. Values are initially represented in ventromedial prefrontal cortex (vmPFC), with neuronal activity therein ultimately signaling the value of accepted offers. Foregone offer values are signaled in dACC. The inputs from recently experienced (vmPFC) and counterfactual (dACC) rewards are integrated with historic reward rate information (possibly encoded in basal ganglia dopamine [DA] neurons). This integrated signal sets decision thresholds for use in the rate rule (see text). Optimal foraging is regulated by gain modulations in this threshold, such as by sudden shifts in environmental states, changes in the space of possible actions, or updates to state–action–outcome contingencies. These different variables are integrated, and their influence on adaptive foraging is possibly mediated by PCC. Current offer values are integrated over time until a threshold is reached (depicted) and the offer is accepted. Decisions to reject offers may also be driven by a similar integration process

threshold-setting and comparison mechanisms for choosing between these options. In addition, memory is needed to store the recent history of the size and location of rewards, as well as any foraging paths or strategies adopted. Finally, a set of computational mechanisms that update the estimate of the environmental state, including detecting changes in the environment, exploring for new information, or searching for alternative options, augments the uncertainty of the estimated average reward rate and hence the threshold used to make a decision.

A standard threshold decision model serves as a useful starting point for understanding the computational operations underlying the foraging choice (Gold and Shadlen 2007; Kacelnik et al. 2011; Calhoun and Hayden 2015). The value of accepting the current option is compared to the value of rejecting it, with the background determining the threshold for accepting the foreground option. The threshold is typically related to the rate of accumulation of energy, information, or some other resource (Charnov 1976; Stephens and Krebs 1986; Pirolli 2007; Hills et al. 2008; Freidin et al. 2009). Besides basic perceptual machinery, computing the value of the current option requires determining the sizes of the associated rewards and probabilities of obtaining those rewards (Bernoulli 1738), as well as the time and energetic costs of choosing the different options (Stephens and Krebs 1986).

The value of rejecting the foreground option is typically governed by the richness of the environment (Charnov 1976). Computing long-term reward rates requires updating a stored value that integrates over different types of information. First and foremost, rewards gained over some time horizon must be integrated into the average value for the environment (Constantino and Daw 2015; Barack and Gold 2016). Second, information about the number and value of other possible rewarding locations must also be incorporated to obtain a better estimate of the environment's overall richness (Reboreda and Kacelnik 1991; Dukas and Jim 2009). Third, assessment of the richness of the environment must be scaled by the uncertainty associated with each source of reward or information, as well as by the overall density of other foragers (Fretwell and Calver 1969), probability of predation (Stephens and Krebs 1986), and other factors.

A control system hypothetically governs the trade-off between the accept and reject values using local reward rates (Stephens and Anderson 2001; Kacelnik et al. 2011, Calhoun and Hayden 2015). The controller will act as a comparator (Carpenter 1988) of the value of accepting to that of rejecting, as well as gating the decision signals for action selection. The controller sets the threshold for the value comparison, utilizing the rate rule (Charnov 1976; Stephens and Krebs 1986; Stephens and Anderson 2001): Select the foreground offer if and only if $G_i/T_i > \overline{G}/\overline{T}$, that is, if the gain in reward from type *i* options, G_i, divided by the time cost, T_i, exceeds the average offer across types. Hence, the threshold is governed by the average offer in the environment.

In general, there are many ways to set this threshold. For example, the controller may explicitly set a general threshold governed by the above-mentioned factors. Or, there may be multiple value-governed thresholds for accepting or rejecting the option facing the organism, with a decision emerging from the interactive race between them (Kacelnik et al. 2011). When the comparator determines that the integration over the value of the current foreground offer reaches the threshold, the organism accepts the foreground option. The threshold can be augmented by new information either in the form of environmental information or in the form of reassessment of the actions available to the organism. Since the threshold is set by the average reward rate, and the reward rate is computed over some time horizon, the threshold can be augmented either by clearing the stored value of the average reward rate or by adaptively setting the horizon over which the history of rewards is to be computed.

In addition to the threshold for accept-or-reject decisions, the challenge of determining when to alter the background is also governed by average reward rates. For some foraging decisions, the problem reduces to a comparison of the current reward rate, computed over a local time horizon, and the average for the environment, computed over a longer one (Charnov 1976). Here, organisms can use the marginal value theorem (Charnov 1976), which is formally equivalent to the rate rule: Background context should shift when $\overline{R} > \delta R/\delta t$, that is, when the average reward rate across the environment is greater than the instantaneous reward rate $\delta R/\delta t$ being offered right now. In these situations, the forager should switch when the reward rate determined by recent offers drops below the average for the environment, that is, when anywhere else on average is better than where the forager is now.

Organisms may use the more myopic rate rule, above, to make decisions about both whether to accept or reject a foreground offer and whether to change the background option (Stephens and Anderson 2001). For other foraging decisions, the problem reduces to a determination of when new information such as evidence of newly available large rewards suggests that switching may be beneficial, augmenting either the relative value of the current offers or the estimate of the average richness of the environment. These factors can induce a change in the organism's strategy, shifting its background option. Hence, foraging is intrinsically hierarchical: A series of accept-or-reject decisions are made while engaged in a particular behavior, while simultaneously informing the organism about whether to continue with that type of behavior or switch to a new one.

Since choices are made sequentially, the alternative foreground options from successive choices may not all be present at the same time, imposing memory and planning demands on foraging. With a single current offer, the alternatives are not simultaneously posed to the forager. And yet, whether or not to accept the current offer will depend on its value relative to other recent offers and to the average offer in the environment. Hence, organisms must remember the history of such offers in order to know whether the current offer should be consumed.

In addition to remembering recent options, foragers also need to estimate the relevant time horizon over which to encode past options and to integrate recent history. This time horizon governs the extent to which memory for past choices influences the current foraging decisions. The entire history of recent offers may not be relevant, especially if there was recently a change in their distribution. Foragers thus must also keep track of the relative stability of the environment (Nassar et al. 2010) and determine how far back in time to filter recent offers (Barack and Gold 2016). The recent history of offers will then be integrated over this relevant time horizon.

Finally, advanced planning and strategic assessment, possibly governed by a hippocampal–striatal–prefrontal cortical mechanism (Redish 2012), must guide the order of future choices. Different sequences of offers will differently impact reward rates. Planning as much as possible also reduces uncertainty and increases the accuracy of estimates of various reward rates. Context too influences the trade-off between risk and reward. Different resources at different locations in the environment will offer different rewards and hence promise different reward rates, and these differing offers may be preferred in different contexts, such as cases where a minimal level of reward is required for continued survival (Caraco 1981; Kolling et al. 2014).

While the basic choice model outlined above—evaluating foreground options, tracking local reward history, a method for comparing foreground offers and local history, and a threshold for switching background contexts—is a beginning framework, additional computational operations are necessary to explain adaptive foraging behavior. As noted, these adaptations occur by changing the stored value of the average reward rates—computed over recent rewards for foreground choices and over long-term history for background changes. These operations include interrupt processes that can initiate shifts in systemic processing, environmental exploration that can determine when to accept rewards on offer and potentially invalidate environmental assumptions, and action optimization that can induce changes for more efficient behavior. Fundamentally, primates are adaptive foragers, and these computational functions all serve to aid in such adaptive behavior.

First, interrupts in the environment, such as uncovering unexpected options or the appearance of predators, can shift foragers out of their foreground/background context into a new one. In computer science, an interrupt is a signal to the system that halts the system's current processing to switch to processing the cause of the interrupt, such as providing keyboard input to a computer. The concept of interrupts has been usefully appropriated in cognitive psychology to understand how cognitive systems apportion attention and process events (Pylyshyn 2007). In the case of foraging, an interrupt is an unexpected signal informing the system that the environment has changed, possibly invalidating assumptions about the current or background environment and requiring changes in strategy such as shifting from foraging to defending against a predator. However, the cortical circuits that mediate the influence of such interrupts, balancing continued operation against the urgency of shifting processing to the source of the interrupt and reassessing the current environment, have not been detailed nor incorporated into foraging decision circuitry.

Second, environmental exploration can increase an organism's knowledge of the environment by gathering information about differentially informative options (Krebs et al. 1978; Wilson et al. 2014), changing foraging strategy to maximize the encounter rate (Bartumeus et al. 2002), the rate at which options in the environment become available, or by expanding the set of states (Sutton and Barto 1998), the possibilities that enter into either the foreground or background decisions. Here, we understand the investigation and discovery of the environment as the exploration of state space using known actions. Such environmental exploration can act as a gain controller that scales the value of recent rewards or the time horizon over which average reward rates are calculated. Either effect can modulate the threshold for choice.

Third, optimization routines can improve foraging efficiency by allowing cognitive systems to explore the possible actions available in an environment. Optimization routines are central to computer science, where they have a number of uses, including minimizing loss functions during curve fitting (van Laarhoven and Aarts 1987; Tan 2008), as well as to psychology, where they have been proposed for understanding the nature of probabilistic inference (Griffiths et al. 2012). Here, we understand these operations as the exploration of action space for a given state of the environment. New actions may make available new information about the environment, effectively shifting the estimated average rate either up or down and hence modulating the threshold.

All three of these additional computational operations can influence the basic foraging choice mechanism in at least two ways. First, unexpected changes in the environment and information about either new states or possible actions can change the uncertainty associated with the estimate of the average reward rate of the environment. Since this reward rate informs the background option in the choice problem posed to the agent, these computations influence the agent's estimate of the background value. This influence thus changes the decision calculus associated with the basic choice mechanism; a noisier estimate of the average reward rate will result in noisier choice behavior as the system will have a wider range over which to infer that the threshold has been exceeded. Second, these operations can influence the threshold operation that dictates the trade-off between foreground and background choices. Unexpected changes or new possibilities may shift the organism into an action selection regime that corresponds to a radical and rapid downshift in the threshold for accepting foreground options or for switching background ones. These changes or possibilities may also curtail the variability in the organism's choices as the current option increases in value relative to the average rate.

A Foraging Circuit in the Brain

The analysis above provides a framework in the form of a process model, adaptive integration to a threshold, which can be used to guide investigation into the neural circuits of foraging decisions. The features of foraging choices, such as their iterative, non-exclusive, sequential nature, the foreground/background context, and the need to integrate information over multiple choices, outline the processing problem facing foragers. Given this description, the characterization of variables in the environment and in the system, such as local and global reward rates and time horizons for reward calculations, and the mathematical operations over these variables provide a theoretical framework for understanding how organisms should forage in their environment. These are the two essential components in understanding the problem that foraging poses to organisms, why they need to keep track of those properties and what computations they need to perform to behave efficiently (Marr 1982; Shagrir 2010). By describing the computations operating over these variables in terms of calculating uncertainty, integrating information, and detecting threshold crossing, we have developed a psychologically plausible process model (Shi et al. 2010; Griffiths et al. 2012, 2015) that allows us to evaluate the validity of our foraging analysis and the implementation of foraging computations using neurobiology.

The investigation of the neurophysiological circuits for foraging is just beginning. Many of the aspects of foraging detailed above, such as the integration of evidence over long timescales or value-weighted route planning, have yet to receive focused formal investigation, and we do not currently have an optimal characterization of such behavior. In some cases, such as route planning, the computational complexity of the problem (known as NP-hard problems) may prevent any principled solution. Despite the young state of the field, much recent progress has been made, and in the following discussion, we describe some of the tasks used to reveal the role of different areas in this foraging circuit.

Studying Foraging in the Laboratory

Below, we discuss three different types of foraging behavior: patch foraging, habitual foraging, and adaptive foraging. To varying degrees, all three task types embody the hallmarks of foraging decisions: a series of iterated non-exclusive choices between accepting or rejecting a foreground option in the context of some background that often requires tracking environmental changes and harvesting information as well as harvesting resources to optimize behavior.

First, as mentioned above, we discuss patch-foraging decisions about whether to continue harvesting reward within a patch or to leave for a new one (Fig. 6.1b). The search for resources presents a central foraging challenge: deciding when to depart a current, depleting resource to search for a new, richer one. In an environment where resources are clumped in patches, foraging in a patch will lead to a decrease in the value of the patch. As resources are harvested, the total number that remains in a patch will decrease, and the remaining resources may be harder to harvest and of lower quality. This change in the distribution of remaining rewards in a patch changes the patch's value relative to other patches in the environment, perhaps at unknown locations and of unknown total values. The challenge of deciding when to depart such a depleting resource in search of a fresh one is known as the patch-leaving problem.

Patch-leaving decisions feature all the hallmarks of a foraging choice. When foraging in a patch, organisms must repeatedly decide whether to continue foraging or whether to move on, with the decision to move on providing the foreground decision. Patch-based decisions are not exclusive, as deciding to stay in a patch does not forego deciding to leave later, and decisions to leave or to stay, or to begin foraging or keep hunting, are always sequential. Finally, as organisms make patch-based decisions, they gain information about the environment by learning about the distribution of patches (such as interpatch distance and patch types) and their longer-term rewarding properties (such as the distribution of reward sizes and reward intake rates), environmental features that cover many choices.

The patch-leaving problem has an optimal solution in the marginal value theorem (MVT), which dictates leave times given knowledge of instantaneous and average intake rates across the environment (Charnov 1976). Over 60 species of animals and even plants across the biological spectrum follow the MVT in their foraging behavior (Stephens and Krebs 1986; Nonacs 2001). The computational principles such as the MVT underlying these fundamental foraging behaviors have been applied to searches through task space during the flexible control of behavior (Payne et al. 2007; Farmer et al. 2011; Janssen et al. 2011), conceptual space during memory tasks (Hills et al. 2012, 2015), and study space during student test preparation (Metcalfe and Jacobs 2010).

A close analogue of patch-foraging tasks are bandit tasks (Gittins and Jones 1974; Gittins 1979; Steyvers et al. 2009). In a bandit task, subjects choose between two or more rewarding locations in the environment, the equivalent of patches. Imagine you are at a casino, playing the slot machines. Some machines may pay out well and others poorly (in actuality, they are all random, but imagine there is some underlying structure to their randomness). Your task is to determine the best slot machine and set your playing policy accordingly (Sutton and Barto 1998). Bandit tasks have the same structure as the slot machine problem. In some cases, the environment is variable (non-stationary bandit problems), and these present a particularly challenging choice context for the subject, as they must trade off exploiting the current best option against exploring for an alternative that is now better.

Second, we discuss decisions about planning and traveling between multiple rewarding locations in the environment (Fig. 6.1c). Many foragers face the challenge of planning a route to harvest resources from multiple well-known locations. An essential aspect of real-world foraging is learning how to forage efficiently through such an environment. Many primates are frugivores, and fruiting times and locations can be learned and then repeatedly navigated to reduce energy expenditures (Menzel 1973; Noser and Byrne 2010). Hence, formation of habitual behaviors, such as repeated path following or traplining, can also be analyzed through a foraging lens. Navigation in general involves a series of sequential decisions, which can be conceptualized as deciding to continue along a route or deciding to deviate from that route, one of the hallmarks of foraging decisions. In addition, navigating the same path over and over is a type of habit. Finally, in foraging, organisms often determine a path for collecting resources. Habitual navigation for environmental resources possesses all of the hallmarks of a foraging decision, and traplining is essentially habitual navigation for food or other resources.

Traplining involves planning a multi-stop route in the most efficient manner possible (Altshuler and Clark 2003; Ohashi and Thomson 2005; Berger-Tal and Bar-David 2015). Traplining decisions have only recently been studied neurobiologically, but they correspond both to a class of traveling salesmen problem, extensively discussed in the psychological literature (MacGregor and Chu 2011), and to a class of habitual decisions, which have been the focus of extensive neurobiological investigation (Graybiel 2008). In traplines, organisms repeatedly choose to visit the same locations (Berger-Tal and Bar-David 2015), and choosing to visit one location before another does not preclude visiting the other locations or novel locations later (Ohashi and Thomson 2005, 2009). Traplines are often routinized, with rare deviations driven by information from the environment (Tinklepaugh 1932; Menzel 1991, 1996; Hemmi and Menzel 1995; Janmaat et al. 2006), and so organisms decide whether to continue with their routine (background choice) or to investigate the local environment (foreground choice). Deciding the order in which to visit a location reflects sequential choices, and deviations from the typical order reflect information gleaned from recent choices. Hence, like patch-leaving decisions, traplining decisions are also made in a foraging choice context.

Third, we discuss changepoint detection decisions in which the organism must sift signal from noise to detect an underlying change in the environment (Fig. 6.1d). Changepoint detection problems also feature many of the hallmarks of foraging decisions. Organisms repeatedly pursue a course of action until an unexpected series of returns from the environment indicates that a change in the environment's structure, or changepoint, may have occurred. Foregoing one option does not prevent returning to it once a change in the environment indicates the relative value of that option has increased. In changepoint detection problems, organisms must choose whether to vary their choice strategy (foreground choice) or continue with the same strategy (background choice). They must keep track of the uncertainty associated with the current best option as well as the probability of a changepoint. By integrating evidence over multiple decisions, organisms can estimate when a change has occurred and shift their behavior accordingly to return to a reward maximizing state.

The Mammalian Foraging Circuit

Using insights gleaned from multiple studies reflecting the above computational demands, we discuss several nodes in a foraging circuit in the brain, mapping different computations required for foraging to different brain areas (Fig. 6.3). This

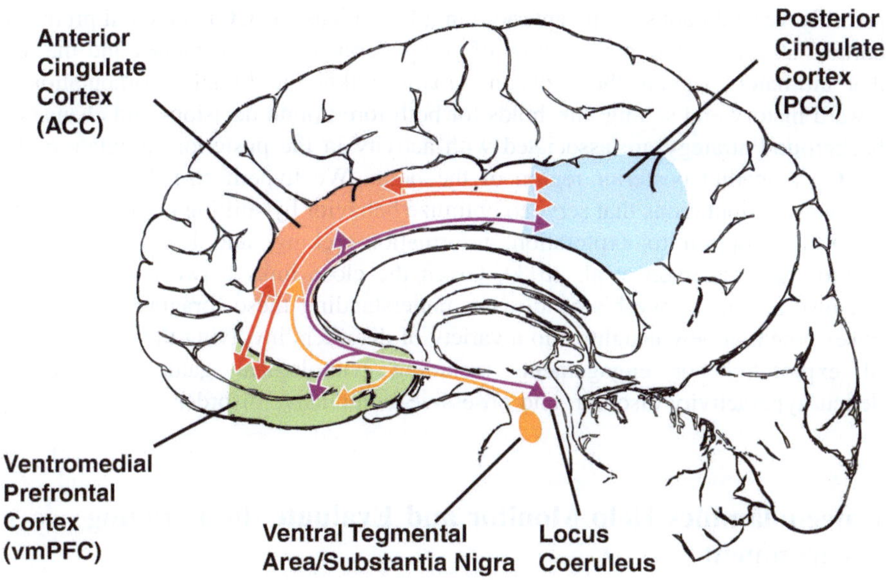

Fig. 6.3 Neural areas and connections discussed herein. The ventromedial prefrontal cortex (vmPFC, *light green*), the dorsal anterior cingulate cortex (dACC, *light red*), and the posterior cingulate cortex (PCC, *light blue*) form an interconnected circuit (*red arrows*) that regulates adaptive foraging decisions. Innervation from dopaminergic (*orange*) and noradrenergic (*purple*) nuclei in the basal ganglia signal rewards and environmental changes that are integrated in the regulation of decision thresholds during foraging

circuit is comprised of three interconnected cortical regions: the ventromedial prefrontal cortex, the anterior cingulate cortex, and the posterior cingulate cortex (Vogt et al. 1979; Heilbronner and Haber 2014; Heilbronner and Hayden 2016), with inputs from subcortical dopamine neurons to prefrontal areas (Williams and Goldman-Rakic 1993; Björklund and Dunnett 2007) and brainstem norepinephrine neurons throughout (Aston-Jones and Cohen 2005).

Catecholamines play important roles in regulating foraging behavior. Dopamine neurons signal the instantaneous deviation of recent outcomes from the predicted environmental returns (Schultz et al. 1997, 1998; Schultz 1998) as well environmental richness—two key variables needed to compute option values and long-term reward rates. Norepinephrine signals may serve to regulate this circuitry to match foraging strategies to internal states and the state of the environment (Aston-Jones and Cohen 2005) and possibly prime systems to respond to unexpected changes in the environment (Jepma and Nieuwenhuis 2011; Nassar et al. 2012) or learn novel environmental contingencies (Sara and Bouret 2012).

Following these computations, a fundamental aspect of foraging decisions is the accept-or-reject nature of foreground choices. Accept choices are driven by computations executed in a valuation network with a main node in the ventromedial prefrontal cortex (vmPFC). As noted above, the decision to reject the foreground option is determined in part by the local reward rate determined by the background context, including the local history of rewards, which is tracked by the dorsal and possibly ventral banks of the anterior cingulate sulcus (dACC), a medial prefrontal cortical structure. The main source of comparison of the two values and the area that ultimately signals the decision remains unknown. Finally, computation of reward history and setting thresholds for both foreground decisions and changes in background strategy are associated with activity in the posterior cingulate cortex (PCC), a medial posterior region of the brain. We hypothesize that this region executes computations that serve to optimize behavior by shifting organisms from a foreground option to exploration, information-seeking, and learning about the environment (Pearson et al. 2011). Given the close links between nodes in this circuitry and neuropsychiatric disease, understanding these foraging circuits promises potential new insights into a variety of disorders involving the dysregulation of exploration or engagement, including pathological gambling, attention deficit/hyperactivity disorder, and obsessive–compulsive disorder.

Catecholamines Help Monitor and Evaluate the Foraging Environment

The first step in foraging decisions requires the nervous system to estimate the value of the options under consideration. Dopaminergic circuits play a key role in value computations, originating with food tracking in simpler organisms (Hills et al. 2004), and manifest in the regulation of both reward (Schultz 2006) and movement

(Vallone et al. 2000). Dopaminergic circuits in the basal ganglia project heavily to the vmPFC and ACC (Williams and Goldman-Rakic 1993; Björklund and Dunnett 2007) and provide a primary reward signal for tracking value (Schultz et al. 1997, 1998; Schultz 1998), with a variety of recent evidence suggesting that dopaminergic neurons integrate multiple sources of information to construct representations of reward (Deserno et al. 2015; Sharp et al. 2015; Doll et al. 2016; Sadacca et al. 2016; Tian et al. 2016). These circuits execute fundamental reward-related prediction error computations that allow animals to update the values associated with different options and learn about their environments (Schultz et al. 1997, 1998; Schultz 1998; Sutton and Barto 1998; Tremblay et al. 1998). Dopamine plays a central role in signaling satiety as well, via the hormone leptin (DiLeone 2009). Some evidence from patients with Parkinson's disease, a disease characterized by the degeneration of dopamine neurons, suggests that dopamine may also play a crucial role in signaling the richness of the environment (Rutledge et al. 2009). Recent research shows that polymorphisms in genes coding for G protein-coupled catecholamine receptors are associated with different thresholds for patch-leaving decisions in the nematode *C. elegans* (Bendesky et al. 2011). Hence, the role of dopamine in regulating foraging decisions may be ancestral and widespread.

In addition to dopamine, norepinephrine plays a key role in regulating the focus of behavior and the demands of the environment. Noradrenergic pathways begin in the locus coeruleus and send projections throughout cortex (Aston-Jones 2004; Aston-Jones and Cohen 2005; Aston-Jones and Waterhouse 2016), including PCC (Levitt and Moore 1978; Joshi et al. 2016), ACC (Chandler et al. 2013), and vmPFC (Chandler et al. 2014). The baseline level of noradrenergic neuronal activity in the locus coeruleus is hypothesized to regulate the balance between focus, distraction, and alertness, with low levels of tonic activity reflecting drowsiness or quiescence, high levels reflecting distractibility, and moderate levels of activity punctuated by goal-relevant, phasic, short-duration periods of high activity reflecting focused behavior (Aston-Jones and Cohen 2005). These phasic spikes may serve as interrupts that propagate from the locus coeruleus (Sara and Bouret 2012) into a distributed cortical network of frontoparietal regions (Corbetta and Shulman 2002; Corbetta et al. 2008). By regulating focus and mediating the influence of environmental changes on cognition, norepinephrine plays a key role in managing the adaptation of behavior during foraging.

VmPFC Signals the Value of Foreground Options

In foraging decisions, the vmPFC represents the value of the current offer, which mirrors its role in decision making more generally (Rangel and Hare 2010; Glimcher and Fehr 2013). The proposed function for vmPFC in computing the relative value of the current choice facing the organism is consistent with a large literature studying value-based decision making, both within and outside foraging contexts, which identifies the vmPFC, the striatum, and the posterior cingulate cortex (PCC; also discussed below) as central nodes in a valuation network (Rushworth et al. 2011; Bartra et al. 2013; Clithero and Rangel 2014; Platt and Plassmann 2014). Computationally, both single-unit recording and neuroimaging studies suggest that vmPFC activity signals the value of the foreground, accept-or-reject offer.

In a short-term versus long-term reward trade-off task, Boorman and colleagues presented participants with a sequential multi-alternative decision-making problem (Boorman et al. 2013). Agents confronted three alternatives, each with a signaled reward magnitude and underlying reward probabilities that could be estimated from the recent history of outcomes. Reward magnitudes varied randomly from trial to trial, whereas reward probabilities were sampled from a distribution centered on the previous trial's probability for that option. Participants first chose one of the three options and received a reward if that option was a winner on that trial. Then, one of three events occurred. On one-third of trials, a new trial began. On another third of trials, participants were permitted to choose one of the foregone options, without any change in the associated reward magnitude. In the final third, participants could again make a second choice with the same reward probabilities, but the reward values were reset to a common, large value. This task design separates short-term expected values (from the offered reward size × probability) from the best long-term option (the highest long-term probability, since rewards varied randomly).

Although not designed as a foraging task, the opportunity to revisit previously foregone options, the sequential nature of the choices, and the connected underlying reward probabilities make this task a nice example of a foraging-type problem. Boorman and colleagues found that vmPFC activity correlated positively with the expected value of the chosen option and negatively with the best unchosen option, but not the worst option (Boorman et al. 2013). vmPFC activity further signaled the relative value of the chosen offer but not the relative long-term value. Finally, activation associated with value transferred from the first to second option, by negatively encoding the best unchosen option during the first choice and positively encoding the value of that option during the second. Hence, vmPFC activity signals the value of the current choice depending on the context, consistent with the value of the foreground offer in foraging contexts.

Another recent study reinforced the role of the vmPFC in signaling the value of a chosen option in a foraging context (McGuire and Kable 2015). In a willingness-to-wait task, participants waited a variable amount of time for an offered token to mature to its full value, at which point they pressed a button to accept the reward. Participants could decide to pass on a token at any point to move on to the next trial without reward. They experienced two temporal environments: in the high persistence (HP) environment, waiting for the full value of a reward to mature made sense, whereas in the low persistence (LP) environment, after 20s, the best option was for the participant to sell their token and move on to the next offer. Activity in vmPFC correlated with the difference in the subjective value between the two conditions, as participants were more likely to wait for higher yields in high-persistence environments, with this preference reflected in vmPFC activity (McGuire and Kable 2015). Moreover, there was an interaction between the environment type (HP or LP) and the time-in-trial on vmPFC activity, as predicted by the difference in the value of leaving early across the environments (McGuire and Kable 2015). These results also suggest that vmPFC activity tracks the value of the foreground option.

A number of other studies have confirmed the role of vmPFC in both foraging and non-foraging contexts. Many studies have shown that vmPFC activity reflects reward expectation at time of decision (Gershman et al. 2009; Lebreton et al. 2009; Noonan et al. 2010; Plassmann et al. 2010; Smith et al. 2010; Litt et al. 2011) and others that vmPFC represents the values of the different options or their value difference (Boorman et al. 2009; Wunderlich et al. 2010; Hunt et al. 2013), though this latter interpretation is challenged by the evidence that the signal reflects the option currently attended to by the chooser (Krajbich et al. 2010; Lim et al. 2011). Still other studies have shown that vmPFC activity (1) signals the probability of choosing a particular option (Daw et al. 2006) and the expected value of options (Payzan-LeNestour et al. 2013) in bandit tasks, (2) tracks value in both habit- and goal-based decisions (Wunderlich et al. 2012), and (3) signals the value of foreground offers independently of search values or costs when choosing to harvest reward during patch-based foraging (Kolling et al. 2012).

At the level of single neurons, the best evidence for the importance of the vmPFC in value computations comes from traditional non-foraging paradigms (Bouret and Richmond 2010; Strait et al. 2014). In forced response paradigms, monkeys initiate a trial and then sometimes perform follow-up actions to receive a reward (Bouret and Richmond 2010). vmPFC neurons signaled the expected reward to be gained from the current trial (Bouret and Richmond 2010). In non-foraging choice paradigms, monkeys are simultaneously offered a choice between typically two but sometimes more options and make a choice based on the reward magnitudes and probabilities of the offers (cf. Platt and Glimcher 1999). In these situations, vmPFC neurons initially signal the value of each option on offer but ultimately shift to signaling the value of the chosen option (Strait et al. 2014). These neurophysiological findings broadly align with the results of neuroimaging studies indicating vmPFC signals the value of foreground options. Future studies are needed to confirm a selective role for vmPFC neurons in computing values in both foraging and non-foraging contexts.

Generally, our understanding of neural circuits must be shaped by the demands of the selective environments that resulted in their organization and dynamics. Describing the contribution of the vmPFC to foraging decisions provides an explanatory scaffold for understanding why the region tracks the value of momentary choices. With heavy reciprocal connectivity with the amygdala, important for processing rewards (Paton et al. 2006; Saez et al. 2015), the striatum, central to reward-based learning (Schultz et al. 1997; Tremblay et al. 1998), and different areas of the cingulate, such as the ACC (Heilbronner and Hayden 2016) and PCC (Heilbronner and Haber 2014), important for control of cognition and comportment, the vmPFC can mediate the influence of experienced rewards on estimating reward rates and help transform computed values into choices via the rate rule (Fig. 6.2).

ACC Signals the Value of Foregone Options and Background Rates

ACC is a central node in the brain's foraging circuitry. This region shows activity in both humans and monkeys as agents prepare to disengage from exploiting a foreground option and shift to foraging for alternatives. The first study to demonstrate this pattern was conducted by Hayden and colleagues, who devised a laboratory version of the patch-leaving problem suitable for neural recordings in monkeys (Hayden et al. 2011). In this task, the agent chooses between continuing to exploit the current patch, thereby receiving a juice reward which decreases in size with repeated exploitation, or leaving the current patch for a new one. Although agents did not physically travel between patches, they experienced a temporal delay for choosing to forage (Constantino and Daw 2015). As predicted by the MVT, behavior was sensitive to the travel time to the next patch. Although monkeys persisted in patches longer than optimal, they were efficient patch foragers with near-optimal leaving times (Hayden et al. 2011; Blanchard and Hayden 2014). Human foragers also show this perseverative tendency (Constantino and Daw 2015).

Hayden and colleagues found that neurons in the dACC responded phasically around the time of each choice and that the magnitude of these responses increased with each successive decision to remain in the patch, reaching a peak just prior to the decision to leave the patch (Hayden et al. 2011). This "accumulation" across successive decisions is reminiscent of integrate-to-bound systems active in perceptual decision making (Roitman and Shadlen 2002; Gold and Shadlen 2007). Notably, the apparent firing rate threshold for patch departure varied systematically with travel time. Longer travel times reflect a greater investment of time (and, in the wild, energy) in moving on, influencing the assessment of the richness of the environment. Modulating firing rate thresholds for deciding to leave a patch thus provides a mechanism for translating the richness of the environment into patch residence times and, hence, changing foraging strategy. These findings are consistent with the hypothesis that dACC neurons gather evidence favoring foraging for an alternative.

A number of previous primate electrophysiology studies have observed similar dynamics in ACCs (Procyk et al. 2000; Shidara and Richmond 2002). In a sequence repetition task where monkeys had to search for the correct motor sequence to receive a reward, dACC neurons showed a stereotyped increase in firing around the time of movement until reward was received (Procyk et al. 2000). In a different sequential action task, dACC neurons also showed phasic increases in firing rate time-locked to cue onset or movement onset (Shidara and Richmond 2002).

The temporal dynamics in neuronal responses observed in dACC in these studies were remarkably similar to those reported by Hayden and colleagues despite differences in task design. Hence, though the phasic increases in dACC firing rates may signal the value of the foregone or not-yet-harvested reward, it may alternatively signal the control processes implemented to persist in a course of action.

Another recent study showed that activity of dACC neurons signals the value of foregone options in an accept-or-reject choice task (Blanchard and Hayden 2014). Blanchard and Hayden presented rhesus monkeys with an accept-or-reject offer on a computer screen one at a time. Monkeys were adept foragers and showed near-optimal diet selection behavior by rejecting unprofitable items and consuming profitable ones (cf. Stephens and Krebs 1986). Activity of dACC neurons signaled the value of the foregone option and was differentially modulated by the relative value of accepted and rejected offers. Since these modulations in neuronal activity followed decisions, they signaled the value of the foregone option rather than the value of other alternatives. Such "counterfactual" reward signals in the activity of dACC neurons are consistent with the idea that this area computes the value of foregone options (Hayden et al. 2009; Westendorff et al. 2016).

Human neuroimaging studies of patch-based foraging broadly endorse these conclusions (Kolling et al. 2012; Shenhav et al. 2014). In a seminal study (Kolling et al. 2012), human participants encountered a patch with two reward options and chose between harvesting one of those two items and searching for a new patch. After choosing to harvest, reward probabilities for each option were revealed and participants then made their selection. After choosing to search, participants lost some points, reflecting the costs of searching, and were once again confronted with the choice between searching or harvesting. When participants chose to harvest rather than search, dACC blood-oxygen-level-dependent (BOLD) activity, taken as an index of overall neural metabolic activity and assessed in functional magnetic resonance imaging, signaled the value of searching and was negatively correlated with the value of harvest. When participants instead chose to search rather than harvest, dACC BOLD activity was higher and correlated positively with the value of search and negatively with search cost. Hence, dACC activity reflected the value of searching when choosing whether or not to enter a patch. The value of searching was determined by the search alternatives minus the costs of searching, a composite relevant to updating the running average of switching background options. Efficiently switching background options is governed by the MVT, which determines the threshold for changing context by the average reward rate across the environment. Hence, dACC activity may reflect integration of estimations of environmental richness into long-term reward rates.

In addition, following selection of one of the harvest offers, dACC BOLD activity was correlated with the value of the unchosen option relative to the chosen one, reminiscent of how single dACC neurons signal the value of foregone options. While the harvest phase of the task was a classic two-alternative forced-choice decision context, our framework can still make sense of these foregone value signals. Unchosen options provide valuable information about the average richness of a patch, for use in calculating the average local reward rate and setting the threshold in the rate rule. Whereas chosen options can directly influence these reward rates via experienced rewards, unchosen options need dedicated vicarious pathways for value computations. In both forage and harvest phases of the task, rewards that were not experienced but merely observed can influence future decisions, via the contribution of counterfactual reward signals carried by dACC (Hayden et al. 2009) to estimates of local or global reward rates.

These findings are echoed by a recent study using a patch-based design to assess the neurobiology of decision making under risk (Meder et al. 2016). In a sequential gambling task, participants rolled a die repeatedly, accumulating the number of points displayed, unless a “1” was rolled, in which case they lost their earnings. Participants could cash out at any time to receive the accumulated sum of points as reward. The estimated cumulative gamble value, incorporating the combined effects of expected reward, risk, and other variables, was correlated with activity in dACC, in addition to a number of other areas. When participants chose to continue accumulating points, dACC activity was correlated with the probability that they would choose the foregone option, to cash in their earnings throughout the duration of a bout. Here again, dACC activity signals the value of the foregone option, possibly updating average local reward rates with the value of cashing in.

A study by Wittmann and colleagues indicates activity in this area tracks average as well as recent rewards (Wittmann et al. 2016). In a foraging-type task, participants were permitted to leave a patch only once in the middle of a block of forced-choice trials. The recent history of rewards influenced decisions to stay in the patch, whereas the rewards earned further into the past reduced the preference to stay. dACC BOLD activity matched the influence of reward history on behavior, with negative effects of distant rewards and positive effects of recent rewards, as well as correlating with decisions to stay or leave (Wittmann et al. 2016). These findings suggest that foregone reward signals in dACC reflect computation of reward rates over multiple timescales, consistent with the observation that the activity of single neurons tracks reward rates over multiple timescales in dACC (Seo and Lee 2007; Bernacchia et al. 2011).

In sum, neurons in the dACCs signal the value of foregone options during foraging, with suggestive evidence that these computations contribute to tracking local and long-term reward rates (Fig. 6.2). In the context of the neural computations necessary for foraging, the value of foregone options must be included in the different reward rate calculations. Decisions to accept or reject offers are grounded in the reward rate calculations for the different types of offers as well as the corresponding average offer in the environment. Foregone offers, though their values are not directly experienced, still possess valuable information about what is available in the environment. Similarly, decisions to shift background context reflect reward rate calculations for the environment, which integrate over all offers, including foregone options. In both cases, foraging decisions are driven by estimates of average reward rates, estimates that are more accurate for having incorporated such counterfactual rewards. In fact, failing to adequately estimate these reward rates, such as by failing to incorporate the value of unexperienced but available options, can lead to impulsive choices due to inaccurate estimates of reward rates. Furthermore, exploration for new options can be driven by a lack of such counterfactual information and the need for better estimates of the richness of the environment. In sum, these findings suggest that ACC is central to updating estimates of reward rates, a key computational variable in foraging decisions.

PCC Adjusts Foraging Strategy

In order to shift between exploiting the current patch and searching for new patches, foraging requires memory for resource locations in the environment, evaluation of the value of these locations, and, more speculatively, the regulation of attention to the current patch against attention to the wider environment. With connections to mnemonic networks including the hippocampus, frontal and parietal areas implicated in attention, and reciprocal connections with medial prefrontal structures such as dACC and vmPFC (Vogt et al. 1979; Heilbronner and Haber 2014), the posterior cingulate cortex (PCC) is a central hub in the hypothesized foraging circuit. The shift from exploitation to exploration or the need to adjust behavioral regime to reflect changes in the environment requires integration of multimodal inputs and a comparison of the value of local options with the current estimates of the reward rate. The PCC is uniquely situated to coordinate the process of comparing the value of the current location to the relative values of other locations to determine the best time to move on and to update reward rate computations by changing the time horizon for integration or by overwriting computed values for average rates. These same computational principles can be applied to a range of cognitive domains, including regulation of complex behaviors such as exploring concepts, memory, or the space of actions (Hills et al. 2010). The PCC fundamentally regulates behavioral optimization by context-driven exploration of both environmental states and the space of actions.

Several lines of evidence support the idea that PCC performs computations that regulate the balance of exploration and exploitation at the heart of foraging. In a 4-armed bandit task in monkeys, Pearson and colleagues discovered signals in PCC that tracked the decision to explore a new bandit or exploit the current one (Pearson et al. 2009). Monkeys faced a decision between four different bandits, each of which underwent a biased random walk around a mean value, and monkeys shifted between exploration and exploitation depending on the recent history of rewards (Pearson et al. 2009). Tonic firing rates of PCC neurons signaled decisions to explore or exploit, and also predicted the probability of exploring on the next trial. Overall average population activity also favored exploration. In addition, PCC neurons showed both linear and quadratic tuning curves for reward size, which may be important for detecting deviations from a default reward in order to update time horizons, detect change, and adjust reward rate estimates. Activity of PCC neurons signals the influence of reward and behavioral state during foraging, potentially indicating a role in adaptive updating of instantaneous reward rates or active modulation of decision thresholds in the foraging circuit.

A neuroimaging study using probabilistic bandit task revealed a more specific computational correlate of novelty in the human PCC. Wittman and colleagues designed a bandit task in which each location was baited with an image, each of which was associated with different, non-varying probability of reward (Wittmann et al. 2008). Some images were familiar and some new over the course of a run, and a reinforcement learning model fit to choices revealed a novelty bonus for the value of new pictures, triggering increased exploration (Wittmann et al. 2008). The authors found that in addition to a number of other areas, PCC was activated by novelty and exploration (Wittmann et al. 2008).

Further evidence from numerous imaging studies supports a role for PCC in assessment of long-term reward rates to optimize behavior. In an early investigation of the neural circuits mediating changepoint detection and behavioral adaptation, Summerfield and colleagues discovered that PCC activity reflected the combined effect of a number of relevant variables (Summerfield et al. 2011). Participants classified sinusoidal gratings called Gabor patches by their orientation in one of two categories. The mean and variance of these samples underwent unsignaled switches every 10–20 trials. vmPFC and PCC were active when the probability of selecting a particular category was high. Moreover, there was a strong three-way interaction of angular update (the prediction error between the observed Gabor and the outcome category mean), variance (sigma for the Gabor samples), and volatility (probability of a changepoint) on activity in PCC (Summerfield et al. 2011). Hence, PCC appears to signal the integration of evidence from the environment when used to update behavior.

In a study directly examining the neural circuitry mediating changepoint detection, McGuire and colleagues asked participants to predict a rewarding location on a screen to gather either high or neutral rewards (McGuire et al. 2014). The rewarding location was drawn from a distribution whose mean underwent occasional unsignaled shifts (changepoints), and participants experienced both low-noise environments, with a narrow distribution of possible rewarding locations, and high-noise ones with a wide distribution (McGuire et al. 2014). To maximize reward rate, participants should track relative uncertainty and changepoint probability while ignoring reward size (Nassar et al. 2010). The authors found that in fact, reward size, changepoint probability, and uncertainty all influenced choices. Participants tended to underweight both changepoint probability and relative uncertainty and used reward size to update their estimate of the location of the money drop. One region in PCC was more active for larger changepoint probabilities, and a second more ventral locus was less active for greater relative uncertainty (McGuire et al. 2014), suggesting functional specializations within PCC (cf. Leech et al. 2011). In addition, overlapping regions in PCC as well as occipitoparietal, anterior insula, dorsomedial frontal, and right lateral prefrontal cortices signaled reward, changepoint probability, and relative uncertainty, indicating a role in computing overall learning rates. Unlike other brain regions in this network, higher BOLD signal in PCC and parietal cortex predicted greater updating of estimates of the location of the next money drop by participants (McGuire et al.

2014). This central role for PCC in adaptive learning confirms and extends its role in updating during categorization (Summerfield et al. 2011).

What computational role does the integration of information about environmental states play in foraging? Further evidence comes from a recent study of decision making under risk (Kolling et al. 2014). The goal of the task was to gain as many points as possible while making safe (low reward, high probability) or risky (high reward, but low probability) choices and only earning rewards if a threshold number of points were achieved within a block (Kolling et al. 2014). Participants were generally risk averse, but more risk prone if they had not yet reached the threshold as the end of a block approached, mimicking the shift from risk aversion to risk-seeking behavior in birds when their energetic reserves approach starvation thresholds (Caraco 1981; Kacelnik and Bateson 1996; Bateson and Kacelnik 1997). Activity in PCC was more strongly coupled with activity in dACC when participants made risky choices in contexts where riskier choices made sense, whereas PCC was more strongly linked with vmPFC when participants made safe choices in safer contexts (Kolling et al. 2014). The authors concluded that PCC mediates effect of context on choice by selective coupling with dACC or vmPFC.

Though choices were made in a two-alternative forced-choice context (Kolling et al. 2014), the foraging analysis above can provide some insight into these observations. The risky and safe options are akin to two different types of resources. Recall above that accept-or-reject decisions for foreground choices are made using the rate rule: if the reward rate associated with the type of foreground offer exceeds the average over all types, then the foreground offer should be accepted. Also recall above that default choices can be considered foreground offers, whereas non-default choices can be considered part of the background. In risky contexts, PCC coupled more with dACC, which tracks foregone offer values and background reward rates. Perhaps, then, PCC could be resetting the stored value for the background, i.e., non-default, option in riskier contexts, shortening the time horizon over which to incorporate foregone offers or explicitly lowering the threshold setting on the basis of the history of stored offers. In contrast, in safer contexts, PCC coupled more with vmPFC, which tracks foreground offer values. Perhaps when selecting the foreground, i.e., default, option in safer contexts, PCC is tracking the benefit of the default option in the current environment.

When cast in a foraging light, these findings suggest a role for PCC in optimizing behavior. PCC appears to integrate evidence over multiple actions and compares this evidence to the recent history of rewards derived from both foreground accepted (vmPFC) and counterfactual (dACC) rewards to generate a non-specific signal when behavior drifts outside the expected efficiency for longer-term outcomes within the current behavioral regime. That is, PCC forecasts market downturns, thereby triggering action selection mechanisms to shift the agent into a more efficient behavioral regime. As noted above, the threshold for patch departure can be directly modulated, through gain control that increases or decreases the evidence necessary for departing a patch, or indirectly modulated, by changing long-term reward rate calculations, such as by augmenting the time horizon over which the history of rewards contributes to reward rate calculations.

Optimal threshold setting requires keeping track of the state of the environment, and PCC integrates multiple sources of information, including the relative uncertainty of the current rewards on offer, the probability of a shift in environmental state, the risk pressure generated by the environment, and the size of the discrepancy between predicted and observed states and rewards in order to optimize behavior for the current environment.

Recent work supports this proposed role for PCC in regulating foraging decisions. In a follow-up to the patch-leaving study discussed above (Hayden et al. 2011), Barack and colleagues recorded from PCC neurons, while monkeys made patch-leaving decisions in a simulated foraging environment (Barack et al. 2012; Barack and Platt 2013). They found slow modulations of PCC firing rates evolved over the course of several seconds at the beginning and end of patches. These modulations signaled information about properties of the foraging environment, such as the travel time delay to begin foraging in a new patch, and aspects of the agent, such as the urgency with which monkeys depart the current patch. These two features of PCC neuronal activity during patch-based foraging carry sufficient information for setting thresholds for deciding when to leave the current patch (Barack et al. 2012; Barack and Platt 2013).

PCC's role in regulating adaptation to changing environments is complemented by its role in action sequence learning. Action sequence learning plays an important role in establishing and maintaining traplines, routine foraging paths to rewarding locations in the environment. Neural regions important for navigation, sequence or pattern formation, and memory presumably contribute to the establishment and maintenance of trapline foraging. Such sequences invoke motor sequence learning circuits in the brain (Willingham 1998) including the basal ganglia (Graybiel 2008). Lesions or illness that disrupts the basal ganglia impairs motor sequence learning (Boyd et al. 2009; Tremblay et al. 2010). Motor sequence learning proceeds via segmentation of a series of motor movements into larger segments (Sakai et al. 2003) followed by the concatenation of such segments into larger chunks (Verwey 1996, 2001; Sakai et al. 2003). Once these chunks are in place, executing the motor sequence can become a routine habit.

Formation of habitual sequences like routine foraging along traplines engages dopaminergic circuitry in the basal ganglia. These dopamine-regulated routines allow animals to efficiently maneuver in their environments. Trapline foraging—repeatedly moving along a preplanned route to harvest renewing resources—is emblematic of habits, automated repetitive sequences of motor or cognitive behaviors, engaged by organisms in the natural world (Graybiel 2008). Learning routine route-following behavior appears to be executed by the basal ganglia (Jin et al. 2014) through reinforcement learning algorithms (Desrochers et al. 2010). Trapline initiation and termination may be executed by neurons in the dorsolateral prefrontal cortex (dlPFC; Fujii and Graybiel 2003) and the striatum (Fujii and Graybiel 2005). Start- and end-point signals in these areas may be part of an action-chunking mechanism for learning and maintaining habits.

Wymbs and colleagues investigated how people learn to execute a sequence of key presses over the course of several days (Wymbs et al. 2012). The authors segregated chunking—the production of a sequence of connected movements—from concatenation—stringing together chunks into longer sequences. They found that increases in chunking behavior were associated with increasing activity in bilateral putamen and PCC. By contrast, dlPFC activity decreased with increasing concatenation. The contribution of PCC to learning action sequences is further supported by evidence showing activity in this area during early sequence learning (Pammi et al. 2012). Hence, in addition to regulating the use of information from the environment to update behavior, PCC also seems to play a role in regulating the learning of sequences of choices.

Combining these two key roles for the PCC—namely environmental tracking and the regulation of response sequences—three electrophysiological studies endorse a key role for PCC in changing behavior in response to changes in the environment. Hayden and colleagues investigated the causal role for PCC in driving shifts in strategy in a two-alternative forced-choice paradigm (Hayden et al. 2008). Monkeys chose between a safe option that delivered a medium reward all the time and a risky one that delivered a small reward half the time and a large reward otherwise. Following a risky choice, monkeys tended to follow a win-stay, lost-shift strategy, sticking with the risky option when their choice resulted in a large reward and abandoning it for the safe option when their choice resulted in a small reward. Electrical stimulation in the PCC following receipt of the large reward on a risky choice induced shifts to the safe option, as though the monkey had received a small reward. This preliminary evidence suggests a role for the PCC in optimizing behavior in an environmentally dependent fashion.

In a recent study investigating the neural circuits of conditional visuomotor learning, Heilbronner and Platt compared neural activity in PCC during the use of well-learned visual motor rules to newly introduced ones (Heilbronner and Platt 2013). Monkeys observed a cue instructing them to shift gaze to the right or left. During a given session, half the cues were well learned, and half were novel. Monkeys used trial-and-error sampling to learn where to look following presentation of a novel cue, and for each trial type, they could receive either a large or small reward. PCC neurons fired more for incorrect movements than for correct ones during a trial's outcome epoch, for both well-learned and novel scenes. For low-value novel scenes, inactivation of PCC with an inhibitory pharmacological agent resulted in poorer performance than for high-value novel scenes or well-learned ones. Once again, this causal evidence suggests a role for PCC in the integration of environmental information and subsequent change in behavior to adapt to new contexts.

If PCC does regulate behavior on the basis of information harvested from the environment, then PCC neurons should both represent the state of the environment and predict behavioral variability. Barack, Gariépy, and Platt uncovered startling evidence that PCC neurons carry precisely these signals (Barack et al. 2014). Monkeys foraged through a circular array of targets, two of which were randomly baited on each trial, one with a small and one with a large reward. The design of the task allowed the size of rewards to be decorrelated from environmental information, operationalized as the sequence of rewards corresponding to the current trial. Monkeys spontaneously adopted traplines, moving in circular patterns from one target to its next nearest neighbor. However, the probability of monkeys diverging from these traplines on a given choice during the trial was dictated by the amount of information the monkey had received about the current trial's pattern of rewards. Firing rates of PCC neurons signaled more information about the spatial pattern of rewards in the environment than about reward size and predicted monkeys' tendency to deviate from traplines when the spatial pattern of rewards was revealed. These findings suggest PCC tracks the state of the environment to regulate subsequent behavior.

In sum, PCC neurons are more active during exploratory decisions (Pearson et al. 2009), signal the properties of foraging environments and agents with changes in activity time-locked to changes in foraging strategy (Barack et al. 2012; Barack and Platt 2013), and forecast deviations from routine foraging (Barack et al. 2014). Furthermore, causal interventions in PCC can trigger switches in strategy (Hayden et al. 2008) and influence learning of stimulus action contingencies (Heilbronner and Platt 2013). PCC activity reflects the novelty of choices (Wittmann et al. 2008; Heilbronner and Platt 2013); outcomes, uncertainty, and environmental volatility (Summerfield et al. 2011; McGuire et al. 2014); behavioral optimization driven by reward context (Kolling et al. 2014) and sequence learning (Wymbs et al. 2012; Barack et al. 2014); and adaptive regulation of both cognitive (Leech and Sharp 2014) and behavioral (Hayden et al. 2008; Wymbs et al. 2012; Heilbronner and Platt 2013) routines. Together, these observations invite the hypothesis that PCC serves to adaptively regulate foraging thresholds in novel, noisy, unstable, and unpredictable environments (Fig. 6.2).

Conclusion

Impulsivity leads us to make maladaptive choices due to failures to consider the long-term consequences of our choices. These regrettable choices can be analyzed as a result of malfunctioning neural circuits designed by evolution for foraging decisions, choices made in iterated non-exclusive foreground–background accept-or-reject contexts. Rational analysis of optimal behavior on such choices established the need for tracking reward rates—those associated with foreground offers, as well as those associated with long-term averages in the environment. In order to forage adaptively, responding to changes in the environment and the rewards on offer, agents can manipulate decision thresholds based on these reward rates.

Recent and ongoing investigation of the neural circuits mediating foraging has revealed tantalizing evidence for the neural mechanisms of our process model (Fig. 6.3). The vmPFC represents the value of foreground offers, while the dACC represents the value of unchosen offers and background options. dACC also seems to represent reward rates at multiple timescales. Finally, the PCC tracks the environment and the recent history of choices, seemingly modulating foraging thresholds to regulate behavioral variability and the learning of reward–outcome contingencies. Subcortical dopamine neurons provide inputs on instantaneous forecasts of environmental returns as well as possibly long-term reward rates. Brainstem norepinephrine neurons may serve to regulate the entire circuit to match foraging thresholds to internal state or environmental uncertainty.

Our analysis of foraging behavior may provide insight into psychiatric dysfunction involving impulsive decisions, such as obsessive–compulsive disorder (OCD), pathological gambling (PG), or attention deficit/hyperactivity disorder (ADHD). Characterized by disturbing intrusive thoughts (obsessions) and repetitive aversive actions (compulsions) (Graybiel and Rauch 2000; Maia et al. 2008; Menzies et al. 2008; Nenadic 2008; Greenberg et al. 2010), aberrant neurobiological circuitry in OCD patients includes the anterior cingulate (Saxena et al. 1998, Cosgrove and Rauch 2003; Maia et al. 2008). The compulsions that characterize OCD can be seen as resulting from dysregulation of reward rates, resulting in repetitive behavior that is akin to a forager failing to efficiently leave a patch.

Similarly, PG may result from malfunctioning foraging circuitry. Frequency of gambling-related patterns of thought negatively correlates with performance on patchy foraging tasks (Addicott et al. 2015), and dysfunctional circuitry in PG includes vmPFC (Potenza 2008). PG may result from an inability to correctly assess the reward rates of foreground offers, yielding inflated estimates of incomes and hence perseverative foraging behavior. The aberrant processes that give rise to impulse control disorders may be revealed by situating the neural circuits of decision making in their evolutionary context and considering the decision ecology of real-world agents, with potentially important implications for treatment.

ADHD, like OCD and PG, features atypical behavioral adaptation to changing environments, a key process in adaptive foraging. ADHD is characterized by inattention and hyperactivity and impulsivity (American Psychiatric Association, 2013). Patients have deficits in executive functioning (Woods et al. 2002; Marije Boonstra et al. 2005), including difficulty inhibiting prepotent responses in a conflict processing task (Sergeant et al. 2002) and difficulty ignoring irrelevant cues in a cued choice task (van Meel et al. 2007). These deficits could result from an inability to accurately regulate foraging thresholds, the inappropriate integration of information for setting thresholds resulting in overly eager switching between behavioral plans. Viewing psychiatric dysfunction through the foraging lens yields insight into the computational processes that go awry in such afflictions and the relationship between our ancestral neural circuitry and the maladaptive responses to modern life engendered by neural malfunction.

References

Abbott, J. T., Austerweil, J. L., & Griffiths, T. L. (2015). *Random walks on semantic networks can resemble optimal foraging*. Neural Information Processing Systems Conference; A preliminary version of this work was presented at the aforementined conference., American Psychological Association.

Addicott, M. A., Pearson, J. M., Kaiser, N., Platt, M. L., & McClernon, F. J. (2015). Suboptimal foraging behavior: A new perspective on gambling. *Behavioral Neuroscience, 129*(5), 656.

Altshuler, D. L., & Clark, C. J. (2003). Darwin's hummingbirds. *Science, 300*(5619), 588–589.

American Psychiatric Association. (2013). *The diagnostic and statistical manual of mental disorders: DSM 5*. Washington, DC: American Psychiatric Association.

Anderson, D. E., Vogel, E. K., & Awh, E. (2013). A common discrete resource for visual working memory and visual search. *Psychological Science*, 24(6).

Aston-Jones, G. (2004). Locus coeruleus, A5 and A7 noradrenergic cell groups. In G. Paxinos (Ed.), *The rat nervous system* (pp. 259–294). San Diego: Elsevier Academic Press.

Aston-Jones, G., & Cohen, J. D. (2005). An integrative theory of locus coeruleus-norepinephrine function: Adaptive gain and optimal performance. *Annual Review of Neuroscience, 28,* 403–450.

Aston-Jones, G., & Waterhouse, B. (2016). Locus coeruleus: From global projection system to adaptive regulation of behavior. *Brain Research, 1645,* 75–78.

Barack, D. L., Gariépy, J.-F., & Platt, M. L. (2014). Expected value and expected information encoding in the posterior cingulate. *Poster presented at Computational and Systems Neuroscience Conference 11*, Salt Lake City, UT.

Barack, D. L., & Gold, J. I. (2016). Temporal trade-offs in psychophysics. *Current Opinion in Neurobiology, 37,* 121–125.

Barack, D. L., Hayden, B. Y., Pearson, J. M., & Platt, M. L. (2012). Neural threshold for foraging decisions in posterior cingulate cortex. *Poster presented at Computational and Systems Neuroscience Conference 9*, Salt Lake City, UT.

Barack, D. L., & Platt, M. L. (2013). Components of strategic decision mechanisms in posterior cingulate cortex. *Poster presented at Computational and Systems Neuroscience Conference 10*, Salt Lake City, UT.

Bartra, O., McGuire, J. T., & Kable, J. W. (2013). The valuation system: A coordinate-based meta-analysis of BOLD fMRI experiments examining neural correlates of subjective value. *Neuroimage, 76,* 412–427.

Bartumeus, F., Catalan, J., Fulco, U., Lyra, M., & Viswanathan, G. (2002). Optimizing the encounter rate in biological interactions: Lévy versus Brownian strategies. *Physical Review Letters, 88*(9), 097901.

Bateson, M., & Kacelnik, A. (1997). Starlings' preferences for predictable and unpredictable delays to food. *Animal Behaviour, 53*(6), 1129–1142.

Beierholm, U., Guitart-Masip, M., Economides, M., Chowdhury, R., Düzel, E., Dolan, R., et al. (2013). Dopamine modulates reward-related vigor. *Neuropsychopharmacology, 38*(8), 1495–1503.

Bendesky, A., Tsunozaki, M., Rockman, M. V., Kruglyak, L., & Bargmann, C. I. (2011). Catecholamine receptor polymorphisms affect decision-making in *C. elegans*. *Nature, 472* (7343), 313–318.

Berger-Tal, O., & Bar-David, S. (2015). Recursive movement patterns: Review and synthesis across species. *Ecosphere, 6*(9), 149.

Bernacchia, A., Seo, H., Lee, D., & Wang, X.-J. (2011). A reservoir of time constants for memory traces in cortical neurons. *Nature Neuroscience, 14*(3), 366–372.

Bernoulli, D. (1738). Specimen theoriae novae de mensura sortis (Exposition of a new theory on the measurement of risk). Comentarii Acad. Scient. Petropolis (translated in *Econometrica*), *5* (22), 23–36.

Bickel, W., & Marsch, L. A. (2001). Toward a behavioral economic understanding of drug dependence: Delay discounting processes. *Addiction, 96*(1), 73–86.

Bickel, W., Miller, M. L., Yi, R., Kowal, B. P., Lindquist, D. M., & Pitcock, J. A. (2007). Behavioral and neuroeconomics of drug addiction: Competing neural systems and temporal discounting processes. *Drug and Alcohol Dependence, 90,* S85–S91.

Björklund, A., & Dunnett, S. B. (2007). Dopamine neuron systems in the brain: An update. *Trends in Neurosciences, 30*(5), 194–202.

Blanchard, T. C., & Hayden, B. Y. (2014). Neurons in dorsal anterior cingulate cortex signal postdecisional variables in a foraging task. *The Journal of Neuroscience, 34*(2), 646–655.

Boorman, E. D., Behrens, T. E. J., Woolrich, M. W., & Rushworth, M. F. S. (2009). How green is the grass on the other side? Frontopolar cortex and the evidence in favor of alternative courses of action. *Neuron, 62*(5), 733–743.

Boorman, E. D., Rushworth, M. F., & Behrens, T. E. (2013). Ventromedial prefrontal and anterior cingulate cortex adopt choice and default reference frames during sequential multi-alternative choice. *The Journal of Neuroscience, 33*(6), 2242–2253.

Bouret, S., & Richmond, B. J. (2010). Ventromedial and orbital prefrontal neurons differentially encode internally and externally driven motivational values in monkeys. *The Journal of Neuroscience, 30*(25), 8591–8601.

Boyd, L., Edwards, J., Siengsukon, C., Vidoni, E., Wessel, B., & Linsdell, M. (2009). Motor sequence chunking is impaired by basal ganglia stroke. *Neurobiology of Learning and Memory, 92*(1), 35–44.

Cain, M. S., Vul, E., Clark, K., & Mitroff, S. R. (2012). A Bayesian optimal foraging model of human visual search. *Psychological Science, 23*(9), 1047–1054.

Calhoun, A. J., & Hayden, B. Y. (2015). The foraging brain. *Current Opinion in Behavioral Sciences, 5,* 24–31.

Caraco, T. (1981). Energy budgets, risk and foraging preferences in dark-eyed juncos (*Junco hyemalis*). *Behavioral Ecology and Sociobiology, 8*(3), 213–217.

Carpenter, R. H. (1988). *Movements of the eyes*. London: Pion Limited.

Chandler, D. J., Gao, W.-J., & Waterhouse, B. D. (2014). Heterogeneous organization of the locus coeruleus projections to prefrontal and motor cortices. *Proceedings of the National Academy of Sciences (USA), 111*(18), 6816–6821.

Chandler, D. J., Lamperski, C. S., & Waterhouse, B. D. (2013). Identification and distribution of projections from monoaminergic and cholinergic nuclei to functionally differentiated subregions of prefrontal cortex. *Brain Research, 1522,* 38–58.

Charnov, E. L. (1976). Optimal foraging, the marginal value theorem. *Theoretical Population Biology, 19*(2), 129–136.

Clithero, J. A., & Rangel, A. (2014). Informatic parcellation of the network involved in the computation of subjective value. *Social Cognitive and Affective Neuroscience, 9*(9), 1289–1302.

Clutton-Brock, T., & Harvey, P. H. (1980). Primates, brains and ecology. *Journal of Zoology, 190* (3), 309–323.

Constantino, S. M., & Daw, N. D. (2015). Learning the opportunity cost of time in a patch-foraging task. *Cognitive, Affective, & Behavioral Neuroscience, 15*(4), 837–853.

Corbetta, M., Patel, G., & Shulman, G. L. (2008). The reorienting system of the human brain: From environment to theory of mind. *Neuron, 58*(3), 306–324.

Corbetta, M., & Shulman, G. L. (2002). Control of goal-directed and stimulus-driven attention in the brain. *Nature Reviews Neuroscience, 3*(3), 201–215.

Cosgrove, G. R., & Rauch, S. L. (2003). Stereotactic cingulotomy. *Neurosurgery Clinics of North America, 14*(2), 225–235.

Daw, N. D., O'Doherty, J. P., Dayan, P., Seymour, B., & Dolan, R. J. (2006). Cortical substrates for exploratory decisions in humans. *Nature, 441*(7095), 876–879.

Deserno, L., Huys, Q. J., Boehme, R., Buchert, R., Heinze, H.-J., Grace, A. A., et al. (2015). Ventral striatal dopamine reflects behavioral and neural signatures of model-based control during sequential decision making. *Proceedings of the National Academy of Sciences (USA), 112*(5), 1595–1600.

Desrochers, T. M., Jin, D. Z., Goodman, N. D., & Graybiel, A. M. (2010). Optimal habits can develop spontaneously through sensitivity to local cost. *Proceedings of the National Academy of Sciences (USA), 107*(47), 20512–20517.

DiLeone, R. J. (2009). The influence of leptin on the dopamine system and implications for ingestive behavior. *International Journal of Obesity, 33,* S25–S29.

Doll, B. B., Bath, K. G., Daw, N. D., & Frank, M. J. (2016). Variability in dopamine genes dissociates model-based and model-free reinforcement learning. *The Journal of Neuroscience, 36*(4), 1211–1222.

Dukas, R. (2002). Behavioural and ecological consequences of limited attention. *Philosophical Transactions of the Royal Society of London B: Biological Sciences, 357*(1427), 1539–1547.

Dukas, R. R., & Jim, (2009). *Cognitive ecology II.* Chicago, IL: University of Chicago Press.

Farmer, G. D., Janssen, C. P., & Brumby, D. P. (2011). How long have I got? Making optimal visit durations in a dual-task setting. *Proceedings of the 33rd annual meeting of the Cognitive Science Society.*

Frederick, S., Loewenstein, G., & O'Donoghue, T. (2002). Time discounting and time preference: A critical review. *Journal of Economic Literature, 40,* 351–401.

Freidin, E., Aw, J., & Kacelnik, A. (2009). Sequential and simultaneous choices: Testing the diet selection and sequential choice models. *Behavioural Processes, 80*(3), 218–223.

Fretwell, S. D., & Calver, J. S. (1969). On territorial behavior and other factors influencing habitat distribution in birds. *Acta Biotheoretica, 19*(1), 37–44.

Fu, W.-T., & Pirolli, P. (2007). SNIF-ACT: A cognitive model of user navigation on the World Wide Web. *Human-Computer Interaction, 22*(4), 355–412.

Fujii, N., & Graybiel, A. M. (2003). Representation of action sequence boundaries by macaque prefrontal cortical neurons. *Science, 301*(5637), 1246–1249.

Fujii, N., & Graybiel, A. M. (2005). Time-varying covariance of neural activities recorded in striatum and frontal cortex as monkeys perform sequential-saccade tasks. *Proceedings of the National Academy of Sciences (USA), 102*(25), 9032–9037.

Gallistel, C. R., & Gibbon, J. (2000). Time, rate, and conditioning. *Psychological Review, 107*(2), 289.

Genovesio, A., Wise, S. P., & Passingham, R. E. (2014). Prefrontal–parietal function: From foraging to foresight. *Trends in Cognitive Sciences, 18*(2), 72–81.

Gershman, S. J., Pesaran, B., & Daw, N. D. (2009). Human reinforcement learning subdivides structured action spaces by learning effector-specific values. *The Journal of Neuroscience, 29* (43), 13524–13531.

Gilzenrat, M. S., Nieuwenhuis, S., Jepma, M., & Cohen, J. D. (2010). Pupil diameter tracks changes in control state predicted by the adaptive gain theory of locus coeruleus function. *Cognitive, Affective, & Behavioral Neuroscience, 10*(2), 252–269.

Gittins, J. C. (1979). Bandit processes and dynamic allocation indices. *Journal of the Royal Statistical Society: Series B (Methodological), 41*(2), 148–177.

Gittins, J., & Jones, D. (1974). A dynamic allocation index for the sequential allocation of experiments. In J. M. Gani, K. Sarkadi, & I. Vincze (Eds.), *Progress in statistics.* Amsterdam: North Holland.

Glimcher, P., & Fehr, E. (2013). *Neuroeconomics: Decision making and the brain.* San Diego, CA: Academic Press.

Glimcher, P., Kable, J., & Louie, K. (2007). Neuroeconomic studies of impulsivity: Now or just as soon as possible? *The American Economic Review, 97*(2), 142–147.

Gold, J. I., & Shadlen, M. N. (2007). The neural basis of decision making. *Annual Review of Neuroscience, 30,* 535–574.

Graybiel, A. M. (2008). Habits, rituals, and the evaluative brain. *Annual Review of Neuroscience, 31,* 359–387.

Graybiel, A. M., & Rauch, S. L. (2000). Toward a neurobiology of obsessive-compulsive disorder. *Neuron, 28*(2), 343–347.

Greenberg, B. D., Rauch, S. L., & Haber, S. N. (2010). Invasive circuitry-based neurotherapeutics: Stereotactic ablation and deep brain stimulation for OCD. *Neuropsychopharmacology, 35*(1), 317–336.

Griffiths, T. L., Lieder, F., & Goodman, N. D. (2015). Rational use of cognitive resources: Levels of analysis between the computational and the algorithmic. *Topics in Cognitive Science, 7*(2), 217–229.

Griffiths, T. L., Vul, E., & Sanborn, A. N. (2012). Bridging levels of analysis for probabilistic models of cognition. *Current Directions in Psychological Science, 21*(4), 263–268.

Guitart-Masip, M., Fuentemilla, L., Bach, D. R., Huys, Q. J., Dayan, P., Dolan, R. J., et al. (2011). Action dominates valence in anticipatory representations in the human striatum and dopaminergic midbrain. *The Journal of Neuroscience, 31*(21), 7867–7875.

Hamilton, W. D. (1964). The genetical evolution of social behaviour. I. *Journal of Theoretical Biology, 7*(1), 1–16.

Harding, R. S., & Teleki, G. (1981). *Omnivorous primates: Gathering and hunting in human evolution*. New York: Columbia University Press.

Hayden, B. Y., Nair, A. C., McCoy, A. N., & Platt, M. L. (2008). Posterior cingulate cortex mediates outcome-contingent allocation of behavior. *Neuron, 60*(1), 19–25.

Hayden, B. Y., Pearson, J. M., & Platt, M. L. (2009). Fictive reward signals in the anterior cingulate cortex. *Science, 324*(5929), 948–950.

Hayden, B. Y., Pearson, J. M., & Platt, M. L. (2011). Neuronal basis of sequential foraging decisions in a patchy environment. *Nature Neuroscience, 14*(7), 933–939.

Heilbronner, S. R., & Haber, S. N. (2014). Frontal cortical and subcortical projections provide a basis for segmenting the cingulum bundle: Implications for neuroimaging and psychiatric disorders. *The Journal of Neuroscience, 34*(30), 10041–10054.

Heilbronner, S. R., & Hayden, B. Y. (2016). Dorsal anterior cingulate cortex: A bottom-up view. *Annual Review of Neuroscience, 39,* 149–170.

Heilbronner, S. R., & Platt, M. L. (2013). Causal evidence of performance monitoring by neurons in posterior cingulate cortex during learning. *Neuron, 80*(6), 1384–1391.

Hemmi, J. M., & Menzel, C. R. (1995). Foraging strategies of long-tailed macaques, *Macaca fascicularis*: Directional extrapolation. *Animal Behaviour, 49*(2), 457–464.

Hills, T. (2010). Investigating mathematical search behavior using network analysis. In R. Lesh, P. L. Galbraith, C. R. Hains, & A. Hurford (Eds.), *Modeling students' mathematical modeling competencies* (pp. 571–581). New York: Springer.

Hills, T., Brockie, P. J., & Maricq, A. V. (2004). Dopamine and glutamate control area-restricted search behavior in *Caenorhabditis elegans*. *The Journal of neuroscience, 24*(5), 1217–1225.

Hills, T. T., Jones, M. N., & Todd, P. M. (2012). Optimal foraging in semantic memory. *Psychological Review, 119*(2), 431.

Hills, T. T., Mata, R., Wilke, A., & Samanez-Larkin, G. R. (2013). Mechanisms of age-related decline in memory search across the adult life span. *Developmental Psychology, 49*(12), 2396.

Hills, T. T., & Pachur, T. (2012). Dynamic search and working memory in social recall. *Journal of Experimental Psychology. Learning, Memory, and Cognition, 38*(1), 218.

Hills, T. T., Todd, P. M., & Goldstone, R. L. (2008). Search in external and internal spaces evidence for generalized cognitive search processes. *Psychological Science, 19*(8), 802–808.

Hills, T. T., Todd, P. M., & Goldstone, R. L. (2010). The central executive as a search process: Priming exploration and exploitation across domains. *Journal of Experimental Psychology: General, 139*(4), 590.

Hills, T. T., Todd, P. M., & Jones, M. N. (2015). Foraging in semantic fields: How we search through memory. *Topics in Cognitive Science, 7*(3), 513–534.

Hunt, L. T., Woolrich, M. W., Rushworth, M. F., & Behrens, T. E. (2013). Trial-type dependent frames of reference for value comparison. *PLoS Computational Biology, 9*(9), e1003225.

Janmaat, K. R. L., Byrne, R. W., & Zuberbühler, K. (2006). Evidence for a spatial memory of fruiting states of rainforest trees in wild mangabeys. *Animal Behaviour, 72*(4), 797–807.

Janssen, C. P., Brumby, D. P., Dowell, J., Chater, N., & Howes, A. (2011). Identifying optimum performance trade-offs using a cognitively bounded rational analysis model of discretionary task interleaving. *Topics in Cognitive Science, 3*(1), 123–139.

Jepma, M., & Nieuwenhuis, S. (2011). Pupil diameter predicts changes in the exploration–exploitation trade-off: Evidence for the adaptive gain theory. *Journal of Cognitive Neuroscience, 23*(7), 1587–1596.

Jin, X., Tecuapetla, F., & Costa, R. M. (2014). Basal ganglia subcircuits distinctively encode the parsing and concatenation of action sequences. *Nature Neuroscience, 17*(3), 423–430.

Joshi, S., Li, Y., Kalwani, R. M., & Gold, J. I. (2016). Relationships between pupil diameter and neuronal activity in the locus coeruleus, colliculi, and cingulate cortex. *Neuron, 89*(1), 221–234.

Kacelnik, A. (1997). Normative and descriptive models of decision making: Time discounting and risk sensitivity. In G. R. Bock & G. Cardew (Eds.), *Characterizing human psychological adaptations* (pp. 51–67). Chichester, UK: Wiley.

Kacelnik, A., & Bateson, M. (1996). Risky theories: The effects of variance on foraging decisions. *American Zoologist, 36,* 402–434.

Kacelnik, A., Vasconcelos, M., Monteiro, T., & Aw, J. (2011). Darwin's tug-of-war vs. starlings' horse-racing: How adaptations for sequential encounters drive simultaneous choice. *Behavioral Ecology and Sociobiology, 65*(3), 547–558.

Kolling, N., Behrens, T. E. J., Mars, R. B., & Rushworth, M. F. S. (2012). Neural mechanisms of foraging. *Science, 336*(6077), 95–98.

Kolling, N., Behrens, T., Wittmann, M., & Rushworth, M. (2016). Multiple signals in anterior cingulate cortex. *Current Opinion in Neurobiology, 37,* 36–43.

Kolling, N., Wittmann, M., & Rushworth, M. F. (2014). Multiple neural mechanisms of decision making and their competition under changing risk pressure. *Neuron, 81*(5), 1190–1202.

Krajbich, I., Armel, C., & Rangel, A. (2010). Visual fixations and the computation and comparison of value in simple choice. *Nature Neuroscience, 13*(10), 1292–1298.

Krebs, J. R., Kacelnik, A., & Taylor, P. (1978). Test of optimal sampling by foraging great tits. *Nature, 275*(5675), 27–31.

Lebreton, M., Jorge, S., Michel, V., Thirion, B., & Pessiglione, M. (2009). An automatic valuation system in the human brain: Evidence from functional neuroimaging. *Neuron, 64*(3), 431–439.

Leech, R., Kamourieh, S., Beckmann, C. F., & Sharp, D. J. (2011). Fractionating the default mode network: Distinct contributions of the ventral and dorsal posterior cingulate cortex to cognitive control. *The Journal of Neuroscience, 31*(9), 3217–3224.

Leech, R., & Sharp, D. J. (2014). The role of the posterior cingulate cortex in cognition and disease. *Brain, 137*(1), 12–32.

Levitt, P., & Moore, R. Y. (1978). Noradrenaline neuron innervation of the neocortex in the rat. *Brain Research, 139*(2), 219–231.

Lim, S.-L., O'Doherty, J. P., & Rangel, A. (2011). The decision value computations in the vmPFC and striatum use a relative value code that is guided by visual attention. *The Journal of Neuroscience, 31*(37), 13214–13223.

Litt, A., Plassmann, H., Shiv, B., & Rangel, A. (2011). Dissociating valuation and saliency signals during decision-making. *Cerebral Cortex, 21*(1), 95–102.

Loewenstein, G. (1996). Out of control: Visceral influences on behavior. *Organizational Behavior and Human Decision Processes, 65*(3), 272–292.

MacGregor, J. N., & Chu, Y. (2011). Human performance on the traveling salesman and related problems: A review. *The Journal of Problem Solving, 3*(2), 2.

Maia, T. V., Cooney, R. E., & Peterson, B. S. (2008). The neural bases of obsessive–compulsive disorder in children and adults. *Development and Psychopathology, 20*(4), 1251–1283.

Marije Boonstra, A., Oosterlaan, J., Sergeant, J. A., & Buitelaar, J. K. (2005). Executive functioning in adult ADHD: A meta-analytic review. *Psychological Medicine, 35*(08), 1097–1108.

Marr, D. (1982). *Vision: A computational investigation into the human representation and processing of visual information* New York: Henry Holt and Co Inc.

McGuire, J. T., & Kable, J. W. (2015). Medial prefrontal cortical activity reflects dynamic re-evaluation during voluntary persistence. *Nature Neuroscience, 18*(5), 760–766.

McGuire, J. T., Nassar, M. R., Gold, J. I., & Kable, J. W. (2014). Functionally dissociable influences on learning rate in a dynamic environment. *Neuron, 84*(4), 870–881.

Meder, D., Haagensen, B. N., Hulme, O., Morville, T., Gelskov, S., Herz, D. M., et al. (2016). Tuning the brake while raising the stake: Network dynamics during sequential decision-making. *The Journal of Neuroscience, 36*(19), 5417–5426.

Menzel, E. W. (1973). Chimpanzee spatial memory organization. *Science, 182*(4115), 943–945.

Menzel, C. R. (1991). Cognitive aspects of foraging in Japanese monkeys. *Animal Behaviour, 41* (3), 397–402.

Menzel, C. (1996). Structure-guided foraging in long-tailed macaques. *American Journal of Primatology, 38*(2), 117–132.

Menzies, L., Chamberlain, S. R., Laird, A. R., Thelen, S. M., Sahakian, B. J., & Bullmore, E. T. (2008). Integrating evidence from neuroimaging and neuropsychological studies of obsessive-compulsive disorder: The orbitofronto-striatal model revisited. *Neuroscience and Biobehavioral Reviews, 32*(3), 525–549.

Metcalfe, J., & Jacobs, W. J. (2010). People's study time allocation and its relation to animal foraging. *Behavioural Processes, 83*(2), 213–221.

Milton, K. (1981). Distribution patterns of tropical plant foods as an evolutionary stimulus to primate mental development. *American Anthropologist, 83*(3), 534–548.

Milton, K. (1988). Foraging behaviour and the evolution of primate intelligence. In A. W. R. W. Byrne (Ed.), *Machiavellian intelligence: Social expertise and the evolution of intellect in monkeys, apes, and humans* (pp. 285–305). New York: Clarendon Press.

Nassar, M. R., Rumsey, K. M., Wilson, R. C., Parikh, K., Heasly, B., & Gold, J. I. (2012). Rational regulation of learning dynamics by pupil-linked arousal systems. *Nature Neuroscience, 15*(7), 1040–1046.

Nassar, M. R., Wilson, R. C., Heasly, B., & Gold, J. I. (2010). An approximately Bayesian delta-rule model explains the dynamics of belief updating in a changing environment. *The Journal of Neuroscience, 30*(37), 12366–12378.

Nenadic, I. (2008). Targeting brain regions and symptoms: Neuronal single-unit recordings and deep brain stimulation in obsessive-compulsive disorder. *Biological Psychiatry, 63*(6), 542–543.

Newell, A. (1994). *Unified theories of cognition*. Cambridge, MA: Harvard University Press.

Niv, Y., Daw, N. D., & Dayan, P. (2005). How fast to work: Response vigor, motivation and tonic dopamine. *Proceedings of the 18th International Conference on Neural Information Processing Systems, NIPS'05* (pp. 1019–1026). Cambridge, MA: MIT Press.

Niv, Y., Daw, N. D., Joel, D., & Dayan, P. (2007). Tonic dopamine: Opportunity costs and the control of response vigor. *Psychopharmacology (Berl), 191*(3), 507–520.

Nonacs, P. (2001). State dependent behavior and the marginal value theorem. *Behavioral Ecology, 12*(1), 71–83.

Noonan, M. P., Walton, M. E., Behrens, T. E. J., Sallet, J., Buckley, M. J., & Rushworth, M. F. S. (2010). Separate value comparison and learning mechanisms in macaque medial and lateral orbitofrontal cortex. *Proceedings of the National Academy of Sciences (USA), 107*(47), 20547–20552.

Noser, R., & Byrne, R. W. (2010). How do wild baboons (*Papio ursinus*) plan their routes? Travel among multiple high-quality food sources with inter-group competition. *Animal Cognition, 13* (1), 145–155.

Ohashi, K., & Thomson, J. D. (2005). Efficient harvesting of renewing resources. *Behavioral Ecology, 16*(3), 592–605.

Ohashi, K., & Thomson, J. D. (2009). Trapline foraging by pollinators: Its ontogeny, economics and possible consequences for plants. *Annals of Botany, 103*(9), 1365–1378.

Pammi, V. C., Miyapuram, K. P., Samejima, K., Bapi, R. S., & Doya, K. (2012). Changing the structure of complex visuo-motor sequences selectively activates the fronto-parietal network. *Neuroimage, 59*(2), 1180–1189.

Passingham, R. E., & Wise, S. P. (2012). *The neurobiology of the prefrontal cortex: Anatomy, evolution, and the origin of insight*. Oxford: Oxford University Press.

Paton, J. J., Belova, M. A., Morrison, S. E., & Salzman, C. D. (2006). The primate amygdala represents the positive and negative value of visual stimuli during learning. *Nature, 439*(7078), 865–870.

Payne, S., & Duggan, G. (2011). Giving up problem solving. *Memory & Cognition, 39*(5), 902–913.

Payne, S. J., Duggan, G. B., & Neth, H. (2007). Discretionary task interleaving: Heuristics for time allocation in cognitive foraging. *Journal of Experimental Psychology: General, 136*(3), 370.

Payzan-LeNestour, E., Dunne, S., Bossaerts, P., & O'Doherty, J. P. (2013). The neural representation of unexpected uncertainty during value-based decision making. *Neuron, 79*(1), 191–201.

Pearson, J. M., Hayden, B. Y., Raghavachari, S., & Platt, M. L. (2009). Neurons in posterior cingulate cortex signal exploratory decisions in a dynamic multioption choice task. *Currrent Biology, 19*(18), 1532–1537.

Pearson, J. M., Heilbronner, S. R., Barack, D. L., Hayden, B. Y., & Platt, M. L. (2011). Posterior cingulate cortex: Adapting behavior to a changing world. *Trends in Cognitive Sciences, 15*(4), 143–151.

Pirolli, P. L. T. (2007). *Information foraging theory: Adaptive interaction with information*. Oxford: Oxford University Press.

Plassmann, H., O'Doherty, J. P., & Rangel, A. (2010). Appetitive and aversive goal values are encoded in the medial orbitofrontal cortex at the time of decision making. *The Journal of Neuroscience, 30*(32), 10799–10808.

Platt, M. L., & Glimcher, P. W. (1999). Neural correlates of decision variables in parietal cortex. *Nature, 400*(6741), 233–238.

Platt, M., & Plassmann, H. (2014). Multistage valuation signals and common neural currencies. In P. W. Glimcher & E. Fehr (Eds.), *Neuroeconomics* (2nd ed., pp. 237–258). San Diego, CA: Academic Press.

Potenza, M. N. (2008). The neurobiology of pathological gambling and drug addiction: An overview and new findings. *Philosophical Transactions of the Royal Society of London B: Biological Sciences, 363*(1507), 3181–3189.

Procyk, E., Tanaka, Y. L., & Joseph, J. P. (2000). Anterior cingulate activity during routine and non-routine sequential behaviors in macaques. *Nature Neuroscience, 3*(5), 502–508.

Pylyshyn, Z. W. (2007). *Things and places: How the mind connects with the world*. Cambridge, MA: MIT press.

Ranade, S., Hangya, B., & Kepecs, A. (2013). Multiple modes of phase locking between sniffing and whisking during active exploration. *The Journal of Neuroscience, 33*(19), 8250–8256.

Rangel, A., & Hare, T. (2010). Neural computations associated with goal-directed choice. *Current Opinion in Neurobiology, 20*(2), 262–270.

Real, L. A. (1991). Animal choice behavior and the evolution of cognitive architecture. *Science, 253*(5023), 980–986.

Reboreda, J., & Kacelnik, A. (1991). Risk sensitivity in starlines: Variability in food amount and food delay. *Behavioral Ecology, 2*, 301–308.

Redish, A. (2012). Search processes and hippocampus. In P. M. Todd, T. T. Hills, & T. W. Robbins (Eds.), *Cognitive search: Evolution, algorithms, and the brain* (pp. 81–95). Cambridge, MA: MIT Press.

Roitman, J. D., & Shadlen, M. N. (2002). Response of neurons in the lateral intraparietal area during a combined visual discrimination reaction time task. *The Journal of Neuroscience, 22* (21), 9475–9489.

Rushworth, M. F., Noonan, M. P., Boorman, E. D., Walton, M. E., & Behrens, T. E. (2011). Frontal cortex and reward-guided learning and decision-making. *Neuron, 70*(6), 1054–1069.

Rutledge, R. B., Lazzaro, S. C., Lau, B., Myers, C. E., Gluck, M. A., & Glimcher, P. W. (2009). Dopaminergic drugs modulate learning rates and perseveration in Parkinson's patients in a dynamic foraging task. *The Journal of Neuroscience, 29*(48), 15104–15114.

Sadacca, B. F., Jones, J. L., & Schoenbaum, G. (2016). Midbrain dopamine neurons compute inferred and cached value prediction errors in a common framework. *eLife, 5*, e13665.
Saez, A., Rigotti, M., Ostojic, S., Fusi, S., & Salzman, C. (2015). Abstract context representations in primate amygdala and prefrontal cortex. *Neuron, 87*(4), 869–881.
Sakai, K., Kitaguchi, K., & Hikosaka, O. (2003). Chunking during human visuomotor sequence learning. *Experimental Brain Research, 152*(2), 229–242.
Sara, S. J., & Bouret, S. (2012). Orienting and reorienting: The locus coeruleus mediates cognition through arousal. *Neuron, 76*(1), 130–141.
Saxena, S., Brody, A. L., Schwartz, J. M., & Baxter, L. R. (1998). Neuroimaging and frontal-subcortical circuitry in obsessive-compulsive disorder. *British Journal of Psychiatry, Suppl*(35), 26–37.
Schultz, W. (1998). The phasic reward signal of primate dopamine neurons. *Advances in Pharmacology, 42,* 686–690.
Schultz, W. (2006). Behavioral theories and the neurophysiology of reward. *Annual Review of Psychology, 57,* 87–115.
Schultz, W., Dayan, P., & Montague, P. R. (1997). A neural substrate of prediction and reward. *Science, 275*(5306), 1593–1599.
Schultz, W., Tremblay, L., & Hollerman, J. R. (1998). Reward prediction in primate basal ganglia and frontal cortex. *Neuropharmacology, 37*(4–5), 421–429.
Seo, H., & Lee, D. (2007). Temporal filtering of reward signals in the dorsal anterior cingulate cortex during a mixed-strategy game. *The Journal of Neuroscience, 27*(31), 8366–8377.
Sergeant, J. A., Geurts, H., & Oosterlaan, J. (2002). How specific is a deficit of executive functioning for attention-deficit/hyperactivity disorder? *Behavioural Brain Research, 130*(1), 3–28.
Shagrir, O. (2010). Marr on computational-level theories. *Philosophy of Science, 77*(4), 477–500.
Sharp, M. E., Foerde, K., Daw, N. D., & Shohamy, D. (2015). Dopamine selectively remediates 'model-based' reward learning: A computational approach. *Brain, 139,* 355–364.
Shenhav, A., Cohen, J. D., & Botvinick, M. M. (2016). Dorsal anterior cingulate cortex and the value of control. *Nature Neuroscience, 19*(10), 1286–1291.
Shenhav, A., Straccia, M. A., Cohen, J. D., & Botvinick, M. M. (2014). Anterior cingulate engagement in a foraging context reflects choice difficulty, not foraging value. *Nature Neuroscience, 17*(9), 1249–1254.
Shi, L., Griffiths, T. L., Feldman, N. H., & Sanborn, A. N. (2010). Exemplar models as a mechanism for performing Bayesian inference. *Psychonomic Bulletin & Review, 17*(4), 443–464.
Shidara, M., & Richmond, B. J. (2002). Anterior cingulate: Single neuronal signals related to degree of reward expectancy. *Science, 296*(5573), 1709–1711.
Smith, D. V., Hayden, B. Y., Truong, T. K., Song, A. W., Platt, M. L., & Huettel, S. A. (2010). Distinct value signals in anterior and posterior ventromedial prefrontal cortex. *The Journal of Neuroscience, 30*(7), 2490–2495.
Stephens, D. (2008). Decision ecology: Foraging and the ecology of animal decision making. *Cognitive, Affective, & Behavioral Neuroscience, 8*(4), 475–484.
Stephens, D. W., & Anderson, D. (2001). The adaptive value of preference for immediacy: When shortsighted rules have farsighted consequences. *Behavioral Ecology, 12*(3), 330–339.
Stephens, D., Couzin, I. D., & Giraldeau, L. (2012). Ecological and behavioral approaches to search behavior. In P. M. Todd, T. T. Hills, & T. W. Robbins (Eds.), *Cognitive search: Evolution, algorithms, and the brain* (pp. 25–45). Cambridge, MA: MIT Press.
Stephens, D. W., & Krebs, J. R. (1986). *Foraging theory*. Princeton, NJ: Princeton University Press.
Steyvers, M., Lee, M. D., & Wagenmakers, E.-J. (2009). A Bayesian analysis of human decision-making on bandit problems. *Journal of Mathematical Psychology, 53*(3), 168–179.
Strait, C. E., Blanchard, T. C., & Hayden, B. Y. (2014). Reward value comparison via mutual inhibition in ventromedial prefrontal cortex. *Neuron, 82*(6), 1357–1366.

Summerfield, C., Behrens, T. E., & Koechlin, E. (2011). Perceptual classification in a rapidly changing environment. *Neuron, 71*(4), 725–736.

Sutton, R. S., & Barto, A. G. (1998). *Reinforcement learning: An introduction*. Cambridge, MA: MIT Press.

Tan, C. M. (2008). *Simulated annealing*. Croatia: InTech.

Tian, J., Huang, R., Cohen, J. Y., Osakada, F., Kobak, D., Machens, C. K., et al. (2016). Distributed and mixed information in monosynaptic inputs to dopamine neurons. *Neuron, 91* (6), 1374–1389.

Tinklepaugh, O. L. (1932). The multiple delayed reaction with chimpanzees and monkeys. *Journal of Comparative Psychology, 13*(2), 207.

Tremblay, P.-L., Bedard, M.-A., Langlois, D., Blanchet, P. J., Lemay, M., & Parent, M. (2010). Movement chunking during sequence learning is a dopamine-dependant process: A study conducted in Parkinson's disease. *Experimental Brain Research, 205*(3), 375–385.

Tremblay, L., Hollerman, J. R., & Schultz, W. (1998). Modifications of reward expectation-related neuronal activity during learning in primate striatum. *Journal of Neurophysiology, 80*(2), 964–977.

Trivers, R. L. (1971). The evolution of reciprocal altruism. *Quarterly Review of Biology, 46*(1), 35–57.

Trivers, R. L. (1972). Parental investment and sexual selection. In B. Campbell (Ed.), *Sexual selection and the descent of man* (pp. 136–179). Chicago: Aldine de Gruyter.

Vallone, D., Picetti, R., & Borrelli, E. (2000). Structure and function of dopamine receptors. *Neuroscience and Biobehavioral Reviews, 24*(1), 125–132.

van Laarhoven, P., & Aarts, E. (1987). *Simulated annealing: Theory and applications*. New York: Springer Science & Business Media.

van Meel, C. S., Heslenfeld, D. J., Oosterlaan, J., & Sergeant, J. A. (2007). Adaptive control deficits in attention-deficit/hyperactivity disorder (ADHD): The role of error processing. *Psychiatry Research, 151*(3), 211–220.

Verwey, W. B. (1996). Buffer loading and chunking in sequential keypressing. *Journal of Experimental Psychology: Human Perception and Performance, 22*(3), 544.

Verwey, W. B. (2001). Concatenating familiar movement sequences: The versatile cognitive processor. *Acta Psychologica, 106*(1), 69–95.

Vogt, B. A., Rosene, D. L., & Pandya, D. N. (1979). Thalamic and cortical afferents differentiate anterior from posterior cingulate cortex in the monkey. *Science, 204*(4389), 205–207.

Westendorff, S., D., Everling, K. S., & Womelsdorf, T. (2016). Prefrontal and anterior cingulate cortex neurons encode attentional targets even when they do not apparently bias behavior. *Journal of Neurophysiology*, (in press).

Wilke, A., Hutchinson, J., Todd, P. M., & Czienskowski, U. (2009). Fishing for the right words: Decision rules for human foraging behavior in internal search tasks. *Cognitive Science, 33*(3), 497–529.

Williams, G. C. (1966). Natural selection, the costs of reproduction, and a refinement of Lack's principle. *The American Naturalist, 100*(916), 687–690.

Williams, S. M., & Goldman-Rakic, P. S. (1993). Characterization of the dopaminergic innervation of the primate frontal cortex using a dopamine-specific antibody. *Cerebral Cortex, 3*(3), 199–222.

Willingham, D. B. (1998). A neuropsychological theory of motor skill learning. *Psychological Review, 105*(3), 558.

Wilson, R. C., Geana, A., White, J. M., Ludvig, E. A., & Cohen, J. D. (2014). Humans use directed and random exploration to solve the explore–exploit dilemma. *Journal of Experimental Psychology: General, 143*(6), 2074.

Wittmann, B. C., Daw, N. D., Seymour, B., & Dolan, R. J. (2008). Striatal activity underlies novelty-based choice in humans. *Neuron, 58*(6), 967–973.

Wittmann, M. K., Kolling, N., Akaishi, R., Chau, B. K., Brown, J. W., Nelissen, N., et al. (2016). Predictive decision making driven by multiple time-linked reward representations in the anterior cingulate cortex. *Nature Communications, 7,* 12327.

Wolfe, J. M. (2013). When is it time to move to the next raspberry bush? Foraging rules in human visual search. *Journal of Vision, 13*(3), 10–10.

Woods, S. P., Lovejoy, D. W., & Ball, J. D. (2002). Neuropsychological characteristics of adults with ADHD: A comprehensive review of initial studies. *The Clinical Neuropsychologist, 16* (1), 12–34.

Wunderlich, K., Dayan, P., & Dolan, R. J. (2012). Mapping value based planning and extensively trained choice in the human brain. *Nature Neuroscience, 15*(5), 786–791.

Wunderlich, K., Rangel, A., & O'Doherty, J. P. (2010). Economic choices can be made using only stimulus values. *Proceedings of the National Academy of Sciences (USA), 107*(34), 15005–15010.

Wymbs, N. F., Bassett, D. S., Mucha, P. J., Porter, M. A., & Grafton, S. T. (2012). Differential recruitment of the sensorimotor putamen and frontoparietal cortex during motor chunking in humans. *Neuron, 74*(5), 936–946.

Chapter 7
Dissecting Impulsivity: Brain Mechanisms and Neuropsychiatric Implications

Trevor W. Robbins and Jeffrey W. Dalley

Introduction

The notion of impulsivity continues to attract enormous research interest. Of a total of 12,480 items associated with the construct on the Web of Science (and a further 2586, with the related 'impulsiveness'), 5343 have appeared in the last 5 years (compared with 3254 from 2005 to 2010). This compares favorably with many other psychiatric 'trait-related' constructs such as apathy, anhedonia, extraversion, schizotypy, sensation seeking, and compulsivity (Table 7.1). Definitions of impulsivity can be quite broad-based and subsume the notions both of premature, out-of-control responding and of excessively risky behavior—although these aspects may be somewhat independent. Another essential aspect of a definition of impulsivity is that it is recognized that this trait can presumably have beneficial consequences in certain situations and for certain individuals. However, it is generally agreed that impulsivity is often likely to lead to adverse consequences and may then assume importance as a cross-diagnostic symptom in disorders such as attention-deficit/hyperactivity disorder (ADHD), substance abuse, Gilles de la Tourette's syndrome, mania, and antisocial behavior (Dalley et al. 2011).

Research into impulsivity gained enormous impetus from the invention of the Barratt Impulsiveness Scale (BIS) and related self-report instruments (such as the behavioral avoidance and approach systems: BIS/BAS) The Barratt Scale includes such subjective evaluations of one's performance as: 'I plan for the future'; 'I say things without thinking'; and 'I am restless at lectures' (Patton et al. 1995). This scale recognized from an early stage that there may be distinct forms of impulsivity, by its definition of subscales for 'motor', 'attentional,' and 'non-planning' impulsivity and this theme will be pursued further in this article. What is also highly

T.W. Robbins (✉) · J.W. Dalley
Department of Psychology, University of Cambridge, Downing St, Cambridge CB2 3EB, UK
e-mail: twr2@cam.ac.uk

J.R. Stevens (ed.), *Impulsivity*, Nebraska Symposium on Motivation 64,
DOI 10.1007/978-3-319-51721-6_7

Table 7.1 References to trait-like concepts of impulsivity on the Web of science

By year	References
1995–1999	706
2000–2004	1348
2005–2010	3609
2011–2016	5375
By category	**References**
Impulsiveness	2595
Apathy	4542
Anhedonia	3567
Extraversion	6428
Schizotypy	1980
Sensation seeking	5358
Compulsivity	624
Total	12,502

Note As of 8 Oct 2016

germane is the lack of relationship between measures derived from the BIS and more objective, laboratory measures of impulsivity attempting to capture some of the main elements of the main definition. A recent example of this comes from the paper by Nombela et al. (2014) which tested 60 adults (30 diagnosed with Parkinson's disease) with a range of objective tests of impulsivity as well as the Barratt and BIS/BAS scales (Carver and White 1994). A principal component analysis of the data revealed four orthogonal factors with suitably high eigenvalues which showed clear dissociations among the test measures including the subjective scales. Thus, the BIS score correlated with a general test battery for measuring 'frontal' deficits and the Stroop test score, but not with other commonly used tests such as temporal discounting and go/no-go error score.

This article takes a more neuroscientifically oriented approach to dissecting a unitary notion of impulsivity and also therefore inevitably considers animal models of the construct. This is relatively easy to do because, at a behavioral level, there are many parallel tests of impulsivity in humans and other animals, especially rodents and non-human primates (Table 7.2). We will consider the neural bases of these tasks across species to provide further information concerning their common and overlapping, as well as of their distinctive, neural processing requirements. This may enable a new taxonomy of such tasks and their implications for subdividing the impulsivity construct. Previously, a distinction has been made between tasks that measure impulsive action as distinct from impulsive choice, the implication being that impulsive action measures 'motor' or 'response' inhibition, whereas impulsive choice is governed by parameters of reinforcement (Winstanley et al. 2006). A similar scheme has suggested a distinction between 'impulsive disinhibition' and 'impulsive decision making' (Reynolds et al. 2006). In this chapter, we will show that such distinctions, although useful, do not always capture the relevant dimensions of impulsivity and their neuropsychological basis. We will also go on to show

Table 7.2 Paradigms for measuring different forms of impulsivity in humans and rodents

Waiting/stopping	Choice/action	Type/task	References
Waiting impulsivity	Impulsive choice	Reflective impulsivity	**Clark et al.** (2006), Evenden (1999), **Kagan** (1966)
		Delayed gratification/reinforcement	Ainslie (1975), Evenden (1999), **Green and Myerson** (2004), Mazur (1991), Rachlin et al. (1986)
		Temporal discounting	**Kirby and Petry** (2004)
		Probability discounting	Mazur (1991)
Waiting impulsivity	Impulsive action	4/5-choice serial reaction time task (premature responses)	Carli et al. (1983), Robbins (2002), **Sanchez-Roige et al.** (2014), **Voon et al.** (2014)
Stopping impulsivity	Impulsive action	Stop-signal reaction time task	de Wit and Richards (2004), Eagle et al. (2008), **Logan** (1994)

Note References in **bold** are for human studies and non-bold are for rodent studies

how fractionating the impulsivity construct in different ways may be a useful step to understanding its relevance to neuropsychiatric disorders.

Some of the main tasks that have been used to infer impulsivity include the temporal discounting of reward which, by providing a choice decision to be made between small, sooner rewards versus larger, delayed rewards, has thus been said to quantify 'impulsive choice' (see Bickel et al. and Mitchell, this volume). Temporal discounting of reward is often related to so-called delayed gratification, when the capacity to tolerate delays of reinforcement may result in larger rewards, or 'delay aversion,' where any delays in reward are experienced as sufficiently frustrating to motivate choosing the smaller, sooner reward option. Probability discounting is an apparently related process to temporal discounting, requiring a 'risky' choice between a small, certain and a larger, uncertain reward. By contrast, Logan's stop-signal reaction time task (SSRTT) focuses more obviously on motor inhibition and requires subjects to cancel an already initiated response (Logan 1994); it provides parallel measures of 'Go-reaction time' (RT) and 'Stop-RT' (SSRT) and could be described as a test of 'impulsive action.' However, it is also clear that such a task (and the go/no-go task with which it is often, probably mistakenly, equated) also implies a choice, namely of whether to respond or not. (The main difference between the SSRTT and the go/no-go task is that the latter requires response inhibition at an earlier stage of response processing).

We will take a novel approach to analyzing underlying mechanisms of impulsivity using such paradigms by suggesting a relationship to the processing of reward and motivation at the level of the nucleus accumbens of the ventral striatum for some forms of impulsivity and to controlling aspects of motor response control for others that depend alternatively upon neural networks that include the dorsal rather than ventral striatum. We will also show how this distinction can involve both elements in tasks that require animals to respond to the presentation of reward-related cues, as occurs in the 5-choice serial reaction time task (5CSRTT) (Robbins 2002). In this situation, which is based on a human continuous performance test of sustained attention, rodents are trained to detect brief visual targets that predict food reward by responding appropriately in a row of apertures set into one wall of the test chamber. Responding is rewarded for correct detections but punished with time-out from positive reinforcement (the house light is dimmed) upon an error of commission in one of the other apertures or an error of omission in failing to respond to the target at all. More relevant to the present theme is what happens if the rodent responds in apertures prior to the occurrence of the visual target—in fact, this again leads to time-out and the animal has to initiate the next trial after a short delay period in darkness. These responses are thus premature as well as maladaptive and fulfill the operational requirements of impulsive behavior. They resemble the situation defined by Grey Walter's phenomenon of contingent negative variation in which humans await reward in the presence of a reward-predictive stimulus (Tecce 1972). Although premature responding in the 5CSRTT has been described, like the SSRT, as an example of impulsive action, it will be shown that these two forms of behavior are actually mediated by quite different neural systems. In fact, because it involves mediating delays to reward prior to response selection, premature responding in the 5CSRTT has more in common with impulsive choice tasks such as temporal discounting and indeed will be shown to depend in part on some common neural circuitry. By contrast, the SSRTT requires inhibition of a response that has already been initiated. Hence, we have made another distinction between 'waiting impulsivity' and 'stopping impulsivity' (Dalley et al. 2011). Table 7.2 shows the various ways in which these three commonly used paradigms can be categorized according to these classifications.

Neural Basis of Premature Responding: Opponent and DA-dependent Mechanisms in the Nucleus Accumbens

The nucleus accumbens is well known to be an important component of the 'reward system' which identifies goals for action and provides motivational support for reward-seeking behavior. This system includes other structures such as the medial orbital cortex and insula, as well as limbic afferents, for example, from the amygdala. Dopamine (DA)-containing neurons in the ventral tegmental area that project to the accumbens have been shown in rhesus monkeys to encode a prediction error by their fast phasic firing that initially accompanies the occurrence of reward and is then displaced earlier in time to the occurrence of conditioned cues that predict the occurrence of reward (such as a food pellet or fruit juice). Further work has shown that the tonic level of DA cell firing may also encode reward uncertainty, relevant to risk (Fiorillo et al. 2003). Human functional resonance imaging studies using the monetary incentive delay (MID) task (Knutson et al.

2000) have shown analogous responses (in terms of the hemodynamic blood-oxygen-level-dependent [BOLD] response) to reward-predictive cues that precede an opportunity to make a discriminative response for reward and may respond proportionately to expected reward magnitude (which is generally, but not exclusively, monetary in nature). However, the human participant must defer responding following the predictive cue, until the discriminative stimuli are available; this is reminiscent of the 5CSRTT, where there is a similar requirement for inhibitory response control in the expectation of reward, though one probably more demanding than in the human MID paradigm.

Much previous research has found that performance on the 5CSRTT by rats requires the coordinated functioning of several different neural circuits (Chudasama et al. 2003) and this is largely beyond the scope of the present article. However, premature responding was already known to be dependent on the nucleus accumbens and the infralimbic cortex from studies employing fiber-sparing excitotoxic lesions or other neurotoxins (Cole and Robbins 1989), intracerebral infusions, e.g., to affect dopamine (D-amphetamine; Cole and Robbins 1989), and GABA and glutamate receptors (Murphy et al. 2005) (Fig. 7.1). The infralimbic cortex innervates the shell region of the nucleus accumbens and this is congruent with evidence that excitotoxic lesions of the shell attenuate the increase in premature responding induced by amphetamine that is a consequence of its actions to enhance DA function (Murphy et al. 2008). Significantly, excitotoxic lesions of the core subregion of the nucleus accumbens have quite the opposite effect, to enhance the premature responding produced by amphetamine (Murphy et al. 2008). Hence, there appears to be a degree of functional opponency in the interactions between these two regions of the nucleus accumbens, the shell apparently promoting and the core inhibiting impulsive behavior.

The other significant point about premature responding is that it is the measure showing greatest individual variation among the Lister-hooded rat population. About 8–10% of this strain respond prematurely at a much higher level than the rest of the population and persist consistently in this tendency suggesting that it is trait related. Indeed, further experiments (S Pitzoi, E Petretto, B Jupp, AB Fernando, AC Mar, W Sommer, O Staehlin, R Spanagel, TW Robbins, TJ Aitman, JW Dalley, unpublished observations) have shown that the impulsive tendency breeds true in this population. A genome-wide linkage analysis of the first five generations revealed a significant quantitative trait locus (QTL) for premature responding on chromosome 1q31–1q34, spanning approximately 20 cM, with a maximum logarithm of the odds (LOD) score of 4.07. Further analysis in this region of linkage on chromosome 1, carried out by combining generation 6 genotypes, confirmed the QTL and increased the strength of the linkage on chromosome 1 to a maximum LOD of 5.2.

The impulsive tendency is exacerbated when the delay before presentation of the discriminative stimuli (the inter-trial interval or ITI) is experimentally lengthened from its usual 5–7 s or longer. It may well be asked whether the tendency to impulsivity mainly becomes apparent when rats fail to learn to inhibit their premature responses as a consequence of the punishing feedback over the many (often 40)

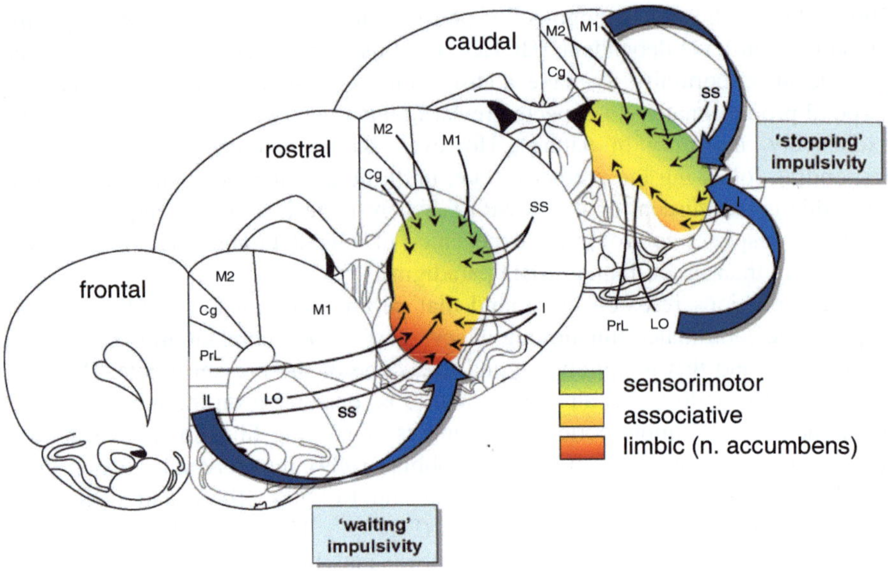

Fig. 7.1 Simplified neuroanatomical circuitry of 'waiting' and 'stopping' impulsivity depicted on coronal sections of the rat brain (Paxinos and Watson 1997). Redrawn and adapted from Van Waes et al. (2012). Waiting impulsivity depends on the ventromedial prefrontal cortex (IL and PrL) and inputs from this region to the shell and core subregions of the nucleus accumbens (see text for details). Stopping impulsivity depends on the primary and supplementary motor cortices, lateral orbitofrontal cortex, and the dorsal striatum. Abbreviations: *Cg* cingulate cortex; *IL* infralimbic cortex; *I* insula cortex; *LO* lateral orbitofrontal cortex; *PrL* prelimbic cortex; *M1* primary motor cortex; *M2* supplementary motor cortex; *SS* somatosensory cortex

sessions required to obtain stable 5CSRTT performance. This predicts that initially all rats tend to exhibit impulsive behavior, but that the 'high impulsives' emerge gradually as a function of further training. However, this does not appear to be the case. First, high-impulsive rats can be identified in the earliest stages of training, even in young (35-day-old) animals. Second, if the time course of responding is measured during those sessions in which long, 'challenge' ITIs are interpolated, it is evident that performance improves over the 30-min session (Dalley, J.W. and Robbins, T.W., unpublished observations). However, as shown in Fig. 7.2, this is equally so in the 'high-' and 'low-' impulsive rats, suggesting that the high-impulsive rats are responding normally to negative feedback, but that they simply have an overall higher level of premature responding.

The phenotype of the high-impulsive rat is remarkably selective (Dalley et al. 2007; Molander et al. 2011; Dilleen et al. 2012). A common assumption has been that such rats would show more locomotor activity in photocell cages, but this is not the case—if anything they are less active than normal. They do have small, sometimes significant impairments in attention, as measured by their capacity to identify the visual targets in the 5CSRTT. They exhibit normal Pavlovian appetitive conditioning and patterns of behavior in the elevated plus maze that suggest that

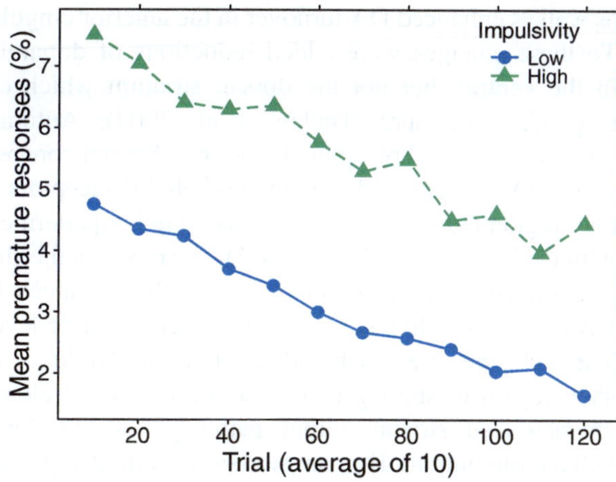

Fig. 7.2 Premature responses in the 5CSRTT as a function of time on task following interpolation of a single session with a longer inter-trial interval of 7 s. High-impulsive rats make more premature responses than low-impulsive rats. Premature responses decline at the same rate in both groups of animals over the course of the session (J.W. Dalley and T.W. Robbins, unpublished findings)

they are not more anxious, nor do they appear more stressed in terms of corticosterone responses. There is a tendency to exhibit a significantly greater (albeit small) novelty preference when given the choice between being located in a novel versus familiar environment. However, by far the most dramatic aspect of their phenotype is their significant tendency to self-administer cocaine in a binge-access chronic paradigm to a significantly greater extent than normal, 'low-impulsive' rats (Dalley et al. 2007). These animals also showed greater evidence of relapse in a procedure in which abstinence (or the voluntary cessation of drug-taking) is promoted by punishment (rather than by the commonly employed extinction-reinstatement procedure, which may have less ecological validity) (Economidou et al. 2009). There was a similar pattern of effects for nicotine self-administration and relapse (Diergaarde et al. 2008), although not for heroin (McNamara et al. 2010), suggesting that impulsivity is related specifically to stimulant drug self-administration (Poulos et al. 1995; Pena-Oliver et al. 2015). The relationship for alcohol self-administration is more complicated, but impulsivity may promote certain forms of alcohol intake. Of even greater importance, the enhanced intake of stimulants such as cocaine had a compulsive quality, as shown specifically by the tendency of high-impulsive rats most unusually to continue to work under a 'seeking-taking' schedules of cocaine seeking when electric foot-shock punishment was also occasionally delivered under the same schedule (Belin et al. 2008). This effect clearly adequately fulfills a definition of compulsive behavior, given the adverse consequences of electric foot shock, and led further support to the hypothesis of stimulant drug addiction proceeding from impulsive to compulsive behavior (and from initial control by the ventral, to the dorsal, striatum) (Everitt and Robbins 2005, 2016).

In parallel with these behavioral characteristics, the high-impulsive rats exhibited a number of significant neural and neurochemical correlates. High-impulsive rats show neurochemical and pharmacological evidence of enhanced serotonin levels and release in the medial prefrontal cortex (mPFC, including the intra-limbic cortex), as well as enhanced DA turnover in the anterior cingulate cortex (Dalley et al. 2002). To these changes were added reductions of dopamine D2/3 receptor availability in the ventral, but not the dorsal, striatum which correlated with the premature responding measure (Dalley et al. 2007). Autoradiographic studies indicated reductions of D2/3 receptors in the shell but not core region, together with reductions in the DA transporter (DAT) in the shell. D1 receptors in contrast were reduced in the core region (Jupp et al. 2013). This complex pattern of changes appeared consistent with the hypothesis of enhanced DA turnover in the shell (the D2/3 receptor changes could have reflected an adaptation to the enhanced DA turnover and the reduced DAT levels would have led to increased synaptic levels of DA in the shell region). These changes presumably affected the striatal direct and indirect pathways from the shell region (assuming that these are organized along the same lines as the better characterized striatal output pathways of the dorsal striatum) that influenced behavioral output. Human studies of impulsivity are consistent with low D2/3 receptor binding in the midbrain predicting impulsivity as measured by the BIS; this would also lead to elevated DA release in terminal domains in the ventral striatum (Buckholtz et al. 2010).

Although the shell output was thus identified as being important for the increased impulsivity, further evidence indicated an additional contribution of the core region. Thus, magnetic resonance imaging highlighted reduced gray matter in the region of the accumbens core of the left hemisphere especially that was also strongly correlated with impulsive responding (Caprioli et al. 2014). GABA decarboxylase (GAD) activity was also reduced in the core region suggesting that medium spiny cells may have been reduced in this area. An infusion of an antisense oligonucleotide sequence for GAD into the nucleus accumbens core also induced impulsive responding in normally low-impulsive rats. Therefore, it appears that the hypothesised functional opponency of the shell and core alluded to above in relation to the findings of Murphy et al. (2008) might result from an enhanced, DA-dependent output of the shell being inadequately gated by a compromised core subregion—although this hypothesis awaits further testing. Other evidence for opponency of these two regions comes from similarly contrasting effects of intra-core and intra-shell infusions of the D3 receptor antagonist nafadotride (Besson et al. 2010), as well as the effects of deep brain stimulation of these two accumbens subregions (Sesia et al. 2008).

Neural Basis of Impulsive Choice: Overlapping Circuits and the Impulsivity Construct

The involvement of the core subregion in the construct of impulsivity is further supported by its implication in impulsive choice. Thus, excitotoxic lesions of the nucleus accumbens core region induced rats to choose a small, sooner food reward rather than waiting for a delayed larger reward (Cardinal et al. 2001). Much subsequent work, reviewed elsewhere (Robbins and Dalley 2016), is consistent with this conclusion—and in contrast, lesions of the shell have been reported to have no effect on impulsive choice (Pothuizen et al. 2005). Moreover, an early result that supports this interpretation is the finding that whereas delayed gratification was found to be related to decreased DA release in the nucleus accumbens core, impulsive premature responding was associated with decreased DA release in the core as well as increased DA release in the shell subregion (Diergaarde et al. 2008), as postulated above. High-impulsive rats do show steeper discounting of reward than controls with delay (Robinson et al. 2009). These data suggest that there is some commonality in the neural substrates that underpin premature responding and also impulsive choice (both examples of what we have termed 'waiting impulsivity'; Dalley et al. 2011), giving credibility to the notion of a unitary construct of impulsivity. However, there is also evidence of subtle differences in this neural network, supporting the view that the construct can be fractionated, as demonstrated by the analysis of impulsivity in rodents according to different measures described above (Winstanley et al. 2004a). By contrast, we will show below how 'stopping impulsivity' is mediated by a different neural system that involves a different sector of the striatum.

This hypothesis of overlapping and distinct circuitries may be supported by further studies of the neural mechanisms affecting temporal discounting of reward: Selective lesion studies support roles for the basolateral amygdala, ventral hippocampus, and the medial and lateral orbitofrontal cortex, but not the mPFC (Cardinal et al. 2001; Winstanley et al. 2004b; Mar et al. 2011). The lack of effect of mPFC lesions contrasts with control mechanisms over premature responding, which include the anterior cingulate and infralimbic cortex (Muir et al. 1996; Chudasama et al. 2003). Eventually, the new neuroscience tools provided by optogenetics and chemogenetics will be deployed to confirm and elaborate on the circuit control of these behavioral responses. Additionally, in vivo electrophysiology will be useful to examine network-like activity in relation to premature responding. Initial analyses (Donnelly et al. 2015) have shown a ramping of neuronal activity in relation to premature responses in the nucleus accumbens and ventromedial prefrontal cortex (PFC)—also in relationship to rewarded trials, a finding which may be relevant to data suggesting that premature responses may be more likely after an immediately previous incorrect trial as compared to a rewarded one (Christakou et al. 2004).

Chemical Neuromodulation of Waiting Impulsivity

Similarly, there are overlapping and contrasting effects of serotonin (or 5-hydroxytryptamine, 5-HT) manipulations on premature responding and temporal discounting. Forebrain 5-HT depletion greatly increases premature responding

(Harrison et al. 1997) but does not have dramatic effects on temporal discounting (Winstanley et al. 2004a), although acutely the 5-HT1A receptor agonist 8-OHDPAT does induce impulsive choice (Winstanley et al. 2005), and recent electrophysiological data show that dorsal raphe neurons fire during the waiting period of temporal discounting for food reward (Miyazaki et al. 2011).

A systemically administered 5-HT2C receptor antagonist exacerbated premature responding produced by 5-HT depletion (Winstanley et al. 2004c), whereas 5-HT2A receptor antagonism provided in the mPFC (Winstanley et al. 2003) or nucleus accumbens (Robinson et al. 2008a) blocks this measure of impulsivity. To test this hypothesis of dissociable effects of different 5-HT receptors further, the behavioral effects of two partially selective serotonergic (5-HT) ligands, ketanserin (5-HT2A,C receptor antagonist), and SER-082 (5-HT2C,B receptor antagonist) were compared in the two tests of impulsivity. Dissociation was seen between the effects of ketanserin, which decreased impulsivity in the 5-CSRTT, but had no effect on the temporal discounting of reward task, and SER-082, which had no effect on performance of the 5CSRTT, but decreased impulsive responding in the temporal discounting task (Talpos et al. 2006).

The dopaminergic modulation of waiting impulsivity described above has implications for human attention-deficit/hyperactivity disorder (ADHD). Early on, (Dalley et al. 2007) it was noticed that cocaine self-administration appeared to blunt the high impulsivity expressed as increased premature responding; this was reminiscent of effects of agents such as methylphenidate (Ritalin®) in combating impulsive behavior in ADHD and presumably arises from the effects of these drugs to increase catecholamine (i.e., DA and noradrenaline [NA] levels) in the synaptic cleft, by virtue of their actions, for example, to block the DA and NA transporters and hence block the reuptake of these neurotransmitters. More recently, this has been explored in further detail both with intravenously self-administered cocaine (Caprioli et al. 2013) and orally administered methylphenidate (Caprioli et al. 2015). In both cases, the stimulant drug reduced premature responding significantly in high-impulsive rats while increasing it in rats with lower (i.e., normal) baseline levels of premature responding (Fig. 7.3). This corresponds to the well-known 'rate dependency' (Dews and Wenger 1977; Robbins 1981) of the effects of stimulant drugs. Additionally, these behavioral changes were matched by corresponding changes in D2/D3 receptors throughout the striatum; in other words, the low D2/D3 receptors in high-impulsive rats were increased by the drugs and vice versa. Further analysis revealed that while this was a significant correlate of the behavioral effect, it could not be the only contributory mechanism. Another significant influence was shown to work through noradrenergic mechanisms; the NA-reuptake blocker atomoxetine (also used to treat ADHD, as Strattera®) dose-dependently reduced high impulsivity (Robinson et al. 2008b)—though without increasing premature responding in normal rats, as does methylphenidate. Atomoxetine (like methylphenidate) achieved this reduction in impulsivity without significantly affecting accuracy to detect the brief visual targets, i.e., in the absence of any sedative effects.

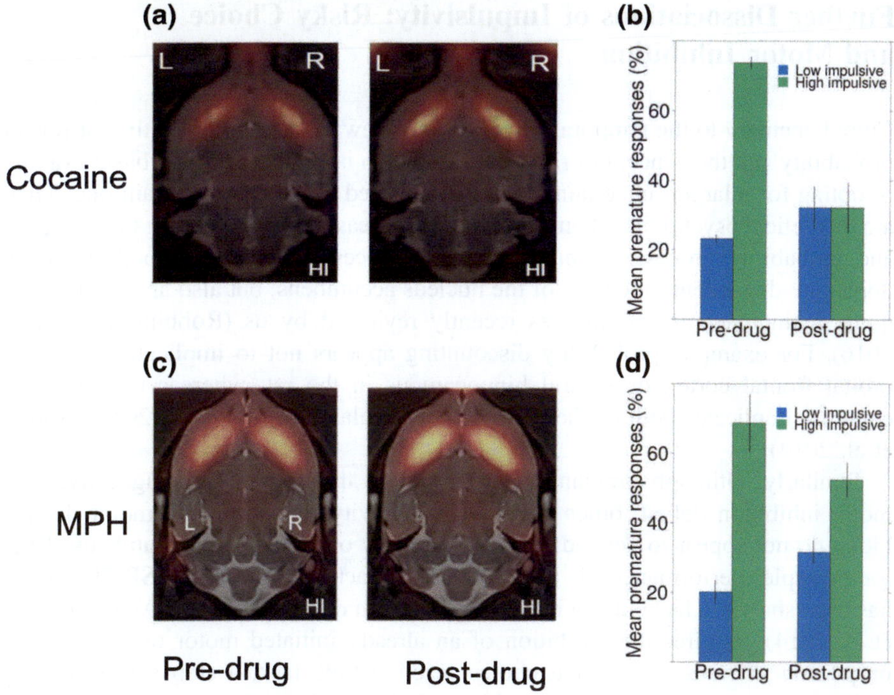

Fig. 7.3 Baseline dependency in the effects of intravenously self-administered cocaine (*upper graphs*) and oral methylphenidate (MPH, *lower graphs*) on DA D2 receptor availability in the ventral striatum (**a**, **c**) and behavior (**b**, **d**). High-impulsive rats exhibit a diminished availability of D2 receptors in the ventral striatum compared with low-impulsive rats (Dalley et al. 2007). This deficit (left scans) is corrected by cocaine and methylphenidate (right scans) with a corresponding reduction in behavioral impulsivity in the 5CSRTT (**b, d,** respectively). From Caprioli et al. (2015) and Caprioli et al. (2013) with permission

Further studies showed that atomoxetine produced the same effects when infused into the shell, but not the core regions of the nucleus accumbens, nor into the prefrontal cortex (Economidou et al. 2012). Thus, part of the opponency within the nucleus accumbens may also comprise NA–DA interactions there, as originally postulated by Alexander Cools (e.g., Tuinstra and Cools 2000). The assumption must be that regulation of DA leads to fluctuations of premature responding, high levels of which are antagonized by increased NA, presumably released from sub-coeruleal projections to the shell region (Delfs et al. 1998). The implications are that atomoxetine might be a more effective regulator of impulsive responding than methylphenidate in ADHD, despite the latter's greater clinical efficacy, which extends to other symptoms besides impulsive behavior. Atomoxetine has also been shown to reduce impulsive choice when given systemically (Robinson et al. 2008b), and indeed to oppose other forms of impulsive behavior to be discussed below, although via its actions in PFC, rather than the striatum.

Further Dissociations of Impulsivity: Risky Choice and Motor Inhibition

Complementary to the temporal discounting of reward is the discounting of reward probability and the concept of risky choice, which is embodied in the basic example of opting for a larger, uncertain reward as opposed to a smaller, certain one. There are theoretical psychological and computational reasons for supposing that temporal and probability processing shares common processes. They also both implicate dopamine-dependent processes of the nucleus accumbens, but also appear to utilize quite distinct neural circuitry, as recently reviewed by us (Robbins and Dalley 2016). For example, probability discounting appears not to implicate the medial orbital frontal cortex or ventral hippocampus in the rat, whereas temporal discounting implicates both of these structures (Abela and Chudasama 2013; Stopper et al. 2014).

Similarly, although premature responding in the 5CSRTT is suggestive of a motor inhibition deficit, other forms of impulsivity resulting from motor disinhibition do not appear to depend upon the integrity of the nucleus accumbens. Thus, for example, performance on the stop-signal reaction time task (SSRTT), which has been shown to have utility in studies of human disorders such as ADHD (Logan et al. 2014), requires the inhibition of an already initiated motor response: On a proportion of trials of a visual choice reaction time task, a stop signal (usually auditory) is presented a short, variable period after the imperative cue to indicate that no response should be made. Impulsive responding here is represented by the failure or slowness to brake the response, with a corresponding prolongation of the stop reaction time, which is computed from the response time distribution according to a 'race' model. There has been considerable attention paid to the neural network that underpins SSRTT performance in humans which we will return to below. However, in the immediate context of animal studies, the SSRTT has been implemented in rats and the underlying neural systems explored by interventions using fiber-sparing cell body lesions and intracerebral infusions. These studies have shown that damage to the nucleus accumbens core has no effects on SSRT performance (Eagle and Robbins 2003), contrasting remarkably with the powerful effects of such lesions on other forms of impulsivity, as in the 5CSRTT and the temporal discounting paradigm (see above). By contrast, dorsal striatal lesions and infusions of a D2 receptor antagonist into the dorsal but not the ventral striatum produce a significant lengthening of the SSRT (and the D1 receptor antagonist has the opposite effects) (Eagle et al. 2011). A human positron emission tomography (PET) study employing the DA ligands [^{11}C]NNC-112 and [^{18}F]fallypride, respectively, has examined individual differences in D1 and D2 receptors in relation to SSRT performance and importantly confirmed significant relationships of SSRT with DA receptor binding potentials in the dorsal and not the ventral striatum with reduced D2 receptor binding being correlated with inferior SSRT performance (Robertson et al. 2015).

The rodent homologue of the caudate receives overlapping neural inputs from the lateral orbitofrontal cortex and the anterior cingulate cortex, and lesions in rats of both structures (but not the mPFC), specifically lengthen the SSRT (Eagle and Robbins 2003; Eagle et al. 2008). This neural network thus contrasts quite strongly with that controlling premature responding on the 5CSRTT, which includes more ventral aspects of mPFC and the nucleus accumbens. One way of conceptualizing this is to suppose that the 5CSRTT premature response and delayed reward discounting test paradigms tap into different stages of the response sequence, representing the beginning of the sequence prior to response selection, whereas the SSRTT relates to the regulation of responding post-initiation. We have previously characterized SSRT deficits as exemplifying stopping impulsivity rather than waiting impulsivity (Dalley et al. 2011). The two tasks clearly further refine the notion of impulsive action. The SSRTT is often considered to be a sophisticated version of another well-known go/no-go task in which subjects respond to one cue but inhibit responding to the other. Despite their superficial similarities, which probably also involve some common processing demands, these two paradigms differ in the sense that in the SSRTT, a response has already been selected but then has to be canceled, whereas in the go/no-go task, the inhibition of responding is imposed as part of response selection—in other words, the inhibition comes at an earlier stage in the production of the response sequence, and this might also be reflected in which fronto-striatal loop is implicated and how it is modulated. Thus, for example, performance of the SSRTT is much less sensitive to pharmacological manipulation of 5-HT than the go/no-go task (Eagle et al. 2008).

There is further evidence of differential chemical modulation of the different forms of impulsivity. SSRTT performance is especially sensitive to the improvement by systemic atomoxetine, inducing blockade of NA uptake, providing a third example of the beneficial effects of this drug on impulsivity (Robinson et al. 2008b). Moreover, a similar beneficial effect was also obtained when infusing the drug into the lateral orbitofrontal cortex, consistent with the evidence of effects of lesions of this area, further pharmacological manipulations being consistent with a NA-ergic action of atomoxetine (Bari et al. 2011). By contrast, citalopram, the selective serotonin reuptake inhibitor (SSRI), had little effect on SSRT performance over a wide acute dose range (Bari et al. 2009). Additionally, forebrain 5-HT depletion also had little effect, in marked contrast to its effects on premature responding in the 5CSRTT (Eagle et al. 2009).

Translation from Laboratory to Clinic of Findings on Impulsivity

Whereas the body of preclinical work reviewed above provides several valuable pointers concerning the theoretical construct of impulsivity and its neural basis, parallel studies, sometimes inspired by the basic advances and sometimes inspiring them, have shown the utility of the research for several clinical constructs. Reference has already been made to ADHD, but another prominent example is of stimulant drug addiction. There is considerable evidence for low levels of striatal D2/3 receptors in chronic drug abusers, as well as hypometabolism of the orbitofrontal cortex (Volkow et al. 1993) and impaired decision making, including temporal discounting and impulsive behavior (Perry and Carroll 2008). It is not entirely clear, however, whether these effects result from neurotoxic actions of stimulant drug abuse, or else whether they may precede and even cause some aspects of drug abuse. The findings of increased stimulant drug self-administration and compulsive drug seeking in combination with low D2/3 receptors in high-impulsive rats (Dalley et al. 2007) suggest that impulsivity could contribute to vulnerability to stimulant addiction in humans and hence be an endophenotype, i.e., a characteristic also shown to be present in non-affected family members, suggestive, but not conclusive, of heritable factors that confer possible vulnerability or predisposition to an disorder (Gottesman and Gould 2003).

This hypothesis was tested directly in a number of ways by Ersche and colleagues. Individuals with stimulant dependence had very high BIS scores relative to healthy age- and IQ-matched controls, as would be expected. However, the non-drug-abusing siblings of the stimulant-dependent addicts were intermediate in their BIS scores between these two groups, also being significantly higher than controls (Ersche et al. 2010), just as would be predicted by the endophenotype hypothesis. Therefore, the tendency to respond impulsively was present in the family and not simply due to stimulant drug abuse. Moreover, for a sensation-seeking scale, there was no difference between the siblings and controls, showing that the impulsivity trait was more selectively present in the family. Recreational stimulant users also had high sensation-seeking scores but had no tendency to high BIS scores, consistent with the hypothesis that there are considerable individual differences in the propensity to stimulant drug addiction (Ersche et al. 2012b). These findings were largely borne out by a later study using instead the SSRTT. Both the stimulant-dependent individuals and their siblings showed lengthened SSRTs, the former confirming many previous findings. Slowness of SSRT, and hence the tendency to impulsivity, was related to reduced white matter (fractional anisotropy) in the arcuate fasciculus innervating the inferior frontal cortex, as indexed by diffusion tensor imaging, a finding consistent with previous evidence of frontal damage and functional neuroimaging implicating, in particular, the right inferior frontal gyrus (RIFG) in SSRT performance (Ersche et al. 2011; Ersche et al. 2012a). Consequently, it appears that individuals with reduced white matter (as well as gray matter) in this region may be susceptible to stimulant use disorder. Further evidence is provided by fMRI data from a number of laboratories indicating similarly reduced BOLD responses in inhibitory tasks such as the SSRTT in stimulant abusers, indicating inefficient control of responding (Morein-Zamir and Robbins 2015). One study has compared stimulant abusers with their siblings and found that the latter actually overactivated the RIFG compared with healthy control volunteers (Morein-Zamir et al. 2013). This intriguing result conceivably indicates a tendency to impose inhibitory voluntary control to a greater extent than normal, perhaps helping to explain the resilience of the siblings to resist drug abuse.

An entirely different approach to establishing vulnerability to drug abuse comes from a longitudinal approach, as exemplified by the IMAGEN project (Schumann et al. 2010). Two thousand healthy 14-year-old adolescent volunteers were investigated with a multidisciplinary battery comprising neuropsychological testing, neuroimaging, and genomics in order to identify markers or characteristics to gauge possible risk for drug (including alcohol and nicotine) use. One of the studies utilized fMRI with the SSRTT and the large sample size enabled the use of principal component analysis to analyze which neural networks were associated with performance (Whelan et al. 2012). On successful stop trials, seven orthogonal neural 'clusters' were identified with suitably large eigenvalues (Fig. 7.4). These included the lateral orbitofrontal cortex, the medial frontal cortex, the right inferior cortex and cingulate cortex, the pre-supplementary area, the parietal cortex, and basal ganglia. On failed trials, where stopping was unsuccessful, the same circuits were engaged with the exception of the pre-supplementary cortex, suggesting that this region implements the motor inhibitory braking effect on action. Performance on a go/no-go task was related to reduced RIFG activity, consistent with earlier data. These neural networks are consistent with what had been found previously with fMRI tasks using similar behavioral test paradigms (Aron and Poldrack 2006).

Importantly, the degree of activation of certain regions correlated with questionnaire data on drug use. Experience with alcohol and nicotine correlated with orbitofrontal hypoactivation and with illicit drugs (predominantly cocaine) with an overactivation of the RIFG/cingulate cluster. Hence, it appears that the activity of neural circuits implicated in response control is predictive of drug use. The seemingly paradoxically increased activity of the RIFG region may relate to the initiation of drug use when there is an attempt to impose control (like the siblings of

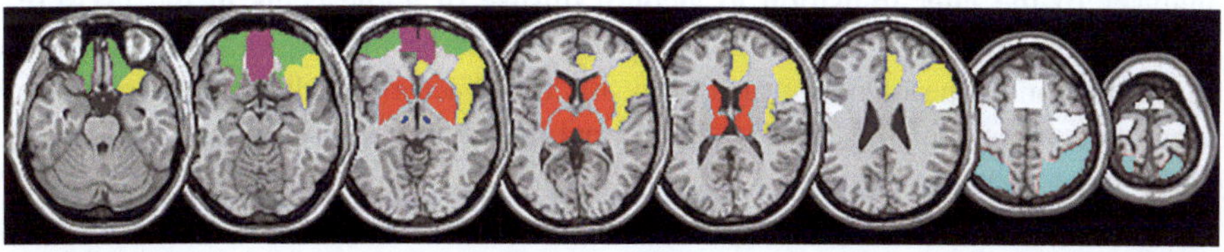

Fig. 7.4 Neuroimaging of the stop-signal reaction time task in 14-year-old adolescents from the IMAGEN project ($N = 1252$). Different networks were associated with different aspects of impulse control as measured by significant BOLD activations on successful stopping trials in the stop-signal reaction time task. Seven orthogonal clusters were identified by principal component analysis (six shown here): medial prefrontal cortex (*purple*); basal ganglia (*red*); pre-supplementary motor cortex/parietal cortex (*white*); parieto-occipital cortex (*light blue*). Adolescents reporting drug use (alcohol or nicotine or both) had reduced activity in the lateral orbitofrontal cortex (*green*). Adolescents additionally reporting illicit drug use; *increased* activity in right inferior frontal/anterior cingulate network (*yellow*). This figure represents an interim analysis of 1252, adolescents, the results being essentially the same as the final analysis of $N = 2000$ adolescents (see Whelan et al. 2012). Figure provided by kind permission of Hugh Garavan and Robert Whelan

the study described above). Additionally, individuals scoring high in ADHD-like symptoms also displayed alterations in the inferior frontal cortex region, though bilaterally, as well as in the basal ganglia cluster but on failed stop trials only. These data may indicate that there is some overlap in the neural substrates underlying a propensity for drug use and a tendency toward ADHD-like symptoms but also differences.

Another correlate of reduced activity of the RIFG region was with activity of the noradrenaline/norepinephrine transporter (NET), which is of particular interest given the beneficial effects of the NA reuptake blocker atomoxetine on SSRT in individuals with adult ADHD as well as healthy volunteers (Chamberlain et al. 2007). It was further shown that the improved SSRT performance in healthy volunteers is correlated with an increased BOLD response in the RIFG region (Chamberlain et al. 2009). Recently, these beneficial effects have been confirmed and extended to certain patients with Parkinson's disease. Task-free resting state functional connectivity analysis showed that atomoxetine enhanced connectivity between the RIFG and the dorsal anterior cingulate in Parkinson's disease, hence generally boosting the fronto-striatal circuitry associated with SSRT performance (Borchert et al. 2016). More specifically, the fMRI results with Parkinson's disease patients suggest that atomoxetine increases sensitivity of the inferior frontal gyrus to afferent inputs from the pre-supplementary motor cortex; and further that atomoxetine enhances downstream modulation of frontal-subcortical connections for response inhibition (Rae et al. 2016). These effects may correspond to the effects of intra-PFC atomoxetine in rats described above and provide a possible explanation of some of the therapeutic effects of the drug in ADHD, as well as Parkinson's disease. Whether atomoxetine can be used effectively in substance abusers seeking treatments to help with response control remains to be seen.

It should be made clear that this work establishing impulsivity as a possible endophenotype or trait marker for drug abuse needs much further work. Further analyses of the later transition to alcohol misuse of adolescents in the IMAGEN sample have indicated that impulsivity may well be an important predisposing factor, but only one of many factors in this multifactorially determined condition. Moreover, the promising links to the animal literature could be made even tighter. There have been no studies to data of how individual variation in SSRT performance in rodents might relate to the compulsive drug-seeking tendency. Likewise, the high-impulsive, premature responding phenotype in the rodent 5CSRTT has not yet been shown directly to predict stimulant drug dependence in humans. However, a 4CSRTT analogue of this task in humans has been shown to be capable of detecting increased premature responding in both methamphetamine and cannabis abusers (Voon et al. 2014). Another elegant analogue of the rodent 5CSRTT similarly shows impulsive responding in alcohol-dependent individuals (Sanchez-Roige et al. 2014). Analysis of the neuroanatomical substrates of 5CSRTT performance in binge drinkers and abstinent subjects with alcohol use disorders shows that the premature responding is linked to reduced structural connectivity of the ventral striatum and subgenual cingulate cortex with the subthalamic nucleus (STN), consistent with the critical infralimbic–nucleus accumbens–STN circuitry as established from rodent studies (Morris et al. 2016). Such studies encourage the use of these tests to probe the precise nature and breadth of a neuroendophenotype (i.e., an endophenotype with both a behavioral and a neural element) of impulsivity relevant to drug abuse. It was of particular interest that these pathological drinking groups were not differentiated in terms of their SSRT performance, and an analysis of distinct forms of impulsivity is certainly relevant. In the same way, it may be useful to compare with the motor inhibition paradigms the predictive capabilities of temporal and probability discounting, as these also may predict some degree of susceptibility to stimulants. However, although impulsivity may be a predisposing factor for several forms of substance abuse, including alcoholism, a detailed analysis of such factors from the IMAGEN sample indicates that it is far from being the only such factor (Whelan et al. 2014).

The possible utility of the dissociations we have shown in different aspects of impulsivity for the purposes of psychiatric classification or nosology has been illustrated in studies of the heterogeneity of symptoms in ADHD. Solanto and coworkers showed that, consistent with the findings described by (Nombela et al. 2014), for a large population of juvenile ADHD patients, performance on the tests of choice impulsivity (temporal discounting) and the SSRTT was essentially uncorrelated, although there were large deficits in both indicating impulsive behavior, and the tests were predictive of the overall diagnosis (Solanto et al. 2001). This suggests that ADHD may implicate different aspects of fronto-striatal cognitive control systems according to specific dysfunctional neural circuitries.

Theoretical Implications for the Impulsivity Construct: The Role of Cognitive Control

The evidence reviewed so far suggests that the psychometric evidence of dissociable aspects of impulsivity can be matched by the neural dissociations described. There is evidence for a central role for fronto-striatal circuitry in the expression of impulsive behavior, but, as in the case of waiting versus stopping impulsivity, these are probably mediated to some extent by parallel pathways. Moreover, probabilistic, 'risky' discounting appears separate from temporal discounting, suggesting that uncertainty and delay of reward are mediated through separate systems.

We should consider additional manifestations of impulsivity, such as 'reflection' impulsivity, which can be defined as the tendency to make rapid decisions without adequate accumulation and consideration of the available evidence (Kagan 1966); this can include perceptual decision making as well as value-based decision making. In contrast to the original Matching Familiar Figures Task which focuses on perceptual discriminations, the Information Sampling Task (IFT); (Clark et al. 2006) and the Beads Task represent different aspects of information gathering prior to decision making. The former was used to show deficits through early decisions in current and abstinent amphetamine and opiate abusers, although these effects failed to correlate with BIS ratings (Clark et al. 2006). Abstaining alcohol-dependent individuals and compulsive gamblers have been shown to have analogous impairments (Lawrence et al. 2009). Banca et al. found that binge drinkers more reliably showed deficits on the Beads Task than the IST, but intriguingly also that the two tests were correlated with different cortical substrates: Poor performance on the Beads Task was associated with smaller dorsolateral PFC and inferior parietal volumes, whereas for the IST, lower evidence accumulation was associated with greater dorsal cingulate and precuneus volumes (Banca et al. 2016); it is possible that these differences arise because of the more explicit nature of the problem in the IST makes it less prone to impulsive decisions. Although these tasks are associated with cortical substrates, it seems plausible that they represent further examples of waiting impulsivity given that the urge to make a decision has to be inhibited to enable further evidence accumulation. Further evidence is required to determine whether reflection impulsivity represents an entirely different form of impulsivity, operating, for example, at the level of decision making implemented by cognitive networks in the cerebral cortex. There has been some discussion of possible animal models by Evenden (1999).

More generally, these different aspects resemble instances of 'cognitive control,' although this broad-based concept seems to invoke mechanisms of response selection and rule use as well as inhibitory response control (which also help to distinguish, for example, go/no-go paradigms from the SSRTT (Eagle et al. 2008). Some of these issues have been described in recent reviews that have focused on inhibitory response control as the primary control mechanism (Bari and Robbins 2013; Aron et al. 2014), which may, however, be applied to distinct streams of processing in distinct fronto-striatal functional loops. In the case of stopping impulsivity and the role of inferior PFC circuitry in SSRT performance, alternative arguments have been advanced about the nature of the cognitive control processes. Thus, it has been suggested that, although the SSRTT incontrovertibly engages specific behavioral inhibitory processes (including most recently, the 'braking' of initiated responses), fMRI studies of its underlying circuitry may nonetheless be confounded with attentional requirements of the task (Erika-Florence et al. 2014). This controversy has been discussed in great detail in a recent review (Aron et al. 2014). Perhaps the most relevant evidence is a meta-analysis of 70 fMRI studies (Cai et al. 2014), which identified two adjacent clusters of activation in the right insula and inferior frontal cortex that exhibited distinct functional characteristics. The insula cluster was more closely coupled to the anterior cingulate and showed greater activation on unsuccessful SSRT trials, whereas the inferior frontal cluster was functionally connected to the parietal and dorsomedial PFC activations, exhibited relatively greater activation on successful trials, and was closely related to individual differences in SSRT performance. This analysis thus implies a more important role for the inferior frontal cluster in response inhibition rather than in monitoring outcomes of the task. However, additional functions for this control 'hub,' interacting with other neural networks, cannot be ruled out.

The concept of self-control and consequent resistance to temptation is undoubtedly central to theoretical accounts of impulsivity but self-control may

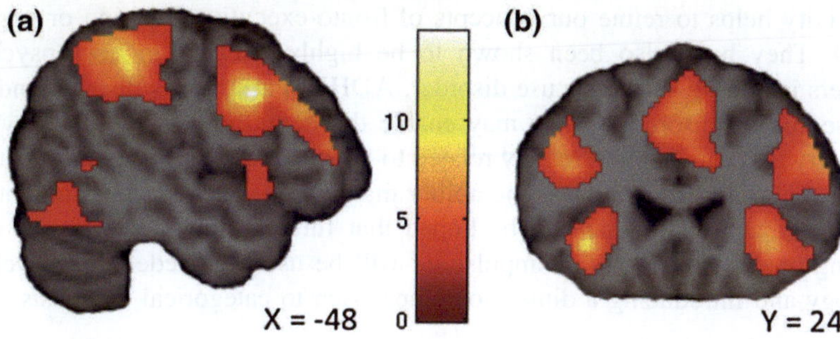

Fig. 7.5 The neural network underlying the resistance of temptation by willpower. **a** Bilateral dorsolateral PFC, bilateral posterior parietal cortex and **b** bilateral inferior frontal gyrus (compare Fig. 7.4) were more activated when the temptation to choose the smaller, sooner reward during the delay had to be suppressed. Images are displayed at a threshold of $p < 0.005$ uncorrected with an extent of >10 voxels. From Crockett et al. (2013) with kind permission

implicate additional mechanisms. An important higher-order strategy is pre-commitment, in which self-control difficulties are anticipated and exposure to temptation is voluntarily avoided. In a recent fMRI study of pre-commitment in humans, the effects of 'willpower' (i.e., the capacity for self-control) and pre-commitment were directly compared (Crockett et al. 2013). Whereas willpower or voluntary inhibitory control predictably engaged the dorsolateral and inferior PFC and parietal cortex, pre-commitment specifically activated the lateral frontopolar cortex (LFPC) (Fig. 7.5). Moreover, during pre-commitment, the LFPC had increased functional connectivity with DLPFC and PPC, particularly in more impulsive individuals, and the relationship between impulsivity and LFPC connectivity was mediated by value-based activations of the ventromedial PFC. These findings hence support a hierarchical model of self-control in which LFPC orchestrates pre-commitment by controlling action plans in more caudal PFC regions, as a function of their expected value. This example well illustrates the complexity of mechanisms governing impulsivity; in the absence of a strategic decision, such a pre-commitment, an individual may more readily find themselves compromised by the need to engage active voluntary processes that may consume considerable effort and be susceptible to lapse during stress or 'hot' emotional circumstances.

Conclusions

This article has shown the utility of a neuroscience approach to the concept of impulsivity, by demonstrating that different forms of impulsivity may exist that are related to distinct neural systems or distinct forms of chemical neuromodulation, sometimes apparently conserved across species. Investigation of these forms of impulsivity helps to refine our concepts of fronto-executive function or cognitive control. They have also been shown to be highly relevant to neuropsychiatric disorders including substance use disorder, ADHD, Parkinson's disease, and other impulse control disorders. They may enable the definition of new phenotypes in psychiatry that can be more readily related to genetics, useful in the stratification of clinical trials and as potential vulnerability markers, for example, for susceptibility to drugs of abuse. It is thus to be hoped that further refinements in our understanding of different forms of impulsivity will be useful in redefining psychiatric nosology and introducing a dimensional approach to categorical diagnosis.

Acknowledgements The authors acknowledge support from the Wellcome Trust (grant 104631/Z/14/Z), UK Medical Research Council (grants G0701500, G0802729, G9536855), and the European Commission ('Imagen' LSHM–CT–2007–037286). The Cambridge University Behavioural and Clinical Neuroscience Institute is supported by a joint award from the Wellcome Trust (093875/Z/10/Z) and Medical Research Council (G1000183). We thank our colleagues and many collaborators for their contributions.

References

Abela, A. R., & Chudasama, Y. (2013). Dissociable contributions of the ventral hippocampus and orbitofrontal cortex to decision-making with a delayed or uncertain outcome. *European Journal of Neuroscience, 37*(4), 640–647. doi:10.1111/ejn.12071

Ainslie, G. (1975). Specious reward: A behavioral theory of impulsiveness and impulse control. *Psychological Bulletin, 82*(4), 463–496.

Aron, A. R., & Poldrack, R. A. (2006). Cortical and subcortical contributions to Stop signal response inhibition: Role of the subthalamic nucleus. *Journal of Neuroscience, 26*(9), 2424–2433. doi:10.1523/JNEUROSCI.4682-05.2006

Aron, A. R., Robbins, T. W., & Poldrack, R. A. (2014). Inhibition and the right inferior frontal cortex: One decade on. *Trends Cognitive Sciences, 18*(4), 177–185. doi:10.1016/j.tics.2013.12.003

Banca, P., Lange, I., Worbe, Y., Howell, N. A., Irvine, M., Harrison, N. A., et al. (2016). Reflection impulsivity in binge drinking: Behavioural and volumetric correlates. *Addiction Biology, 21*(2), 504–515. doi:10.1111/adb.12227

Bari, A., Eagle, D. M., Mar, A. C., Robinson, E. S., & Robbins, T. W. (2009). Dissociable effects of noradrenaline, dopamine, and serotonin uptake blockade on stop task performance in rats. *Psychopharmacology (Berl), 205*(2), 273–283. doi:10.1007/s00213-009-1537-0

Bari, A., Mar, A. C., Theobald, D. E., Elands, S. A., Oganya, K. C., Eagle, D. M., et al. (2011). Prefrontal and monoaminergic contributions to stop-signal task performance in rats. *Journal of Neuroscience, 31*(25), 9254–9263. doi:10.1523/JNEUROSCI.1543-11.2011

Bari, A., & Robbins, T. W. (2013). Inhibition and impulsivity: Behavioral and neural basis of response control. *Progress in Neurobiology, 108,* 44–79. doi:10.1016/j.pneurobio.2013.06.005

Belin, D., Mar, A. C., Dalley, J. W., Robbins, T. W., & Everitt, B. J. (2008). High impulsivity predicts the switch to compulsive cocaine-taking. *Science, 320*(5881), 1352–1355. doi:10.1126/science.1158136

Besson, M., Belin, D., McNamara, R., Theobald, D. E., Castel, A., Beckett, V. L., et al. (2010). Dissociable control of impulsivity in rats by dopamine D2/3 receptors in the core and shell subregions of the nucleus accumbens. *Neuropsychopharmacology, 35*(2), 560–569. doi:10.1038/npp.2009.162

Borchert, R. J., Rittman, T., Passamonti, L., Ye, Z., Sami, S., Jones, S. P., et al. (2016). Atomoxetine enhances connectivity of prefrontal networks in Parkinson's disease. *Neuropsychopharmacology, 41*(8), 2188. doi:10.1038/npp.2016.46

Buckholtz, J. W., Treadway, M. T., Cowan, R. L., Woodward, N. D., Li, R., Ansari, M. S., et al. (2010). Dopaminergic network differences in human impulsivity. *Science, 329*(5991), 532. doi:10.1126/science.1185778

Cai, W., Ryali, S., Chen, T., Li, C. S., & Menon, V. (2014). Dissociable roles of right inferior frontal cortex and anterior insula in inhibitory control: Evidence from intrinsic and task-related functional parcellation, connectivity, and response profile analyses across multiple datasets. *Journal of Neuroscience, 34*(44), 14652–14667. doi:10.1523/JNEUROSCI.3048-14.2014

Caprioli, D., Hong, Y. T., Sawiak, S. J., Ferrari, V., Williamson, D. J., Jupp, B., et al. (2013). Baseline-dependent effects of cocaine pre-exposure on impulsivity and D2/3 receptor availability in the rat striatum: Possible relevance to the attention-deficit hyperactivity syndrome. *Neuropsychopharmacology, 38*(8), 1460–1471. doi:10.1038/npp.2013.44

Caprioli, D., Jupp, B., Hong, Y. T., Sawiak, S. J., Ferrari, V., Wharton, L., et al. (2015). Dissociable rate-dependent effects of oral methylphenidate on impulsivity and D2/3 receptor availability in the striatum. *Journal of Neuroscience, 35*(9), 3747–3755. doi:10.1523/JNEUROSCI.3890-14.2015

Caprioli, D., Sawiak, S. J., Merlo, E., Theobald, D. E., Spoelder, M., Jupp, B., et al. (2014). Gamma aminobutyric acidergic and neuronal structural markers in the nucleus accumbens core underlie trait-like impulsive behavior. *Biological Psychiatry, 75*(2), 115–123. doi:10.1016/j.biopsych.2013.07.013

Cardinal, R. N., Pennicott, D. R., Sugathapala, C. L., Robbins, T. W., & Everitt, B. J. (2001). Impulsive choice induced in rats by lesions of the nucleus accumbens core. *Science, 292*(5526), 2499–2501. doi:10.1126/science.1060818

Carli, M., Robbins, T. W., Evenden, J. L., & Everitt, B. J. (1983). Effects of lesions to ascending noradrenergic neurones on performance of a 5-choice serial reaction task in rats: Implications for theories of dorsal noradrenergic bundle function based on selective attention and arousal. *Behavioural Brain Research, 9*(3), 361–380.

Carver, C. S., & White, T. (1994). Behavioral inhibition, behavioral activation and affective response to impending reward and punishment: The BIS/BAS scales. *Journal of Personality and Social Psychology, 67,* 319–333.

Chamberlain, S. R., Del Campo, N., Dowson, J., Muller, U., Clark, L., Robbins, T. W., et al. (2007). Atomoxetine improved response inhibition in adults with attention deficit/hyperactivity disorder. *Biological Psychiatry, 62*(9), 977–984. doi:10.1016/j.biopsych.2007.03.003

Chamberlain, S. R., Hampshire, A., Muller, U., Rubia, K., Del Campo, N., Craig, K., et al. (2009). Atomoxetine modulates right inferior frontal activation during inhibitory control: A pharmacological functional magnetic resonance imaging study. *Biological Psychiatry, 65*(7), 550–555. doi:10.1016/j.biopsych.2008.10.014

Christakou, A., Robbins, T. W., & Everitt, B. J. (2004). Prefrontal cortical-ventral striatal interactions involved in affective modulation of attentional performance: Implications for corticostriatal circuit function. *Journal of Neuroscience, 24*(4), 773–780. doi:10.1523/JNEUROSCI.0949-03.2004

Chudasama, Y., Passetti, F., Rhodes, S. E., Lopian, D., Desai, A., & Robbins, T. W. (2003). Dissociable aspects of performance on the 5-choice serial reaction time task following lesions of the dorsal anterior cingulate, infralimbic and orbitofrontal cortex in the rat: Differential effects on selectivity, impulsivity and compulsivity. *Behavioural Brain Research, 146*(1–2), 105–119.

Clark, L., Robbins, T. W., Ersche, K. D., & Sahakian, B. J. (2006). Reflection impulsivity in current and former substance users. *Biological Psychiatry, 60*(5), 515–522. doi:10.1016/j.biopsych.2005.11.007

Cole, B. J., & Robbins, T. W. (1989). Effects of 6-hydroxydopamine lesions of the nucleus accumbens septi on performance of a 5-choice serial reaction time task in rats: Implications for theories of selective attention and arousal. *Behavioural Brain Research, 33*(2), 165–179.

Crockett, M. J., Braams, B. R., Clark, L., Tobler, P. N., Robbins, T. W., & Kalenscher, T. (2013). Restricting temptations: Neural mechanisms of precommitment. *Neuron, 79*(2), 391–401. doi:10.1016/j.neuron.2013.05.028

Dalley, J. W., Everitt, B. J., & Robbins, T. W. (2011). Impulsivity, compulsivity, and top-down cognitive control. *Neuron, 69*(4), 680–694. doi:10.1016/j.neuron.2011.01.020

Dalley, J. W., Fryer, T. D., Brichard, L., Robinson, E. S., Theobald, D. E., Laane, K., et al. (2007). Nucleus accumbens D2/3 receptors predict trait impulsivity and cocaine reinforcement. *Science, 315*(5816), 1267–1270. doi:10.1126/science.1137073

Dalley, J. W., Theobald, D. E., Eagle, D. M., Passetti, F., & Robbins, T. W. (2002). Deficits in impulse control associated with tonically-elevated serotonergic function in rat prefrontal cortex. *Neuropsychopharmacology, 26*(6), 716–728. doi:10.1016/S0893-133X(01)00412-2

de Wit, H., & Richards, J. B. (2004). Dual determinants of drug use in humans: Reward and impulsivity. In R. A. Bevins & M. T. Bardo (Eds.), *Motivational factors in the etiology of drug abuse of the Nebraska symposium on motivation* (Vol. 50, pp. 19–55). Lincoln, NE: University of Nebraska Press.

Delfs, J. M., Zhu, Y., Druhan, J. P., & Aston-Jones, G. S. (1998). Origin of noradrenergic afferents to the shell subregion of the nucleus accumbens: Anterograde and retrograde tract-tracing studies in the rat. *Brain Research, 806*(2), 127–140.

Dews, P. B., & Wenger, G. R. (1977). Rate-dependency of the behavioral effects of amphetamine. *Advances in Behavioral Pharmacology, 1*, 167–227.

Diergaarde, L., Pattij, T., Poortvliet, I., Hogenboom, F., de Vries, W., Schoffelmeer, A. N., et al. (2008). Impulsive choice and impulsive action predict vulnerability to distinct stages of nicotine seeking in rats. *Biological Psychiatry, 63*(3), 301–308. doi:10.1016/j.biopsych.2007.07.011

Dilleen, R., Pelloux, Y., Mar, A. C., Molander, A., Robbins, T. W., Everitt, B. J., et al. (2012). High anxiety is a predisposing endophenotype for loss of control over cocaine, but not heroin, self-administration in rats. *Psychopharmacology (Berl), 222*(1), 89–97. doi:10.1007/s00213-011-2626-4

Donnelly, N. A., Paulsen, O., Robbins, T. W., & Dalley, J. W. (2015). Ramping single unit activity in the medial prefrontal cortex and ventral striatum reflects the onset of waiting but not imminent impulsive actions. *European Journal of Neuroscience, 41*(12), 1524–1537. doi:10.1111/ejn.12895

Eagle, D. M., Bari, A., & Robbins, T. W. (2008a). The neuropsychopharmacology of action inhibition: Cross-species translation of the stop-signal and go/no-go tasks. *Psychopharmacology (Berl), 199*(3), 439–456. doi:10.1007/s00213-008-1127-6

Eagle, D. M., Baunez, C., Hutcheson, D. M., Lehmann, O., Shah, A. P., & Robbins, T. W. (2008b). Stop-signal reaction-time task performance: Role of prefrontal cortex and subthalamic nucleus. *Cerebral Cortex, 18*(1), 178–188. doi:10.1093/cercor/bhm044

Eagle, D. M., Lehmann, O., Theobald, D. E., Pena, Y., Zakaria, R., Ghosh, R., et al. (2009). Serotonin depletion impairs waiting but not stop-signal reaction time in rats: Implications for theories of the role of 5-HT in behavioral inhibition. *Neuropsychopharmacology, 34*(5), 1311–1321. doi:10.1038/npp.2008.202

Eagle, D. M., & Robbins, T. W. (2003). Lesions of the medial prefrontal cortex or nucleus accumbens core do not impair inhibitory control in rats performing a stop-signal reaction time task. *Behavioural Brain Research, 146*(1–2), 131–144.

Eagle, D. M., Wong, J. C., Allan, M. E., Mar, A. C., Theobald, D. E., & Robbins, T. W. (2011). Contrasting roles for dopamine D1 and D2 receptor subtypes in the dorsomedial striatum but not the nucleus accumbens core during behavioral inhibition in the stop-signal task in rats. *Journal of Neuroscience, 31*(20), 7349–7356. doi:10.1523/JNEUROSCI.6182-10.2011

Economidou, D., Pelloux, Y., Robbins, T. W., Dalley, J. W., & Everitt, B. J. (2009). High impulsivity predicts relapse to cocaine-seeking after punishment-induced abstinence. *Biological Psychiatry, 65*(10), 851–856. doi:10.1016/j.biopsych.2008.12.008

Economidou, D., Theobald, D. E., Robbins, T. W., Everitt, B. J., & Dalley, J. W. (2012). Norepinephrine and dopamine modulate impulsivity on the five-choice serial reaction time task through opponent actions in the shell and core sub-regions of the nucleus accumbens. *Neuropsychopharmacology, 37*(9), 2057–2066. doi:10.1038/npp.2012.53

Erika-Florence, M., Leech, R., & Hampshire, A. (2014). A functional network perspective on response inhibition and attentional control. *Nature Communications, 5,* 4073. doi:10.1038/ncomms5073

Ersche, K. D., Barnes, A., Jones, P. S., Morein-Zamir, S., Robbins, T. W., & Bullmore, E. T. (2011). Abnormal structure of frontostriatal brain systems is associated with aspects of impulsivity and compulsivity in cocaine dependence. *Brain, 134*(Pt 7), 2013–2024. doi:10.1093/brain/awr138

Ersche, K. D., Jones, P. S., Williams, G. B., Turton, A. J., Robbins, T. W., & Bullmore, E. T. (2012a). Abnormal brain structure implicated in stimulant drug addiction. *Science, 335*(6068), 601–604. doi:10.1126/science.1214463

Ersche, K. D., Turton, A. J., Chamberlain, S. R., Muller, U., Bullmore, E. T., & Robbins, T. W. (2012b). Cognitive dysfunction and anxious-impulsive personality traits are endophenotypes for drug dependence. *American Journal of Psychiatry, 169*(9), 926–936. doi:10.1176/appi.ajp.2012.11091421

Ersche, K. D., Turton, A. J., Pradhan, S., Bullmore, E. T., & Robbins, T. W. (2010). Drug addiction endophenotypes: Impulsive versus sensation-seeking personality traits. *Biological Psychiatry, 68*(8), 770–773. doi:10.1016/j.biopsych.2010.06.015

Evenden, J. L. (1999). Varieties of impulsivity. *Psychopharmacology (Berl), 146*(4), 348–361.

Everitt, B. J., & Robbins, T. W. (2005). Neural systems of reinforcement for drug addiction: From actions to habits to compulsion. *Nature Neuroscience, 8*(11), 1481–1489. doi:10.1038/nn1579

Everitt, B. J., & Robbins, T. W. (2016). Drug addiction: Updating actions to habits to compulsions ten years on. *Annual Review of Psychology, 67,* 23–50. doi:10.1146/annurev-psych-122414-033457

Fiorillo, C. D., Tobler, P. N., & Schultz, W. (2003). Discrete coding of reward probability and uncertainty by dopamine neurons. *Science, 299*(5614), 1898–1902. doi:10.1126/science.1077349

Gottesman, I. I., & Gould, T. D. (2003). The endophenotype concept in psychiatry: Etymology and strategic intentions. *American Journal of Psychiatry, 160*(4), 636–645. doi:10.1176/appi.ajp.160.4.636

Green, L., & Myerson, J. (2004). A discounting framework for choice with delayed and probabilistic rewards. *Psychological Bulletin, 130*(5), 769–792. doi:10.1037/0033-2909.130.5.769

Harrison, A. A., Everitt, B. J., & Robbins, T. W. (1997). Central 5-HT depletion enhances impulsive responding without affecting the accuracy of attentional performance: Interactions with dopaminergic mechanisms. *Psychopharmacology (Berl), 133*(4), 329–342.

Jupp, B., Caprioli, D., Saigal, N., Reverte, I., Shrestha, S., Cumming, P., et al. (2013). Dopaminergic and GABA-ergic markers of impulsivity in rats: Evidence for anatomical localisation in ventral striatum and prefrontal cortex. *European Journal of Neuroscience, 37*(9), 1519–1528. doi:10.1111/ejn.12146

Kagan, J. (1966). Reflection-impulsivity: The generality and dynamics of conceptual tempo. *Journal of Abnormal Psychology, 71,* 17–24.

Kirby, K. N., & Petry, N. M. (2004). Heroin and cocaine abusers have higher discount rates for delayed rewards than alcoholics or non-drug-using controls. *Addiction, 99*(4), 461–471. doi:10.1111/j.1360-0443.2003.00669.x

Knutson, B., Westdorp, A., Kaiser, E., & Hommer, D. (2000). FMRI visualization of brain activity during a monetary incentive delay task. *Neuroimage, 12*(1), 20–27. doi:10.1006/nimg.2000.0593

Lawrence, A. J., Luty, J., Bogdan, N. A., Sahakian, B. J., & Clark, L. (2009). Problem gamblers share deficits in impulsive decision-making with alcohol-dependent individuals. *Addiction, 104*(6), 1006–1015. doi:10.1111/j.1360-0443.2009.02533.x

Logan, G. D. (1994). On the ability to inhibit thought and action. A user's guide to the stop signal paradigm. In D. Dagenbach & T. H. Carr (Eds.), *Inhibitory processes in attention, memory and language*. San Diego, CA: Academic Press.

Logan, G. D., Van Zandt, T., Verbruggen, F., & Wagenmakers, E. J. (2014). On the ability to inhibit thought and action: General and special theories of an act of control. *Psychological Review, 121*(1), 66–95. doi:10.1037/a0035230

Mar, A. C., Walker, A. L., Theobald, D. E., Eagle, D. M., & Robbins, T. W. (2011). Dissociable effects of lesions to orbitofrontal cortex subregions on impulsive choice in the rat. *Journal of Neuroscience, 31*(17), 6398–6404. doi:10.1523/JNEUROSCI.6620-10.2011

Mazur, J. E. (1991). Choice with probabilistic reinforcement: Effects of delay and conditioned reinforcers. *Journal of the Experimental Analysis of Behavior, 55*(1), 63–77. doi:10.1901/jeab.1991.55-63

McNamara, R., Dalley, J. W., Robbins, T. W., Everitt, B. J., & Belin, D. (2010). Trait-like impulsivity does not predict escalation of heroin self-administration in the rat. *Psychopharmacology (Berl), 212*(4), 453–464. doi:10.1007/s00213-010-1974-9

Miyazaki, K., Miyazaki, K. W., & Doya, K. (2011). Activation of dorsal raphe serotonin neurons underlies waiting for delayed rewards. *Journal of Neuroscience, 31*(2), 469–479. doi:10.1523/JNEUROSCI.3714-10.2011

Molander, A. C., Mar, A., Norbury, A., Steventon, S., Moreno, M., Caprioli, D., et al. (2011). High impulsivity predicting vulnerability to cocaine addiction in rats: Some relationship with novelty preference but not novelty reactivity, anxiety or stress. *Psychopharmacology (Berl), 215*(4), 721–731. doi:10.1007/s00213-011-2167-x

Morein-Zamir, S., & Robbins, T. W. (2015). Fronto-striatal circuits in response-inhibition: Relevance to addiction. *Brain Research, 1628*(Pt A), 117–129. doi:10.1016/j.brainres.2014.09.012

Morein-Zamir, S., Simon Jones, P., Bullmore, E. T., Robbins, T. W., & Ersche, K. D. (2013). Prefrontal hypoactivity associated with impaired inhibition in stimulant-dependent individuals but evidence for hyperactivation in their unaffected siblings. *Neuropsychopharmacology, 38*(10), 1945–1953. doi:10.1038/npp.2013.90

Morris, L. S., Kundu, P., Baek, K., Irvine, M. A., Mechelmans, D. J., Wood, J., et al. (2016). Jumping the gun: Mapping neural correlates of waiting impulsivity and relevance across alcohol misuse. *Biological Psychiatry, 79*(6), 499–507. doi:10.1016/j.biopsych.2015.06.009

Muir, J. L., Everitt, B. J., & Robbins, T. W. (1996). The cerebral cortex of the rat and visual attentional function: Dissociable effects of mediofrontal, cingulate, anterior dorsolateral, and parietal cortex lesions on a five-choice serial reaction time task. *Cerebral Cortex, 6*(3), 470–481.

Murphy, E. R., Dalley, J. W., & Robbins, T. W. (2005). Local glutamate receptor antagonism in the rat prefrontal cortex disrupts response inhibition in a visuospatial attentional task. *Psychopharmacology (Berl), 179*(1), 99–107. doi:10.1007/s00213-004-2068-3

Murphy, E. R., Robinson, E. S., Theobald, D. E., Dalley, J. W., & Robbins, T. W. (2008). Contrasting effects of selective lesions of nucleus accumbens core or shell on inhibitory control and amphetamine-induced impulsive behaviour. *European Journal of Neuroscience, 28*(2), 353–363. doi:10.1111/j.1460-9568.2008.06309.x

Nombela, C., Rittman, T., Robbins, T. W., & Rowe, J. B. (2014). Multiple modes of impulsivity in Parkinson's disease. *PLoS ONE, 9*(1), e85747. doi:10.1371/journal.pone.0085747

Patton, J. H., Stanford, M. S., & Barratt, E. S. (1995). Factor structure of the Barratt impulsiveness scale. *Journal of Clinical Psychology, 51*(6), 768–774.

Paxinos, G., & Watson, C. (1997). *The rat brain in stereotaxic coordinates* (3rd ed.). San Diego: Academic Press.

Pena-Oliver, Y., Giuliano, C., Economidou, D., Goodlett, C. R., Robbins, T. W., Dalley, J. W., et al. (2015). Alcohol-preferring rats show goal oriented behaviour to food incentives but are neither sign-trackers nor impulsive. *PLoS ONE, 10*(6), e0131016. doi:10.1371/journal.pone.0131016

Perry, J. L., & Carroll, M. E. (2008). The role of impulsive behavior in drug abuse. *Psychopharmacology (Berl), 200*(1), 1–26. doi:10.1007/s00213-008-1173-0

Pothuizen, H. H., Jongen-Relo, A. L., Feldon, J., & Yee, B. K. (2005). Double dissociation of the effects of selective nucleus accumbens core and shell lesions on impulsive-choice behaviour and salience learning in rats. *European Journal of Neuroscience, 22*(10), 2605–2616. doi:10.1111/j.1460-9568.2005.04388.x

Poulos, C. X., Le, A. D., & Parker, J. L. (1995). Impulsivity predicts individual susceptibility to high levels of alcohol self-administration. *Behavioural Pharmacology, 6*(8), 810–814.

Rachlin, H., Logue, A. W., Gibbon, J., & Frankel, M. (1986). Cognition and behavior in studies of choice. *Psychological Review, 93,* 33–45.

Rae, C. L., Nombela, C., Rodriguez, P. V., Ye, Z., Hughes, L. E., Jones, P. S., et al. (2016). Atomoxetine restores the response inhibition network in Parkinson's disease. *Brain, 139*(Pt 8), 2235–2248. doi:10.1093/brain/aww138

Reynolds, B., Ortengren, A., Richards, J. B., & de Wit, H. (2006). Dimensions of impulsive behavior: Personality and behavioral measures. *Personality and Individual Differences, 40,* 305–315. doi:10.1016/j.paid.2005.03.024

Robbins, T. W. (1981). Behavioural determinants of drug action: Rate-dependency revisited. In S. J. Cooper (Ed.), *Theory in psychopharmacology* (Vol. 1, pp. 1–63). London: Academic Press.

Robbins, T. W. (2002). The 5-choice serial reaction time task: Behavioural pharmacology and functional neurochemistry. *Psychopharmacology (Berl), 163*(3–4), 362–380. doi:10.1007/s00213-002-1154-7

Robbins, T. W., & Dalley, J. W. (2016). Impulsivity, risky choice, and impulse control disorders: Animal models. In J.-L. Dreher & L. Tremblay (Eds.), *Decision neuroscience: Handbook of reward and decision-making*. Amsterdam: Academic Press Elsevier.

Robertson, C. L., Ishibashi, K., Mandelkern, M. A., Brown, A. K., Ghahremani, D. G., Sabb, F., et al. (2015). Striatal D1- and D2-type dopamine receptors are linked to motor response inhibition in human subjects. *Journal of Neuroscience, 35*(15), 5990–5997. doi:10.1523/JNEUROSCI.4850-14.2015

Robinson, E. S., Dalley, J. W., Theobald, D. E., Glennon, J. C., Pezze, M. A., Murphy, E. R., et al. (2008a). Opposing roles for 5-HT2A and 5-HT2C receptors in the nucleus accumbens on inhibitory response control in the 5-choice serial reaction time task. *Neuropsychopharmacology, 33*(10), 2398–2406. doi:10.1038/sj.npp.1301636

Robinson, E. S., Eagle, D. M., Economidou, D., Theobald, D. E., Mar, A. C., Murphy, E. R., et al. (2009). Behavioural characterisation of high impulsivity on the 5-choice serial reaction time task: Specific deficits in 'waiting' versus 'stopping'. *Behavioural Brain Research, 196*(2), 310–316. doi:10.1016/j.bbr.2008.09.021

Robinson, E. S., Eagle, D. M., Mar, A. C., Bari, A., Banerjee, G., Jiang, X., et al. (2008b). Similar effects of the selective noradrenaline reuptake inhibitor atomoxetine on three distinct forms of impulsivity in the rat. *Neuropsychopharmacology, 33*(5), 1028–1037. doi:10.1038/sj.npp.1301487

Sanchez-Roige, S., Baro, V., Trick, L., Pena-Oliver, Y., Stephens, D. N., & Duka, T. (2014). Exaggerated waiting impulsivity associated with human binge drinking, and high alcohol consumption in mice. *Neuropsychopharmacology, 39*(13), 2919–2927. doi:10.1038/npp.2014.151

Schumann, G., Loth, E., Banaschewski, T., Barbot, A., Barker, G., Buchel, C., et al. (2010). The IMAGEN study: Reinforcement-related behaviour in normal brain function and psychopathology. *Molecular Psychiatry, 15*(12), 1128–1139. doi:10.1038/mp.2010.4

Sesia, T., Temel, Y., Lim, L. W., Blokland, A., Steinbusch, H. W., & Visser-Vandewalle, V. (2008). Deep brain stimulation of the nucleus accumbens core and shell: Opposite effects on impulsive action. *Experimental Neurology, 214*(1), 135–139. doi:10.1016/j.expneurol.2008.07.015

Solanto, M. V., Abikoff, H., Sonuga-Barke, E., Schachar, R., Logan, G. D., Wigal, T., et al. (2001). The ecological validity of delay aversion and response inhibition as measures of impulsivity in AD/HD: A supplement to the NIMH multimodal treatment study of AD/HD. *Journal of Abnormal Child Psychology, 29*(3), 215–228.

Stopper, C. M., Green, E. B., & Floresco, S. B. (2014). Selective involvement by the medial orbitofrontal cortex in biasing risky, but not impulsive, choice. *Cerebral Cortex, 24*(1), 154–162. doi:10.1093/cercor/bhs297

Talpos, J. C., Wilkinson, L. S., & Robbins, T. W. (2006). A comparison of multiple 5-HT receptors in two tasks measuring impulsivity. *Journal of Psychopharmacology, 20*(1), 47–58. doi:10.1177/0269881105056639

Tecce, J. J. (1972). Contingent negative variation (CNV) and psychological processes in man. *Psychological Bulletin, 77*(2), 73–108.

Tuinstra, T., & Cools, A. R. (2000). Newly synthesized dopamine in the nucleus accumbens is regulated by beta-adrenergic, but not alpha-adrenergic, receptors. *Neuroscience, 98*(4), 743–747.

Van Waes, V., Beverley, J. A., Siman, H., Tseng, K. Y., & Steiner, H. (2012). CB1 cannabinoid receptor expression in the striatum: Association with corticostriatal circuits and developmental regulation. *Frontiers in Pharmacology, 3,* 21. doi:10.3389/fphar.2012.00021

Volkow, N. D., Fowler, J. S., Wang, G. J., Hitzemann, R., Logan, J., Schlyer, D. J., et al. (1993). Decreased dopamine D2 receptor availability is associated with reduced frontal metabolism in cocaine abusers. *Synapse (New York, N. Y.), 14*(2), 169–177. doi:10.1002/syn.890140210

Voon, V., Irvine, M. A., Derbyshire, K., Worbe, Y., Lange, I., Abbott, S., et al. (2014). Measuring "waiting" impulsivity in substance addictions and binge eating disorder in a novel analogue of rodent serial reaction time task. *Biological Psychiatry, 75*(2), 148–155. doi:10.1016/j.biopsych.2013.05.013

Whelan, R., Conrod, P. J., Poline, J. B., Lourdusamy, A., Banaschewski, T., Barker, G. J., … Consortium, I. (2012). Adolescent impulsivity phenotypes characterized by distinct brain networks. *Nature Neuroscience, 15*(6), 920–925. doi:10.1038/nn.3092

Whelan, R., Watts, R., Orr, C. A., Althoff, R. R., Artiges, E., Banaschewski, T., … Consortium, I. (2014). Neuropsychosocial profiles of current and future adolescent alcohol misusers. *Nature, 512*(7513), 185–189. doi:10.1038/nature13402

Winstanley, C. A., Chudasama, Y., Dalley, J. W., Theobald, D. E., Glennon, J. C., & Robbins, T. W. (2003). Intra-prefrontal 8-OH-DPAT and M100907 improve visuospatial attention and decrease impulsivity on the five-choice serial reaction time task in rats. *Psychopharmacology (Berl), 167*(3), 304–314. doi:10.1007/s00213-003-1398-x

Winstanley, C. A., Dalley, J. W., Theobald, D. E., & Robbins, T. W. (2004a). Fractionating impulsivity: Contrasting effects of central 5-HT depletion on different measures of impulsive behavior. *Neuropsychopharmacology, 29*(7), 1331–1343. doi:10.1038/sj.npp.1300434

Winstanley, C. A., Theobald, D. E., Cardinal, R. N., & Robbins, T. W. (2004b). Contrasting roles of basolateral amygdala and orbitofrontal cortex in impulsive choice. *Journal of Neuroscience, 24*(20), 4718–4722. doi:10.1523/JNEUROSCI.5606-03.2004

Winstanley, C. A., Theobald, D. E., Dalley, J. W., Glennon, J. C., & Robbins, T. W. (2004c). 5-HT2A and 5-HT2C receptor antagonists have opposing effects on a measure of impulsivity: Interactions with global 5-HT depletion. *Psychopharmacology (Berl), 176*(3–4), 376–385. doi:10.1007/s00213-004-1884-9

Winstanley, C. A., Theobald, D. E., Dalley, J. W., & Robbins, T. W. (2005). Interactions between serotonin and dopamine in the control of impulsive choice in rats: Therapeutic implications for impulse control disorders. *Neuropsychopharmacology, 30*(4), 669–682. doi:10.1038/sj.npp.1300610

Winstanley, C. A., Eagle, D. M., & Robbins, T. W. (2006). Behavioral models of impulsivity in relation to ADHD: Translation between clinical and preclinical studies. *Clinical Psychology Review, 26*(4), 379–395. doi:10.1016/j.cpr.2006.01.001

Chapter 8
Toward Narrative Theory: Interventions for Reinforcer Pathology in Health Behavior

Warren K. Bickel, Jeffrey S. Stein, Lara N. Moody, Sarah E. Snider, Alexandra M. Mellis and Amanda J. Quisenberry

O God, that men should put an enemy in their mouths to steal away their brains!
—the character Cassio from Shakespeare's Othello, Act II Scene iii

Introduction

In Shakespeare's Othello, Cassio laments that man knowingly chooses to consume harmful substances without regard for the consequences. Nonetheless, human consumption of psychoactive drug compounds is as old as the compounds themselves (Crocq 2007). Although drug use is immediately rewarding, its delayed consequences can be devastating. When I (W.K.B.) was a postdoctoral fellow at Johns Hopkins University, an interaction with one particular man exemplified this concept and became a pivotal moment in my career. The man, a chronic heroin user I will call "Dennis," was a participant in an ongoing study in the laboratory.

Dennis tested positive for illicit opioids and had visible track marks on his neck from intravenous heroin injection into his jugular vein. The veins at other, less conspicuous injection sites had collapsed due to Dennis' long history with heroin use; thus, his jugular vein was one of the last viable options through which to administer his fix. When I inquired about Dennis' positive urine sample and his wounds, he said that the local paper, *The Baltimore Sun*, reported that a spate of fatal heroin overdoses in the area was due to an increase in the availability of high-purity heroin. Dennis went on to say that if the heroin was *that* pure, he definitely needed to try some. As I listened to Dennis' enthusiasm, I could not help but wonder how someone could do something so risky without regard for the consequences. Did Dennis devalue his life that much? Perhaps, many cascading

W.K. Bickel (✉) · J.S. Stein · L.N. Moody · S.E. Snider
A.M. Mellis · A.J. Quisenberry
Virginia Tech Carilion Research Institute, 2 Riverside Circle,
Roanoke, VA 24016, USA
e-mail: wkbickel@vtc.vt.edu

J.R. Stevens (ed.), *Impulsivity*, Nebraska Symposium on Motivation 64,
DOI 10.1007/978-3-319-51721-6_8

issues that come with chronic heroin use made his life intolerable. However, the ultimate consequence of overdose for a chemically induced high is arguably not a rational valuation of any life. So, again, I asked, "Why?"

Dennis' myopic behavior was a self-control failure that could lead to the ultimate sacrifice. Dennis and others like him seek immediate rewards from drugs of abuse while sacrificing delayed outcomes such as improved health, employment, or stable family and social relationships. Such shortsighted behavior demonstrates a lack of concern for, or a devaluation of, the future. To explore this phenomenon, we empirically measured responses to a future time perspective task (Petry et al. 1998). Specifically, we read the beginnings of a number of open-ended stories and asked 34 heroin-addicted participants and 59 healthy control participants to generate the ending of these stories. In particular, one of the stories during this task began, "After awakening, Bill began to think about his future. In general, he expected to…" Participants in the study were asked to complete the story in any way they wish and then give an approximation of the time in which the story took place. We, as researchers, were not interested in the story's content, but rather its *time frame*. The healthy control participants' stories took place, on average, 4.7 years in the future. In contrast, heroin-addicted participants' stories took place only 9 days in the future, demonstrating the significantly shorter time horizon observed in drug addiction. From this perspective, one could ask how an individual who cannot see beyond the next nine days would value a reward that is beyond that frame? Dennis may have been incapable of valuing a healthy life because he may not have been able to imagine a future past next week.

Myopic time horizons and valuation of the future can be more finely measured by examining temporal (or delay) discounting, the process in which the value of a reward declines with increasing delay to its receipt (Kirby 1997; Bickel and Marsch 2001; Madden and Johnson 2010). For example, an immediately available reward may be highly valued, whereas having to wait for the same reward decreases its value with increasing wait times. The rate of the decline in reward valuation can be measured using a choice task that estimates the rate at which individuals discount delayed rewards (see Box 8.1). If Dennis had completed a discounting task, we would likely have observed rapid devaluation of delayed rewards. Unfortunately, however, Dennis' perspective is not uncommon among individuals with self-control failure and is the basis for a large and still growing field of research examining discount rates and maladaptive behaviors.

In this chapter, we expand our understanding of temporal discounting both as a behavioral process and as a tool to measure impulsive decision making. The extant evidence indicates that excessive discounting of delayed rewards is a trans-disease process, that is, a process evident in a wide range of diseases, disorders, and maladaptive health behaviors. We describe the evidence supporting this claim and discuss how this process can be explained using a common mechanism, the competing neurobehavioral decision systems (CNDS). Next, we expand our discussion to reinforcer pathology, the interaction between temporal discounting and the overvaluation of specific commodities, such as drugs of abuse. Finally, we end by presenting a review of recent evidence that temporal discounting and reward valuation can be altered using methods of *narrative theory*, a novel intervention framework which entails examining the impact of participant- and researcher-generated narratives on measures of reinforcer pathology.

Box 8.1: Temporal Discounting

Temporal discounting is the process in which a delayed reward loses its value as a function of the delay to its receipt. The rate at which the delayed reward loses its value can be empirically measured using one of several hypothetical or potentially real choice tasks (Koffarnus and Bickel 2014; Madden and Johnson 2010).

One of these tasks used to measure delay discounting is the **adjusting-amount task**. This task offers repeating choices between a smaller, immediate reward and a larger, delayed reward. Across trials, the amount of the larger, delayed reward stays constant (e.g., \$100 in one week from now), while the amount of the smaller, immediate reward is titrated until an **indifference point** is reached (Richards et al. 1997; Bickel et al. 1999; Du et al. 2002). That is, some smaller immediate amount of money now will be subjectively equivalent to the delayed \$100. Figure 8.1 provides example trials from this task; for space, we present only three trials, although six trials are most commonly used to estimate an indifference point (Du et al. 2002). This titration procedure is iterated over multiple delays (e.g., one day, one week, one month, three months, one year, and 25 years) to obtain a discounting curve (i.e., discounted value as a function of delay). Derivations of this task have also been studied in which a number of parameters have been manipulated, including magnitude of the rewards, the probability of the rewards, whether rewards occur in the past or future, whether rewards are to be gained or lost, and the social distance between the participant and the reward recipient (Rachlin et al. 1991; Baker et al. 2003; Yi et al. 2006a, b; Rachlin and Jones 2008).

Once indifference points are calculated, they are often fit to a nonlinear regression model. Again, multiple theoretical models are used to fit the indifference points (see Franck et al. 2015; Killeen 2009; Madden and Johnson 2010); however, Mazur's (1987) **hyperbolic model**

$$V = \frac{A}{1 + kD}, \tag{8.1}$$

is most common in the addiction literature (MacKillop et al. 2011). Here, V is the present value of the reward (i.e., indifference point), A represents the amount of the delayed reward, D is the delay, and k is a free parameter which indexes discount rate. Higher values of k indicate a more rapid decline in value of delayed rewards (Odum 2011).

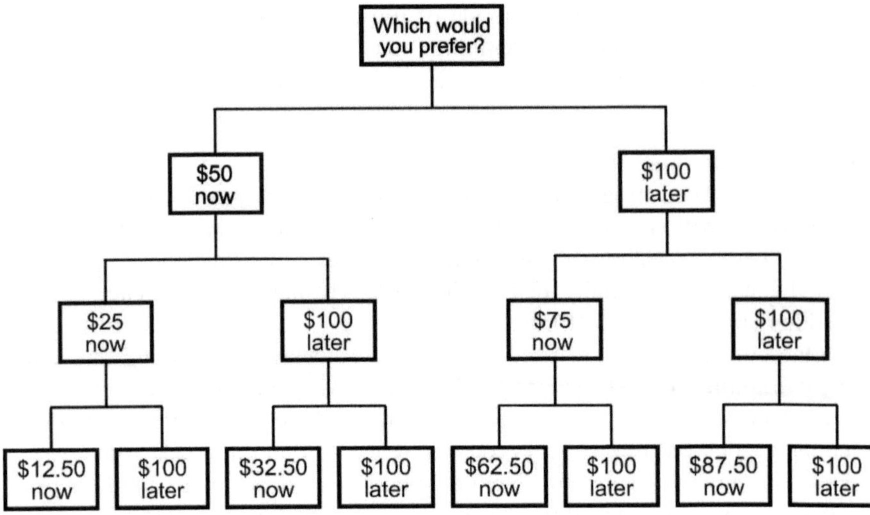

Fig. 8.1 Three example trials of the adjusting-amount temporal discounting task. With each choice, the smaller, immediate amount increases or decreases by half of the previous amount. The traditional adjusting-amount task titrates a total of five times to determine an estimated indifference point at each delay

Trans-disease Study of Health Behaviors

Given the state of health in the USA, namely that it lags behind other developed countries in several common metrics of health, identifying ways to prevent poor health and intervene on the behavior that causes it is of utmost importance. The National Research Committee and the Institute of Medicine, in a report titled *US Health in International Perspective*: *Shorter Lives*, *Poorer Health*, examined several metrics of health and in the USA and compared them to other developed countries (Woolf et al. 2013). Key findings from the report include shortcomings in the USA across six health behaviors: smoking, diet, physical inactivity, substance use, sexual practices, and injurious behaviors, implicating these behaviors as contributors to increased morbidity and mortality.

Health disparities in the USA necessitate improvements in how we study health and disease. One challenge to the study of disease is the assumption that diseases have unique etiologies which should be studied and treated as distinct from one another. This perspective is evident in disease-specific scientific societies, in journals, and even in the organization of the National Institutes of Health in which each institute is charged with the study of overlapping disease states (e.g., National Institute on Drug Abuse and National Institute on Alcohol Abuse and Alcoholism). In addition, science largely follows a reductionistic approach; that is, we study smaller and smaller phenomena with the hope that by breaking diseases into their component parts, the solution to the problem will become clear at a lower level of analysis (Skurvydas 2005; Strange 2005). Reductionistic approaches have resulted in remarkable productivity (e.g., DNA sequencing), evidenced by a rapidly increasing body of published research (Evans 2008) that has engrained this approach as the dominant scientific paradigm (Mitchell 2009). This approach, however, may have unintended consequences as scientists are compelled to learn more about progressively finer points related to their specialty. Specifically, the cause of some diseases may not be found by delving deeper, and specialization comes at the cost of less communication across specialty areas, creating "intellectual silos." An emphasis on deep, but narrow, specialization may result in failure to identify similar phenomena across specialties that could otherwise help in the characterization of many disease states.

Adding to this challenge is that a variety of diseases are both complex in cause and presentation. In particular, the symptoms of mental health and substance-use disorders are heterogeneous and diffuse; that is, many symptom profiles may result in the diagnosis of the same disorder. For example, in the current version of the *Diagnostic and Statistical Manual* (American Psychiatric Association 2013), substance-use disorders are comprised of eleven different symptoms; however, to be diagnosed with mild substance-use disorder, an individual must only present with two of those symptoms. Thus, several different individuals diagnosed with substance-use disorder may not share a single common symptom. The heterogeneous presentation of symptoms in diseases necessitates the consideration of possible common factors across diseases to elucidate those that may share similar etiologies or disease trajectories.

Here, we discuss a recent application, summarized by physicist and philosopher Ernst Mach: "Thence is imposed the task of everywhere seeking out in the natural phenomena those elements that are the same, and that amid all multiplicity are ever present" (Mach and McCormack 1907, p. 5). These ever-present phenomena are identified through the study of trans-disease processes, where the goal "is to understand the processes that operate in more than one disease and use that information to better understand, in principle, all the diseases in which they operate" (Bickel and Mueller 2009, p. 2). Trans-disease processes offer a means of dealing with the heterogeneous and diffuse manifestations of disorders and maladaptive behaviors by elucidating underlying characteristics that are present across multiple pathologies and to then use that information to better understand disease (cf. Insel et al. 2010).

Over the past two decades, temporal discounting has emerged as a candidate trans-disease process (see Box 8.2 for illustration of a foundational study). Tables 8.1, 8.2, and 8.3 (adapted from Bickel and Stein, under review) summarize the results of studies providing examinations of the relation between temporal discounting and a wide variety of health behaviors. Table 8.1 focuses on omissions of behavior that improve or maintain health (e.g., medical screening), Table 8.2 focuses on commissions of behavior that worsen health directly (e.g., substance

Table 8.1 Summary of study findings describing the association between delay discounting and health behavior omissions

	Finding	Study population	Study
Medical screening			
Blood pressure tests	–	Hypertensive patients, ≥ age 20	Axon et al. (2009)
Cholesterol tests	–	≥ age 50	Bradford (2010)
Mammograms	–	≥ age 50	Bradford (2010)
Breast examinations	–	≥ age 50	Bradford (2010)
Pap smears	–	≥ age 50	Bradford (2010)
Prostate examinations	–	≥ age 50	Bradford (2010)
Dental visits	–	≥ age 50	Bradford (2010)
		College graduates (mostly)	Chabris et al. (2008); Exp. 3
Doctor/dental visits		College students	Daugherty and Brase (2010)
HSV-2 tests	–	STI clinic patients	Chesson et al. (2006)
		General clinic patients	Chesson et al. (2006)
		Teenage clinic patients	Chesson et al. (2006)
		College students	Chesson et al. (2006)
Prevention and treatment			
Exercise frequency	–	Normal weight, overweight, and obese	Chabris et al. (2008); Exp. 1
	–	≥ age 50	Bradford (2010)
		College students	Daugherty and Brase (2010)
		College students and community residents	Chabris et al. (2008); Exp. 2
		College graduates (mostly)	Chabris et al. (2008); Exp. 3
On a diet		Normal weight, overweight, and obese	Chabris et al. (2008); Exp. 1
Eating healthy food		College graduates (mostly)	Chabris et al. (2008); Exp. 3
		Overweight and obese females	Appelhans et al. (2012)
Eating breakfast	–	College students	Daugherty and Brase (2010)
Flu shots	–	≥ age 50	Bradford (2010)
	–	Corporate workplace employees	Chapman and Coups (1999)
	–	College faculty/staff	Chapman et al. (2001); Exp. 1
Wearing sunscreen	–	College students	Daugherty and Brase (2010)
Wearing sunscreen	–	Adults	Bradford et al. (2014)
Flossing	–		Chabris et al. (2008)

(continued)

Table 8.1 (continued)

	Finding	Study population	Study
		College graduates (mostly)	
Bike/motorcycle helmet use		College students	Daugherty and Brase (2010)
Seatbelt use	−	College students	Daugherty and Brase (2010)
Seatbelt use	−	Adults	Bradford et al. (2014)
Condom use with alcohol intoxication	−	Problem drinkers	Celio et al. (2016)
Condom use, general		Problem drinkers	Celio et al. (2016)
		General clinic patients	Chesson et al. (2006)
		Teenage clinic patients	Chesson et al. (2006)
		College students	Chesson et al. (2006)
Prescription compliance	−	Type 2 diabetes patients	Reach et al. (2011)
	−	Type 2 diabetes patients	Lebeau et al. (2016)
	−	College graduates (mostly)	Chabris et al. (2008); Exp. 3
		Elderly	Chapman et al. (2001); Exp. 2
Diet/exercise	−	Hypertensive patients, $\geq$ age 20	Axon et al. (2009)
Treatment compliance, general		Hypertensive patients, $\geq$ age 20	Axon et al. (2009)

Note Adapted from Bickel and Stein (under review)
− indicates a significant negative association between the behavior and delay discounting
Blank cells in this column indicate no significant relation

Table 8.2 Summary of study findings describing the association between delay discounting and health behavior commissions

	Finding	Study population	Study
Substance abuse			
Opioids[a]	+	Opioid-dependent versus controls	Madden et al. (1997)
Alcohol[a]	+	Problem drinkers versus controls	Vuchinich and Simpson (1998)
Tobacco[a]	+	Smokers versus controls	Mitchell (1999)
Other stimulants[a]	+	Cocaine-dependent versus controls	Coffey et al. (2003)
Marijuana[a]		Marijuana-dependent versus controls	Johnson et al. (2010)
Needle sharing	+	Opioid users	Odum et al. (2000)

(continued)

Table 8.2 (continued)

	Finding	Study population	Study
Gambling			
Pathological gambling[a]	+	Pathological gamblers versus controls	Petry (2001b)
Problem gambling plus substance abuse[a]	+	Problem gambling substance abusers versus controls	Petry and Casarella (1999)
Diet			
Binge-eating disorder	+	Females, aged 25–45	Davis et al. (2010)
Fast/convenience food consumption	+	College employees	Garza et al. (2016)
		Overweight and obese females	Appelhans et al. (2012)
Snack consumption	+	General sample	Bradford et al. (2014)
Overeating		College graduates (mostly)	Chabris et al. (2008); Exp. 3
Sexual behavior			
Intercourse (ever)		STI clinic patients	Chesson et al. (2006)
		General clinic patients	Chesson et al. (2006)
		Teenage clinic patients	Chesson et al. (2006)
	+	College students	Chesson et al. (2006)
Earlier sexual experiences		STI clinic patients	Chesson et al. (2006)
	+	General clinic patients	Chesson et al. (2006)
		Teenage clinic patients	Chesson et al. (2006)
		College students	Chesson et al. (2006)
	+	General sample	Reimers et al. (2009)
Multiple partners		Problem drinkers	Celio et al. (2016)
		STI clinic patients	Chesson et al. (2006)
		General clinic patients	Chesson et al. (2006)
		Teenage clinic patients	Chesson et al. (2006)
	+	College students	Chesson et al. (2006)
Sexual infidelity	+	General sample	Reimers et al. (2009)
Pornography use	+	College students	Negash et al. (2016)
Other risky behavior			
Texting while driving	+	College students	Hayashi et al. (2015)
		College students	Hayashi et al. (2016)

Note Adapted from Bickel and Stein (under review)
+ indicates a significant positive association between the behavior and delay discounting
− indicates significant negative association
Blank cells in this column indicate no significant relation
[a]Indicates seminal finding; more detailed reviews and meta-analyses of this robust finding may be found elsewhere (MacKillop et al. 2011; Amlung et al. 2016b)

Table 8.3 Summary of study findings describing the association between delay discounting and health outcomes and other disorders

	Finding	Study population	Study
Outcome			
Obesity[a]	+	Female college students	Weller et al. (2008)
High body fat		College students	Rasmussen et al. (2010)
		Adolescent boys	Lu et al. (2014)
	+	Adolescent girls	Lu et al. (2014)
		College students	Daly et al. (2009)
Poor response to weight-loss treatment	+	Adolescents	Best et al. (2012)
High blood pressure		Elderly	Chapman et al. (2001); Exp. 2
	+	College students	Daly et al. (2009)
Heart rate		College students	Daly et al. (2009)
Heart rate invariance	+	College students	Daly et al. (2009)
Poor glycemic control	+	Type 2 diabetes patients	Reach et al. (2011)
	+	Type 2 diabetes patients	Lebeau et al. (2016)
		College students	Daly et al. (2009)
Pregnancy (ever)		STI clinic patients	Chesson et al. (2006)
	+	General clinic patients	Chesson et al. (2006)
		Teenage clinic patients	Chesson et al. (2006)
		College students	Chesson et al. (2006)
Disorder			
Attention deficit/hyperactivity disorder	+	Adolescent boys	Paloyelis et al. (2010)
	+[b]	Children, aged 7–9	Wilson et al. (2011)
		Children and adolescents, ages 6–17	Scheres et al. (2006)
		College students	Scheres et al. (2008); hypothetical rewards
	+	College students	Scheres et al. (2008); real rewards
	+	College students	Hurst et al. (2011)
Anorexia	−	Anorexia patients versus controls	Steinglass et al. (2012)
	−	Anorexia patients versus controls	Decker et al. (2015)
		Anorexia patients versus controls	King et al. (2016)
		Anorexia patients versus controls	Ritschel et al. (2015)

(continued)

Table 8.3 (continued)

	Finding	Study population	Study
		Weight-recovered anorexia patients versus controls	Decker et al. (2015)
		Weight-recovered anorexia patients versus controls	Ritschel et al. (2015)
Bulimia	+	Bulimia patients versus controls	Kekic et al. (2016)
Obsessive–compulsive personality disorder	–	OCPD patients versus controls	Pinto et al. (2014)
Schizophrenia	+	Schizophrenia patients versus controls	Heerey et al. (2007)
		Schizophrenia patients versus controls	Wing et al. (2012)
		Schizophrenia patients who smoke versus controls who smoke	Wing et al. (2012)
		Schizophrenia patients who smoke versus controls who smoke	MacKillop and Tidey (2011)

Note Adapted from Bickel and Stein (under review)
+ indicates a significant positive association between the behavior/disorder and delay discounting
Blank cells in this column indicate no significant relation
[a]Indicates seminal finding; a more detailed review and meta-analysis of this robust finding may be found elsewhere (Amlung et al. 2016a)
[b]Indicates an effect of delay discounting was no longer observed when controlling for intelligence

abuse), and Table 8.3 focuses on behavioral outcomes (e.g., obesity) and psychiatric disorders. As these findings show, elevated rates of discounting are associated with virtually every form of addictive substance (for meta-analysis, see MacKillop et al. 2011; Amlung et al. 2016b), including cigarettes (Bickel et al. 1999; Baker et al. 2003; Reynolds et al. 2004), cocaine (Coffey et al. 2003; Bickel et al. 2011; Moody et al. 2016), opioids (Madden et al. 1997; Stoltman et al. 2015), and alcohol (Petry 2001a; Moallem and Ray 2012; Moody et al. 2016).

Box 8.2: Temporal Discounting and Addiction

In a foundational study, Madden et al. (1997) compared temporal discounting in **opioid users** to **demographically matched, non-drug-using controls** (see Fig. 8.2). Opioid users showed dramatically higher rates of discounting of a \$1000 reward that is depicted by the curves, fit using Eq. 8.1, where the more closely the curves hug the axes, the steeper the discounting. The effective delay 50 (ED_{50}), or delay at which the commodity (in this case \$1000) loses half of its value, is calculated as the inverse of the *k* parameter from Eq. 8.1

(Yoon and Higgins 2008). In this case, the ED_{50} of the control group was more than a month (ED_{50} = 37.04 months), while the ED_{50} of the opioid-dependent group was less than a week (ED_{50} = 4.55 months)—more than an eightfold difference. The strikingly high rate of discounting observed in opioid-dependent individuals depicts the restricted perspective from which these individuals view the future and makes evident how future negative consequences of poor health behaviors may carry little value for these individuals.

Excessive temporal discounting has also been reported in problem gambling (Dixon et al. 2003; Miedl et al. 2012), obesity (Weller et al. 2008; Epstein et al. 2010), and binge-eating disorder (Davis et al. 2010), as well as frequent consumption of fast food (Garza et al. 2016), earlier sexual encounters (Chesson et al. 2006; Reimers et al. 2009), and texting while driving (Hayashi et al. 2015). Likewise, excessive discounting has been observed in those who less frequently engage in health-promoting behaviors such as eating breakfast (Daugherty and Brase 2010), receiving flu shots (Bradford 2010), wearing sunscreen (Daugherty and Brase 2010), flossing (Chabris et al. 2008), wearing a helmet when biking or motorcycling (Daugherty and Brase 2010), wearing seatbelts (Chesson et al. 2006), using condoms (Chesson et al. 2006), and complying with prescribed medical advice (Chabris et al. 2008; Reach et al. 2011; Lebeau et al. 2016). In sum, the pervasiveness of excessive temporal discounting in this wide range of diseases, disorders, and health behaviors (see Tables 8.1, 8.2 and 8.3) supports temporal discounting as a trans-disease process and occasions investigation of its underlying mechanisms.

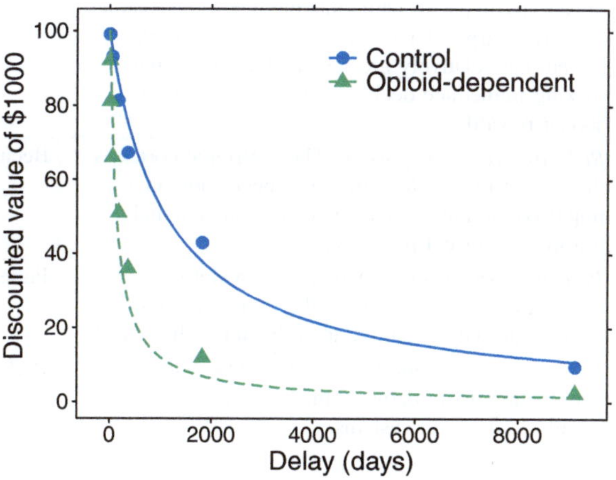

Fig. 8.2 Evidence of greater discounting in opioid users compared to controls. Data replotted from Madden et al. (1997)

Table 8.4 Dual-systems theories of decision making

System	Researchers
Controlled versus automatic: A theory of information processing in which two systems are required to parse categorical and individual information from the environment	Schneider and Shiffrin (1977)
Planner versus doer: A farsighted planner and a myopic doer are fundamental to the agency conflict of economic systems	Shefrin and Thaler (1977)
Verbatim versus gist: Fuzzy trace theory is a dual-process theory of judgment and decision making focusing on verbatim (literal surface form) and gist (bottom-line meaning) representations of stimuli	Reyna and Brainerd (1995), Rahimi-Golkhandan et al. (2017)
Conscious versus unconscious: Emotional states that are not consciously experienced can still impact behavior, implying a distinct conscious center and emotional center	Damasio et al. (1996)
Cool versus hot: A two-system framework for the underpinnings of self-control, in which a "cool, cognitive 'know'" system and a "hot, emotional 'go'" system strategically self-regulate	Metcalfe and Mischel (1999)
System 2 versus System 1 (also deliberative versus impulsive and slow versus fast): A dual-process model of thought and decision where system 2 (the slower, rule-based system) assesses associative and deductive components of information and system 1 (the fast, associative system) provides heuristics	Frederick (2002), Kahneman (2011), Kahneman and Frederick (2002)
Abstract versus visceral: An ideal, diffuse, abstract goal and a more immediate and environmentally cued visceral goal compete in self-controlled decisions	Bernheim and Rangel (2002)
PFC versus mesolimbic: The PFC has relatively greater involvement while making delayed decisions that favor larger, later rewards. The mesolimbic system has relatively greater involvement while making immediate decisions that favor smaller, sooner rewards	McClure et al. (2004)
Reflective versus impulsive: The prefrontal cortex is the seat of reward for future prospects, and an impulsive and amygdala-centered system signals reward for current prospects	Bechara (2005)
Patient versus myopic: A dual-self model that describes why reinforcers in the future are less valued and why cognitive load disrupts self-control	Fudenberg and Levine (2006)
Executive versus impulsive: The CNDS described here distinguishes between the executive and impulsive decision systems	Bickel et al. (2007)

Competing Neurobehavioral Decision Systems Theory

The maladaptive decision making that characterizes the various diseases, disorders, and health behaviors presented in Tables 8.1–8.3 can be modeled as the product of two distinct systems which form the basis of the *competing neurobehavioral decision systems* (CNDS) theory: (1) the reward-driven, present-oriented system and (2) the controlled, future-oriented system. The two systems, termed the "impulsive" and "executive" systems (Bickel et al. 2007), provide an engine of reward and an engineer of future plans to direct it. However, the CNDS theory is not the only dual-systems model applied to decision making. Displayed in Table 8.4 are other dual systems relevant to the study of choice previously described in the literature (see also Rahimi-Golkhandan et al. 2017).

The biologic substrates of dual systems have been described both in isolation and as interacting systems that produce the neurophenotypes associated with disease (see also Robbins and Dalley, this volume). For example, McClure et al. (2004) identified two distinct categories of neural activation during completion of a temporal discounting task in a functional magnetic resonance imaging (fMRI) scanner. Individual choices between the smaller, immediate rewards and larger, delayed rewards reflect relatively greater activation in distinct regions associated with different components of decision making. For example, when participants made choices that reflected their preference for smaller, immediate rewards, they showed relatively greater activation of impulsive reward centers (i.e., the paralimbic cortex). In contrast, when individuals made more self-controlled decisions to select larger, later rewards, they demonstrated relatively greater activity in executive control centers (i.e., lateral prefrontal cortex and parietal prefrontal cortex). Extrapolating from these observations, one might predict diminished activity in the prefrontal cortex (i.e., the executive decision system) would be associated with the various disease states reviewed previously.

So long as these impulsive and executive systems of the CNDS are in balance, individuals will be both sensitive to reinforcement and also able to delay reward in order to consider how their decisions may interact with long-term consequences. Specifically, both systems must be capable of influence and sensitive to context for an individual to engage in healthy behavior. For example, during periods of immediate threat or other conditions in which proximal events are of primary concern, relative control by the impulsive system is desirable. In contrast, relative control by the executive system is desirable in decisions regarding retirement savings or other long-term outcomes. With disease states, however, comes a persistent imbalance in relative control of these systems. Insensitivity to reward is associated with distinct pathologies of anhedonia (i.e., inability to experience pleasure) and depression (Liu et al. 2016). Hyperactivation of the left ventromedial prefrontal cortex in response to putatively rewarding cues (pictures of food) is associated with anorexia nervosa (Uher et al. 2004), a condition of excessive self-control (Steinglass et al. 2012; Decker et al. 2015; Ritschel et al. 2015). Conversely, diminished executive control compared to impulsive control has been identified in addiction (Goldstein and Volkow 2011). Thus, relative dominance of either the executive or impulsive decisions appears to produce disorder. Only regulatory balance between systems is likely to produce consistently adaptive decision making.

Although individual drug classes have different acute actions on prefrontal cortex activity (Goldstein and Volkow 2011), pathological states of addiction are associated with decreased activity in the lateral prefrontal cortex during working-memory tasks (Wang et al. 2010), decreased performance on executive function tasks (Chanraud et al. 2007), and decreased gray matter density in the broader prefrontal cortex (Fein et al. 2002). These structural changes may be the result of, rather than the cause of, substance use at least in the case of alcohol and marijuana in adolescence (Medina et al. 2008, 2009); however, executive dysfunction may also precede excessive drug taking (Heitzeg et al. 2008). This suggests a cycle in which disrupted executive control (as demonstrated by increased discounting of future rewards) predisposes an individual to addiction; in turn, this drug use associated with addiction then further disrupts function executive control and compounds the decision-making dysfunction.

Again, the CNDS theory of addiction relies on the interplay between both the executive and impulsive decision systems. For example, diminished functional connectivity between executive control centers of the prefrontal cortex and dopaminergic reward centers of the midbrain and paralimbic cortex is associated with longer duration of drug use in heroin-dependent individuals (Yuan et al. 2010). In addition, smokers who experience greater craving while abstinent from nicotine show altered functional connectivity between executive and reward centers compared to smokers who report less craving (Cole et al. 2010). Thus, in addiction and other health behaviors described here, an imbalance between activity of the executive and impulsive decision systems is apparent.

Reinforcer Pathology

The dysregulation between the two decision systems of the CNDS may result in a process that undergirds the various diseases and maladaptive health behaviors described above. This process, which we have called *reinforcer pathology* (Bickel et al. 2014a), is the interaction between (1) excessive temporal discounting (see Box 8.2) and (2) overvaluation of specific commodities that may damage health (see Box 8.3). Substance-use disorders, obesity, and other maladaptive health behaviors (see Tables 8.1–8.3) are associated with a history of health decisions that offer short-term rewards despite negative, long-term consequences. Moreover, commodities that are chronically overconsumed in reinforcer pathology, such as drugs of abuse and food, share a common reinforcement timeline in that they offer their greatest rewards in the immediate period after consumption (e.g., alcohol intoxication or the taste of a snack food; see Fig. 8.3) and their greatest costs at some point in the future (e.g., liver disease or type 2 diabetes).

Box 8.3: Measuring Commodity Valuation through Behavioral Economic Demand

Demand for reinforcers in humans can be understood by investigating the variance in purchasing of a commodity as a function of price. Price can be manipulated by either increasing or decreasing the amount of a commodity available for purchase at a set price, or by increasing or decreasing the monetary price of a commodity available for purchase at a set quantity. Altering either of these two price components results in a functionally equivalent change in the **unit price** of the commodity (DeGrandpre et al. 1993). Purchasing behavior can then be understood over different commodity unit prices, with demand for a commodity typically decreasing as the price of the commodity increases. This sensitivity to price is termed **elasticity of demand** and varies in degree of responsiveness of purchasing to price changes. Relative insensitivity to price increases represents a higher valuation of the commodity, where an individual will defend purchasing behavior despite increasing costs. Individual valuation of a commodity can also be understood using **intensity of demand**, that is demand for a commodity at marginally low prices.

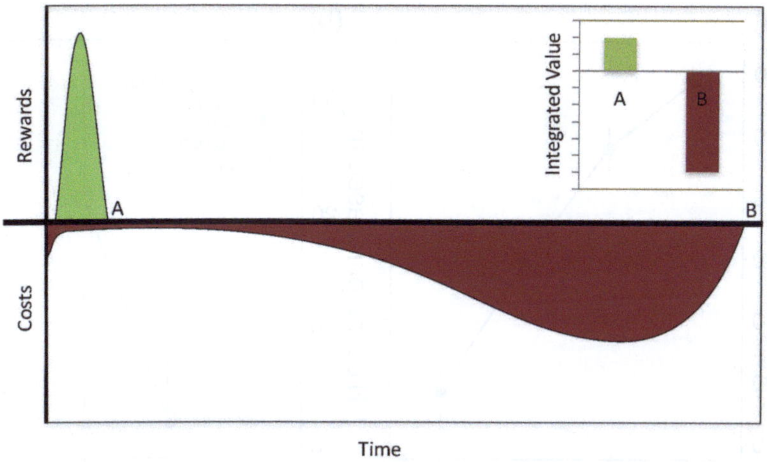

Fig. 8.3 The temporal window of valuation. The commodities overconsumed in reinforcer pathology deliver their rewards and costs over a common timeline. That is, they may come with some marginal, initial monetary or search costs, but they also offer their greatest rewards soon after consumption. If the overall value of the reward is subjectively calculated as the benefits minus the costs up to point A, consumption of the commodity is rational and highly reinforcing. However, if the temporal window is extended to point B, the long-term costs may be of a greater magnitude than the immediate rewards. Comparing the total benefits minus costs of the commodity at the two points (see *inset graph*) demonstrates how an abbreviated temporal window can lead to reinforcer pathology

These components of demand can be assessed through many laboratory procedures and naturalistic observations (for a detailed discussion of these historical and contemporary procedures, see Bickel et al. 2016a). One assay to measure demand is a **self-administration** task, during which an individual is given the opportunity to work for a single unit of a commodity. For example, individuals may be given access to a preferred food at costs which vary in number of lever presses or duration of work at a task, with the opportunity to consume that food within an experimental setting. Demand assessment may also involve **purchase tasks**, where a participant is given the choice to purchase units of the commodity at varying prices. These purchases can be real (where choices are actualized at the end of the experiment), potentially real (where some subset of purchasing choices are actualized), or purely hypothetical. Thus far, evidence suggests that data obtained from each type of task are functionally equivalent (Amlung et al. 2012; Amlung and MacKillop 2015; Wilson et al. 2016).

Recent innovations in methods of demand assessment have allowed for observation of purchasing behavior in complex marketplaces filled not just with single commodities, but also economic **substitutes** and **complements** (other commodities which either replace, or are used in conjunction with, a primary commodity). One novel example is the **experimental tobacco marketplace** (Quisenberry et al. 2015b), which simulates an online storefront featuring both cigarettes and alternative tobacco

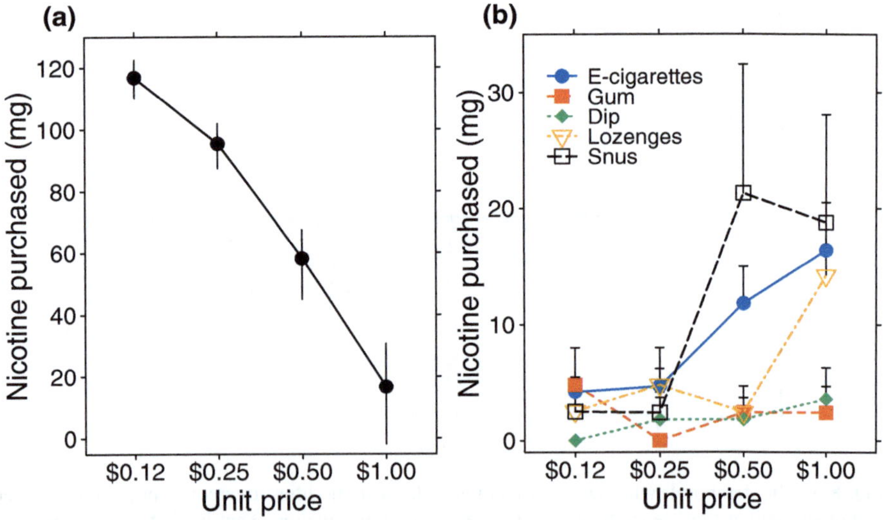

Fig. 8.4 Demand and substitution curves for tobacco products. **a** The elasticity of demand for cigarettes decreases as they increase in price. **b** The cigarette price effects purchasing of other commodities, demonstrating that consumption of other products increases as the price of cigarettes increases (i.e., a substitution effect). Data shown were obtained from the experimental tobacco marketplace (Quisenberry et al. 2015b)

products (e.g., snus, e-cigarettes, dip, cigarillos, lozenges, and gum). Participants can navigate this store and select commodities to purchase during experimentally determined conditions, with varying prices, incomes, and product labeling.

The end result of many of the assays described above is the generation of a **demand curve**, or representation of how demand for a commodity decreases over increasing price (see Fig. 8.4), which can be modeled exponentially (Hursh and Silberberg 2008; see also Koffarnus et al. 2015).

Individuals suffering from addiction demonstrate the two components of reinforcer pathology: increased discounting of the future (MacKillop et al. 2011; Bickel et al. 2016a, c) and increased demand for drugs of abuse (Wilson et al. 2016). They may seek out drugs at great personal costs, not only in terms of the monetary price or search costs, but also in terms of alternative reinforcers that are sacrificed in favor of drug-seeking or drug-taking behavior (e.g., loss of health, employment, or family time). However, to the individual, the rewards of drug use are still worth the immediate costs of drug seeking and purchasing. The valuation of these drugs can be observed through the investigation of *behavioral economic demand* (see Box 8.3), which measures sensitivity of consumption of a given commodity to increases in its price (Bickel et al. 2017).

Addiction is not the only disorder that follows the reinforcer pathology model of excessive discounting and commodity overvaluation. Individuals who are overweight or obese demonstrate both excessive temporal discounting and high demand for food (Epstein et al. 2010). First, like addiction, high rates of temporal discounting are robustly associated with obesity (Weller et al. 2008; Amlung et al. 2016a). Second, individuals with high body mass index (BMI) will expend a greater amount of effort to earn a single unit of preferred food than their lower BMI counterparts (Giesen et al. 2010). Moreover, the interaction of both demand and discounting is a better predictor of BMI (Best et al. 2012) and energy intake (Rollins et al. 2010) than either measure alone.

A trans-disease understanding of fundamental pathologies may also lead us to treatment options for addiction and obesity, as well as other maladaptive health behaviors which may fit within the reinforcer pathology model (e.g., indoor tanning, Reed 2015). These interventions may come from novel applications of treatments currently found effective in other disease states; alternatively, novel treatments may be developed to specifically correct the underlying imbalances of the CNDS that may contribute to reinforcer pathology (Bickel et al. 2016a, c).

Narrative Theory and Methods

The CNDS theory suggests that reinforcer pathology results from an imbalance between dual decision systems such that the executive decision system is relatively weaker than the impulsive decision system. One way to treat reinforcer pathology is to strengthen the components of the executive system and, as a result, approximate regulatory balance between impulsive and executive decision systems. Several methods along these lines have been explored and discussed elsewhere (Bickel et al. 2016a, c). Here, however, we address a new approach to such interventions that we explicate for the first time, namely narrative theory and methods.

To understand the rationale for this approach, consider the important evolutionary reason for our highly developed prefrontal cortex and associated executive function. Robin Dunbar (Dunbar 1992; Dunbar and Shultz 2007) sought to identify correlates of the size of the neocortex among human and non-human primates proportional to the rest of the brain. Although he considered many factors, such as diet and foraging patterns, among others, the only variables that showed a strong relationship with proportional neocortex size were social factors such as group size, social play, and grooming. Thus, Dunbar's (1998) social brain hypothesis suggests that the relative size of the neocortex and therefore the executive decision system is not the result of the contingencies of survival, but rather the contingencies of social interactions.

Apes and monkeys form social alliances with conspecifics through grooming or other forms of direct physical contact. However, humans can interact with a much larger number of conspecifics with the use of language. Interestingly, most human conversations are about gossip. Indeed, gossip accounts for approximately 65% of conversations (Dunbar 2004). When humans communicate with each other, they use distinct storylike structures (Mar 2004) and humans learn more information when it is presented as a story than when given as factual information (Baumeister et al. 2004). Moreover, the centrality of narratives to our species is evident in that we see narratives where none exist (Gazzaniga 1998; Gottschall 2012). For example, Heider and Simmel (1944) showed 144 undergraduates a film that depicted a big stationary square with a flap that opens and closes and two triangles and a circle that move around the screen. When asked what they saw, only three students said that they saw geometric shapes move about on the screen. The remainder provided narratives of various types that suggested motives and a storyline. Consider a brief portion of what one participant said about the film: "Triangle number-one shuts his door (or should we say line) and the two innocent young things walk in. Lovers in the two-dimensional world no doubt; little triangle-two and sweet circle. Triangle one (here-after known as the villain) spies the young love…." (p. 247). This and other examples suggest that narratives are a key feature of human behavior and that narratives may provide more than mere information. They convey story and emotion in a way that is uniquely salient in human society.

Importantly, Huth et al. (2016) asked participants to listen to two hours of narratives while in an fMRI scanner. Subsequent principal component analysis of language content and brain regions found four distinct components involved in processing these narratives: social, emotional, communal, and violent components. Results showed intricate patterns of activation in numerous brain regions that were consistent across participants, including portions of the prefrontal cortex and the

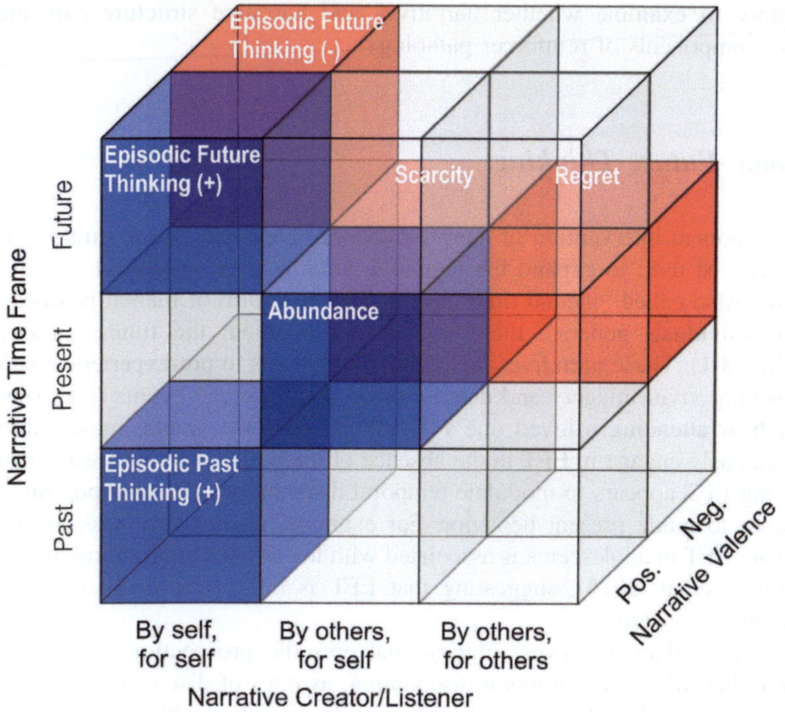

Fig. 8.5 A narrative theory framework depicting the three-dimensional space in which narratives may be manipulated: narrative creator/listener (*x*-axis), time frame (*y*-axis), and valence (*z*-axis). *Shaded cells* depict areas we and others have investigated in prior research (see Table 8.5 for results). Narratives describing mortality cues (Griskevicius et al. 2011) are not pictured due to space limitations, as the diffuse nature of these narratives could be considered to span multiple cells on two separate axes (time frame and narrative creator/listener)

limbic system. Thus, listening to narratives may result in greater utilization and perhaps interaction than information without such stories (see also Nummenmaa et al. 2014).

If narratives engage multiple neural structures from both the impulsive and executive decision systems, then perhaps narratives can be used to rebalance the dysregulation between these systems seen in addiction. Narratives can vary in at least three dimensions (see Fig. 8.5). The first dimension refers to the narrative creator/listener; that is, narratives can be created by the research participant for the research participant, by the experimenter for the research participant, or by the experimenter about someone else for the research participant. The second dimension is time; that is, narratives can occur in the past, the present, or the future. The third dimension is valence; that is, narratives can address negative or positive outcomes. Collectively, these dimensions describe in broad outline how narratives can be manipulated. In the following sections, we review data from the field and our laboratory to examine whether narratives and narrative structure can alter the distinct components of reinforcer pathology.

Episodic Future Thinking

One component intervention of narrative theory is episodic future thinking (EFT), which can be used to expand the temporal window over which individuals value rewards. Also called "mental time travel," EFT is a form of mental prospection in which individuals generate their own narratives about the future (Atance and O'Neill 2001). These narratives then allow individuals to pre-experience the future by invoking vivid imagery and details surrounding specific events (e.g., starting a new job or attending a loved one's wedding). To some extent, most individuals spontaneously engage in EFT in the absence of intervention. In turn, such naturally occurring EFT appears to modulate temporal discounting, allowing possible future outcomes to guide present behavior. For example, greater vividness of naturally occurring EFT in adolescents is associated with lower rates of temporal discounting (Bromberg et al. 2015), suggesting that EFT is integral to decisions involving valuation of the future.

Additional data, however, suggest that episodic prospection is not the only variable that influences temporal discounting, as rates of discounting are undifferentiated between healthy controls and amnesic patients unable to engage in EFT (Kwan et al. 2013, 2015). Moreover, quality of EFT is undifferentiated between healthy controls and pathological gamblers (Wiehler et al. 2015), despite pathological gambling otherwise being associated with excessive temporal discounting (Petry 2001b; Dixon et al. 2003; Miedl et al. 2012). Thus, a clearer understanding of the role of EFT in temporal discounting awaits further investigation. Nonetheless, explicit intervention designed to evoke highly vivid narratives involving EFT robustly reduces temporal discounting. A summary of the methods used in these studies may be found in Box 8.4. These effects have been demonstrated in a range of populations, including obese participants (Daniel et al. 2013a, b), cigarette smokers (Stein et al. 2016), and healthy volunteers (Peters and Büchel 2010), an effect likely mediated in part by enhanced activation of brain areas associated with the executive decision system (e.g., medial rostral prefrontal cortex; Peters and Büchel 2010).

Additional data indicate that EFT narratives produce therapeutic effects on the second component of reinforcer pathology: commodity overvaluation. Specifically, EFT has been shown to reduce behavioral economic demand for highly palatable food in obese populations (Sze et al. under review), alcohol in alcohol-dependent populations (Snider et al. 2016a), and cigarettes in cigarette smokers (Stein and Bickel, unpublished data). Importantly, data from both the laboratory and naturalistic contexts indicate that EFT also reduces direct measures of consumption, including cigarette smoking (Stein et al. 2016) and food intake (Daniel et al. 2013b, 2015; Sze et al. 2015; O'Neill et al. 2016).

Table 8.5 Summary of narrative studies to date and their effects on delay discounting and food or drug consumption

Narrative type			Temporal discounting		Food/drug consumption	
	Reference	Study sample	Effect	Commodity	Effect	Commodity
Positive EFT						
	Peters and Büchel (2010)	Young adults	↓	Hypothetical money		
	Benoit et al. (2011)	Adults	↓	Hypothetical money		
	Daniel et al. (2013b)	Overweight/obese adult females	↓	Hypothetical money	↓	Real food
	Daniel et al. (2013a)	Overweight/obese adult females	↓	Hypothetical money		
		Lean adult females	↓	Hypothetical money		
	Liu et al. (2013)	Young adults	↓	Hypothetical money		
	Lin and Epstein (2014)	Adults	↓	Hypothetical money		
	Daniel et al. (2015)	Overweight/obese children	↓	Hypothetical money	↓	Real food
	Sze et al. (2015)	Overweight/obese parent–child dyads			↓	Real food
	Dassen et al. (2016)	Young adult females	↓	Hypothetical money	↓[b]	Real food
	O'Neill et al. (2016)	Overweight/obese adult females			↓	Real food
	Snider et al. (2016a)	Alcohol-dependent adults	↓	Hypothetical money	↓[a]	Hypothetical alcohol
	Stein et al. (2016)	Cigarette-smoking adults	↓	Hypothetical money	↓	Real cigarettes
	Stein and Bickel (unpublished data)	Cigarette-smoking adults			↓[a]	Hypothetical cigarettes

(continued)

Table 8.5 (continued)

Narrative type			Temporal discounting		Food/drug consumption	
	Reference	Study sample	Effect	Commodity	Effect	Commodity
	Sze et al. (under review)	Overweight/obese adults	↓	Hypothetical money	↓[a]	Hypothetical food
	Daniel et al. (2016)	Adults	↓	Hypothetical money		
Neutral EFT						
	Liu et al. (2013)	Young adults	–	Hypothetical money		
	Lin and Epstein (2014)	Adults	↓	Hypothetical money		
Negative EFT						
	Liu et al. (2013)	Young adults	↑	Hypothetical money		
Positive episodic past thinking (EPT) EFT						
	Daniel et al. (2016)	Adults	–[c]	Hypothetical money		
Abundance						
	Bickel et al. (2016d)	Adults	–	Hypothetical money		
	Dixon et al. (2016)	Pathological gamblers	↓	Hypothetical money		
Scarcity						
	Bickel et al. (2016d)	Adults	↑	Hypothetical money		
	Sze et al. (under review)	Overweight/obese adults	↑	Hypothetical money	↑	Hypothetical food[a]
	Dixon et al. (2016)	Pathological gamblers	–	Hypothetical money		
Mortality cues						
	Griskevicius et al. (2011)	Adults from low childhood SES	↑	Hypothetical money		
		Adult from high childhood SES	↓	Hypothetical money		

(continued)

Table 8.5 (continued)

Narrative type			Temporal discounting		Food/drug consumption	
	Reference	Study sample	Effect	Commodity	Effect	Commodity
Sexual regret expression						
	Quisenberry et al. (2015a)	Adults	↓	Hypothetical condom-protected sex		
	Quisenberry et al. (2015a)	Adults	–	Hypothetical money		

Note Effects on specified measures are summarized as follows: ↓ = reduced; – = no change; ↑ = increased; blank = not investigated
[a]Indicates consumption investigated in a demand context
[b]Indicates EFT only reduced consumption when using food-based cues
[c]Did not affect discounting of future monetary rewards, but did reduce discounting of past monetary rewards

Table 8.5 provides a summary of studies examining the effects of EFT narratives on temporal discounting and either drug or food consumption. Collectively, these data support the use of EFT as an intervention for the reinforcer pathology associated with addiction and other maladaptive health behaviors.

Box 8.4: Narrative Methods Used in EFT, Scarcity, Abundance, and Regret Studies

Some procedures are common to many narrative theory studies, regardless of whether those narratives involve EFT, scarcity, abundance, or other manipulations. Namely, a participant is asked to read and consider a narrative, whether that narrative is self- or experimenter-generated or varies along any other dimension depicted in Fig. 8.5. Participants then complete behavioral tasks, often while text or audio reminders of the narratives are presented.

Below, we outline the specific procedures used in each narrative theory method. See the main text for additional details.

Episodic Future Thinking

Participants first complete a guided task designed to generate narratives about events that could occur at multiple time points in the future (EFT) or occurred in the recent past (ERT). Care is taken to elicit as much vivid detail as possible (e.g., "Who were you with?" and "What were you doing?"). This narrative generation task is most often administered by research staff (e.g., Daniel et al. 2013a, b); however, an effective self-guided task has recently been developed for use online and other instances in which availability of research staff is limited (Sze et al. under review).

During the completion of one or more behavioral tasks, participants are asked to vividly think about their events. A short textual cue reminding participants of their narrative appears on the computer monitor. Occasionally, participants record themselves reading a written description of the events to use as subsequent audio cues (e.g., Stein et al. 2016), especially in instances in which behavioral tasks do not require continuous attention to the computer monitor.

Scarcity and Abundance

Participants read a short narrative describing an abrupt change in income and related lifestyle, consider it for a period of time (e.g., 15 s; Sze et al. under review), and assume they are experiencing the conditions described. Narratives remain on the screen for a predetermined period of time to allow careful reading and consideration (Bickel et al. 2016d). Participants then complete one or more behavioral tasks. Although other narratives have been used (Dixon et al. 2016), below we present the scarcity and abundance narratives, as well as the neutral control narrative, used by Bickel et al. (2016d).

Scarcity. You have just been fired from your job. You will now have to move in with a relative who lives in a part of the country you dislike, and you will have to spend all of your savings to move there. You do not qualify for unemployment, so you will not be making any income until you find another job.

Neutral. At your job, you have just been transferred to a different department in a location across town. It is a similar distance from where you live so you will not have to move. You will be making 2% more than you previously were.

Abundance. At your job you have just been promoted. You will have the opportunity to move to a part of the country you always wanted to live in OR you may choose to stay where you are. Either way, the company gives you a large amount of money to cover moving expenses, and tells you to keep what you don't spend. You will be making 100% more than you previously were.

Regret

Like scarcity and abundance, participants are asked to read short narratives, consider them for some period of time, and then complete one or behavioral tasks. However, specific details of the narrative are individualized to the participants to make the details more salient and relatable. Below are the narratives used by Quisenberry et al. (2015a) in an examination of the effects of regret on discounting of delayed sexual gratification.

Negative narrative, with regret expression. Taylor, your best friend who is also [*male/female*], [*X*] years old, and engages in sexual behavior similar to yours, just called to tell you about a social gathering [*s/he*] attended where [*s/he*] met someone [*s/he*] was interested in. They ended up having sex without using protection and Taylor expressed extreme regret. [*S/he*] said, "I knew I should have used protection that night. What was I thinking?!" Soon after the experience, Taylor experienced a sore throat, fever, rash, fatigue, headache, and muscle pain and described it as "the worst flu ever". Taylor went to the doctor for these symptoms and tested positive for the HIV virus that causes AIDS. Taylor is profoundly devastated, afraid [*his/her*] whole life is over, and wishes [*s/he*] never made the mistake.

Negative narrative. Taylor, your best friend who is also [*male/female*], [*X*] years old, and engages in sexual behavior similar to yours, just called to tell you about a social gathering [*s/he*] attended where [*s/he*] met someone [*s/he*] was interested in. They ended up having sex without using protection and Taylor expressed extreme excitement. said, "I had a great time and my partner was very attractive. I'm excited to see them again!" Soon after the experience, Taylor experienced a sore throat, fever, rash, fatigue, headache, and muscle pain and described it as "the worst flu ever". Taylor went to the doctor for these symptoms and tested positive for the HIV virus that causes AIDS. Taylor is profoundly devastated, afraid [*his/her*] whole life is over, and crying uncontrollably.

Positive narrative. Taylor, your best friend who is also [*male/female*], [*X*] years old, and engages in sexual behavior similar to yours, just called to tell you about a social gathering [*s/he*] attended where [*s/he*] met someone [*s/he*] was interested in. They ended up having sex without using protection and Taylor expressed extreme excitement. [*S/he*] said, "I had such a good time and my partner was very attractive. I can't wait to see them again!" Soon after the experience, Taylor experienced a sore throat, fever, rash, fatigue, headache, and muscle pain and described it as "the worst flu ever". Taylor went to the doctor for these symptoms and tested negative for the HIV virus that causes AIDS. Taylor is extremely happy and called you jumping for joy.

Control Conditions

Historically, several comparison conditions have been implemented to isolate the effects of prospection involved in EFT. These include the completion of behavioral tasks in the absence of any episodic thinking (Liu et al. 2013) and non-autobiographical episodic thinking, such as imagining details from a third-party narrative (Daniel et al. 2013b). However, perhaps the most appropriate control condition (and the most frequently used in the study of temporal discounting) is episodic recent thinking (ERT), in which participants imagine real events that occurred over the past several hours or days (Daniel et al. 2015; O'Neill et al. 2016; Snider et al. 2016a; Stein et al. 2016). Like EFT, the ERT condition invokes episodic memory and vivid imagery, but isolates the prospective component of EFT in its effects on temporal discounting and commodity valuation.

Episodic Future Versus Past Thinking

Recent data suggest that discounting in response to the ERT control condition is undifferentiated from an additional control condition in which discounting was measured under typical circumstances (i.e., featuring no episodic thinking; Sze et al. under review). However, by definition, the absolute temporal distances typically used in ERT and EFT differ in magnitude, with ERT evoking imagery from the last several hours or days and EFT evoking imagery from up to a year in the future (e.g., Stein et al. 2016). Possible effects of episodic thinking of the more distant past on temporal discounting have, until recently, not been examined. Daniel et al. (2016), however, recently reported that such *episodic past thinking* over time frames comparable to traditional EFT did not affect discounting of future rewards; rather, episodic thinking of the distant past reduced only the discounting of past rewards, in which participants report preference between having received smaller rewards in the recent past or larger rewards in the more distant past (Yi et al. 2006b). Conversely, EFT reduced only discounting of future rewards and did not affect discounting of past rewards. Thus, the effects of episodic thinking on discounting appear specific to the time frame (past or future) of episodic imagery and rewards being evaluated.

Episodic Future Thinking Valence

To date, most studies investigating the effects of EFT on reinforcer pathology have used EFT featuring positive future events (see Table 8.5). However, the effects of EFT featuring neutral, or even negative, content have not been well explored. Some data suggest that valence is not critical in determining EFT's effects on temporal discounting. For example, effects of positive EFT content on discounting remain even when controlling for effects of EFT on affect (Sze et al. under review), as well as ratings of enjoyment, excitement, and other dimensions of episodic content

(Snider et al. 2016a). In addition, neutral EFT content has been shown to produce similar reductions in temporal discounting as positive EFT content in healthy volunteers (Lin and Epstein 2014). In contrast, however, additional data from one study suggest that EFT featuring *negative* content increases temporal discounting in healthy volunteers (Liu et al. 2013), an effect opposite to that observed with positive content in the same and other studies. These preliminary data on EFT featuring negative content outline a clear course for future research before firm conclusions can be reached regarding the role of EFT valence (positive, negative, and neutral) on measures of reinforcer pathology.

Effects of Episodic Future Thinking on Alternative Forms of Discounting

As discussed in Box 8.1, the discounting framework has also been used to study the effects of variables other than delay on valuation of rewards. These include probability discounting, defined as valuation of a reward as a function of the odds against its receipt (Rachlin et al. 1991), and social discounting, defined as valuation of a reward as a function of the social distance between the participant and the reward recipient. The former may be considered a measure of risk aversion, while the latter may be considered a measure of altruism.

Importantly, emerging data (not summarized in Table 8.5) suggest that EFT reduces these varied forms of discounting in a manner similar to that observed in a typical temporal discounting framework. Specifically, Kaplan et al. (2015) reported that EFT reduced discounting in a task that combined probability and temporal discounting. Likewise, some evidence suggests that episodic thinking of both the self and others, and in both the present and the future, reduces social discounting (Yi et al. 2016). These extensions of the foundational findings on EFT and discounting demonstrate the flexibility and robustness of the methods and their ability to address a wide variety of psychological phenomena.

Although some unresolved questions remain regarding EFT, its robust therapeutic effects on both components of reinforcer pathology served as a progenitor to narrative theory, leading us, in part, to systematically explore the various narrative dimensions depicted in Fig. 8.5. In the remainder of this chapter, we review evidence from this ongoing line of inquiry.

Scarcity and Abundance

Effects of both economic scarcity and abundance on reinforcer pathology can be modeled using narrative manipulations. A long-standing association between poverty and psychological distress, including impaired decision making, has been previously documented (Shah et al. 2012; Mani et al. 2013; Haushofer and Fehr 2014). Moreover, momentary or enduring executive dysfunction has been observed in individuals under conditions of poverty, resulting in suboptimal decision making, including steep temporal discounting (Haushofer et al. 2013; Bickel et al. 2014c). These established relations serve as the foundation on which scarcity narrative manipulations are based.

Exposure to hypothetical scarcity conditions in the laboratory has modified racial perception (Krosch and Amodio 2014), cognitive performance (Mani et al. 2013), and the effect of contextual cues (Shah et al. 2012). More germane to this chapter, direct investigations of the effects of scarcity on monetary decision making have demonstrated a relation with scarcity conditions in both the laboratory and real world. For example, a within-subjects investigation of farmers pre- and postharvest found that cognitive control measures were more impaired in a preharvest period in which the farmers were poorer compared to a postharvest period in which they had recently been paid (Mani et al. 2013). In addition, in an investigation of the effects of a narrative invoking mortality cues on discounting, socioeconomic status in childhood predicted discounting outcomes (Griskevicius et al. 2011). That is, mortality narratives increased and decreased discounting in adults with low and high childhood socioeconomic status, respectively. Generally, the data reviewed above are consistent with the conclusion that scarce resources refocus attention toward immediate choices (Shah et al. 2012); that is, scarcity constricts the temporal window of reward valuation.

In our exploration of scarcity and temporal discounting using narrative theory methods, the effect of varying economic conditions on a modified temporal discounting task was investigated in Amazon Mechanical Turk control participants (Bickel et al. 2016d). The 5-trial adjusting temporal discounting task is a rapid version of the adjusting-amount task typically used (see Box 8.1), and it returns the traditional fitted discount rate parameter, k (see Koffarnus and Bickel 2014 for details). In this experiment, participants were asked to read narratives describing either conditions of economic scarcity, abundance, or neutrality and assume that these narratives were true (see Box 8.4 for the specific narratives used). Figure 8.6

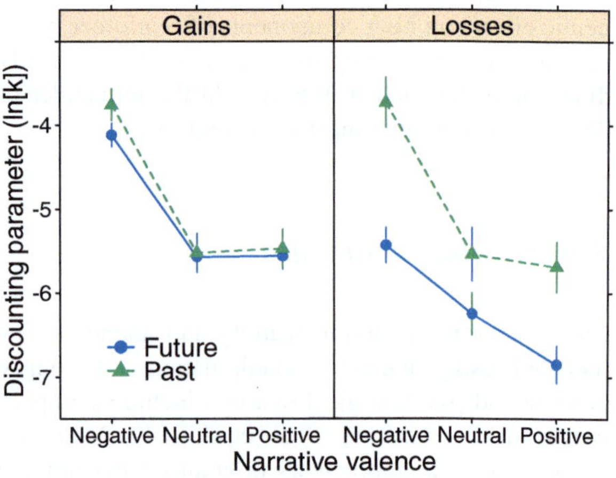

Fig. 8.6 The scarcity narrative significantly increased discount rate, compared to the neutral and abundance income narratives, in all four discounting conditions spanning the future and the past and with both monetary gains and losses. Data regraphed from Bickel et al. (2016d)

depicts the results of this experiment. Exposure to the scarcity narrative, compared to the neutral and abundance narratives, increased discount rate for both future gains and losses, and past gains and losses (see Box 8.1 for further explanation of these task variations). In contrast, no effects of the abundance narrative compared to the neutral narrative were observed in any condition.

However, different effects of scarcity and abundance narratives were observed in pathological gamblers in a recent study (Dixon et al. 2016). In this sample, exposure to a brief narrative about reducing income by half (i.e., scarcity) had no effect on temporal discounting, whereas exposure to a narrative about doubling income (i.e., abundance) reduced temporal discounting. Perhaps, the particular scarcity narrative used in this study did not reflect a change sizable enough to evoke an effect. Alternatively, a more likely explanation for these discrepant effects across studies involves rate dependence, a phenomenon in which response to intervention depends on baseline values of the dependent measure (Bickel et al. 2014b, 2016b; Snider et al. 2016b). Because pathological gamblers show high baseline discount rates compared to healthy controls (Dixon et al. 2003; Petry 2001b), the scarcity narrative in the study by Dixon et al. (2016) may have had little room to further increase discount rate, thereby producing no effect. Conversely, these same baseline discount rates would have provided ample opportunity to show a rate-decreasing effect of the abundance scenario. Indeed, visual inspection of the figure presented in this study corroborates this hypothesis. Nonetheless, this possibility should be systematically explored in future experiments.

Combined Effects of Economic Scarcity and Episodic Future Thinking

In a recent study, we sought to examine the combined effects of economic scarcity and EFT in overweight/obese participants on Amazon Mechanical Turk (Sze et al. under review). Because these narrative interventions affect components of reinforcer pathology in opposing directions, the effects of combining them might reveal their relative strengths and suggest treatment options for reinforcer pathology associated with economic poverty. Participants were randomly assigned to one of four possible two-way combinations of episodic thinking conditions (EFT or ERT) and income narrative conditions (the scarcity or neutral narratives described earlier).

Data revealed that compared to ERT, EFT reduced temporal discounting and behavioral economic demand for highly palatable food; conversely, compared to the neutral narrative, scarcity increased temporal discounting and demand for food regardless of episodic thinking condition. Moreover, little interaction was observed between episodic thinking and income conditions, suggesting that these interventions affect measures of reinforcer pathology independently of one another. Perhaps more importantly, these data suggest that EFT can be used clinically to partially attenuate the harmful effects of economic scarcity.

Regret

Regret aversion is among the biases that influence human decision making and is defined as the propensity to make decisions in order to minimize future regret (Zeelenberg and Pieters 2004). As such, the anticipation of future regret affects our current choices (Bell 1982; Loomes and Sugden 1982). Two distinct varieties of regret have been described in the decision-making literature, that is, regret resulting from short-term actions (i.e., errors of commission) that cause negative, more immediate consequences and regret following long-term inaction (i.e., errors of omission; Gilovich 1994; Gilovich and Medvec 1995). Both types of regret may be used to inform narrative theory; however, here, we refer to the first variety of regret, resulting from errors of commission.

To our knowledge, the first study of regret and discounting using narrative theory methods investigated delay to sexual gratification following exposure to researcher-generated narratives about individuals who are close to the participant (Quisenberry et al. 2015a). Delay to condom-protected sexual gratification was measured by the sexual discounting task, a behavioral task modeled from traditional temporal discounting (Johnson and Bruner 2012, 2013). Responses represent the choice to engage in risky unprotected sex now or wait some delay for condom-protected sex. To complete the task, participants first chose, from an array of 60 picture options, the individuals with whom they would have casual sex. Afterward, participants chose from this subset the most and least attractive potential partners and the most and least likely to have a sexually transmitted infection (STI). For each of the four chosen images, participants used a visual analog scale to answer questions such as, "Would you rather have sex now without a condom or *at some delay* with a condom?" (0 indicates engaging in immediate unprotected sex, and 100 indicates waiting the specified delay for condom-protected sex). This process is repeated at multiple delays to condom-protected sex, including now (no delay), 1 h, 3 h, 6 h, 1 day, 1 week, 1 month, and 3 months.

In this study, Amazon Mechanical Turk users were presented with a textual and auditory narrative about a best friend's recent sexual encounter that highlighted either a positive outcome, a negative outcome, or a negative outcome with the friend expressing regret (see Box 8.4), all containing an identical number of characters and information (Quisenberry et al. 2015a). After reading and listening to the narrative, participants completed the sexual discounting task and a monetary temporal discounting task. Figure 8.7 depicts the effects of these narratives on delay to sexual gratification. Panels a–d represent the distribution of answers across each condition. In the conditions with the most attractive partners (i.e., panel b) and partners least likely to have an STI (i.e., a safety signal; panel c), sexual discounting was decreased after hearing the narrative that involved a negative health outcome with regret expression. In the condition for the least attractive partner (i.e., panel a), discounting was decreased in both of the negative health outcome narratives with no effect of regret. Finally, in the condition with the partner most likely to have an STI (i.e., a warning signal, panel d), sexual discounting was similar across all

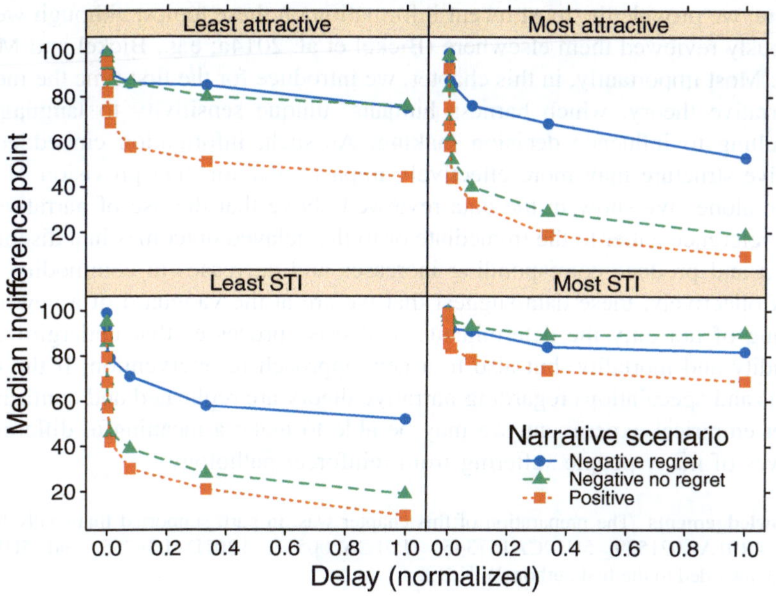

Fig. 8.7 Discounting curves by narrative scenario for each of the sexual discounting task partner conditions. In the most attractive and least STI conditions, experiencing a narrative regarding a friend expressing regret after undergoing a negative health consequence increased delay to sexual gratification. Data reprinted from Quisenberry et al. (2015a)

narratives. Importantly, no significant differences in monetary temporal discounting were observed between narratives demonstrating that these narratives produce change specific to behavioral tasks associated with risky sexual behavior.

Our results suggest that this laboratory measure could be used to prospectively study the effects of public health initiatives concerning risky sexual behavior. Moreover, evidence that a well-documented bias can change measures of risky behavior supports future research on other human biases integrated into narratives.

Conclusions

In this chapter, we summarized the extant evidence on temporal discounting as a measure of self-control. The failure of self-control is evident in a wide variety of disorders, providing evidence that it is a trans-disease process. Excessive discounting of future rewards results from regulatory imbalance of CNDS, a dual-decision process, in which the impulsive decision system exerts greater control relative to the executive decision system. Temporal discounting also interacts with reinforcer valuation to produce reinforcer pathology. Evidence suggests that reinforcer pathology is relevant to several disorders, including drug abuse and obesity.

Here, we provide the most recent information on these topics, although we have previously reviewed them elsewhere (Bickel et al. 2014a; e.g., Bickel and Mueller 2009). Most importantly, in this chapter, we introduce for the first time the methods of narrative theory, which harness humans' unique sensitivity to language and storytelling to influence decision making. As such, information embedded in a narrative structure may more effectively impact behavior than provision of information alone. We show in the data reviewed above that the use of narratives can shift preference either to the immediate or to the delayed outcomes in a discounting context and produce corresponding increases and decreases in commodity valuation. Collectively, these data suggest that we are at the vanguard of a new understanding of not only the determinants of disease processes that undergird excess morbidity and mortality, but also to a new approach to intervention. If the observations and speculations regarding narrative theory are replicated and confirmed by further empirical experiment, we may be able to make a meaningful difference in the lives of many people suffering from reinforcer pathology.

Acknowledgements The preparation of this chapter was, in part, supported financially by NIH grants 4R01AA021529, 5U19CA157345, 1P01CA200512, 4R01DA034755, and 5UH2DK-109543, awarded to the first author (W.K.B.).

References

American Psychiatric Association. (2013). *Diagnostic and statistical manual of mental disorders: DSM-5*. Arlington, VA: American Psychiatric Publishing.

Amlung, M., & MacKillop, J. (2015). Further evidence of close correspondence for alcohol demand decision making for hypothetical and incentivized rewards. *Behavioural Processes, 113,* 187–191.

Amlung, M., Petker, T., Jackson, J., & Balodis, I. (2016a). Steep discounting of delayed monetary and food rewards in obesity: A meta-analysis. *Psychological Medicine, 46,* 2423–2434.

Amlung, M. T., Acker, J., Stojek, M. K., Murphy, J. G., & MacKillop, J. (2012). Is talk "cheap"? An initial investigation of the equivalence of alcohol purchase task performance for hypothetical and actual rewards. *Alcoholism, Clinical and Experimental Research, 36*(4), 716–724.

Amlung, M., Vedelago, L., Acker, J., Balodis, I., & MacKillop, J. (2016b). Steep delay discounting and addictive behavior: A meta-analysis of continuous associations. *Addiction* (in press).

Appelhans, B. M., Waring, M. E., Schneider, K. L., Pagoto, S. L., DeBiasse, M. A., Debiasse, M. A., et al. (2012). Delay discounting and intake of ready-to-eat and away-from-home foods in overweight and obese women. *Appetite, 59*(2), 576–584.

Atance, C. M., & O'Neill, D. K. (2001). Episodic future thinking. *Trends in Cognitive Sciences, 5*(12), 533–539.

Axon, R. N., Bradford, W. D., & Egan, B. M. (2009). The role of individual time preferences in health behaviors among hypertensive adults: A pilot study. *Journal of the American Society of Hypertension, 3*(1), 35–41.

Baker, F., Johnson, M. W., & Bickel, W. K. (2003). Delay discounting in current and never-before cigarette smokers: Similarities and differences across commodity, sign, and magnitude. *Journal of Abnormal Psychology, 112*(3), 382–392.

Baumeister, R. F., Zhang, L., & Vohs, K. D. (2004). Gossip as cultural learning. *Review of General Psychology, 8*(2), 111.

Bechara, A. (2005). Decision making, impulse control and loss of willpower to resist drugs: A neurocognitive perspective. *Nature Neuroscience, 8*(11), 1458–1463.

Bell, D. E. (1982). Regret in decision making under uncertainty. *Operations Research, 30,* 961–981.

Benoit, R. G., Gilbert, S. J., & Burgess, P. W. (2011). A neural mechanism mediating the impact of episodic prospection on farsighted decisions. *The Journal of Neuroscience, 31*(18), 6771–6779.

Bernheim, B. D., & Rangel, A. (2002). *Addiction and cue-conditioned cognitive processes (No. w9329).* Cambridge: National Bureau of Economic Research.

Best, J. R., Theim, K. R., Gredysa, D. M., Stein, R. I., Welch, R. R., Saelens, B. E., et al. (2012). Behavioral economic predictors of overweight children's weight loss. *Journal of Consulting and Clinical Psychology, 80*(6), 1086–1096.

Bickel, W. K., Johnson, M. W., Koffarnus, M. N., MacKillop, J., & Murphy, J. G. (2014a). The behavioral economics of substance use disorders: Reinforcement pathologies and their repair. *Annual Review of Clinical Psychology, 10,* 641–677.

Bickel, W. K., Landes, R. D., Christensen, D. R., Jackson, L., Jones, B. A., Kurth-Nelson, Z., et al. (2011). Single- and cross-commodity discounting among cocaine addicts: The commodity and its temporal location determine discounting rate. *Psychopharmacology (Berlin), 217*(2), 177–187.

Bickel, W. K., Landes, R. D., & Kurth-Nelson, Z. (2014b). A quantitative signature of self-control repair rate-dependent effects of successful addiction treatment. *Clinical Psychological Science, 2*(6), 685–695.

Bickel, W. K., & Marsch, L. A. (2001). Toward a behavioral economic understanding of drug dependence: Delay discounting processes. *Addiction, 96*(1), 73–86.

Bickel, W. K., Mellis, A. M., Snider, S. E., Moody, L., Stein, J. S., & Quisenberry, A. J. (2016a). Novel Therapeutics for Addiction: Behavioral Economic and Neuroeconomic Approaches. *Current treatment options in psychiatry, 3*(3), 277–292.

Bickel, W. K., Miller, M. L., Yi, R., Kowal, B. P., Lindquist, D. M., & Pitcock, J. A. (2007). Behavioral and neuroeconomics of drug addiction: Competing neural systems and temporal discounting processes. *Drug and Alcohol Dependence, 90*(Suppl 1), S85–S91.

Bickel, W. K., Moody, L., Quisenberry, A. J., Ramey, C. T., & Sheffer, C. E. (2014c). A competing neurobehavioral decision systems model of SES-related health and behavioral disparities. *Preventive Medicine, 68,* 37–43.

Bickel, W. K., Moody, L., Snider, S., Mellis, A., Stein, J., & Quisenberry, A. (2017). The behavioural economics of tobacco products: Innovations in laboratory methods to inform regulatory science. In Y. Hanoch & T. Rice (Eds.), Behavioral economics and health behaviors: Key concepts and current research (in press).

Bickel, W. K., & Mueller, E. T. (2009). Toward the study of trans-disease processes: A novel approach with special reference to the study of co-morbidity. *Journal of Dual Diagnosis, 5*(2), 131–138.

Bickel, W. K., Odum, A. L., & Madden, G. J. (1999). Impulsivity and cigarette smoking: Delay discounting in current, never, and ex-smokers. *Psychopharmacology (Berlin), 146*(4), 447–454.

Bickel, W. K., Quisenberry, A. J., & Snider, S. E. (2016b). Does impulsivity change rate dependently following stimulant administration? A translational selective review and re-analysis. *Psychopharmacology, 233*(1), 1–18.

Bickel, W. K., Snider, S. E., Quisenberry, A. J., Stein, J. S., & Hanlon, C. A. (2016c). Competing neurobehavioral decision systems theory of cocaine addiction: From mechanisms to therapeutic opportunities. *Progress in brain research, 223,* 269–293.

Bickel, W. K., & Stein, J. S. (under review). Self-control and its failure: Intertemporal dimensions of health behavior.

Bickel, W. K., Wilson, A. G., Chen, C., Koffarnus, M. N., & Franck, C. T. (2016d). Stuck in time: negative income shock constricts the temporal window of valuation spanning the future and the past. *PloS one, 11*(9), e0163051.

Bradford, D., Courtemanche, C., Heutel, G., McAlvanah, P., & Ruhm, C. (2014). *Time preferences and consumer behavior (No. w20320)*. Cambridge: National Bureau of Economic Research.
Bradford, W. D. (2010). The association between individual time preferences and health maintenance habits. *Medical Decision Making, 30*(1), 99–112.
Bromberg, U., Wiehler, A., & Peters, J. (2015). Episodic future thinking is related to impulsive decision making in healthy adolescents. *Child Development, 86*(5), 1458–1468.
Celio, M. A., MacKillop, J., & Caswell, A. J. (2016). Interactive relationships between sex-related alcohol expectancies and delay discounting on risky sex. *Alcoholism, Clinical and Experimental Research, 40*(3), 638–646.
Chabris, C. F., Laibson, D., Morris, C. L., Schuldt, J. P., & Taubinsky, D. (2008). Individual laboratory-measured discount rates predict field behavior. *Journal of Risk and Uncertainty, 37*(2–3), 237–269.
Chanraud, S., Martelli, C., Delain, F., Kostogianni, N., Douaud, G., Aubin, H.-J., et al. (2007). Brain morphometry and cognitive performance in detoxified alcohol-dependents with preserved psychosocial functioning. *Neuropsychopharmacology, 32*(2), 429–438.
Chapman, G. B., Brewer, N. T., Coups, E. J., Brownlee, S., Leventhal, H., & Leventhal, E. A. (2001). Value for the future and preventive health behavior. *Journal of Experimental Psychology: Applied, 7*(3), 235–250.
Chapman, G. B., & Coups, E. J. (1999). Time preferences and preventive health behavior acceptance of the influenza vaccine. *Medical Decision Making, 19*(3), 307–314.
Chesson, H. W., Leichliter, J. S., Zimet, G. D., Rosenthal, S. L., Bernstein, D. I., & Fife, K. H. (2006). Discount rates and risky sexual behaviors among teenagers and young adults. *Journal of Risk and Uncertainty, 32*(3), 217–230.
Coffey, S. F., Gudleski, G. D., Saladin, M. E., & Brady, K. T. (2003). Impulsivity and rapid discounting of delayed hypothetical rewards in cocaine-dependent individuals. *Experimental and Clinical Psychopharmacology, 11*(1), 18–25.
Cole, D. M., Beckmann, C. F., Long, C. J., Matthews, P. M., Durcan, M. J., & Beaver, J. D. (2010). Nicotine replacement in abstinent smokers improves cognitive withdrawal symptoms with modulation of resting brain network dynamics. *Neuroimage, 52*(2), 590–599.
Crocq, M.-A. (2007). Historical and cultural aspects of man's relationship with addictive drugs. *Dialogues in Clinical Neuroscience, 9*(4), 355–361.
Daly, M., Harmon, C. P., & Delaney, L. (2009). Psychological and biological foundations of time preference. *Journal of the European Economic Association, 7*(2–3), 659–669.
Damasio, A. R., Everitt, B. J., & Bishop, D. (1996). The somatic marker hypothesis and the possible functions of the prefrontal cortex. *Philosophical Transactions of the Royal Society of London. Series B, Biological Sciences, 351*(1346), 1413–1420.
Daniel, T. O., Said, M., Stanton, C. M., & Epstein, L. H. (2015). Episodic future thinking reduces delay discounting and energy intake in children. *Eating Behaviors, 18,* 20–24.
Daniel, T. O., Sawyer, A., Dong, Y., Bickel, W. K., & Epstein, L. H. (2016). Remembering versus imagining: When does episodic retrospection and episodic prospection aid decision making? *Journal of Applied Research in Memory and Cognition, 5*(3), 352–358.
Daniel, T. O., Stanton, C. M., & Epstein, L. H. (2013a). The future is now: Comparing the effect of episodic future thinking on impulsivity in lean and obese individuals. *Appetite, 71,* 120–125.
Daniel, T. O., Stanton, C. M., & Epstein, L. H. (2013b). The future is now: Reducing impulsivity and energy intake using episodic future thinking. *Psychological Science, 24*(11), 2339–2342.
Dassen, F. C. M., Jansen, A., Nederkoorn, C., & Houben, K. (2016). Focus on the future: Episodic future thinking reduces discount rate and snacking. *Appetite, 96,* 327–332.
Daugherty, J. R., & Brase, G. L. (2010). Taking time to be healthy: Predicting health behaviors with delay discounting and time perspective. *Personality and Individual Differences, 48*(2), 202–207.
Davis, C., Patte, K., Curtis, C., & Reid, C. (2010). Immediate pleasures and future consequences: A neuropsychological study of binge eating and obesity. *Appetite, 54*(1), 208–213.

Decker, J. H., Figner, B., & Steinglass, J. E. (2015). On weight and waiting: Delay discounting in anorexia nervosa pretreatment and posttreatment. *Biological Psychiatry, 78*(9), 606–614.
DeGrandpre, R. J., Bickel, W. K., Hughes, J. R., Layng, M. P., & Badger, G. (1993). Unit price as a useful metric in analyzing effects of reinforcer magnitude. *Journal of the Experimental Analysis of Behavior, 60*(3), 641–666.
Dixon, M. R., Buono, F. D., & Belisle, J. (2016). Contrived motivating operations alter delay-discounting values of disordered gamblers. *Journal of Applied Behavior Analysis, 49*(4), 986–990.
Dixon, M. R., Marley, J., & Jacobs, E. A. (2003). Delay discounting by pathological gamblers. *Journal of Applied Behavior Analysis, 36*(4), 449–458.
Dunbar, R. I. (1998). The social brain hypothesis. *Evolutionary Anthropology, 6*(5), 178–190.
Dunbar, R. I. M. (1992). Neocortex size as a constraint on group size in primates. *Journal of Human Evolution, 22*(6), 469–493.
Dunbar, R. I. M. (2004). Gossip in evolutionary perspective. *Review of General Psychology, 8*(2), 100–110.
Dunbar, R. I. M., & Shultz, S. (2007). Evolution in the social brain. *Science, 317*(5843), 1344–1347.
Du, W., Green, L., & Myerson, J. (2002). Cross-cultural comparisons of discounting delayed and probabilistic rewards. *The Psychological Record, 52*(4), 479.
Epstein, L. H., Salvy, S. J., Carr, K. A., Dearing, K. K., & Bickel, W. K. (2010). Food reinforcement, delay discounting and obesity. *Physiology & Behavior, 100*(5), 438–445.
Evans, J. A. (2008). Electronic publication and the narrowing of science and scholarship. *Science, 321*(5887), 395–399.
Fein, G., Di Sclafani, V., Cardenas, V. A., Goldmann, H., Tolou-Shams, M., & Meyerhoff, D. J. (2002). Cortical gray matter loss in treatment-naïve alcohol dependent individuals. *Alcoholism, Clinical and Experimental Research, 26*(4), 558–564.
Franck, C. T., Koffarnus, M. N., House, L. L., & Bickel, W. K. (2015). Accurate characterization of delay discounting: A multiple model approach using approximate Bayesian model selection and a unified discounting measure. *Journal of the Experimental Analysis of Behavior, 103*(1), 218–233.
Frederick, S. (2002). Automated choice heuristics. In T. Gilovich, D. Griffin, & D. Kahneman (Eds.), *Heuristics and biases: The psychology of intuitive judgment* (pp. 548–558). New York, NY: Cambridge University Press.
Fudenberg, D., & Levine, D. K. (2006). A dual-self model of impulse control. *The American Economic Review, 96*(5), 1449–1476.
Garza, K. B., Ding, M., Owensby, J. K., & Zizza, C. A. (2016). Impulsivity and fast-food consumption: A cross-sectional study among working adults. *Journal of the Academy of Nutrition and Dietetics, 116*(1), 61–68.
Gazzaniga, M. S. (1998). *The mind's past*. Berkeley, CA: University of California Press.
Giesen, J. C. A. H., Havermans, R. C., Douven, A., Tekelenburg, M., & Jansen, A. (2010). Will work for snack food: The association of BMI and snack reinforcement. *Obesity, 18*(5), 966–970.
Gilovich, T. (1994). The temporal pattern to the experience of regret. *Journal of Personality and Social Psychology, 67*(3), 357–365.
Gilovich, T., & Medvec, V. H. (1995). The experience of regret: What, when, and why. *Psychological Review, 102*(2), 379–395.
Goldstein, R. Z., & Volkow, N. D. (2011). Dysfunction of the prefrontal cortex in addiction: Neuroimaging findings and clinical implications. *Nature Reviews Neuroscience, 12*(11), 652–669.
Gottschall, J. (2012). *The storytelling animal: How stories make us human*. Boston: Houghton Mifflin Harcourt.
Griskevicius, V., Tybur, J. M., Delton, A. W., & Robertson, T. E. (2011). The influence of mortality and socioeconomic status on risk and delayed rewards: A life history theory approach. *Journal of Personality and Social Psychology, 100*(6), 1015–1026.

Haushofer, J., & Fehr, E. (2014). On the psychology of poverty. *Science, 344*(6186), 862–867.

Haushofer, J., Schunk, D., & Fehr, E. (2013). *Negative income shocks increase discount rates*. Zurich: University of Zurich. (Working Paper).

Hayashi, Y., Miller, K., Foreman, A. M., & Wirth, O. (2016). A behavioral economic analysis of texting while driving: Delay discounting processes. *Accident Analysis and Prevention, 97,* 132–140.

Hayashi, Y., Russo, C. T., & Wirth, O. (2015). Texting while driving as impulsive choice: A behavioral economic analysis. *Accident Analysis and Prevention, 83,* 182–189.

Heerey, E. A., Robinson, B. M., McMahon, R. P., & Gold, J. M. (2007). Delay discounting in schizophrenia. *Cognitive Neuropsychiatry, 12*(3), 213–221.

Heider, F., & Simmel, M. (1944). An experimental study of apparent behavior. *The American Journal of Psychology, 57*(2), 243–259.

Heitzeg, M. M., Nigg, J. T., Yau, W.-Y. W., Zubieta, J.-K., & Zucker, R. A. (2008). Affective circuitry and risk for alcoholism in late adolescence: Differences in frontostriatal responses between vulnerable and resilient children of alcoholic parents. *Alcoholism, Clinical and Experimental Research, 32*(3), 414–426.

Hursh, S. R., & Silberberg, A. (2008). Economic demand and essential value. *Psychological Review, 115*(1), 186–198.

Hurst, R. M., Kepley, H. O., McCalla, M. K., & Livermore, M. K. (2011). Internal consistency and discriminant validity of a delay-discounting task with an adult self-reported ADHD sample. *Journal of Attention Disorders, 15*(5), 412–422.

Huth, A. G., de Heer, W. A., Griffiths, T. L., Theunissen, F. E., & Gallant, J. L. (2016). Natural speech reveals the semantic maps that tile human cerebral cortex. *Nature, 532*(7600), 453–458.

Insel, T., Cuthbert, B., Garvey, M., Heinssen, R., Pine, D. S., Quinn, K., et al. (2010). Research domain criteria (RDoC): Toward a new classification framework for research on mental disorders. *The American Journal of Psychiatry, 167*(7), 748–751.

Johnson, M. W., Bickel, W. K., Baker, F., Moore, B. A., Badger, G. J., & Budney, A. J. (2010). Delay discounting in current and former marijuana-dependent individuals. *Experimental and Clinical Psychopharmacology, 18*(1), 99–107.

Johnson, M. W., & Bruner, N. R. (2012). The sexual discounting task: HIV risk behavior and the discounting of delayed sexual rewards in cocaine dependence. *Drug and Alcohol Dependence, 123,* 15–21.

Johnson, M. W., & Bruner, N. R. (2013). Test-retest reliability and gender differences in the sexual discounting task among cocaine-dependent individuals. *Experimental and Clinical Psychopharmacology, 21*(4), 997–1003.

Kahneman, D. (2011). *Thinking, fast and slow*. New York: Macmillan.

Kahneman, D., & Frederick, S. (2002). Representativeness revisited: Attribute substitution in intuitive judgment. In T. Gilovich, D. Griffin, & D. Kahneman (Eds.), *Heuristics and biases: The psychology of intuitive judgment* (pp. 49–81). New York, NY: Cambridge University Press.

Kaplan, B. A., Reed, D. D., & Jarmolowicz, D. P. (2015). Effects of episodic future thinking on discounting: Personalized age-progressed pictures improve risky long-term health decisions. *Journal of Applied Behavior Analysis, 49,* 148–169.

Kekic, M., Bartholdy, S., Cheng, J., McClelland, J., Boysen, E., Musiat, P., et al. (2016). Increased temporal discounting in bulimia nervosa. *The International Journal of Eating Disorders* (in press).

Killeen, P. R. (2009). An additive-utility model of delay discounting. *Psychological Review, 116* (3), 602–619.

King, J. A., Geisler, D., Bernardoni, F., Ritschel, F., Böhm, I., Seidel, M., et al. (2016). Altered neural efficiency of decision making during temporal reward discounting in anorexia nervosa. *Journal of the American Academy of Child and Adolescent Psychiatry, 55*(11), 972–979.

Kirby, K. N. (1997). Bidding on the future: Evidence against normative discounting of delayed rewards. *Journal of Experimental Psychology: General, 126*(1), 54.

Koffarnus, M. N., & Bickel, W. K. (2014). A 5-trial adjusting delay discounting task: Accurate discount rates in less than one minute. *Experimental and Clinical Psychopharmacology, 22*(3), 222–228.

Koffarnus, M. N., Franck, C. T., Stein, J. S., & Bickel, W. K. (2015). A modified exponential behavioral economic demand model to better describe consumption data. *Experimental and Clinical Psychopharmacology, 23*(6), 504–512.

Krosch, A. R., & Amodio, D. M. (2014). Economic scarcity alters the perception of race. *Proceedings of the National Academy of Sciences (USA), 111*(25), 9079–9084.

Kwan, D., Craver, C. F., Green, L., Myerson, J., Gao, F., Black, S. E., et al. (2015). Cueing the personal future to reduce discounting in intertemporal choice: Is episodic prospection necessary? *Hippocampus, 25*(4), 432–443.

Kwan, D., Craver, C. F., Green, L., Myerson, J., & Rosenbaum, R. S. (2013). Dissociations in future thinking following hippocampal damage: Evidence from discounting and time perspective in episodic amnesia. *Journal of Experimental Psychology: General, 142*(4), 1355–1369.

Lebeau, G., Consoli, S. M., Le Bouc, R., Sola-Gazagnes, A., Hartemann, A., Simon, D., et al. (2016). Delay discounting of gains and losses, glycemic control and therapeutic adherence in type 2 diabetes. *Behavioural Processes, 132,* 42–48.

Lin, H., & Epstein, L. H. (2014). Living in the moment: Effects of time perspective and emotional valence of episodic thinking on delay discounting. *Behavioral Neuroscience, 128*(1), 12–19.

Liu, L., Feng, T., Chen, J., & Li, H. (2013). The value of emotion: How does episodic prospection modulate delay discounting? *PLoS ONE, 8*(11), e81717.

Liu, W.-H., Roiser, J. P., Wang, L.-Z., Zhu, Y.-H., Huang, J., Neumann, D. L., et al. (2016). Anhedonia is associated with blunted reward sensitivity in first-degree relatives of patients with major depression. *Journal of Affective Disorders, 190,* 640–648.

Loomes, G., & Sugden, R. (1982). Regret theory: An alternative theory of rational choice under uncertainty. *The Economic Journal of Nepal, 92*(368), 805–824.

Lu, Q., Tao, F., Hou, F., Zhang, Z., Sun, Y., Xu, Y., et al. (2014). Cortisol reactivity, delay discounting and percent body fat in Chinese urban young adolescents. *Appetite, 72,* 13–20.

Mach, E., & McCormack, T. J. (1907). *The science of mechanics: A critical and historical exposition of its principles*. Chicago: Open Court Publishing Company.

MacKillop, J., Amlung, M. T., Few, L. R., Ray, L. A., Sweet, L. H., & Munafò, M. R. (2011). Delayed reward discounting and addictive behavior: A meta-analysis. *Psychopharmacology (Berlin), 216*(3), 305–321.

MacKillop, J., & Tidey, J. W. (2011). Cigarette demand and delayed reward discounting in nicotine-dependent individuals with schizophrenia and controls: An initial study. *Psychopharmacology (Berlin), 216*(1), 91–99.

Madden, G. J., & Johnson, P. S. (2010). A delay-discounting primer. In G. J. Madden & W. K. Bickel (Eds.), *Impulsivity: The behavioral and neurological science of discounting* (pp. 11–37). Washington, DC: American Psychological Association.

Madden, G. J., Petry, N. M., Badger, G. J., & Bickel, W. K. (1997). Impulsive and self-control choices in opioid-dependent patients and non-drug-using control patients: Drug and monetary rewards. *Experimental and Clinical Psychopharmacology, 5*(3), 256.

Mani, A., Mullainathan, S., Shafir, E., & Zhao, J. (2013). Poverty impedes cognitive function. *Science, 341*(6149), 976–980.

Mar, R. A. (2004). The neuropsychology of narrative: Story comprehension, story production and their interrelation. *Neuropsychologia, 42*(10), 1414–1434.

Mazur, J. E. (1987). An adjusting procedure for studying delayed reinforcement. In M. L. Commons, J. E. Mazur, J. A. Nevin, & H. Rachlin (Eds.), *Quantitative analysis of behavior: Vol. 5. The effect of delay and of intervening events of reinforcement value*. (pp. 55–73). Hillsdale, NJ: Erlbaum.

McClure, S. M., Laibson, D. I., Loewenstein, G., & Cohen, J. D. (2004). Separate neural systems value immediate and delayed monetary rewards. *Science, 306*(5695), 503–507.

Medina, K. L., McQueeny, T., Nagel, B. J., Hanson, K. L., Schweinsburg, A. D., & Tapert, S. F. (2008). Prefrontal cortex volumes in adolescents with alcohol use disorders: Unique gender effects. *Alcoholism, Clinical and Experimental Research, 32*(3), 386–394.

Medina, K. L., McQueeny, T., Nagel, B. J., Hanson, K. L., Yang, T. T., & Tapert, S. F. (2009). Prefrontal cortex morphometry in abstinent adolescent marijuana users: Subtle gender effects. *Addiction Biology, 14*(4), 457–468.

Metcalfe, J., & Mischel, W. (1999). A hot/cool-system analysis of delay of gratification: Dynamics of willpower. *Psychological Review, 106*(1), 3–19.

Miedl, S. F., Peters, J., & Büchel, C. (2012). Altered neural reward representations in pathological gamblers revealed by delay and probability discounting. *Archives of General Psychiatry, 69*(2), 177–186.

Mitchell, S. D. (2009). *Unsimple truths: Science, complexity, and policy*. Chicago: University of Chicago Press.

Mitchell, S. H. (1999). Measures of impulsivity in cigarette smokers and non-smokers. *Psychopharmacology (Berlin), 146*(4), 455–464.

Moallem, N. R., & Ray, L. A. (2012). Dimensions of impulsivity among heavy drinkers, smokers, and heavy drinking smokers: Singular and combined effects. *Addictive Behaviors, 37*(7), 871–874.

Moody, L., Franck, C., Hatz, L., & Bickel, W. K. (2016). Impulsivity and polysubstance use: A systematic comparison of delay discounting in Mono-, Dual-, and Trisubstance use. *Experimental and Clinical Psychopharmacology, 24*(1), 30–37.

Negash, S., Sheppard, N. V. N., Lambert, N. M., & Fincham, F. D. (2016). Trading later rewards for current pleasure: Pornography consumption and delay discounting. *Journal of Sex Research, 53*(6), 689–700.

Nummenmaa, L., Saarimäki, H., Glerean, E., Gotsopoulos, A., Jääskeläinen, I. P., Hari, R., et al. (2014). Emotional speech synchronizes brains across listeners and engages large-scale dynamic brain networks. *NeuroImage, 102,* 498–509.

Odum, A. L. (2011). Delay discounting: I'm ak, you're ak. *Journal of the Experimental Analysis of Behavior, 96*(3), 427–439.

Odum, A. L., Madden, G. J., Badger, G. J., & Bickel, W. K. (2000). Needle sharing in opioid-dependent outpatients: Psychological processes underlying risk. *Drug and Alcohol Dependence, 60*(3), 259–266.

O'Neill, J., Daniel, T. O., & Epstein, L. H. (2016). Episodic future thinking reduces eating in a food court. *Eating Behaviors, 20,* 9–13.

Paloyelis, Y., Asherson, P., Mehta, M. A., Faraone, S. V., & Kuntsi, J. (2010). DAT1 and COMT effects on delay discounting and trait impulsivity in male adolescents with attention deficit/hyperactivity disorder and healthy controls. *Neuropsychopharmacology, 35*(12), 2414–2426.

Peters, J., & Büchel, C. (2010). Episodic future thinking reduces reward delay discounting through an enhancement of prefrontal-mediotemporal interactions. *Neuron, 66*(1), 138–148.

Petry, N. M. (2001a). Delay discounting of money and alcohol in actively using alcoholics, currently abstinent alcoholics, and controls. *Psychopharmacology (Berlin), 154*(3), 243–250.

Petry, N. M. (2001b). Pathological gamblers, with and without substance abuse disorders, discount delayed rewards at high rates. *Journal of Abnormal Psychology, 110*(3), 482.

Petry, N. M., Bickel, W. K., & Arnett, M. (1998). Shortened time horizons and insensitivity to future consequences in heroin addicts. *Addiction, 93*(5), 72973.

Petry, N. M., & Casarella, T. (1999). Excessive discounting of delayed rewards in substance abusers with gambling problems. *Drug and Alcohol Dependence, 56*(1), 25–32.

Pinto, A., Steinglass, J. E., Greene, A. L., Weber, E. U., & Simpson, H. B. (2014). Capacity to delay reward differentiates obsessive-compulsive disorder and obsessive-compulsive personality disorder. *Biological Psychiatry, 75*(8), 653–659.

Quisenberry, A. J., Eddy, C. R., Patterson, D. L., Franck, C. T., & Bickel, W. K. (2015a). Regret expression and social learning increases delay to sexual gratification. *PLoS ONE, 10*(8), e0135977.

Quisenberry, A. J., Koffarnus, M. N., Hatz, L. E., Epstein, L. H., & Bickel, W. K. (2015b). The experimental tobacco marketplace I: Substitutability as a function of the price of conventional cigarettes. *Nicotine & Tobacco Research, 18*(7), 1642–1648.

Rachlin, H., & Jones, B. A. (2008). Social discounting and delay discounting. *Journal of Behavioral Decision Making, 21*(1), 29–43.

Rachlin, H., Raineri, A., & Cross, D. (1991). Subjective probability and delay. *Journal of the Experimental Analysis of Behavior, 55*(2), 233–244.

Rahimi-Golkhandan, S., Garavito, D. M. N., Reyna-Brainerd, B. B., & Reyna, V. F. (2017). A fuzzy-trace theory of risk and time preferences in decision making: Integrating cognition and motivation. In J. R. Stevens (Ed.), *Impulsivity, Nebraska Symposium on Motivation*. New York: Springer.

Rasmussen, E. B., Lawyer, S. R., & Reilly, W. (2010). Percent body fat is related to delay and probability discounting for food in humans. *Behavioural Processes, 83*(1), 23–30.

Reach, G., Michault, A., Bihan, H., Paulino, C., Cohen, R., & Le Clésiau, H. (2011). Patients' impatience is an independent determinant of poor diabetes control. *Diabetes & Metabolism, 37* (6), 497–504.

Reed, D. D. (2015). Ultra-violet indoor tanning addiction: A reinforcer pathology interpretation. *Addictive Behaviors, 41,* 247–251.

Reimers, S., Maylor, E. A., Stewart, N., & Chater, N. (2009). Associations between a one-shot delay discounting measure and age, income, education and real-world impulsive behavior. *Personality and Individual Differences, 47*(8), 973–978.

Reyna, V. F., & Brainerd, C. J. (1995). Fuzzy-trace theory: An interim synthesis. *Learning and Individual Differences, 7,* 1–75.

Reynolds, B., Richards, J. B., Horn, K., & Karraker, K. (2004). Delay discounting and probability discounting as related to cigarette smoking status in adults. *Behavioural Processes, 65*(1), 35–42.

Richards, J. B., Mitchell, S. H., de Wit, H., & Seiden, L. S. (1997). Determination of discount functions in rats with an adjusting-amount procedure. *Journal of the Experimental Analysis of Behavior, 67*(3), 353–366.

Ritschel, F., King, J. A., Geisler, D., Flohr, L., Neidel, F., Boehm, I., et al. (2015). Temporal delay discounting in acutely ill and weight-recovered patients with anorexia nervosa. *Psychological Medicine, 45*(6), 1229–1239.

Robbins, T. W., & Dalley, J. W. (in press). Dissecting impulsivity: Brain mechanisms and neuropsychiatric implications. In J. Stephens (Ed.), *Impulsivity: How time and risk influence decision-making*. New York: Springer.

Rollins, B. Y., Dearing, K. K., & Epstein, L. H. (2010). Delay discounting moderates the effect of food reinforcement on energy intake among non-obese women. *Appetite, 55*(3), 420–425.

Scheres, A., Dijkstra, M., Ainslie, E., Balkan, J., Reynolds, B., Sonuga-Barke, E., et al. (2006). Temporal and probabilistic discounting of rewards in children and adolescents: Effects of age and ADHD symptoms. *Neuropsychologia, 44*(11), 2092–2103.

Scheres, A., Lee, A., & Sumiya, M. (2008). Temporal reward discounting and ADHD: Task and symptom specific effects. *Journal of Neural Transmission, 115*(2), 221–226.

Schneider, W., & Shiffrin, R. M. (1977). Controlled and automatic human information processing: I. Detection, search, and attention. *Psychological Review, 84*(1), 1.

Shah, A. K., Mullainathan, S., & Shafir, E. (2012). Some consequences of having too little. *Science, 338,* 682–685.

Shefrin, H. M., & Thaler, R. (1977). *An economic theory of self-control (No. w20320)*. Cambridge: National Bureau of Economic Research.

Skurvydas, A. (2005). New methodology in biomedical science: Methodological errors in classical science. *Medicina, 41*(1), 7–16.

Snider, S. E., LaConte, S. M., & Bickel, W. K. (2016a). Episodic future thinking: Expansion of the temporal window in individuals with alcohol dependence. *Alcoholism, Clinical and Experimental Research, 40*(7), 1558–1566.

Snider, S. E., Quisenberry, A. J., & Bickel, W. K. (2016b). Order in the absence of an effect: Identifying rate-dependent relationships. *Behavioural Processes, 127,* 18–24.

Steinglass, J. E., Figner, B., Berkowitz, S., Simpson, H. B., Weber, E. U., & Walsh, B. T. (2012). Increased capacity to delay reward in anorexia nervosa. *Journal of the International Neuropsychological Society, 18*(4), 773–780.

Stein, J. S., & Bickel, W. K. (unpublished data). Effects of episodic future thinking on cigarette demand in smokers.

Stein, J. S., Wilson, A. G., Koffarnus, M. N., Daniel, T. O., Epstein, L. H., & Bickel, W. K. (2016). Unstuck in time: Episodic future thinking reduces delay discounting and cigarette smoking. *Psychopharmacology (Berlin), 233,* 3771.

Stoltman, J. J. K., Woodcock, E. A., Lister, J. J., Lundahl, L. H., & Greenwald, M. K. (2015). Heroin delay discounting: Modulation by pharmacological state, drug-use impulsivity, and intelligence. *Experimental and Clinical Psychopharmacology, 23*(6), 455–463.

Strange, K. (2005). The end of "naive reductionism": Rise of systems biology or renaissance of physiology? *American Journal of Physiology-Cell Physiology, 288*(5), C968–C974.

Sze, Y. Y., Daniel, T. O., Kilanowski, C. K., Collins, R. L., & Epstein, L. H. (2015). Web-based and mobile delivery of an episodic future thinking intervention for overweight and obese families: A feasibility study. *JMIR mHealth and uHealth, 3*(4), e97.

Sze, Y. Y., Stein, J. S., Bickel, W. K., Paluch, R. A., & Epstein, L. A. (under review). Bleak present, bright future: Combined effects of negative income shock and episodic future thinking on delay discounting and food demand in an online sample.

Uher, R., Murphy, T., Brammer, M. J., Dalgleish, T., Phillips, M. L., Ng, V. W., et al. (2004). Medial prefrontal cortex activity associated with symptom provocation in eating disorders. *The American Journal of Psychiatry, 161*(7), 1238–1246.

Vuchinich, R. E., & Simpson, C. A. (1998). Hyperbolic temporal discounting in social drinkers and problem drinkers. *Experimental and Clinical Psychopharmacology, 6*(3), 292–305.

Wang, W., Wang, Y.-R., Qin, W., Yuan, K., Tian, J., Li, Q., et al. (2010). Changes in functional connectivity of ventral anterior cingulate cortex in heroin abusers. *Chinese Medical Journal, 123*(12), 1582–1588.

Weller, R. E., Cook, E. W., 3rd, Avsar, K. B., & Cox, J. E. (2008). Obese women show greater delay discounting than healthy-weight women. *Appetite, 51*(3), 563–569.

Wiehler, A., Bromberg, U., & Peters, J. (2015). The role of prospection in steep temporal reward discounting in gambling addiction. *Frontiers in Psychiatry, 6,* 112.

Wilson, A. G., Franck, C. T., Koffarnus, M. N., & Bickel, W. K. (2016). Behavioral economics of cigarette purchase tasks: Within-subject comparison of real, potentially real, and hypothetical cigarettes. *Nicotine & Tobacco Research, 18*(5), 524–530.

Wilson, V. B., Mitchell, S. H., Musser, E. D., Schmitt, C. F., & Nigg, J. T. (2011). Delay discounting of reward in ADHD: Application in young children. *Journal of Child Psychology and Psychiatry and Allied Disciplines, 52*(3), 256–264.

Wing, V. C., Moss, T. G., Rabin, R. A., & George, T. P. (2012). Effects of cigarette smoking status on delay discounting in schizophrenia and healthy controls. *Addictive Behaviors, 37*(1), 67–72.

Woolf, S. H., Aron, L., et al. (2013). *U.S. health in international perspective: Shorter lives, poorer health.* Washington, D.C.: National Academies Press.

Yi, R., de la Piedad, X., & Bickel, W. K. (2006a). The combined effects of delay and probability in discounting. *Behavioural Processes, 73*(2), 149–155.

Yi, R., Gatchalian, K. M., & Bickel, W. K. (2006b). Discounting of past outcomes. *Experimental and Clinical Psychopharmacology, 14*(3), 311–317.

Yi, R., Pickover, A., Stuppy-Sullivan, A. M., Baker, S., & Landes, R. D. (2016). Impact of episodic thinking on altruism. *Journal of Experimental Social Psychology, 65,* 74–81.

Yoon, J. H., & Higgins, S. T. (2008). Turning k on its head: Comments on use of an ED50 in delay discounting research. *Drug and Alcohol Dependence, 95*(1–2), 169–172.

Yuan, K., Qin, W., Dong, M., Liu, J., Liu, P., Zhang, Y., et al. (2010). Combining spatial and temporal information to explore resting-state networks changes in abstinent heroin-dependent individuals. *Neuroscience Letters, 475*(1), 20–24.

Zeelenberg, M., & Pieters, R. (2004). Consequences of regret aversion in real life: The case of the Dutch postcode lottery. *Organizational Behavior and Human Decision Processes, 93*(2), 155–168.

Index

A
Abstinence, 207
Abundance, 248, 250, 251, 253–255
Academic, 8, 10, 26, 28, 31, 52, 55, 61, 128, 146, 147
Academic achievement, 128
Academic competence, 28
Accelerating-delivery approach, 149
Accept-or-reject decision, 164, 166, 168–170, 185
Accuracy, 42–44, 170, 210
Acetylcholine system, 156
Action optimization, 171
Activity risk, 99, 101
Adaptive foraging, 168, 170, 173, 175, 189
Adaptive functioning, 7, 8, 25, 27, 38, 55
Adaptive self-regulation, 45, 46
Addiction, 5, 207, 214, 228, 229, 236, 240, 243, 245, 250
Adjusting-amount task, 229, 230, 254
Adolescent Coping Questionnaire, 31, 34
Adolescents, 8, 27, 28, 30, 31, 33, 36, 37, 121–123, 125, 133, 135, 136, 215, 216, 235, 246
Adrenergic 2A receptors, 156
Adulthood, 4, 34, 42, 43, 51, 121, 122, 124–126, 132
Age, 4, 12, 13, 31, 34, 35, 38, 40, 49, 55, 62, 72–76, 100, 115, 121, 123–126, 128, 129, 135, 214, 232, 233
Aggression, 8, 37–39
Agriculture, 63, 78, 80, 86, 95, 99, 137
AIDS, 97, 251
Alcohol, 10, 126, 128, 135, 145, 207, 215, 216, 218, 230, 233, 236, 240, 246, 247
Alcohol-associated disease, 145
Alertness, 177
Altruism, 253
Amazon mechanical turk, 254–256
Amnesic patients, 246
Amphetamine, 205, 217
Amygdala, 156, 179, 204, 209, 238
Analytical processing, 120, 122, 124, 127, 132, 135
Anhedonia, 201, 202, 239
Animal models, 147, 149, 202, 218
Anorexia nervosa, 239
Anterior cingulate cortex, 156, 165, 175, 176, 208, 213
Anterior insula, 184
Anthropology, 3, 61, 72
Anticipation, 1, 16, 95–97, 103, 256
Anticipatory utility, 103
Anti-sense oligonucleotide sequence, 208
Anti-social behavior, 201
Anxieties, 37, 66, 79, 98, 103
Apathy, 153, 156, 157, 201, 202
Arbitrage, 103
Arcuate fasciculus, 214
Arousal, 18, 131–133
Arousing, 18–21, 23–25
Assumptions, 11, 66, 102, 171, 206, 211, 230
Astrological fortune, 65, 99
Atomoxetine, 210, 211, 213, 216
Attention, 4, 5, 8, 13–17, 20, 23, 25, 27, 28, 31, 34, 37, 41, 48–52, 55, 61, 132, 133, 148, 156, 171, 176, 183, 189, 201, 204, 206, 210, 212, 235, 250, 254
Attention-deficit/hyperactivity disorder (ADHD), 4, 5, 148, 156, 189, 201, 210–212, 214, 216, 217, 220
Attention-deficit, 4, 5, 148, 156, 201, 210
Attitudes, 10, 75, 128, 129
Automatic, 40, 46, 115, 238
Autoradiographic studies, 208
Azande, 97

J.R. Stevens (ed.), *Impulsivity*, Nebraska Symposium on Motivation 64,
DOI 10.1007/978-3-319-51721-6

B
Background choice, 166, 172, 174, 175
Background reward rates, 185
Bandit tasks, 173, 174, 179, 183, 184
Barratt Impulsiveness, 134, 148, 201
Barriers, 151
Basal ganglia, 168, 175, 177, 186, 215, 216
Base rate frequencies, 96
Basolateral amygdala, 156, 209
Battery, 202, 215
Beads task, 217, 218
Behavioral Avoidance and Approach Systems (BAS), 201
Behavioral correlates, 2
Behavioral economic demand, 241, 243, 246, 255
Behavioral economics, 65, 115, 150
Behavioral outcomes, 236
Behavior optimization, 167
Beliefs, 12, 13, 19, 134
Bell, 8, 9, 13, 14, 25, 53–55, 256
Berries, 165
Biking/motorcycling, 237
Bing Consistency Study, 26
Binge-access chronic paradigm, 207
Binge drinkers, 216, 218
Binge-eating disorder, 234, 237
Bing Longitudinal Study, 25, 27, 28, 30, 31, 34–37, 40–42, 45, 47–49, 52, 54, 56
Bing Nursery School, 13, 55
Biology, 3
Biomarker, 128
Block's California child Q-set, 26
Blood-oxygen-level-dependent (BOLD) activity, 181, 182, 184, 203, 205, 214–216
Boas's, Franz, 66
Body Mass Index (BMI), 34–36, 75, 243
Borderline personality disorder, 39, 40
Boredom, 36
Bottom-line meaning, 115, 117, 118, 121, 122, 135, 238
Bounded rationality, 62, 95
Brainstem, 176, 189
Breakfast, 232, 237
Bridging, 15
Button presses, 42, 151

C
Calculating thinking, 124
Candy, 1, 10, 22, 76, 102
Cannabis, 216
Capability, 48
Cardiovascular disease, 145
Carleton Consistency Study, 26
Catecholamine receptors, 177
Catecholamines, 165, 176, 177, 210
Categorical differences, 119, 122
Categorical distinctions, 122, 129, 132, 133
Caudate, 213
Causality, 66, 67, 95–98, 102
Causal models, 97, 103
Causal narratives, 98
Caenorhabditis elegans, 177
Changepoint detection, 166, 174, 175, 184
Changes in the environment, 168, 171, 176, 183, 187, 188
Chemogenetics, 209
Children, 4, 5, 7, 8–40, 46–56, 75, 96, 98, 102, 121, 122, 124, 125, 133, 135, 136, 235, 247
Chile, 62, 73
Choice, 1–5, 9–13, 22, 24, 46, 48, 52–55, 61, 62, 65–72, 74–79, 81–89, 92–95, 101–103, 116, 118–123, 125–137, 146–149, 151–154, 163–168, 170–182, 184, 185, 187–189, 202–204, 207–212, 217, 228–230, 239, 242, 254, 256
Choice experiments, 61, 62, 67, 68, 70, 71, 79, 83, 94, 95, 101, 102, 104
Chromosome 1, 205
Chromosome 1q31-1q34, 205
Cigarettes, 10, 148–150, 236, 242, 246, 247
Cigarette smokers, 148, 246
Cigarillos, 243
Cingulate cortex, 127, 130, 156, 165, 175, 176, 178, 183, 208, 213, 215, 216
Circuitry, 4, 5, 43, 45, 163, 171, 176, 180, 184, 186, 189, 204, 206, 212, 216–218
Cirrhosis, 145
Citalopram, 213
Classical decision theory, 116
Classification, 44, 45, 204, 217
Climate and ecology, 99
Cocaine, 207, 210, 211, 215, 236
Coefficient of variation (CV), 71
Coefficients of relative, 71
Cognitive Affective Processing System (CAPS), 37
Cognitive assessments, 41
Cognitive biases, 121, 122, 136
Cognitive control, 41, 43, 45, 51, 54, 55, 218, 220, 254
Cognitive effort, 151–154, 157
Cognitively transform, 21, 24
Cognitive mechanism, 4
Cognitive performance, 254
Cognitive reflection, 134
Coin flips, 84, 87

Commodity, 26, 150, 236, 241–243, 246–249, 252, 258
Comparator, 169
Competencies, 12, 28, 33, 36, 41
Competing Neurobehavioral Decision Systems (CNDS), 228, 238–240, 243, 257
Competition, 165
Complements, 119, 120, 133, 186, 242
Compulsions, 189
Compulsive gamblers, 218
Compulsivity, 201, 202
Computational complexity, 172
Computational mechanisms, 168
Computer science, 171
Concave utility, 103
Conceptual space, 173
Conditioned cues, 204
Condom, 233, 237, 256
Conflict processing task, 189
Conformist social learning, 62
Congolese BaYaka, 103
Consequences, 1, 3, 9, 12, 20, 35, 36, 55, 126, 132, 145, 146, 163, 165, 188, 201, 205, 207, 227, 228, 231, 237, 239, 240, 256, 257
Consistency, 11, 26, 27, 37, 72, 92–94, 102, 103, 119
Constant risk aversion, 71
Construal, 131
Consummatory, 20–25, 28, 46, 49
Context, 2, 4, 9, 12, 13, 49, 52, 65, 92, 101–103, 117–119, 124, 126, 131, 163–167, 169–174, 176, 178, 179, 181, 182, 185, 187–189, 212, 239, 246, 249, 258
Contextual cues, 12, 24, 55, 254
Contextual variation, 12
Contingency, 19, 28, 53, 54, 96
Contingent negative variation, 204
Control system, 169
Coping plans, 13
Core region, 208, 211
Corticosterone responses, 207
Cosmological uncertainties, 66
Costs, 2, 46, 68, 79, 83, 150, 152, 166–169, 179, 181, 231, 240, 241, 243
Costs of waiting, 68
Covariation, 96, 97, 101
Creator/listener, 245
Credit markets, 71
Crops, 95, 96, 98
Crossover design, 17, 20, 22
Cued choice task, 189
Cultural differences, 4
Cultural inheritance, 62
Cultural relativism, 66
Culture, 3, 4, 8, 61, 62, 65, 66, 71, 96, 97, 102, 103
Cumulative risk, 123
Curve fitting, 171

D
Dangers, 165
DA transporter (DAT), 208
Death, 65, 66, 97, 128
Decision circuits, 163
Deep brain stimulation, 208
Default and non-default choices, 167, 185
Delay, 1, 2, 4, 7–56, 63, 68, 71, 76, 78, 79, 88, 98, 115, 127, 128, 130–132, 134–137, 146–150, 154, 155, 180, 203–205, 209, 217, 219, 228–230, 232–236, 239, 247, 253, 256, 257
Delay aversion, 146, 203
Delay choice, 2, 10–12, 52, 53
Delay deviation score, 28
Delay discounting, 2, 115, 130, 131, 137, 146, 228, 229, 232–236, 247
Delayed gratification, 2, 8, 203, 209
Delayed rewards, 4, 68, 84, 85, 94, 95, 98, 126, 127, 130, 133, 136, 203, 228, 229, 239
Delay maintenance, 2, 10–12, 31, 53
Delay of gratification, 1, 4, 7–11, 13, 17, 20, 25–27, 30, 31, 35, 38–40, 47, 48, 50, 52, 54–56, 115, 127, 131, 132, 134–137
Deliberative thinking, 124
Demand, 122, 150, 151, 241–243, 246, 249, 255
Demand curve, 243
Demographic, 31, 89, 92, 95
Density, 169, 240
Dental hygiene, 145
Depressant effects, 145
Depression, 4, 37, 156, 239
Desire, 18, 46, 67
Developmental difference, 115, 124, 136
Developmental reversals, 121
Diabetes, 145, 233, 235, 240
Diagnostic and Statistical Manual, 231
Die, 97, 120, 182
Diet, 7, 10, 72, 145, 181, 230, 232–234, 244
Dietary diversity, 89, 90, 91, 93, 105–108, 164
Diffusion tensor imaging, 214
Dip, 243
Directed forgetting task, 43, 46, 47
Discounting, 1–4, 10, 11, 68, 69, 77, 95, 115, 127–137, 146–157, 167, 202–204, 209, 210, 212–214, 217, 228–237, 239, 240, 243, 246–258
Discounting curve, 229, 257

Discounting functions, 11, 151, 152, 154
Discount parameter, 68, 69, 72, 86, 92, 128
Discount rate, 72, 76, 77, 83, 102, 103, 128–130, 133, 136, 228, 229, 254, 255
Disease, 5, 66, 97, 128, 145, 176, 177, 228, 230, 231, 237, 239, 240, 258
Disease trajectories, 231
Dispositions, 12, 24, 48
Dissociation, 202, 210, 217
Distance (or spatial) discounting, 3
Distance travelled, 150
Distraction, 15, 16, 17, 20, 48, 50, 177
Distribution of reward sizes, 173
Diversions, 15, 49
Diviner, 64, 65
Dominoes, 84, 88
Dopamine (DA), 156, 165, 168, 177, 189, 204, 205, 208, 212
Dopaminergic pathways, 165
Dopaminergic receptors, 156
Dorsal, 176, 203, 207, 208, 212
Dorsal raphé neurons, 210
Dorsolateral PFC, 129, 130, 218
Drowsiness, 177
D1 receptors, 208, 212
D2/3 receptor, 208, 214
D3 receptor antagonist nafadotride, 208
Drug use, 8, 135, 215, 216, 227, 240, 243
Dual-process models, 45, 115, 127, 131, 133, 238
Dysregulation, 176, 189, 240, 245

E

E-cigarettes, 243
Economic outcomes, 56
Economics, 3, 61, 102, 115, 150
Educational attainments, 38, 39
Effective delay 50 (ED50), 236
Effort, 2–4, 10, 12, 15, 24, 26, 27, 37, 40, 41, 46, 48, 50, 56, 67, 116, 146, 150–157, 219, 243
Effort discounting, 4, 146, 150–157
Ego-control, 30, 48
Ego-resiliency, 30
Eigenvalues, 202, 215
Electrical stimulation, 187
Electric foot-shock, 207
Elevated plus maze, 206
Emotion, 9, 12, 38, 51, 102, 103, 244
Emotional intelligence, 8
Emotionally laden, 42, 43, 46
Emotionally neutral, 42
Empathy scale, 148
Employment, 228, 243
Encounter rate, 171
Endophenotype, 214–217
Endurance, 98
Energy expenditure, 150, 151, 174
Energy intake, 243
Enjoyment, 252
Environmental exploration, 171
Environmental sciences, 3
Episodic future thinking (EFT), 246–250, 252, 253, 255
Episodic past thinking, 248, 252
Episodic recent thinking (ERT), 250, 252, 255
Episodic thinking, 252, 253, 255
Epistemology, 95, 96
Error of commission, 204
Error of omission, 204
Error rate, 121
Ethical Concerns, 83
Ethnographic, 72
Etiologies, 230, 231
Evidence accumulation, 218
Evolution, 150, 188
Exams, 27, 45, 56, 66, 137, 231, 232, 251
Excitement, 251, 252
Executive systems, 239, 243
Executive control, 40, 41, 239, 240
Executive decision system, 239, 243–246, 257
Exercise, 10, 85, 88, 95, 97, 98, 233
Existential categories, 66
Expectancies, 12
Expectations, 11, 38, 53, 54, 86, 167
Expected utility (EU), 67
Expected utility (EUT), 116
Expect value (EV), 67
Experimental economics, 65
Experimental Tobacco Marketplace, 242
Expertise, 121–125
Exploration/exploitation trade-offs, 167
Exploration, 8, 9, 19, 27, 28, 41, 45, 46, 56, 164, 171, 176, 183, 184, 254
Exponential decay, 68
External validity, 94, 101, 102
Extinction-reinstatement procedure, 207
Extraversion, 201, 202
Eye tracking, 122

F

Faces, 2, 5, 10, 12, 23, 42, 43, 46–48, 54, 98, 174
False alarms, 42, 43
Familial history, 12
Family, 79, 98, 214, 228, 243
Family time, 243
Farmer-herders, 62, 63

Farmers, 63, 72–76, 78, 78, 79, 85, 86, 96, 102, 103, 164, 173, 254
Fast food, 237
Fearful, 32, 42, 43, 46
Fiber-sparing cell body lesions, 212
Fiber-sparing excitotoxic lesions, 205
Finance, 3
Fishermen, 63, 78, 79
Fishing, 63, 66, 71–73, 75, 78–80, 89, 90–95, 97–99, 101
Fishing gear, 63
Fitness, 163
Five Choice serial reaction time task (FCSRTT), 204
Flanker task, 151
Flexible, 12, 30, 35, 48, 54, 92, 164, 173
Flights of stairs, 151
Flossing, 232, 237
Flu shots, 232, 237
FMRI imaging, 41, 50
Folk taxonomies, 65
Food, 46, 78, 79, 83, 89, 98, 126, 134, 150, 164–167, 174, 232, 239, 240, 242, 243, 246, 247, 255
Food insecure, 79
Food insecurity, 89, 90, 91, 93, 105–108
Food pellet, 204
Food resources, 164
Foraging, 4, 5, 72, 78–80, 89, 92–95, 97–99, 101, 103, 106–108, 150, 163–183, 185, 186, 188, 189, 244
Foraging circuit, 165, 172, 175, 176, 183
Foraging decisions, 163, 165, 167, 169, 170, 172–177, 179, 182, 183, 186, 188
Foraging path, 164, 168, 186
Foraging strategy, 167, 171, 180, 188
Foraging theory, 150
Force, 97, 101, 103, 150, 152, 155, 165, 179
Foregone offers, 182, 185
Foreground option, 166–170, 172, 173, 176, 179, 180
Forest foragers, 63, 78
Forethought, 1, 3, 9, 12, 148
Fractional anisotropy, 214
Framing effect, 71, 117, 119–122, 129, 133, 136, 137
Free recall, 164
Fronto-striatal loop, 213
Frugivores, 174
Fruit juice, 204
Frustration, 15, 16, 20, 33, 49
Functional connectivity, 216, 219, 240
Functional opponency, 205, 208
Future anticipation, 97
Future generations, 67
Future rewards, 2, 12, 84, 116, 240, 252, 257
Future thinking, 129
Fuzzy-trace theory (FTT), 115, 117

G

GABA and glutamate receptors, 205
GABA decarboxylase (GAD), 208
GABAergic neurons, 156
Gabor patches, 184
Gains, 16, 24, 62–64, 98, 116–120, 123, 129, 132, 133, 146, 147, 150, 168, 169, 171, 173, 185, 254, 255
Gambles, 65, 67, 69, 70, 75, 102, 117
Gambling, 2, 7, 182, 234, 246
Gambling problems, 128
Gardening, 66
Gathering, 63, 72, 78, 86, 217
Gender roles, 72
Genomics, 215
Genotype, 145, 205
Geometric shapes, 244
Gilles de la Tourette's syndrome, 201
Gist, 4, 115, 117–127, 129–137, 238
Go/no-go task, 42, 43, 45, 46, 203, 213, 215
Goal systems, 12
Go-reaction time (RT), 203
G protein, 177
Gum, 242

H

Habit formation, 103
Habitual behaviors, 174
Habitual foraging, 173
Hand grips, 151
Hangover, 145
Happy, 31, 42, 43, 46, 50, 251
Harvest, 63, 79, 94, 95, 98–100, 163, 166, 173, 174, 181, 182, 186
Health behavior, 5, 228, 230–233, 237, 239, 240, 250
Health disparities, 230
Heroin, 207, 227, 228
Hidden zero, 129, 130, 132, 133, 136, 137
Hierarchical regression, 35
High delayers, 42–45, 47
Hippocampal–striatal–prefrontal cortical mechanism, 170
Hippocampus, 183, 209, 212
HIV, 123, 124, 251
Holistic versus analytical reasoning, 65
Hot/cool processing, 45
5-HT, 209, 210, 213
5-HT1A receptor agonist, 210

5-HT2A receptor antagonism, 210
5-HT2C receptor antagonist, 210
Huinca, 62
Humans, 4, 5, 66, 71, 95–97, 146, 147, 149–151, 154, 165, 180, 202–204, 212, 214, 216, 219, 241, 244
Hunter-gatherers, 72, 76, 78, 103
Hunting, 63, 72, 78, 86, 173
Hyperactivity disorder, 148
Hypoactivation, 215
Hypometabolism, 214
Hypothetical rewards, 72, 75, 83, 84, 151, 235

I

Ideation, 17, 19, 23
Identity groups, 63, 81, 82, 98, 106
IMAGEN project, 215
Imagery, 246, 252
Images, 15, 17, 42, 184, 219, 256
Impressionistic, 117, 124
Impulse control, 8, 9, 47, 53, 215
Impulsive, 2, 47, 102, 124, 131, 136, 165, 206, 207, 210, 238, 239, 243, 245
Impulsive action, 2, 3, 202–204, 213
Impulsive choice, 2, 5, 136, 147, 182, 202–204, 208–211
Impulsive decision making, 125, 202, 228
Impulsive disinhibition, 202
Impulsiveness, 102, 148, 201, 202
Impulsivity, 1–5, 8–10, 12, 24, 30, 48, 55, 102, 115, 124–126, 128–134, 136, 137, 147, 148, 188, 189, 201–214, 216–220
Impulsivity Inventory, 148
Inability to wait, 1, 126
Incentive, 72–74, 76
Income, 62, 63, 72, 73, 76, 78, 89–94, 105–108, 189, 243, 250, 251, 255
Indifference points, 69, 146, 152, 155, 229
Indifference values, 69, 71, 86
Individual difference, 25, 31, 32, 36, 37, 40, 42, 45–47, 49–52, 54, 55, 115, 118, 128, 212, 214, 218
Individualist versus collectivist, 66
Inferences, 55, 125
Inferior frontal cortex, 214, 216, 218
Inferior frontal gyrus, 43, 45, 216
Inflation, 103
Information, 4, 31, 34, 53, 66, 86, 87, 101, 117, 118, 121–123, 125, 126, 164, 167–174, 177, 181–183, 185–189, 202, 231, 238, 244, 245, 256, 258
Informational cue, 18, 20, 23, 24
Information Sampling Task (IFT), 217
Infralimbic cortex, 205, 206, 209
Inhibition, 3, 30, 119, 124, 134, 135, 202–204, 212, 213, 216–218
Inhibitory control, 1, 51, 115
Inhibitory response control, 205, 218
Injurious behaviors, 230
Injury, 99
Insensitivity to consequences, 1
Insensitivity to reward, 239
Institute of Medicine, The, 230
Institutional review board, 83
Insurance premiums, 69, 71
Integrate-to-bound systems, 180
Integrative thinking, 97, 101, 103
Intellectual functioning, 157
Intelligence, 12, 30, 236
Internal validity, 102
Interpatch distance, 173
Interpersonal functioning, 38
Interpretation, 45, 62, 63, 116, 130, 131, 133, 179, 209
Interrupt processes, 171
Intertemporal choice, 1, 2, 62, 66, 89, 102, 146, 163
Inter-trial interval, 205
Intracerebral infusions, 205, 212
Intrusive thoughts (obsessions), 189
Intuition, 96, 115, 123–126, 131, 136
In vivo electrophysiology, 209
IQ, 8
Irrelevant rewards, 17–23

J

Johns Hopkins University, 227
Joystick, 151
Judgment, 4, 29, 33, 42, 61, 71, 103, 115, 122, 124, 125, 135, 137, 149, 151, 238
Jugular vein, 227

K

Kahneman, Daniel, 71, 95, 117, 124, 129, 131, 238
Kalahari San, 72
Ketanserin, 210
Keyboard input, 171
Kinship, 98

L

Laboratory tasks, 119, 125
Land, 63, 75
Lateral orbitofrontal cortex (OFC), 130, 206, 209, 213, 215
Lateral prefrontal, 127, 130, 131, 184, 239, 240
Lateral prefrontal cortex, 127, 186, 239, 240
Leptin, 177

Lever presses, 150, 242
Life, 4, 7, 8, 11, 12, 21, 27, 28, 33–35, 37–39, 41, 43, 45–47, 50, 51, 55, 56, 66, 72, 92, 95, 102, 103, 115, 119, 122, 126, 128, 134, 189, 227, 228, 251
Life outcomes, 4, 7, 8, 27, 35, 37–39, 41, 47, 50
Lifespan, 4, 115
Ligands, 210, 212
Limbic system, 43, 238, 245
Linear discriminant analysis, 44
Lister hooded rat, 205
Livelihoods, 89, 92, 98
Liver disease, 240
Livestock, 62, 63, 89, 97
Locomotor activity, 206
Locus coeruleus, 175, 177
Logarithm of the odds (LOD) score, 205
Longitudinal correlates, 27, 32, 35–37, 51
Longitudinal database, 13
Long-term consequences, 163, 165, 188, 239, 240
Long-term reward rates, 169, 176, 181, 182, 184, 189
Loss aversion, 71
Losses, 62, 63, 67, 74, 87, 116–118, 147, 254, 255
Loss functions, 171
Lottery ticket, 67, 116
Low delayers, 42–45
Lozenges, 242, 243
Lure, 44

M

Madagascar, 61–64, 67, 72, 78, 80–82, 86, 95–98
Magic, 64–66, 97, 98, 100
Magnitude, 72, 79, 116, 123, 127, 128, 130, 131, 133, 151, 178–180, 205, 229, 241, 252
Magnitude of delay, 128, 131
Magnitude of reward, 131
Maize, 79, 80, 82, 84–86, 95, 98
Maladaptive behaviors, 228, 231
Malagasy, 63, 64, 67, 83, 95, 97–99, 101, 103
Mania, 201
Mapuche, 62, 72, 73, 102
Marginal utility, 62, 63, 67, 84, 95
Marginal value theorem, 169, 173
Marine fishers, 63
Market involvement, 72
Market value, 78–80, 89
Marshmallow, 2, 4, 8–11, 13, 16, 17, 20–23, 25–27, 30, 31, 35–37, 41, 42, 45–56, 134
Marshmallow test, 2, 4, 8–11, 13, 17, 22, 23, 25–27, 30, 35–37, 41, 42, 45–56
Masikoro, 63, 64, 72, 78, 79, 81, 82, 87, 90, 91, 93, 97, 98, 105–108
Matching Familiar Figures Task, 217
Mathematical ability, 120
Mathematical education, 84
Mathematical operations, 172
Maximization, 38, 146, 150, 152, 163, 171, 175, 184
Maximum voluntary contraction (MVC), 152, 153
Mazur's hyperbolic discounting, 68, 69
Mean, 15, 16, 31, 44, 66, 69, 71, 72, 74–77, 80, 88, 99, 101, 120, 153, 155, 183, 184, 207
Medial orbital cortex, 204
Medial orbitofrontal cortex (OFC), 130, 165
Medial PFC, 130
Medial prefrontal cortex, 165, 207, 215
Medial rostral prefrontal cortex, 246
Medical advice, 237
Medical screening, 231, 232
Medium spiny cells, 208
Men, 35, 62, 84, 87, 88
Mental images, 15
Mentally devalue rewards, 68
Mental representations, 4, 97, 115, 117, 126, 127, 129, 131, 133, 134, 136, 137
Mental time travel, 246
Meta-analysis, 50, 148, 218, 236
Meta-cognitive monitoring, 119
Methamphetamine, 216
Method of adjustment, 149
Method of constant stimuli, 149
Methylphenidate, 210, 211
Mice, 5, 147
Mikea, 63, 65, 72, 78, 79, 81, 82, 84–87, 90, 91, 93, 94, 97–101, 105–108
Minerals, 164
Mischel, 2, 7, 8, 10–31, 36–38, 41, 45, 46, 48, 50, 51, 53–55, 126, 147, 238
Misfortunes, 64, 65, 97
Monetary Choice Questionnaire, 134, 149
Monetary incentive delay (MID) task, 204
Mood, 252
Morbidity, 230, 258
Mortality, 230, 245, 248, 254, 258
Motivational cue, 18, 24
Motives, 244
Motor/response inhibition, 202, 203, 216, 218
Motor system, 156
Movement, 176, 180, 186, 187

N

Naive physics, 65
Narratives, 86, 98, 103, 229, 244–246, 250, 251, 254–258
National Institute of Child Health and Development (NICHD), 24, 35
National Institute on Alcohol Abuse and Alcoholism, 230
National Institute on Drug Abuse, 230
National Institutes of Health, 137, 230
National politics, 66
National Research Committee, 230
Navigation, 174, 186
N-back memory task, 151
Nematode, 177
Neoclassical economics, 102
Neocortex, 164, 244
Neural circuits, 3–5, 165, 172, 179, 184, 187–189, 205, 215
Neural efficiency, 47
Neural mechanisms, 2, 164, 188, 209
Neural networks, 44, 203, 215, 218
Neural processes, 41, 45–47
Neuroendophenotype, 217
Neurons, 5, 156, 168, 176, 177, 179–183, 186–189, 204, 210
Neurophenotypes, 239
Neuropsychological testing, 215
Neuroscience, 3, 115, 156, 209, 219, 220
Neurotoxins, 205
Neurotransmitters, 4, 210
Nicotine, 207, 215, 240, 242
Noise, 174, 184
Noradrenaline (NA), 81, 210, 211, 213, 216
Norepinephrine, 165, 176, 177, 189, 216
Norepinephrine transporter (NET), 216
Norms, 62, 63, 65, 66, 78, 94
Norms of fairness, 65
Nose poke, 151
Nosology, 217, 220
Novelty, 184, 188, 207
Novelty preference, 207
Novel versus familiar environment, 207
Novices, 122, 123
NP-hard problems, 172
Nucleus accumbens, 50, 203–205, 208–213, 217
Number of responses, 150, 151
Nutrition, 3, 78

O

Obesity, 7, 126, 128, 235–237, 240, 243, 257
Obsessive–compulsive disorder, 176, 189
Occipital areas, 127
Occipitoparietal, 184
Odds, 90–92, 96, 116, 152, 153, 205, 253
Opiate, 217
Opportunity cost, 167, 242
Option, 2, 3, 7, 11, 46, 63, 68–71, 86–94, 103, 105–108, 116, 131, 165, 168, 170, 172, 178, 179, 185, 243, 255, 256
Optogenetics, 209
Ordinal distinctions, 123, 130, 132
Outcomes, 1, 4, 7–12, 14, 15, 18, 27, 35, 38, 41, 44, 47, 50, 52, 56, 66, 67, 75, 101, 102, 116–118, 130, 145, 147, 148, 163, 168, 176, 184, 189, 218, 228, 235, 239, 254, 256, 258
Overactivation, 214, 215
Overeating, 5, 234
Oxygen consumption, 150

P

Pain, 98, 251
Paralimbic, 130, 131, 239, 240
Parallel, 39, 40, 46, 115, 124, 131, 151, 202, 203, 207, 213
Parietal cortex, 127, 184, 215, 219
Parkinson's disease, 5, 177, 202, 216, 220
Pascal, 65, 67
Patch foraging, 173
Patch of resources, 163, 165
Patch types, 166, 173
Patience, 1, 2, 98
Pavlovian appetitive conditioning, 206
Peer acceptance, 38
Pennies, 17
Perception of probabilities, 117–119, 152
Perceptions, 17, 37, 97, 117, 152, 254
Perceptual decision making, 180, 217
Perceptual discriminations, 217
Perseverative foraging behavior, 189
Persistence, 178, 179
Personality, 8, 11, 12, 26, 28, 31, 38–42, 147, 148, 236, 243
Personality trait, 147
Personal risk, 101
Pests, 79, 99, 100
Pharmacological manipulation, 213
Phasic spikes, 177
Photocell cages, 206
Physical effort, 151, 152, 154
Physical inactivity, 230
Physical presence, 13, 17, 18, 20, 22, 30
Physical well-being, 35
Pictures, 17, 21–24, 29, 43, 51, 52, 55, 127, 136, 184, 239, 245, 256

Planning, 51, 131, 164, 167, 170, 172, 174, 201
Playing cards, 98
Polymorphisms, 177
Poorer health, 230
Positive functioning, 38, 39
Positive reinforcement, 204
Positron emission tomography (PET), 212
Posterior cingulate cortex (PCC), 127, 130, 165, 175, 176, 178, 183
Pre-commitment, 219
Precuneus, 218
Predation, 165, 169
Prediction error, 177, 184, 204
Predisposing factor, 216, 217
Preference reversals, 68, 71
Preferences, 3–5, 10–12, 55, 61–63, 66, 69, 72, 74, 75, 79, 81–83, 92–95, 102, 103, 115–117, 119, 125–127, 129, 130, 133, 136
Prefrontal cortex (PFC), 43, 127, 156, 165, 168, 175, 176, 186, 206, 207, 209, 211, 215, 218, 219, 238–240, 244, 246
Premature responding, 204–206, 208–213, 216
Prepotent response, 43
Preschool, 8, 25, 27–36, 38–42, 46–52
Presentation, 18–20, 23, 37, 47, 133, 151, 187, 203, 205, 231
Pre-supplementary area, 215
Pretzel, 8, 11, 13, 14, 16, 17, 20–23
Primates, 147, 151, 164, 165, 171, 174, 202, 244
Principal components, 44, 93, 202, 215, 244
Principle of Least Effort, 150
Probabilistic inference, 171
Probability, 2, 3, 12, 63, 65–67, 69, 71, 84, 88, 95, 96, 103, 116–120, 122, 123, 150, 152, 156, 157, 164, 167, 169, 175, 178, 179, 182–186, 188, 203, 212, 217
Probability discounting, 2, 3, 156, 157, 203, 212, 217, 253
Probability premiums, 63, 71
Problem solving, 164
Process model, 5, 45, 115, 127, 131, 133, 135, 136, 167, 168, 172, 188, 238
Progression and treatment of disease, 145
Property, 92
Prospection, 246, 252
Prospect theory, 117–119
Protective mechanism, 131
Protest responses, 85, 86
Psychiatry, 220
Psychic unity, 66
Psychoactive drug, 227
Psychology, 3, 7, 61, 65, 115, 171
Psychopathology, 4, 148, 156, 157
Psychophysical, 149
Public health, 145, 257
Public health initiatives, 257
Punishment, 12, 207
Purchase tasks, 242

Q
Quantitatively measure, 61
Quantitative reasoning, 65
Quantitative trait locus (QTL), 205
Queries, 149
Quiescence, 177

R
Racial perception, 254
Rainfall, 96, 98, 100
Randomness, 96, 174
Rate dependence, 210, 255
Rate of energy gain, 150
Ratings, 26, 28, 29, 31, 32, 36, 38, 41, 42, 99, 152, 218, 252
Rational self-interest, 116
Reaction times, 42
Read, 47, 69, 86, 151, 228, 250, 251, 254
Real-life decision making, 119, 122
Reappraisal, 11, 14
Reasoning, 62, 65, 95, 96, 115, 122, 124–126, 135–137
Recall, 26, 28, 36, 42, 93, 121, 164, 166, 185
Reference point, 117, 118
Reflection, 30, 47, 65, 124, 134, 135, 217, 218
Regret, 249–251, 256, 257
Regret aversion, 256
Reinforcement, 145, 184, 186, 202–204, 239, 240
Reinforcement learning, 184, 186
Reinforcement theory, 145
Reinforcer pathology, 227–229, 240, 241, 243, 246, 250, 252, 253, 255, 257, 258
Rejection sensitivity, 37–41
Relapse, 207
Relative cost, 150
Relevant rewards, 17–20, 22, 23
Reliability, 38, 53, 129
Religion, 66, 96
Renewal times, 164
Representations of reward, 177
Resistance, 150, 218, 219
Response levers, 150
Response vigor, 167
Reward amounts, 69, 131
Reward intake rates, 173
Reward-predictive stimulus, 204

Reward rates, 167, 169–172, 176, 180–185, 188, 189
Reward-seeking behavior, 204
Reward system, 204
Rhesus monkeys, 181, 204
Richness of the environment, 169, 170, 177, 180, 183
Right inferior frontal gyrus (RIFG), 214–216
Risk, 1, 3–5, 61–63, 65–68, 69–73, 75, 78–81, 83, 87–90, 92–99, 101–103, 105, 106, 115–119, 122–127, 129, 130, 132, 135, 136, 145, 146, 167, 170, 182, 185, 186, 204, 215, 253
Risk averse, 62, 63, 69, 70, 75, 102, 117, 185
Risk neutral, 63, 68, 70, 75, 116
Risk preference, 3–5, 61–63, 65, 66, 72, 73, 81, 83, 92, 94, 95, 102, 115–117, 119, 124–127, 129, 130, 136
Risk prone, 62, 63, 69, 70, 72, 75, 88, 185
Risk-reward ratio, 123
Risk sensitivity, 167
Risk taking, 1, 122–125, 132, 136
Risky choice, 1, 2, 66, 83, 102, 119–121, 125–127, 129–131, 133, 137, 165, 185, 187, 203, 212
Risky choice experiments, 83, 102
Risky outcomes, 1, 4
Ritalin®, 210
Rodent operant, 150
Rodents, 151, 152, 154, 202–204, 209, 216
Rote memorization, 120, 123
Route, 126, 136, 167, 172, 174, 186
Rural communities, 83

S
Safe choices, 185
Sailors, 63
Salience, 15, 133
Sample sizes, 15, 31, 36, 215
Samuelson, Paul, 68
Sangu, 62, 72, 73, 102
Savanna farmer-herder, 63
Scarce resources, 254
Scarcity, 248, 250, 251–255
Schizophrenia, 148, 236
Schizotypy, 201, 202
Scholastic Aptitude Test (SAT), 33, 34, 36
Search, 31, 79, 95, 154, 163–166, 173, 179–181, 241, 243
Seatbelts, 233, 237
Sedative effects, 210
Seeking-taking schedules, 207
Selective serotonin reuptake inhibitor, 213
Self-administration, 207, 210, 214, 242
Self-control, 1, 7, 9–11, 13, 16, 34, 36, 41–48, 50, 51, 53–55, 124, 125, 131, 167, 218, 219, 228, 238, 239, 257
Self-esteem, 38
Self-regulation, 27, 28, 33, 45, 46, 56
Self-worth, 8, 37, 38, 40
Selling price, 79
Sensation seeking, 1, 125, 134, 135, 201, 202, 214
Sensitivity to rewards, 115, 239
Sequence learning, 186–188
Sequence repetition task, 180
Sequential decisions, 174
Sequential action task, 180
Sequential gambling task, 182
SER-082, 210
Serotonin, 207, 209, 213
Sex, 2, 30, 35, 62, 72, 85, 89–91, 97, 98, 101, 123, 124, 135, 249, 251, 256
Sexual behavior, 5, 234, 251, 257
Sexual discounting, 256, 257
Sexual gratification, 251, 256, 257
Sexual health, 126
Sexually transmitted infection (STI), 232, 234, 235, 256, 257
Sexual opportunities, 164
Shell region, 205, 208, 211
Shorter lives, 230
Siblings, 214, 215
Signal, 2, 3, 8, 13, 14, 30, 53, 151, 168, 171, 174–177, 179, 181, 182, 184, 185, 188, 203, 212, 215, 256
Signaling satiety, 177
Single-unit recording, 178
Situational cues, 12
Slot machines, 1, 173, 174
Smoking, 149, 230, 246, 247
Snus, 242, 243
Social and moral values, 127, 132, 136
Social capital, 63, 89–91, 93, 105–108
Social competence, 28
Social discounting, 253
Social encounters, 164
Social learning theory, 12
Social lubricant, 145
Social mechanism, 4
Social organization, 72
Social processing, 164
Social values, 115
Societies, 4, 5, 66, 72, 92, 96, 230
Socio-economic status, 129, 254
Sorcerer, 64
South Africa, 96, 97
Spatial cognition, 65

Spatial discounting, 3, 151
Specialization, 78, 184, 231
Spendthrift-Tightwad, 134
Spirit medium, 64, 65
Sports, 66
St. Petersburg Paradox, 67
Stability, 11, 26, 37, 148, 170
Stability of the environment, 170
Standard deviation, 69–71
Starvation thresholds, 185
Statistical correlations, 98
Stimulant, 207, 210, 214, 216, 217, 233
Stimulations, 129, 187, 208
Stochastic environments, 164
Stroop task, 151
Stop-signal reaction time task (SSRTT), 203, 204, 212–215, 217, 218
Stories, 228, 245
Storyline, 244
Storytelling, 5, 258
Strategic attention deployment, 48–50, 52
Strategic planning, 164
Strattera, 210
Stress, 8, 9, 29, 30, 33, 35, 38, 51, 207, 219
Striatum, 43, 45, 130, 178, 179, 186, 203, 206–212, 216
Studying, 3–5, 16, 102, 164, 173, 177
Study of Early Child Care and Youth Development (SECCYD), 25, 35
Study space, 173
Sub-coeruleal projections, 211
Subcortical nuclei, 165
Subjective effects, 145
Subjective expected utility theory, 117
Substance use, 7, 38, 39, 148, 220, 230, 231, 240
Substitutes, 242
Subthalamic nucleus (STN), 216, 217
Sudan, 97
Suffering, 64, 65, 98, 243, 258
Sunscreen, 232, 237
Supernatural causes, 96–102
Supernatural forces, 97, 101, 103
Symbolic rewards, 17, 19, 21, 22
Symptoms, 211, 216, 217, 231, 251
Synaptic cleft, 210
Synthetic thinking, 97
System 1, 124–126, 131, 238
System 2, 124, 125, 238

T
Tanzania, 62, 73, 76
Target-dependent thinking, 97
Task development, 154
Task-switching, 164
Taxonomy, 1, 2, 202
Technologies, 71, 75
Teenagers, 28–31
Template matching, 26
Temporal discounting, 2, 4, 10, 115, 127–137, 146–149, 151, 152, 154, 156, 167, 202–204, 209, 210, 212, 214, 217, 228–231, 236, 237, 239, 240, 243, 246–250, 252–257
Temporal window, 241, 246, 254
Test-retest reliability, 129
Texting, 234, 237
Theoretical framework, 172
Thinking, 16, 17, 19, 23, 24, 50, 66, 97, 101, 103, 117, 124–126, 129, 132, 136, 148, 201, 246, 248, 250–253, 255
Third-party narrative, 252
Threshold, 149, 167–172, 180–182, 185, 186, 219
Time, 2–5, 8–11, 14–19, 21–24, 26, 28, 35, 42, 44, 46, 48–51, 53, 61–63, 65, 66, 68–72, 76, 79, 80, 82–89, 91–96, 98, 101, 102, 107, 108, 115–117, 126–128, 130, 132–134, 147, 152, 155, 156, 163–172, 178–183, 185–188, 203, 204, 206, 207, 212, 215, 228, 243–246, 250–252, 258
Time horizon, 80, 169–171, 183, 185, 228
Time-out, 204
Time preferences, 3, 62, 69, 70, 72, 76, 84, 95, 101, 102, 116, 130, 147
Titration, 69, 75, 81, 82, 84–87, 92, 93, 229
Token, 17, 178
Tolerance, 98
Tolman Edward, 150
Tonic activity, 177
Toy, 16, 17, 24, 31
Track marks, 227
Trade-off, 2, 68, 78, 79, 88, 102, 103, 119, 122, 127, 133, 134, 167, 169, 170, 172, 178
Traffic signal, 3
Trail, 151
Training, 37, 50, 53, 56, 121, 129, 206
Trait, 4, 12, 129, 136, 147, 148, 201, 202, 205, 214, 216
Trans-disease process, 128, 228, 231, 237, 257
Traplining, 166, 174
Traveling salesmen problem, 174
Travel time, 180, 186
Trobrianders, 97
Truncating risky choice, 119, 136
Truncation effects, 119, 137
Trust, 12, 52–54, 84, 220
Tubers, 79, 80, 95

Tversky, Amos, 117
Two-alternative forced-choice, 181, 185, 187
Type 1 and 2 processes, 124

U

Ultimatum game, 65
Uncertainty, 11, 103, 168–170, 172, 175, 184, 186, 188, 189, 204, 217
Unconscious, 115, 124, 238
Undergraduates, 62, 65, 244
Unit price, 150, 241, 242
Unprotected sex, 2, 123, 124, 135, 256
Unsafe sex, 97
UPPS-P Impulsive Behavior Scale, 148
Urine sample, 227
US Health in International Perspective, 230
Utility (U), 67
Utility curve, 62, 67, 94
Utility functions, 62

V

Valuation network, 176, 178
Value, 12, 36, 47, 48, 62, 63, 65, 66–72, 78–80, 82, 84, 86, 88, 89, 93–95, 103, 115, 116, 118, 119, 121, 127, 128, 131–137, 146, 147, 149, 151, 152, 155, 165–185, 187–189, 217, 219, 228, 229, 236, 237, 241, 246, 255
Variance, 31, 35, 49, 66, 99, 101, 103, 116, 134, 135, 137, 184, 241
Variation, 12, 13, 15, 18, 31, 42, 49, 52, 67, 71, 88, 93, 96, 97, 101, 118, 119, 204, 205, 216, 255
Ventral striatum, 43, 45, 130, 203, 208, 211, 212, 216
Ventral tegmental area, 156, 175, 204
Ventromedial prefrontal cortex (vmPFC), 165, 168, 175–179, 183–185, 188, 189
Venturesome, 148
Verbatim, 4, 115, 117–120, 122, 123, 126, 127, 131–137, 238
Vezo, 63, 65, 72, 78, 79, 81, 82, 87, 90, 91, 94, 97–101, 104–108
Visual search, 164
Visual targets, 204, 206, 210
Visuomotor learning, 187
Vocational history, 31
Volatility, 184, 188

W

Waiting, 3, 5, 8, 9, 11, 13–28, 30, 31, 33, 34, 36–38, 40–42, 46–55, 68, 86, 146, 147, 178, 203, 204, 206, 208–210, 213, 217, 218, 256
Waiting strategies, 13
Wait time, 15, 24, 28, 31, 228
Water, 65, 98, 127, 164, 177
Wealth, 62, 63, 67, 68, 72–74, 76, 83, 92–94, 98, 101
Weight and height, 35
WEIRD people, 65, 96
White matter, 214
Willingness-to-accept, 149
Willingness-to-pay, 149
Willingness-to-wait task, 178
Willpower, 9, 12, 24, 47, 48, 55, 219
Witchcraft, 97
Within-subject consistency, 119
Women, 35, 62, 83, 84, 87, 88
Work, 3–5, 10, 12, 14, 17, 19, 21, 23, 26, 27, 30, 33, 37, 38, 45–47, 50, 55, 56, 64, 66, 68, 69, 96, 97, 100, 101, 103, 126, 150, 164, 186, 204, 207, 209, 210, 213, 216, 242
Working memory training, 129
Workload, 72

Y

Yoked control, 156

Z

Zero complement, 119, 120, 133

MIX
Papier aus verantwortungsvollen Quellen
Paper from responsible sources
FSC® C105338

If you have any concerns about our products,
you can contact us on
ProductSafety@springernature.com

In case Publisher is established outside the EU,
the EU authorized representative is:
Springer Nature Customer Service Center GmbH
Europaplatz 3, 69115 Heidelberg, Germany

Printed by Libri Plureos GmbH
in Hamburg, Germany